MAKE YOURSELVES GODS

CLASS | NEW
2 | STUDIES
0 | IN
0 | RELIGION

EDITED BY Kathryn Lofton AND
          John Lardas Modern

MAKE YOURSELVES GODS

Mormons and the Unfinished Business
of American Secularism

PETER COVIELLO

The University of Chicago Press
Chicago and London

The University of Chicago Press, Chicago 60637
The University of Chicago Press, Ltd., London
© 2019 by The University of Chicago
Published 2019

28 27 26 25 24 23 22 21 20 19   1 2 3 4 5

ISBN-13: 978-0-226-47416-8 (cloth)
ISBN-13: 978-0-226-47433-5 (paper)
ISBN-13: 978-0-226-47447-2 (e-book)
DOI: https://doi.org/10.7208/chicago/9780226474472.001.0001

Library of Congress Cataloging-in-Publication Data

Names: Coviello, Peter, author.
Title: Make yourselves gods : Mormons and the unfinished business of American secularism / Peter Coviello.
Description: Chicago : University of Chicago Press, 2019. | Series: Class 200: new studies in religion | Includes bibliographical references and index.
Identifiers: LCCN 2019024283 | ISBN 9780226474168 (cloth) | ISBN 9780226474335 (paperback) | ISBN 9780226474472 (ebook)
Subjects: LCSH: Church of Jesus Christ of Latter-day Saints—History. | Mormon Church—History. | United States—Religion.
Classification: LCC BX8611 .C6485 2019 | DDC 289.3/73—dc23
LC record available at https://lccn.loc.gov/2019024283

"Only the man who sacrifices everything can be a Mormon," said the bishop. "No one will bring the Promised Land to you. You must renounce homeland, family and possessions. That is a Mormon. And if you have nothing but the flowers that people in Iceland call weeds, you must take your leave of them. You lead your young and rosy-cheeked sweetheart out into the wilderness. That is a Mormon. She carries your baby in her arms and hugs it close. You walk and walk, day after day, night after night, for weeks and for months, with your belongings on a handcart. Do you want to be a Mormon? One day she sinks to the ground from hunger and thirst, and dies. You take from her arms your baby daughter who has never learned to smile; and she looks at you with questioning eyes in the middle of this wilderness. A Mormon. But a child cannot get warm against a man's ribs. Few can replace a father, none a mother, my friend. Now you trudge alone across the wilderness for miles and miles with your daughter in your arms; until one night you realize that the biting frost has nipped the life from these tiny limbs. That is a Mormon. You dig a grave with your hands and bury her in the sand, and put up a cross of two straws that blows away at once. That is a Mormon."

HALLDØR LAXNESS, *Paradise Reclaimed*, 1960

CONTENTS

PROLOGUE

Winter Quarters

BEYOND RELIGION

IN THE WINTER OF 1846, TWO years after the murder of founding prophet Joseph Smith, some 3,500 Mormons paused at the outset of the grueling westward exodus that would eventually lead them to Salt Lake. Under the leadership of Brigham Young, they gathered across the Missouri River from Iowa in what would be Nebraska but was then Omaha Indian territory. The environmental historian Jared Farmer sets the scene: "Young needed a wintering place to prepare for the migration. He could have set up camp in Western Iowa, but the Mormon persecution complex propelled him across the Missouri River to unorganized territory. Better to live among the red men than among whites. Young knowingly violated a federal law that forbade contact with Indians on reserved land. He went ahead and negotiated his own extralegal treaties with Omahas and Otoes, both of whom claimed the land at Winter Quarters."[1] Whatever Young's "complex," the Mormons had ample reason to fear persecution; the previous decade—from Ohio to Missouri to Carthage, Illinois, where Smith had been killed—had been overfilled with it. But there was sharper reason still for trepidation at Winter Quarters. For even as the Saints squatted on Native land, even as they negotiated what were from the perspective of the federal government treaties both legally dubious and potentially seditious, they were endeavoring as well to bring into a fuller, clarified practice what Young biographer John G. Turner calls, with careful delicacy, "the church's altered and expanded family structures"—by which he means the practice of polygamy. In the idioms of early Mormonism, this was celestial, or patriarchal plural, marriage.[2]

It is, in so many respects, an irresistible tableau: Mormons and Omaha
and Otoe, with their adjacent histories of violent displacement and erotic
noncompliance, wintering out together on the banks of the Missouri. And
yet what makes the scene only stranger, and denser, and more fractally complex, is the fact that for the Mormons, the Native peoples sharing space
beside them at the Winter Quarters were both more and other than fellow
refugees from an imperial America. More nearly, they were, these peoples,
"Lamanites": the survivors of an ancient race war depicted in the eschatological epic that was Smith's Book of Mormon. (One Mormon term for Native
peoples was "Brother Laman.") But these quasi-fraternal likenesses, however sanctioned by Mormon scripture, ramified in other ways as well. Both
Mormons and Natives were understood to be, after their particular fashions,
deviants, assembling social forms that were conspicuously unstructured by
dyadic monogamy and its arrangements of genders, sex, and property. Both
Mormons and Natives believed themselves to be sovereign people, possessed of a right to self-governance that exceeded the secular powers of the
United States (the Mormons claiming for themselves what Brent M. Rogers has recently described as "an unpopular sovereignty"[3]). And both, from
the perspective of Protestant America, were less nonbelievers or even heathens than they were *zealots*, populations deranged—intellectually, socially,
sexually—by extravagances of belief they chose to name "religion."

Here, for instance, is how a blistering editorial from *Putnam's Monthly*
chose to frame the matter only a few years later, in 1855, in a piece listed
under the simple, stark heading "The Mormons." "Monogamy is sanctioned
by our religion," the editorial opined, but

> goes beyond our religion. . . . Monogamy does not only go with the west-
> ern Caucasian race, the Europeans and their descendants, beyond Chris-
> tianity, it goes beyond Common Law. It is one of the primordial elements
> out of which all law proceeds, or which the law steps in to recognize and
> to protect. . . . It is one of the elementary distinctions—historical and
> actual—between European and Asiatic humanity. . . . It is one of the pre-
> existing conditions of our existence as civilized white men, as much so
> as our being moral entities is a pre-existing condition of the idea of law,
> of the possibility of a revelation. Strike it out, and you destroy our very
> being; and when we say *our*, we mean our race—a race which has its great
> and broad destiny, a solemn aim in the great career of civilization, with
> which no one of us has any right to trifle.[4]

Religion and *beyond* religion: here, in swift miniature, was the very terrain of that perverse intimacy adhering Mormons and Natives. They were peoples marked, in their differing inflections, by deviance, by backwardness, by a threatening acivilizational atavism. And, according to *Putnam's*, they imperiled nothing less than "our existence as civilized white men."

Make Yourselves Gods is a book about the before and after of the scene at Winter Quarters. It gathers together a great wealth of voices from the archive of early Mormonism, Joseph Smith and Brigham Young most prominent among them but a range of others as well: admiring explorers of the West like John W. Gunnison; polemicizing anti-Mormon novelists like Alfreda Eva Bell and Sara Jane Lippincott; Mormon theologians like Orson Pratt and Wilford Woodruff; pioneering polygamist wives and ex-wives like Augusta Cobb and Eliza Snow and Zina Diantha Huntington Jacobs Smith Young; Native leaders like Ute chief Kanosh; and literary appraisers of the Mormon undertaking like Nathaniel Hawthorne and Jack London; as well as a variety of federal officials, Mormon scribes, scandalized editorialists, outraged congressmen and clergy, and ordinary Latter-day Saints, making their way through the tumult and upheaval of the later nineteenth century. And yet, for all this cacophony, the work of *Make Yourselves Gods* might fairly be said to pivot around a single tight nexus of questions. We could put them, most concisely, like this: What would it mean, and what would it require, to build a critical analytics of nineteenth-century American life—colonial, slave made, expansionist, at once rapidly secularizing and boiling over with multiplying faith-practices and devotional enthusiasms—around this layered scene of flight and encounter? How do we best contend with its overlapping but nonidentical violences, its volatile cross-wiring of racialization and erotic errancy and faltering belief? What terms of analysis would be the most salient to such an endeavor, and how, in the light of their mutual entanglement and intermixing—of race with sex with spirit—would we have to torque and reconceive them, each and all? What would we have to conceive anew about the environing disciplines, the managerial codes *and* the uncodified substrates, of nineteenth-century America? What would have to happen to the grammar of our concepts?

THE CARNAL LIFE OF THE SPIRIT

Make Yourselves Gods tells the story of the Mormon nineteenth century. More precisely, it tells *a* story of the Mormons, stretching from their emergence as a dissident sect, notable as much for their post-Protestant heterodoxy as for a dramatically nonnormative sexual imagination, through to their renunciation of polygamy at century's end, in 1890. That renunciation, with which the Mormons would eventually attain statehood for Utah—transforming them into reluctant monogamists and enfranchised US subjects—marked, too, the culmination of a fantastically turbulent history, in which the Mormons appeared by turns as heretics, sex-radicals, American "Mohammedans," racialized refugees, anti-imperialists, colonizers, and eventual white nationalists, protected in their citizenship less by the secular state's offer of official "toleration" than by the complex wages of a sovereign whiteness, at last secured. *Make Yourselves Gods* is distinctive in telling the story of Mormonism *across* these several registers, in a synthesizing idiom that uses archival research and textual exegesis in concert with the conceptual tools of political theology, Native studies, and queer critique. Its aim is to fashion a new framework for imagining orthodoxy, citizenship, and the fate of the flesh in nineteenth-century America. In conversation with but also, in its queerer registers, departing from a vibrant history of scholarship in "Mormon studies," *Make Yourselves Gods* nevertheless shares with this work a disinclination to tune its critical narrative toward the imperative to expose, falsify, or debunk: to surrender Mormonism, in all its intricacy and breadth of vision, to one or another variety of presumptively secularizing delegitimation. Whatever else may be said of *Make Yourselves Gods*, it is not—for reasons I will explain shortly—that kind of book. It is rather a story about the dynamism and violence, but also the wild beauty and extravagant imaginative power, of nineteenth-century Mormonism: a book by an Americanist literary scholar, with a keen interest in the racial history of sexuality, *about* the shape and tenacity of secularist presumption. It is a book whose principal object of scrutiny is the fractious, entangled, ongoing project of secularism.

Part of the ambition in these interlaced inquiries is methodological. The hope, in the first instance, is to produce a critical idiom capable of grasping, in synthesis, the interwoven investments in the flesh and in the spirit that make up the racialization of the soul in nineteenth-century America—what I will call, in the conclusion, the inevitably carnal life of the spirit. At the center of this argument is an account of Mormonism as, in its essence, a radical theory of embodied life: a faith whose cosmology is anchored in visions of a body marked by gender and by race but also, no less crucially, by an incipient divinity. Persons, in early Mormon theology, are not fallen away from God. Rather, they are themselves *embryonic gods*, defined in the grain of their flesh by the possibility of an expansion, via the channels of an engaged carnality, into eternality and godliness itself. Mormon polygamy is both the training ground in which this ungrown divinity develops and also the scene of Mormonism's gravest conflicts and paradoxes. (Among the most crucial unresolved questions of early Mormonism: Do women inhabit the bodies of gods? Or is exaltation solely the province of men?) In their struggle to manage these points of conflict and irresolution, the early Mormons find themselves contending as well, across shifting terrains of race and sex and belief, with some of the ground-level premises of liberal polity that were shaping themselves into solidified form over the course of the century. My claim is that in the elaborate disciplining of the radiant body of early Mormon theology—in those contested, never quite voluntary transformations that mark so conspicuously the last years of the Mormon nineteenth century—we can begin to trace out a different story of secularism than the ones with which we have grown familiar. This is not "secularism" as the climate of belief proper to state neutrality, nor as a welcome relief from the smothering hold of orthodoxy or superstition or benighted credulity. The Mormon story helps us to see, with a new and I think startling clarity, the solidification of secularism as an encompassing and, in its effects, disciplinary force: as, I will contend, a biopolitics.

As that framing suggests, these methodological aspirations place *Make Yourselves Gods* at the heart of a vibrant multidisciplinary critical conversation that, in the exciting efflorescence of scholarly works over the last decade and a half, has been tuned chiefly to the problem of the secular. If this work is broadly "postsecular"—"postsecular critique," as it is sometimes called—it is so perhaps chiefly in the shared critical impatience with what is commonly known as "the secularization thesis." But one especially strong effect of this work has been, as it were, metacritical: an effort toward a remapping of the grammar of our concepts. For even as scholars have grown more incisively skeptical about the clarities offered by the master-trope of secularization—broadly, the idea that modernity is marked by disenchantment, a swing from superstition to rationality, credulity to skepticism, eschatological fanaticism to liberal tolerance—we have begun to learn, too, how deeply secular premises have woven themselves into the fabric of our most indispensable critical paradigms. As scholars like Charles Taylor, Talal Asad, José Casanova, Saba Mahmood, Joan Wallach Scott, Gil Anidjar, and Hussein Ali Agrama have shown us, as well as Americanists like Tracy Fessenden, John Modern, Molly McGarry, and Jared Hickman, "secularism" may be less an object of study than one of the great underinterrogated premises of our long-running modernity: less an event or doctrine than a normative frame, one that lends stability, a perhaps *falsifying* stability, to the categories we know, or think we know.[5] If these divergent and capacious works might be said to cohere around any one moral, it is that unlearning secularism, thinking our paradigms apart from secularist presumption, is an endeavor much more vexed and involving than merely critiquing the historical misapprehensions of the secularization thesis. It requires, it would appear, a more nimble reflexivity, and an altogether more thoroughgoing unloosening.

This is where the theoretical ambitions of *Make Yourselves Gods* are most directly aimed. For one of the principal wagers of the book is that the Mormon story, which is one of a protracted but ultimately failed resistance to the dictates of an increasingly hegemonic liberal secularism, can help us to envision anew much that remains in the grip of implicitly secularizing frameworks. What is "sex" if it is not the liberal-secular linchpin of selfhood Michel Foucault famously suggests? What happens to "race" if we imagine it to be forged as much by rival conceptions of godhead as by the imperatives of settler colonialism? And how do we renovate our most vital critical categories to make them responsive to, rather than unreflexive bearers of, the accumulated force of secularist presumption? *Make Yourselves Gods* in these ways grapples with what I call, borrowing a note from Lauren Berlant, the unfinished business of American secularism.[6] It offers a genealogical account of secularism not as some saving relief from orthodoxy or superstition but as its own brand of orthodoxy and, especially, its own brand of imperial politics. In the intricate and often confounding history of early Mormonism, we witness the halting emergence of, precisely, a biopolitics of secularism: of that fused, disciplinary calibration of sex, racial status, and religiosity that—here in the era of "travel bans," anti-Sharia panics, ongoing inquiries into whether Islam *is a religion*—continues to stratify the fractured postsecular world.

ARGUMENTS, METHODS, GENEALOGIES

The chief arguments of *Make Yourselves Gods* can be mapped out relatively quickly. The book pursues three broad aims. First, the work here offers a reading of early Mormonism keyed to its extravagant carnal imagination, one ventured in the conviction that Mormonism comes into an especially rich relief when figured in the terms of queer historiography and queer critique. *Make Yourselves Gods* means to be, that is, a work of queer theory. Second, the book looks to push back against what I will describe as the liberalizing impulse of Mormon criticism—a criticism that (rightly) resists the debunking imperative in respect to early Mormon theology and practice but replaces it with a sanitizing effort to turn early Mormons into practitioners of *good religion*. This, I will suggest, is a mode of appraisal that counters the secular presumption of the debunking impulse by, in essence, secularizing the Mormons. Third and most largely, *Make Yourselves Gods* wishes to formulate, and to put into circulation, a portable and adaptive analytic vocabulary for critical work on secularism. More particularly, it looks to map out something of the encompassing metaphysics of secularism as they came to be operationalized, in nineteenth-century America, as a set of biopoliticizing disciplines.[7]

To unfold these central claims a bit more methodically: first, an anchoring proposition of *Make Yourselves Gods* is that the Mormon story—Mormon theology especially, though also the drawing-together, in Mormonism, of erotic errancy, racialization, imperial ambition, and the disciplining of bad belief—responds exceptionally well to the conceptual tools of queer historiography and queer critique. This is so, I argue, not solely because of the Mormons' famous commitment to what most of their countrymen took to be a great, impermissible, defiling rupture of the frame of normative intimacy—their devotion, I mean, to polygamy. For polygamy was not some curious liturgical appendage, a minor theological aberration. As I wish to describe it, polygamy was not the simple reflection of a basically fundamentalist restorationism in early Mormonism, nor the coordinated (and quasi-hysterical) countermeasure undertaken by patriarchs who feared the loosening of their hold over a rapidly industrializing social world, nor again the expression, in doctrine, of the private proclivities of a handful of demagogues looking to pursue their illicit desires under the cover of ecclesiastical sanction. Though one can find answering evidence for all these claims, polygamy,

I will insist, is better comprehended as the culminating expression of an entire theology: as the rendering, in the idiom of a lived dailiness, of an orchestrated cosmology whose bedrock insistence was upon the destiny of the human in its divinization, its ascent into godliness. Polygamy, for Smith, was crucial to the notion of *exaltation*. And exaltation, more than anything else, gives to Mormonism its distinctive theological shape.

At the beating heart of Smith's cosmological vision, as we will see, was an insistence that persons in the mortal world were assembling lives on a trajectory that arced, with patient inexorability, toward divinization. Smith would insist, in turn, that it was the calling of persons in the world to *make themselves Gods*: "You have got to learn how to make yourselves Gods," Smith exhorted the faithful in April of 1844, only months before his death, "by going from a small capacity to a great capacity, from a small degree to another, from grace to grace, until the resurrection of the dead from exaltation to exaltation."[8] And in order to do so, persons needed to come into the fantastic knowledge that they were, there in the present tense, living already in the bodies of gods unenlarged. "*All spirit is matter*," we are told in Doctrine and Covenants, in a turn that underscores the fact that in Smith's cosmology there was not heavenly *and* earthly "matter" but only one—which is to say that mortal flesh itself was not different from God's but coterminous with it, made up of the selfsame elements.[9] And again and again in Smith it was a certain irrepressible carnal joyousness—the body's startling capacity for self-confounding, self-enlarging *pleasure*—that vouchsafed the fact that our bodies are not what we had supposed, not the seats of wickedness or Pauline corruption but something else entirely: the vehicles for exaltation. This is what Smith meant when he said, "The great principle of happiness consists in having a body," or when he said that "our Heavenly Father is more liberal in his views, and boundless in his mercies and blessings, than we are ready to believe or receive." As the Book of Mormon observed, "Men are, that they might have joy."[10]

Small wonder, then, that polygamy was a key to exaltation. "*Then shall they be Gods*," Smith wrote of polygamous patriarchs, in his revelation on the sanctity of plural marriage.[11] For polygamy was for Smith the venue built to enable persons to come into the astonishing knowledge that they were in fact living in the bodies of gods not yet unenlarged. (Explicitly, in this revelation, those persons were exclusively and definitively men, though as we will soon see, in chapter-length detail, this was for a crucial window of time a matter of blurred or undercodified certainty in Mormon theology. Smith had left notable room, as early Mormon women well knew, for counterpossibilities, among which was *female power*.) Polygamy, in all, was the intimate form proper to the divinizing flesh.

Make Yourselves Gods is in this respect a work whose deepest conceptual debts are to queer theory and to queer critique. Taking up the thread from accounts like that of Fawn Brodie—who noted long ago that Joseph Smith "was no hair-shirt prophet" but "promised in heaven a continuation of all earthly pleasures"[12]—it looks to restore a vision of Smith as a special sort of *historian of the body*, though to see how this is so we will need to unlock these terms from their sequestration in secular frameworks.[13] Smith, as I want to read him, ceaselessly insisted upon the great consequence of pleasure, refused the diminution of bodily life either for gods or persons, and placed the whole wide theater of the carnal at the very center of a human drama of divinization. But this was not all. For the *effect* of that insistence was not only to render the Mormons deviants in the eyes of their countrymen, heterodox perverts. Rather, and in the very grain of that deviancy, the Saints were persistently *racialized*, in figures as extravagant as they were varied. Listen to Representative Justin Morrill, using polygamy and its counterfeited religiosity to argue against Utah statehood in 1856: "Under the guise of religion this people has established, and seek to maintain and perpetuate, a Mohammedan barbarism revolting to the civilized world."[14] Morrill's was only one among the chorus of voices conjuring the counterfeited whiteness of the Mormons. Again and again they figured as Indian-like in their treachery, Mohammedan in their sensual indulgence, African or Asiatic in their despotism, slave-like in their sycophancy: as, in all, a people whose religiosity made them perverts and whose perversions made them dubious white people (though these links were hardly sequential). As a Jack London character would concisely declare, in respect to the racial constitution of the Latter-day Saints: "They ain't whites . . . they're Mormons."[15]

It is a central premise of *Make Yourselves Gods* that nothing about the eventual Mormon renunciation of polygamy comes especially clear in the absence of an understanding of precisely these multiplying visions of the Mormons as racialized deviants, perverted by misfiring belief. And I will argue, too, that, without contending with these counterstories of racialized Mormon degeneracy, neither can we grasp the Mormons' *own* transformations across the later nineteenth century, those gradual but equally striking self-authored clarifications of Mormon doctrine and Mormon life. For here we find in the Mormons an escalating identification not against but with the racial state: an intensified insistence on racial difference and hierarchy, a striking hyperbolization of gender distinction (in an *already* patriarchal structure of sociality), and the concerted foreclosure of a whole host of errant counterpossibilities to be found in the vast, self-contradicting, profoundly undersystematized theological legacy of Joseph Smith. *Make Yourselves Gods* is thus a story about both the amplitude of early Mormon theology— its extravagant queer affordances, we might say—and the seizure of those counterpossibilities, in what I will describe as a decades-long effort of normalizing codification. Of course, this straining normalization transpired not in any free space of unfettered theological speculation but in anxious, perpetual proximity to the disciplinary force, and the never far-off violence, of a consolidating secularism. And here, too, we are returned to the sharp clarities of queer theory. What we discover in the trajectory of nineteenth-century Mormonism is a semivoluntary accommodation to the secular norms of liberal personhood, family, and erotic life, and this, I will suggest throughout, is a resonant queer story. Or rather—and inasmuch as it depicts vividly what I will call, in the conclusion, a variety of *protohomonationalism*—it is a story that queer theory, and especially queer of color critique, enables us to tell especially exactingly.

Here, then, is the book's second strand of argument. *Make Yourselves Gods* takes its place in a tradition of what we might think of as esoteric Mormon criticism—criticism, that is, that emphasizes the ungoverned imaginative wildness of early Mormon theology, largely in terms of its origins in conceptual precincts apart from those of normative Protestantism. Such appraisal is especially vivid in John L. Brooke's *The Refiner's Fire*, in the metaphysical readings of Catherine Albanese's *A Republic of Mind and Spirit: A Cultural History of American Metaphysical Religion*, and in the adventurous works of D. Michael Quinn (*Early Mormonism and the Magic World View*, perhaps most of all), though elements of it appear as well as far back as Brodie's *No Man Knows My History*.[16] These acute and rigorously nondismissive renderings of the story of Mormon heterodoxy have galvanized the work of *Make Yourselves Gods*, especially in its queerer dimensions, where—in concert with powerful readings of early Mormon cosmology by critics like Terryl Givens and Samuel Morris Brown—I have hoped to grasp something of the countersecularizing force of the early Mormon carnal imagination, as it collided with the violence of secular discipline.[17] That counterrendering has seemed to me important to attempt, and to insist upon. For one striking commonality to be found across a range of more orthodox works in Mormon studies is a tendency not to ignore this multivalent disciplining but to misappraise it. This is especially true of what we might think of as recuperative accounts of early Mormonism: scholarly arguments that wish to separate themselves from basically debunking renderings (about the impossibility of the origin-stories of the Book of Mormon, about Smith's necromantic charlatanism, about belief as subcritical self-deception) by looking less disdainfully at the intricacies of religious devotion and by offering, in turn, critical assessments of the Mormons' persecuting countrymen, who failed so conspicuously to honor the *religious freedom* to which the Saints were, we are told, rightfully entitled. Again, I share wholeheartedly in this antipathy to debunking accounts. (As I have said many, many times when presenting this work: when I read Whitman, it is not to debunk him—to work out if he *really* loved the men he professes himself to have loved, say—and my approach to Smith accords him the same exegetical courtesies.) But I will argue here, too, that what joins these contemporary accounts is an impulse to rescue early Mormons by, in effect, secularizing them: by producing them as though they were *already* in step with the presumptions of liberal personhood, the dictates of liberal rationality, and the (it is always assumed) finally beneficent norms of liberal polity and sociality. They produce early Mormons not as a sect of heterodox sex-radicals about to be disciplined into compliance but as liberals from the start, as believers in free choice, equitable representation, charity, nonviolence, and the holiness of family life. They reduce Mormonism, in all, to "good religion" by the lights of secularism.

The matter is not that there is no trace of any of this in early Mormonism; of course there is. The matter is rather that, in the socialities early Mormonism fostered and the institutions it built and especially in the bodies conjugated by its theologies, the Mormons were *not wholly assimilable* to such iterations of liberalism. This unassimilability can at some moments look like critique, and at others like regressiveness and violence. It is at any rate where much of the abiding force and disquiet of early Mormonism resides, and so we do well not to displace or sanitize it. My own insistence on just that ill-fittedness, and on its consequences, makes for a through-line across all the chapters of *Make Yourselves Gods*, and so too do critical engagements with texts that, in my estimation, hedge Mormon unassimilability. So from Richard Bushman's rendering of Mormon polygamy as a kind of family theology after all, one that "put family first," to Laurel Thatcher Ulrich's account of the polygamous wives of early Mormonism as triumphant in their attainment not of an equivalent godhead but of the ballot; from John Turner's reading of Brigham Young's racism as largely contextual, a reflex-like reflection of racist times, to W. Paul Reeve's reading of the "illogical" accounts of race that would transform the "overwhelmingly white" Mormons into a racially dubious populace—through all this bracing, and generative, and indispensable work, I will argue, we find scholars caught up in the strange labor of producing early Mormonism as *already liberal*, already aligned with the presumptively munificent norms of liberal secularism.[18] Though I am sympathetic to the refusal of secular dismissiveness, I underscore throughout the grim irony entailed in the too-swift consignment even of early Mormonism, with all its carnal extravagance, to the status of good religion.[19] For the Mormons spent much of the century in pitched, multivalent resistance to the disciplining orthodoxies of secularism (even as they hungered for various kinds of inclusion *within* orders of power that had been secularizing). Indeed, much of what I wish to suggest is so lastingly revealing in the Mormon story is their complex, straining, and ultimately failed refusal of the call of the secular—a refusal in which many Mormons understood their eternal fate to be bound up and for which a great number of Saints were willing to stake their lives.

Finally, and most largely, *Make Yourselves Gods* is a book about the accumulating force—the origins and history and ongoingness—of a centuries-long globe-enveloping project whose most familiar name is "secularism." In a real way, this is the book's principal object of scrutiny: it takes the Mormon story as an occasion to anatomize the workings of secularism as a particular mode of liberal discipline, through whose mechanisms devotionality comes to circulate, alongside racial purity and erotic propriety, within an elaborate calculus of viability, capacity, expendability, and threat. Mormonism, I propose, is an immensely revealing object for postsecular critique not least because we find there the story of what was all but universally recognized as an exemplary form of *bad belief* transforming itself—under pain of opprobrium, expulsion, and many escalating forms of what Foucault calls "indirect murder"[20]—into good religion. We find the story of a religion that for decades fails to be secular and is disciplined into becoming so, into shaping itself more and more fully to the dictates of a liberal polity on its way to becoming hegemonic (and achieving that hegemony, in part, in and through the disciplining of errant forms of devotional sociality like that of the Mormons). In the story of nineteenth-century Mormons, in other words, we can see with diagrammatic clarity what the racializing discipline of secularism—secularism as a *biopolitics*—demands and exacts.

The abiding claim throughout *Make Yourselves Gods* is thus that secularism names not the extirpation in sanctioned public life of the religious or the sacred, nor the triumph of cold rationalism, nor some free and recombinant blending of the two. It marks out rather the fashioning of some modes of belief as, actually, religion—as acceptably "spiritual" and not regressively zealous or credulous—to the degree that they comport with the dictates of liberal rationalism and liberal polity. It names religiosity's *enforced compliance* with the many norms (social, sexual, bodily) of liberal selfhood and sociality. Postsecular critique as I understand it, then, attunes us to the way secular religion is belief that adapts to, without rupturing, a hegemonic liberal order, and to the way the sharp division under conditions of secularism is accordingly not between religion and nonreligion but between *good religion* and *bad belief*—between the properly spiritual and the frighteningly zealous, between faith and fundamentalism—with all the intricate racialization that goes along with that distinction. The story of early Mormonism, I hope to show, gives flesh to these processes.

Of course, the many terms at play here—secularism, belief, discipline, biopolitics—can very easily grow entangled and diffuse. This is so not merely because of the contestation and irresolution that invest loaded bits of critical idiom like "secularism" (and its counterparts "secularity" and "the secular"), or even because of the traces of multiple, not always coincident scholarly approaches that condense around them, though that is a pronounced difficulty. As I am using it, "secularism" carries within it a stacked array of inflections: it signifies, all at once and not especially tidily, in registers historical, conceptual, and methodological. Nor is this multiplicity a matter of conceptual imprecision or some want of intellectual fastidiousness. It marks out, rather, something of the recalcitrance of the object itself, its resistance to an easy or commonsensical rendering. And that, too, is among the book's central presumptions. If I am heartened by any one proposition in the work of a whole dynamic generation of postsecular critics—from Asad through Mahmood, Scott, Modern, Lofton, Fessenden, McGarry, Agrama—it is that there can be no simple naming of a thing called "secularism," no brisk determination of its power or its domain, in the absence of a meticulous metacritical reflexivity. It is not always easy to say what we talk about when we talk about secularism.

Accordingly, and in the spirit of Eve Kosofsky Sedgwick—who long ago, in an essay of unsurpassed clarity and generative power, sketched out some of the grounding-points for queer theory—the entirety of the introductory first section of *Make Yourselves Gods* is devoted to mapping out some of what I take to be the most essential voices in, and most necessary grounding-points for, postsecular critique. (That section is entitled, in miniature homage, "Axiomatic.") The ambition there is not only to bring into relief the operative conceptual and methodological presumptions of the book. It is rather to begin to articulate a flexible analytic vocabulary—some usable, portable set of terms—for work on secularism. My hope is to coordinate, and in that way make at least a bit more widely available, the dynamism and revisory conceptual power of work in and around postsecular critique. That collective scholarly effort to renovate our categories, undertaken in the wake of the collapse of secularization stories—efforts offered in the key of anticolonial anthropology, the history of slavery and empire, antiracist feminism, and queer critique—animates all the work of *Make Yourselves Gods*.

CODA: EXPERIMENTS IN PROPHECY

Make Yourselves Gods is thus, in several senses, an experiment. At its most straightforward, the book is a story about Mormonism, and about the intricacies of its nineteenth-century history. It moves, chapter by chapter, through a recounting of the premises of Mormon theology, of some of its knottier complications and indwelling or inchoate possibilities for development, and turns finally to the withdrawal of those counterpossibilities in the teeth of a multifaceted, often violent opposition. The book unfolds in four parts, over six chapters. The first part, "Axiomatic," offers an extended genealogy of work on secularism, in the effort to establish a critical grammar for the book. The second part, which consists of two substantial chapters, is entitled "Joy," and it is here that the book's extended, unhurrying, often granular accounting of Mormon prophecy and doctrinal proposition begins in earnest. Chapter 2 addresses what I call the radiant body of early Mormon theology, taking up Joseph Smith's imaginings of the character and fate of embodied life and reading polygamy as a sort of culminating fabulation, one that looks to write out, in the language of quotidian life, his vision of divinizing flesh. Chapter 3 turns then to the question of *female* embodiment, reading the writings and life stories of a handful of early Mormon polygamous wives to ask if women, too, could be understood to inhabit the bodies of embryonic gods. I focus here not on the antipatriarchality of early Mormon polygamy—it was, from the first, committedly patriarchal—but on what many early Mormon women found to be the ampler, unforeclosed counterpossibilities circulating there, opportunities for sociality and service but *also* for prophecy, power, and divinization.

The next section shifts the terrain of the book definitively to the West, and to Mormon life there. The third part, also two extended and interlinked chapters, is entitled "Extermination." Chapter 4 returns to the foundational text of Mormonism, the Book of Mormon, and scrutinizes the place of race and indigeneity in its singular narrative form. Here I take up the lineaments of anti-imperial critique to be found in the work—its glancing vision of the putative heroes, the Nephites, as self-blinded imperialists—and examine how precisely that anti-imperial reading of the moral of the Book of Mormon played out in the Mormons' ventures into the West, where it came to be routed through the Saints' fractured identifications and disidentifications with Native peoples, the imperial United States, and their scriptural forebears. Chapter 5 considers closely both the racializing delegitimation of the deviant (because polygamous) Mormons that followed them from the first, and the Mormons' mixed responses to these assaults. It reads out a pattern escalating identification *with* the racial state as a strategy self-legitimating distinction: an effort to secure for the increasingly reviled Mormons a place at the table of an American settler-colonial empire by fitting themselves to a sort of *hypernormativity*, one expressed largely in solidifying and expanding commitments to rigid hierarchies in gender and in race. The final section is entitled "Theodicy." Looking back through contemporary entanglements of Mormonism with homosexuality, this chapter frames the book's arguments about the biopolitics of secularism by figuring the Mormons in the key of *homonationalism*: as a population marked out as expendable life and countering such denigration through a hyperbolized identification with the norms of the racial state. Here I show how the Mormon story, and its running together of erotic errancy, racial status, and proper belief, helps us to establish an enlarged critical vocabulary for the workings of biopolitics, one that, in its attention to racialized religion and desecularized races, looks to unwrite the secularizing presumption still sheltered within the idioms of biopolitical critique.

In the first instance, then, the book is an experiment in historical narration. What we might think of as the linear history of nineteenth-century Mormonism provides an essential backdrop to the book, to be sure—though it is not my intention, in what follows, to retell it. Several major turning points in that history will indeed be crucial to the work at hand, and these are worth noting in advance: the 1830 publication of the Book of Mormon; the massacre of the Mormons (following Governor Lilburn Boggs's "extermination order") in Missouri in 1838; the hugely fomenting years (1840–44) in Nauvoo, Illinois, where Smith first wrote down the polygamy revelation and where the first meetings of the Female Relief Society took place; Smith's 1844 murder in Carthage, Illinois, and the subsequent migration to the West under Brigham Young; the decade of renegade world-making in Salt Lake— Young's systematizing consolidation of his own power, and of the Mormon ambition to be free of the incursions of the federal government—and its culmination in the tense stand-off that was the Utah War of 1857–58; the decades of fractious coexistence, with both the Native peoples of the region and with the United States government itself, as the avowedly polygamous Mormons contended with acts of law designed to criminalize plural marriage and to devastate what was widely understood to be Mormonism's imperial ambitions (from the Morrill Anti-Bigamy Act of 1862 to the momentous *Reynolds v. United States* decision of 1879 to the Edmunds-Tucker Act of 1887); and, finally, the "Manifesto," written by Wilford Woodruff in 1890, in which the Mormons renounced polygamy in the effort to gain statehood for Utah— which, at last, in 1896, they did. These are, in effect, the conventional milestones, available in any history of the Saints.

My own telling, the reader will find, charts a somewhat zigzagging path between and among these events. (Chapter 5, for those readers looking for it, offers the most directly chronological narration.) My aspiration in this is not indirection. It is rather toward a differently calibrated sort of historicism—one that, in mapping nineteenth-century Mormonism across different coordinates, hopes to dislodge at least something of the presumption built into conventional renderings of the Mormon nineteenth century. For such chronologies, inasmuch as they install statehood as a kind of culminating telos, tend to transform Mormon history into something like an assimilation story, whose happy (or happyish) ending turns upon the Saints' eventual inclusion within the great empire of American democracy. (These tellings gravitate accordingly around dramas of achieved comity, prejudices overcome, and eventual redemptive enfranchisement.) That is not the story this book tells. An exercise in critical genealogy, *Make Yourselves Gods* offers itself as, in effect, a countermyth. It traces its own, rather less linear path through the thickets of nineteenth-century Mormonism in the book-wide effort to make legible other patterns, and other trajectories, than those that operate under the sign of liberal enfranchisement.

An account of vexed and capacious origins, of ungrown theological possibility, and of a gradual, only semivoluntary suppression: this, in broad strokes, is the story of nineteenth-century Mormonism that *Make Yourselves Gods* aims to tell. But it seems worth avowing up front as well that the *purpose* of telling that story, across just that critical terrain, lies for me considerably beyond the frame of Mormonism itself. The principal ambition of the book is not to reshape or redirect the study of Mormonism itself, or to remake Mormon studies, and it would be disingenuous, I think, not to say so. This is not a book that boasts new archival discoveries, that sets Mormonism in comparativist conversation with other para- or anti-Protestantisms (with the Muslims of the early republic, say, or antebellum Catholics, or American Jews), that excavates the mutual inflections of Mormon and Native cosmologies as the settler projects of Mormonism grew more expansive, that embarks upon a story of comparative polygamies, or that offers a media history of the print circulation of the faith.[21] As edifying and as necessary as any of these pursuits might be, this is not that book. In a way that some readers might find unsatisfying, its ambit is both more narrow and more broad. It is narrow because its focus is rather closely upon early Mormonism, and the fate of its carnal imagination, across a handful of nineteenth-century scenes. But it is more broad as well. For while early Mormonism is the subject of *Make Yourselves Gods*, and while the book works methodically through its theology, its history, and its historiography, its object, properly speaking, is something else. Ultimately, the book aims to shine a light *through* early Mormonism, as it were, in order to reveal, with new precision and detail, the contours of the hegemonic formation that envelops it: to illuminate, I mean, the arrayed and entangled forces that exerted themselves most forcefully upon the Mormons, that shaped and fettered and cajoled them, and that brought about those startling conversions whereby these racialized heretics and deviants became, in a relatively short frame of time, patriots to the United States and its empire of white monogamy. The nearest name I have for these conjoined forces, and for their operative cogency, is secularism.

Make Yourselves Gods is thus, above all else, a work about secularism. It tells the story of secularism through a close accounting of what it exacts from Mormonism: of how and when and why this seemingly least secular of theologies, with its visions of the body and its practices of social life, transformed itself into a religion considerably more in step, if not quite entirely in accord, with the dictates of belonging proper to the secular nation. Watching the pressure under which the Mormons shaped themselves to those dictates—haltingly, protestingly, partially—brings into exceptional relief what I will be calling the biopolitical force of secularism. To grasp that story you need to understand what sex and race and indigeneity mean in nineteenth-century America. But my claim is that you need to grasp as well how the meanings of those very categories, of "race" and "sex" and "indigeneity," are themselves saturated with dictates about proper belief, tolerable devotion, and normative deployments of "spirituality"—in ways that our critical languages, *including* the languages of biopolitical critique, do not yet quite fully describe. The wager of the book is that the labor of telling the Mormon story in this key, across these several conceptual terrains, can help us to begin to establish a critical vocabulary that, in its attention to this weave of investments, is more potently synthesizing than those to which we most commonly defer. The book is, in these senses, an experiment that makes use of the story of early Mormonism in the effort to stage an encounter between the languages of biopolitics and postsecular critique in the hope that both will emerge ampler, and more acute.

Such are the book's meta-ambitions. But the work of the book is experimental in other, perhaps nearer respects as well. Put it like this: I am, by training and practice, a scholar of nineteenth-century American literature and queer studies, and despite this *Make Yourselves Gods* contains startlingly little in the way of what we commonly recognize as "literature." I take up the Book of Mormon, and spend some time with writings by Emerson, Melville, Stowe, Henry Highland Garnet, and Fanny Stenhouse. But the fact is that these do not give the book its critical gravity; they occasion very few of the exegetical set pieces upon which literary-critical scholarship is typically built. In the place of this work is a different sort of endeavor. This is the effort to assemble a nimble, responsive, and above all synthesizing critical idiom that holds in balanced tension the inheritances of an unruly set of scholarly pursuits, ranging from religious history and historiography, Native studies, anticolonial critique, and political theology to Mormon studies, critical race theory, and, of course, queer theory. What you will accordingly find throughout the pages of this book is a protracted contention with just this confusion of tongues: an attempt to speak both as part of and across multiple scholarly conversations, in a way that shortchanges none of them, while in the pursuit of a critical vocabulary that is at the same time not fully in the service of any. It is, you could say, a book-length labor of intellectual style.

That struggle brings us to the final experimental aspect of *Make Yourselves Gods*. When I say that the conceptual ambition of the book—to provide a synthesizing scholarly idiom that gains purchase on the secularizing presumption folded into our languages of critique—is a labor of *style*, I have in mind an especially galvanizing passage from the work of the great scholar of Mormonism, Jan Shipps. In her preface to *Mormonism: The Story of a New Religious Tradition*, from 1985, Shipps pauses to note her own efforts to "establish contexts that would have been recognizable to the Latter-day Saints who lived in the times and places in question." She underscores in turn the ways she has written less at any clinical distance from the early Mormons who are her subject than, as it were, in colloquy with them. "A disadvantage of this manner of proceeding," she goes on, "is its tendency to make my argument appear somehow apologetic at times—an irony since I am not a Mormon—but that disadvantage is far outweighed by the effective means this stylistic strategy provided for reconstructing the picture of early Mormonism *as perceived from the inside*."[22] Though my own critical motivations are different, I have come to understand very, very well this slightly anxious dialectic in what Shipps calls "stylistic strategy." Shipps weighs what she fears might be read as a kind of apologism, an insufficiently detached criticality, against the desire for an ampler historical reconstruction and a more precise verisimilitude. *Make Yourselves Gods*, which is also written by a non-Mormon—this, too, seems worth saying up front—also risks a certain kind of apologism, though its form and terms are different. Mine finds its voice perhaps most prominently in a certain unexpurgated insistence, a strain of borrowed vehemence—what we might think of, at its least restrained, as a kind of free-indirect proselytizing. So, for example, when in the course of presenting the work of this book I have been asked about my sense of the enduring appeal of Mormonism across the centuries, often by auditors not much masking their wary skepticism, I have had a ready answer: Smith, I have said, offered a vision of a God hugely more generous and loving in respect to His human brethren than any Protestantism had quite been willing to venture, in which it was His wish that all the very greatest glories of mortal life (friendship, family, embodiment, sex) would carry on *eternally*, undissolved, in still greater glory, as persons themselves ascended toward their destiny in godhead. And that, I have said, seems to me an exceptional, irreducibly powerful vision.

I can truthfully say, along with Shipps, that the aim in this and other seemingly unchastened identifications with the idioms of early Mormonism has not been to ratify Mormon theology, and even less has it been to shield the Mormons from the rigor of critique. The work of the latter chapters, and especially of the conclusion, should make this clear enough. But that specific quality of investedness, which for me has amounted to a desire to hew closely and a little doggedly to what I take to be the countersecular insistences Smith worked to bring into some legible relief, has seemed to me a valuable way to resist the strong, the veritably tidal pull of contemporary secular presumption. Secularism, I will be arguing throughout, is not an especially easy set of organizing presumptions to get *beneath*; it speaks, very often, in an ordinary and even critical voice, and wears a number of respectable guises. The neutralish, cogitative, deflating, always faintly condescending posture of *tolerant curiosity* proper to liberal skepticism: this is only one of these guises. As allergic as I am to liberalizing accounts of the "good religion" of early Mormonism, I am no less eager to speak in tones other than those of, say, antiquarian bemusement or anthropological delectation.

So when the rhetoric in what follows rises in pitch, when the argumentative style gives more latitude to Smithian prophetic extravagance than might seem proper to the cooler idioms of scholarly inquiry, know that there is a metaclaim at play, a methodological polemic—an effort, let's say, to breathe upon the embers of some still-vital Mormon concepts (the divinizing mortal flesh in its journeying toward exaltation, for instance) in the hope that they might show us some of what yet remains in shadow, even in the glare of so much secular illumination. As Smith never tired of noting, doctrine is one thing, "believing and receiving" another. *Make Yourselves Gods* believes him.

AXIOMATIC

———

INTRODUCTION

What We Talk about When We Talk about Secularism

AXIOMATIC

THE WORK OF *Make Yourselves Gods* mixes, somewhat promiscuously, argument and presumption. In the previous pages I have tried to lay out some of what the book contends, chiefly about Mormonism but more largely about secularism as it gathers strength and coherence across the American nineteenth century. Taking up the nineteenth-century Mormons as an exemplary case, the book examines how a style of liberal discipline, fusing race and sex and devotionality, came to be materialized in the context of an escalatingly biopoliticized secularity. More broadly still, *Make Yourselves Gods* aims to contribute to the ongoing critical conversation about the world-shattering force of what we know, in shorthand, as "1492," and about its enduring afterlives in North America.[1] For this is the context in which Christianity itself was folded into the imperial domination of the globe, with the result that the languages a distinctively *Christian* secularism came to speak—about race and sex and property but also about freedom, tolerance, autonomy, and much else—would be suffused with the imperatives of a planetary theo-racial domination. Or so, in the work of scholars from Sylvia Wynter and Walter Mignolo to Edward Said, Hortense Spillers, and contemporaries like Tomoko Masuzawa and Jared Hickman, we have come to learn. As Gil Anidjar puts it, with syllogistic compression: "Orientalism is secularism, and secularism is Christianity."[2]

Even to begin to pursue such expansive claims as these, though, is to put oneself in colloquy with a tremendous volume of accumulated scholarship. One speaks, necessarily, in and through the critical vernaculars established over several generations of historical and historiographic reconsideration, genealogical critique, methodological clarification, and conceptual polemicizing. The very notion of "secularism" *condenses* these many established traditions of analysis, acting as a potent crossing-point between their varied articulations. In consequence of this, it is an especially fractious sort of concept, susceptible to blurring at the margins, and alive with an internal dissensus brewed up across multiple scenes of inquiry, with their divergent idioms, norms, and presumptions. This is part (though only part) of what Hussein Ali Agrama means when, borrowing a note from David Scott, he describes secularism as a "problem-space"—a scene of distinctions being insisted upon, instantiated, and unraveled, with perplexing velocity. The problem-space of secularism, on this accounting, is one of constant flux and adjustment (where the edges of pluralistic "tolerance" are forever encountering, and rationalizing, what lies beyond), requiring of its observers in turn a recursive, seemingly never-ending labor of calibration.[3] These are not processes to which we can, once and for all, call halt, in some magisterial gesture of summary comprehension. (Given the nature of its object, the work of "secular critique," as John Modern has recently put it, "cannot be reduced to exposure, to greater clarity about how things are in essence.")[4] But this does not mean a clarification of terms is not in order, or without use.

Since so many of my own grounding presumptions reside exactly here, in these conjoined historical and thickly conceptual senses of "secularism," I want now to begin the work of the book by offering a small genealogy—inexhaustive, to be sure—of secularism as a mobile, many-voiced critical formulation. In walking, chamber by chamber, through the handful of works and of thinkers that have most given shape to "secularism" as I understand it, my aim is, in the first instance, to make some of these presumptions explicit. But the larger hope is that, in dwelling in the details of this capsule genealogy, we might also begin to establish a shared set of terms, some transferable and adaptive idioms for work that, while traversing these several disciplines, converges around the matter of secularism. What follows is a preliminary effort in that direction: an attempt to articulate a portable analytic vocabulary—some axioms for secularism, and for postsecular critique—that might be of use even in respect to scenes far afield of nineteenth-century Mormonism.

Fair warning, though: it is likely that a few of the following points will seem to some readers obvious enough not to require belaboring, while to others many of those same points will read as so counterintuitive, or unlikely, or perhaps even counterfactual, as to demand far *more* in the way of critical or historical substantiation. I can make no claim to be satisfying across all such readerly scenes. My inspiration here, as I have mentioned, comes from the luminous work of Eve Kosofsky Sedgwick, whose seven axioms, in her introduction to *Epistemology of the Closet*, many of us have long since been able to recite, catechism-like, by heart. Sedgwick frames her undertaking by noting that anyone doing queer scholarship, "in a culture where same-sex desire is still structured by its distinctive public/private status, at once marginal and central, as *the* open secret, discovers that the line between straining at truths that prove to be imbecilically self-evident, on the one hand, and on the other hand tossing off commonplaces that turn out to retain their power to galvanize and divide, is weirdly unpredictable."[5] One governing presumption of *Make Yourselves Gods* is that secularism is so much a part of our untheorized and offhand real, so much the stuff of naturalized commonsense, that much of Sedgwick's dialectic between the startling and the "imbecilically self-evident" will obtain, if following out different lines of stress than those proper to queer theory. "Will they bore or will they shock?" Sedgwick wonders of her collection of "otherwise unarticulated assumptions and conclusions from a long-term project of anti-homophobic analysis." I proceed here with a similarly eager uncertainty.

Axiom 1: Secularism is not hostile to "religion" as such.

Secularism is not that force or form of social ordering to which the religious is opposed (or spirituality, or devotion, or belief). Nor is it that which remains after the thoroughgoing derogation of religiosity in modern public life, and its replacement by the generous pluralism of state neutrality and official tolerance. Not the rationalized antidote to religion and its various orthodoxies, not the erosion of all possibilities for faith, secularism is, more properly, an orchestrated constellation of all these foregoing terms: an economy, then, that distributes them, and sets them in mutually explanatory relation to one another. In this, Charles Taylor—vexing though his work can be (of which more shortly)—is exactly and illuminatingly correct.

Taylor, in 2007, followed up his monumental *Sources of the Self* with the equally voluminous *A Secular Age*. We come at it now through the scrim of a decade's worth of veneration, appraisal, and—in dutiful turn—critique, but it's worth noting from the start the shape and the force of its polemic.[6] In his account of the disciplinary efforts of early modern clerical elites, of their own elaboration of the spiritual principles of the saeculum and the broad consequences of these internal shifts in Latin Christendom, Taylor's book gives us abundant reason to mistrust accounts of the diminishment of religion after 1500 in, he says at the outset, "the West." He is interested, to be sure, in what happens after religion ceases to be (what he conceives to have been) a given, an unremarkable and in that respect largely uncritical component of mortal life, and becomes instead "an option," "one human possibility among others": a thing one might choose, or decline to choose, among an array of proliferating possibilities.[7] But that proliferation is part of what matters so greatly to Taylor. For what he calls "the nova effect" describes, to the contrary, a spectacular multiplication of religiosities in the aftermath of this titanic shift in the environment of belief, this "fragilization" of all possibilities with respect to immanence and transcendence.[8] And this (whatever we might say about Taylor's subsequent propositions about the "buffered self" in its "disenchanted world") is crucial: as José Casanova glosses the point, "Taylor challenges secularist prejudices that tend to understand the secular as merely the space left behind when this-worldly reality is emptied of religion or to view unbelief as resulting simply from the progress of science and rational inquiry."[9] Hence Taylor's vigorous "polemic against 'subtraction stories,'" those many self-contented accounts of the alleged secularization of modernity that "treat the history of religion as the career of a mistake."[10] Secularism as subtraction, as diminishment, as an *overcoming* of the merely or misbegottenly or benightedly "religious": these, Taylor helps us to see, are not credible accounts of modernity so much as they are stories moderns like to tell themselves, about themselves. (As Jordan Stein astutely turns the point, "The history of secularism is the history of a story we told, not of a thing that happened.")[11] The matter is not merely that something called "secularization" has not in fact accomplished the diminishment or extirpation of religiosity in some neutral, numericized sense (though one could easily pursue that claim).[12] It is rather that in its fragilization, what we know as "religion" has at once mutated and, in that mutation, found for itself a prodigious fecundity.

The condition of belief Taylor describes as definitive for a secular age that commences around 1500 thus does not *cancel* religion, or supersede it, or suppress it: it redefines and redistributes it. Given the "mutual exposure of the religious and the secular"—given the entangled processes by which *the religious and the secular create one another*—we do well, in the light of Taylor's analysis, to resist those visions of modernity that rush to declare "religion" that which has been vanquished, stifled, or otherwise starved of life.[13] Religion flourishes in a secular age, and not as holdover, residue, or unconverted outside.

Axiom 2: Secularism's negative, its enemy, is not religion; it is *bad belief.*

Perhaps more acutely than any other scholar, Talal Asad has anatomized the constitution of "religion" as such not as against but in and through what he names the "doctrine called secularism."[14] Working in an anthropological tradition of anticolonial critique and taking up "the shifting web of concepts making up the secular," Asad argues, in *Formations of the Secular*, that to grasp what secularism is, and to begin any genealogical accounting of its historicity and its force, one must grapple with the interlinked series of binarized distinctions it propagates. For these, as they twist and twine around one another, form something like the DNA of secularism, at least under the broad conditions of a solidifying liberalism that is Asad's object of analysis. Notably, these multiplying binaries are not propped upon a distinction between the religious and the nonreligious. "Religion," more precisely, is what secular distinction causes to appear as such.

How so? Asad begins by noting the "familiar oppositions" that "pervade modern secular discourse, especially in its polemical mode": he lists "*belief* and *knowledge, reason* and *imagination, history* and *fiction, symbol* and *allegory, natural* and *supernatural, sacred* and *profane*" (23). But what Asad's work goes on to delineate is not some authorizing shift in preference, over the course of the expansion of secular orders of power, from one side to the other in these binary pairs. He describes, rather, the deployment and solidification of a universalizing background *against which* these categories assemble themselves and come into their shifting relational value. That background provides the structuring grammar of secularism.

In Asad's reading, for instance, the way secular discourse establishes the primacy of something like "reason" is not by denigrating "faith," or not exactly; rather, secular discourse puts "faith" into circulation in constrained, bifurcated ways. This is what Nancy Bentley, in a trenchant phrase, names "the secularization two-step": she means the processes whereby a single cleavage—*faith* and *reason*, let's say—comes to be followed by a second-order distinction, in which the category leaning away from the secular is itself split and divided. From *that* division, that subsequent cleavage, a new set of distinctions emerges, in which the oppositional category (*faith*) is assembled into contrasting binarized versions of itself: into iterations that

are ennobling or that do harm, that are civilizing or imbruting, that are tolerable or malign.[15] So it is not the case that *faith* itself is necessarily backward
or wrongheaded within secular conditions anchored in the primacy of *reason*. For there is a *kind* of faith that is tolerable and indeed welcome there:
the faith that improves us, that leavens the pain of a coldly rational world,
that makes us ethical, and caring, and sensitive. And there is also, correlatively, a negative version of faith, by which we can be deluded, steered away
from the clarifying paths of the real, and drawn too far over into the anti-
or nonreality of superstition. There is not, that is, a singular heroic reason,
facing off against its maligned opponent, faith. There are, rather, reason and
salving faith and *their* bad shadow, delusive or misbegotten faith. These are
the mechanics of secular distinction.

The pairing of *religion* and *secularism* is, on Asad's account, perhaps the
paradigmatic case of this procedure. So it is demonstrably not the case that
"religion" has no place in the public life of modern democracies that understand themselves as secular and liberal; but this, for Asad, does not exemplify something like "tolerance" on the part of modern states. He argues
rather that this distinction is superseded by a more important, more structurally determining one. For under the regime of secularism, Asad writes,
only those religions that demonstrate themselves "consistent with the basic
requirements of modern society, including democratic governance" can be
tolerated, and indeed can *count*, as valid religion. More precisely: "*Only
religions that have accepted the assumptions of liberal discourse are being
commended*, in which tolerance is sought on the basis of distinctive relation between law and morality" (182, 183, emphasis added).[16] This is what it
means for Asad to say that in a secular world, "religion" names "everything
the modern state can afford to let go." Or again: "From the point of view of
secularism, religion has the option either of confining itself to private belief
and worship or of engaging in public talk that makes no demands on life.
In either case such religion is seen by secularism to take the form it should
properly have. Each is equally the condition of its legitimacy" (147, 199). That
makes no demands on life: in Asad's rendering, the secular state only "toler-
ates" that which does not present itself as a rival claimant, pursuing differing
conceptions of the public, the private, the good, the necessary, and much
besides. As he says at the outset, mapping out the sharply constrained forms
of "tolerance" proper to secularism: "The secular state does not guarantee
toleration; it puts into play different structures of ambition and fear" (8).

The salient distinction, under conditions of secularism as it has been
fomented in and routed through the orders of political liberalism, is thus not

between the religious and the nonreligious. It travels rather between those religions that adhere to the conventions of liberal polity (its socialities, its arrangements of publicity and privacy, its styles of embodiment) and those that do not. Those that do not, Asad argues, do not appear as "religion" at all, or at least not as legitimate religion. Rather, they appear as something intimately worse: a perversion of the properly private, morally persuasive (i.e., committedly nonviolent) character of religion. They appear, in all, as *bad belief*. These are, in the secular order of things, not *really* religions. For religion, true religion, good religion by the lights of secular distinction, is that which elevates us in virtue, teaches us compassion and forbearance, adheres us to senses of awe and wonder before the universe, organizes our charitable impulses, directs our ethical conflicts, nourishes our spirits. Whereas bad belief—and for Asad, the exemplifying twenty-first-century case is *political Islam*—spoils all this.[17] In its departures from the frameworks of liberal being, as they are ratified by the social order and enforced by the state, bad belief depraves religion, turning it to malignant, intolerable use. Accordingly, and in the name and defense of "universalizing reason itself," it must be transformed, set right, *corrected*.

Hence, that great dream of bringing one or another version of good religion, with all of its emancipatory promises, to an array of places united only by their presumed "aspiration toward liberal modernity" (59, 61). These dreams of emancipation from the fetters of self-imprisoning bad belief give shape to the "secular redemptive politics" that have come to define political liberalism in its global, self-universalizing aspirations. At their core is no refusal of "religion" as such, or spirit, or faith, or any of their proximate formations. There is rather a secular commitment to eradicating bad belief. For bad belief, in the scales of secular appraisal, disorders nothing less than its subjects' access to their full, their true humanity. What we find under regimes of secularism, with their fulsome promises of saving relief from the many violences of orthodoxy and superstition, is thus not tolerance, properly speaking, but those "structures of ambition and fear"—or, more precisely, what Asad names "a readiness to cause pain to those who are to be saved by being humanized" (61, 62).

Axiom 3: Secularism is a normative project: a discipline.

Crucial to the foregoing is the making of secularism in and through particular worlds of politics. In this, I would wish to follow Asad, Mahmood, Casanova, Scott, and many others in specifying the *domain* of secularism, or rather the domain of secularism as it figures as an object of postsecular critique. "Secularism" in this formulation gives name to a way of structuring the world: a "conceptual environment," but one fomented in and secured historically through a variety of kinds of power, which would come eventually to cohere in the political orders of liberalism, global in its universalizing self-conception if not (quite) in its territorial reach. This is secularism as part of the political epistemology of liberalism or, more amply, as a *discourse*: a kind of knowledge-power (in the Foucaultian idiom), wedded to a liberalism forged in empire, whose multiple and variant effects exceed calculation in advance.[18]

With respect to precisely that excess, and to the residues of the secular project that are no less efficacious for being not wholly amenable to signification, few writers argue more searchingly than religious historian and genealogical critic John Lardas Modern, whose work on the evanescence or ghostly materiality of secularism helps us further specify the project. Modern's attention in *Secularism in Antebellum America* is, he writes, to the discourse of secularism. But he wishes us to understand "discourse" in a particular sense. His ambition, he says at the outset, is "to glimpse the dynamism of secularism by showing how its metaphysics assumed an almost biological presence—what Foucault calls 'the incorporeal materialism' of discourse."[19] Just that incorporeal materiality—the "searing reality of discourse," as he puts it—is key to his claims about secularism and modernity, and one of Modern's preferred figures for this intimately felt, saturating, yet unformalizable "reality" is *ghosts*. His book, as he avers, "is a particular history of ghosts as they became tangible in the lives of antebellum Americans who, in one way or another, found themselves subject to modernity's effects"—by which he means, ultimately, subject to *discourse*, discourse generally and the discourse of secularism in particular (xviii, xxxiv). For it is discourse, in Modern's formulation, that lives as "an airy substance that presses upon one's actions . . . an amorphous constellation of ideas and moral vectors that cannot be named in the certain terms of empirical analysis"; it is discourse that makes for "a reality" that is "intimate yet exceed[s] the bounds of conceptual formulation"; and it is discourse, in this conception, that comes to feel for its subjects uncanny and possessing, like something (again in Foucault's words) "strange, frightening, perhaps maleficent" (xxviii, xii, xxviii). The discourse of secularism, Modern contends, may be vaporous and diffuse, but it is also envelopingly *material*, a magnetizing power at work in the world.

The work of *Secularism in Antebellum America* is far-ranging, but one way to frame out the project of the book is to say that it traces, with much the same genealogical attentiveness that Foucault brought to "sexuality," the emergence of what we might now call "spirituality" across the American nineteenth century, mapping it not as some ineffable human essence but as a quantity implanted and distributed in persons, solicited and maximized, its circulation the matter of rational calculation and deliberative method. The book is anchored in an attentiveness to an array of antebellum efforts toward the rationalization of the human—that paradigmatically secular undertaking—though for Modern these multiplying processes are not inimical to but wholly intimate with the dissemination of antebellum religiosity. Scrutinizing emergent systems and networks ("the spread of rail lines and telegraph wires as well as the extension of mass-mediated forms into everyday life," as inflected, too, by the rationalities of Scottish Common Sense philosophy), Modern declines to claim that these and other secular calculations of the human amounted ultimately to "mere extensions of Protestantism." Rather, he insists, striking the Asadian note, that "during this eruptive play of forces, both the religiosity of Protestantism and the secularity of the democratic nation-state conformed to an unmarked and unacknowledged metaphysical scheme that made possible and governed them both" (34, 21, 20). This unacknowledged and cohering metaphysics, and the multiplicity of forces engineered and deployed to consolidate it—to transform it into the stuff of the everyday Real—are what Modern is after in his accounts of the ghosts and the machines, the material life of spirits, in antebellum America.

So when Modern looks at the scientized rationalizations of the human in antebellum America, he does not find the agents and discourses of religiosity working in brave, straining opposition to them, clinging to a realm of spirits as against these sterilizing disenchantments of the world. He finds rather *spirits made rational*, enchantments enacted in the idiom of calculability. This, in conversation with familiar figures like Durkheim and Weber, he calls "the normativity of enchantment" (7). But *Secularism in Antebellum America* discloses selves "enchanted" in a particular sense, actuated by "forces only tangentially related to them and never quite in their control." These forces are multiple and varied. "For those living in a secular imaginary," Modern writes, "decisions about religion were often one's own, yet the range of available choices had been patterned and shaped by circumstance. Institutions making their invisible demands. Media generating models of particular choices. Machines enabling you to interact with your decisions and those of others. A choice being made before it presents itself as such. Unseen something haunting the day" (6, 7). *This* is the ghostly secularism, vastly structuring and inapprehensible in its immanent totality, that Modern wishes to restore to the conversation about modernity under the sign of the secular. For together, these forces make up not only "the strange processes by which the religious and the secular were made compatible"; they make up, too, what Modern calls "the disciplinary air of the secular age" (20–21, 6). Indeed, one of the signal clarities of Modern's work is to be found in its insistence on the force of secularism not merely as a state policy or even a fixed episteme but as, rather, a self-masking normativity, a *discipline*: an encompassing metaphysics whose dynamic effects are at once world-suturing and, at the level of first principles, regulatory. By focusing on these effects, as against the self-propagating narratives of liberal progress and an ever-expanding enlightened self-emancipation, Modern's work looks to "unsettle the congealed mythos of religious freedom and pluralistic evolution" and to push back hard against liberalism's proliferating "advertisements" for the uncoerced sovereignty of selves (6).[20] His is, we could say, a vigorous countermyth to liberal apologetics prosecuted in the key of "religious freedom."

But *Secularism in Antebellum America* does more than bring secularism into new and clarified focus as one of the governing disciplinary projects proper to a liberal modernity coming to understand itself as true, agentive, free. In his attentiveness to the enveloping metaphysics of secularism, and to the turning of even its most vaporous qualities into normative material effectivities, Modern gives us as well an essential critical grammar for addressing the prodigious *dynamism* of a disciplinary secularism, its quicksilver adaptivity. His work attunes us to secularism not as object but condition, not as enforceable proposition but as something instead *networked*, animated by a self-replicating systematicity. In Modern's terms, what Casanova calls a "doxa" and Asad a "regime" takes shape rather as an intricate machinery, one that works in a distinctively recursive way. For secularism, as Modern describes it, is forever generating an outside, some element that exceeds its parameters, stretching beyond the reach of its formalizing capacities; but it is just as constantly *domesticating* that excess, triangulating it, bringing it at last into the fold of one or another kind of secular legibility, in a recursive circuit of self-legitimation. (To put it differently, secularism is both the ascent *and* the critique of rationalism, where critique is incorporated as melancholia, as Weberian lament *about* disenchantment, as yearning toward lost plenitude, and the rest.)[21] This is one crucial valence of my use of the phrase *the unfinished business of secularism*: where there is an outside, something unassimilated or unincorporated, there is redemptive work for the machinery of secular enfranchisement yet to do.[22]

For Modern, there is thus no stable outside to the feedback loops of secular metaphysics, no debunking or exposing positions that are not themselves liable to be folded back into the processes of secular legitimation. As he glosses the project elsewhere: "All critique is immanent, analysis of the world being but an effect of that world, an effect that in those rare cases is fed back into the scene in such a way as *to inflect rather than affirm* what already is."[23] Postsecular critique, on this salutary model, is a scene of necessary complicities, partial knowledges, unstable tools. And its aim, in Modern's clarifying summary, is not to expose, to disenchant or reenchant, to stake claim to an ultimate Real. It is rather to discompose the textures of the given—to "inflect rather than affirm" the horizons of the possible—as they are authorized by the metaphysics of secularism.

Axiom 4: Secularism has a body.

To approach secularism in this way as an enveloping normative condition—to consider, as Modern puts it, what it is "to be alive within a secular age whose freedoms carry with them their own coercions and their own madness"[24]—is to grapple, necessarily, with both the historicity of the concept and, correlatively, with its amplitude and variability. Casanova rightly observes of "modern secularism" that it "comes in multiple historical forms, in terms of different normative models of the legal-constitutional separation of the secular state and religion; or in terms of the different types of cognitive differentiation among science, philosophy, and theology; or in terms of the different models of practical differentiation among law, morality, and religion, and so on."[25] Given the intimacy of secularism with the political projects clustered in the vicinity of liberalism, and given the huge circumstantial variability of liberal projects as they are enacted in different settings, in differing relations to histories of nationness, global capital, and empire, this must necessarily be so. (Joan Wallach Scott's *Sex and Secularism*, with its comparative surveying of the markedly different, if densely interrelated, secular projects that unfolded in France, the United States, and Egypt, is exemplary in its attentiveness to exactly the variability Casanova invokes.) Modern's work, like my own in this book, follows on the historical ligaturing of an account like Foucault's in regarding the American nineteenth century as an especially revealing passage in the career of secularism, inasmuch as it witnesses the solidification of a liberal-democratic project while *also*, in simultaneity, ushering in a mad proliferation of competing religiosities. It's a given that the grammar that links up secularism to these and related powers—to liberalism as forged in industrializing empire—will vary considerably, site to site. So too will its corresponding normativities.

But there remains much to say, even at this necessary level of abstraction, about the content of these normativities. From the backward-looking perspective of the twenty-first century, for instance, little seems clearer than that the secular imaginary propagates not only stories about good religion in its opposition to bad belief but, woven in and through these, stories about *the fate of the flesh*: about embodiment, differentiation, and the corporeally liberating and/or imprisoning effects of the life of the spirit. In this, we need only think of the wild proliferation of contemporary stories about religiosity and an always-racialized *gender*. Indeed, ours is a moment in which it appears to be especially easy to take such stories not as instances of disciplinary normativity but as, in essence, the reverse: as testaments to the evidently close and ineradicable ties between secularism and the liberation of women. This presumption has come to speak in many tongues, though perhaps no iteration was quite as crystallized as that of Ronald Inglehart and Pippa Norris, who argued in the pages of *Foreign Policy* in 2003 that what Samuel Huntington famously referred to as a "clash of civilizations" was in fact "more to do with eros than demos." This was because the worrying "gap in values" "between the West and the Muslim world" was, for them, most deeply entailed in commitments to "gender equality and sexual liberalization," both of which—as they would go on to argue in their book *Rising Tide: Gender Equality and Cultural Change around the World*—were the happy offspring of secularization.[26]

This narrative has by now an easy familiarity: in the name of women's rights, as Sara Farris recently put it, Western pundits, conservative politicians, and the neoliberal state—as well as some Western feminisms—assail the backwardness of an unenlightened (and sweepingly homogenized) "Muslim world" and figure that world's putatively uninflected cruelty to women as a function of its *failure to be secular*.[27] Lila Abu-Lughod, in *Do Muslim Women Need Saving?*, calls this the "new common sense about global women's rights and saving Muslim women in particular."[28] As Abu-Lughod makes plain, these are, quite precisely, redemption narratives, at the center of which is a fantasy-figure supersaturated with gendered and racial meaning: the brown women ensnared in and by bad belief (to ring a slight change on Gayatri Spivak's paradigmatic formulation). Secularism, in this telling, *has a body*: liberal, rights-bearing, enjoying the right to choose belief (made maximally legible in oppositionality, the choice to disbelieve). It is, in such redemptive polemics, the body these belief-imprisoned women desire, do not yet have, but might, through the imperial munificence of Western intervention, at last acquire.[29]

The scholarship of Saba Mahmood works especially exactingly to unravel this interweaving of secular self-regard and the fantasy-figure of the cruelly un- or presecularized Muslim woman. It is the labor of *Politics of Piety*, from 2005—and amplified in her newer work, *Religious Difference in a Secular Age: A Minority Report*, from 2015—to disturb the normative presumptions of (late) liberalism as they operate not only in colonial geopolitics but in the idioms of critique itself—and of feminist critique in particular. At the heart of Mahmood's ethnography of female pietist movements in the mosques of late-twentieth-century Cairo is an unwriting of what she argues is the overburdened, ultimately fetishized metaconcept of *agency*. "The ongoing importance of feminist scholarship on women's agency cannot be emphasized enough," she writes, "especially when one remembers that Western popular media continues to portray Muslim women as incomparably bound by the unbreakable chains of religious and patriarchal oppression."[30] Folded into those modes of critique that center agency and its inhibition, Mahmood argues, is a series of presumptions about the character and content of freedom, autonomy, humanness itself—all of which are in alarmingly untroubled accord with the triumphalist self-understanding of liberal secularism (what Asad, marking out the target of his critique, calls "the triumphalist history of the secular"[31]). These presumptions look, in their way, bland and innocuous: "that all human beings have an innate desire for freedom, that we all somehow seek to assert our autonomy when allowed to do so, that human agency primarily consists of acts that challenge social norms and not those that uphold them." But these are precisely the "normative liberal assumptions" that Mahmood asks us to interrogate, "in part because liberal assumptions about what constitutes human nature and human agency have become integral to our humanist intellectual traditions," with distorting and delimiting effects on the enterprise of critique itself.[32] In her engagements with the women's pietist movements Mahmood discloses more than the contingency of these normative propositions, their fealty to universalizing conceptions of the human in which only certain dispositions *count* as autonomy and certain comportments of the self register as agency. She finds, too, a stark narrowing of the aperture of humanness, whereby subjects outside the charmed circle of secular self-understanding find themselves designated as wanting in freedom, deficient in agency, *hindered in the attainment of a full humanness*. From here, of course, it is a short step to violence—to that "readiness to cause pain to those who are to be saved by being humanized."[33] This is the violent promise of secular redemption, whose persistent (though not sole) twenty-first-century fulcrum is the Muslim woman, poised for rescue from the self-cancellation of religious devotion.[34]

Mahmood's point is not that the movements of which the women she studied were a part are insusceptible to coding as patriarchal, or nonliberal, or nonliberatory, or even that they do not or cannot cause (gendered) pain. Nor is it that under secular conditions in which legitimate religion is complexly privatized, women—*as women*—do not bear a special burden in representing the dangerous instability of belief, or in embodying the breathless susceptibility of "good religion" to the incursion of bad belief, whereby the policing of the one can stand in for the stabilization of the other.[35] It is rather that the actions undertaken within those movements, and the forms of life that flourish there, are not resultantly *nonviable*, nonfeminist, necessarily coerced, or for that matter politically or social negligible. Resisting the normative presumptions bundled into what she calls "the trope of *resistance*," and refusing those styles of "progressive politics" whose orientation toward an inevitable teleology "makes it hard for us to see and understand forms of being and action that are not necessarily encapsulated by the narrative of subversion and reinscription of norms," Mahmood asks us to inquire instead after precisely those "forms of life" enabled in these movements "that are not so easily captured in terms of a relationship of negation to the existing hegemonic order."[36] To do otherwise is to consign the movement's women to one or another triumphalist, violently humanizing secular narrative—a narrative that, as Linell E. Cady and Tracy Fessenden remark, "threads the narrative of gender and sexual emancipation into its own triumphal plotline, such that . . . robust expressions of Islamic feminism betoken the victory of *secular* forces, whatever the evidence to the contrary."[37]

Joan Wallach Scott, whose recent volume *Sex and Secularism* leans especially forcefully against the tenacious vision of "secularism as the guarantor of equality between women and men," gives a compelling new valence to Mahmood's work.[38] Against that increasingly hegemonic bit of putative common sense linking secularism to female liberation, Scott marshals the bracing contrary claim that, far from being a merely vestigial or unexpurgated holdover haunting secular regimes, gender inequality has been in fact *hardwired* into the politics of secularism, in varied but widespread and persisting ways. In pursuit of this polemical counterclaim, Scott gives ample consideration to the ways that the secular privatization of religion burdens women in particular with the task of representing all that is potentially unstable, and so in need of coercive discipline, in religiosity itself. But her work also makes a startling turn.

In *Sex and Secularism* Scott directs our attention to the great Weberian subject of *disenchantment*, and in particular to "the transformations that 'disenchantment' brought to the legitimation of political power." Arguing with and alongside Claude Lefort, she notes that with the ultimate fall of the gods—with the recession of divine authorization for political power— comes a distinctive crisis in legitimacy: the absent center or "empty place," in Lefort's terms, of liberal-democratic power. (Democracy, Lefort remarks, "is instituted and sustained by the dissolution of the markers of certainty. It inaugurates a history in which people experience a fundamental indeter- minacy as to the basis of power, law and knowledge.") In Scott's ingenious repurposing of psychoanalytic frameworks, the fundamental unknowability of sex—the impossibility of fixing "the ultimate meaning of the difference of sex"—becomes both a figure for democracy's own foundational indetermi- nacy and, more crucially, *a vehicle for its overcoming.* "Notions of difference based on sex were fundamental to the conceptualization of political moder- nity, and . . . secular subjects," Scott argues, precisely insofar as they "sought to resolve what Lefort referred to as the indeterminacy of democracy—its abstractions (the individual, rights, nations, representation)—by grounding them in a seemingly concrete referent: the visible, sexed bodies of women and men." Scott avers that "the attribution of meaning to sexed bodies"—that is to say, gender—"is the implementation of the always imperfect attempt at discipline."[39] And yet it is precisely there, in the rushes of Weberian dis- enchantment, that the aspiring discourses of science and natural reason— secularism's foot soldiers—come sweeping onto the scene. For these dis- courses promise to stabilize that chaotic indeterminacy and to solidify, as *maximally natural*, what they produce as the most self-evident of human facts: the difference between the sexes. Secular science, as Scott refigures it, is the discourse that speaks the holy truth of sexual difference, and so of secular political legitimacy. For her, gender inequality is in this way a component of secularism, not some fleeting, soon-to-be-righted infirmity: feature, not bug.

As all these examples make plain, the gendered subjects of the secular imaginary are also, in simultaneity, *racialized* subjects—so much so that to speak this way (with the grammatical hiccups of "also" and "in simultane- ity") is finally a poor, distorting way of speaking. The gender of Muslim women is not an addition to, or inflection of, the racialization of Islam, just as the simultaneity of accord and discord in the white woman's relation to universalized "rights" is not ancillary but constitutive. The matter is not that these are equivalent or interchangeable or sequential differences—easily comparable susceptibilities of the flesh to politically efficacious coding—or that the regime of secularism makes use of them as such. The crucial point is rather that *the discourse of secularism conjugates what flesh it encounters*—that it both propounds and depends upon styles of interwoven racialization and sexual difference, that in turn ratify and refigure one another. "Is There a Secular Body?" Charles Hirschkind wondered in a 2011 issue of *Cultural Anthropology*, to which I think we may, in the light of these strong theorizations, answer with an emphatic affirmative.[40] As Foucault is everywhere at pains to remind us, social structures *invent* the objects through and upon which they act. They are, that is, forever in the business of imagining the bodies proper to them: of conceiving the parameters, the capacities and liabilities, and the organizing coherences of a body their cosmologies at once solicit, presume, and enact.[41] In this, secularism is no different.

The vaunted neutrality of secular politics thus does not extend without interruption across corporeal difference. As Scott and Mahmood argue forcefully, such differences are rather made to appear, are invested with heft and live significance, in and through secularism. We ought to observe, too, that these residues of difference do not make for an *inadmissibility* into secular orders, even if they do make for an obliquity to their universalizing terms—an ill-fittedness that, like a bad conscience, can sometimes prickle the secular imaginary, disturbing the benign expansiveness of its self-conception. For the very promise of secular redemption hinges, as we have seen, upon the legitimating toleration of *some* styles of difference and, most of all, upon the offer of *eventual* inclusion. Through the ceaseless production of an *un*included outside, the secular imaginary keeps permanently operative its cruelly optimistic promise of an ultimate, if forever forestalled, enfranchisement. It is this perpetual belatedness that (as scholars like Lauren Berlant, Sara Ahmed, and Jasbir Puar have been especially good at showing) transforms these embodied obliquities into secularism's own authorizing figures, marks of its unfinished business.[42] Asad puts it memorably: "Thus what has often been described as the political exclusion of women, the propertyless, colonial subjects, in liberalism's history can be re-described as the gradual extension of liberalism's incomplete project of universal emancipation."[43]

And for those forms of life that, through all these processes of inclusion and postponement, remain outside the perimeter of secular legitimacy, there is a different fate. We might think again of Modern's contention that under the normative sociality of disciplinary secularism, "ways of knowing the world" found "illegitimate" registered as "failures on the part of individuals and, perhaps, *entire communities*, to assume their full humanity."[44] Subgroups, in other words, can menace the life, the health, and the flourishing of general populations, and so must be managed accordingly. Some forms of embodied life, in their errancy, are more expendable than others.

Axiom 5: Secularism is a biopolitics.

Criticism has not wanted for a conceptual vocabulary to describe the rationalized distribution of capacities across populations in a slatted, hierarchized economy of life, ranging from the healthy to the expendable. One prominent term for these proceedings is, of course, *biopolitics*. The biopolitical names an order of power that operates through a disciplinary investment in the biological life of mass social phenomena, as these are disaggregated into subspecies and micropopulations, and rationalized in an optimizing calculus designed to foster some forms of life, inhibit or disallow others, and regulate them collectively in a flexible economy of interaction. (Kyla Schuller offers a deft and compact definition: "Biopower functions as an umbrella term combining two different yet overlapping instruments of post-sovereign power deployed within the regime of civilization: the discipline of the individual body, which worked to 'integrate the body into a system of economic productivity'; and the 'regulatory controls' of biopolitics, which 'aim to adjust population to economic processes.'")[45] To say that secularism conjugates the flesh it encounters, and offers a kind of body as the redemptive (if never quite habitable) telos toward which its disciplining insistences are aimed, is to begin to frame out matters like the racialization of religion and the desecularization of raced subjects as operative elements within a larger economy of life: what I will be calling, throughout *Make Yourselves Gods*, the biopolitics of secularism.

Such a biopolitical framing of secular discourse can be glimpsed in much of the work we have surveyed already (as in Modern's remarks above about population, say), and particularly in feminist accounts tuned to secularism's mobilization of racial and sexual difference. It borrows especially from the insights of a historian of religion and sexuality like Molly McGarry, whose *Ghosts of Futures Past* reckons exactly with the striking contiguity of our critical narratives of rationalized sex and secularized religion. McGarry's work shows that the emergence of "sexuality"—that great switching-point for disciplinary and biopolitical orders of power, where, in Foucault's phrase, "body and population meet"—is, as Foucault narrates it, another kind of disenchantment story: in the now-canonical genealogy, we move, as McGarry puts it, from "the Catholic confessional . . . to the psychoanalyst's couch."[46] One thrust of McGarry's argument is that such a way of telling the story of sexuality leaves us ill equipped to recognize, *as* sex, those esoteric, fugitive, spirit-fired inhabitations of the flesh that were fomented at quite a distance from the assessing gaze of rationalized medical practice. ("If the confessional is one culturally specific site for producing speech about the self," she argues, "the Protestant evangelical tent, the revival meeting, and the Spiritualist séance may be among its American corollaries.")[47] But the corollary, metahistorical polemic of McGarry's work is equally crucial. It is that the solidification of modern sexuality and that of secular hegemony were conjoined processes, entwined and codeterminant, bound up with one another in strategies of rationalization, differentiation, and above all interiorization. (Spirituality and sexuality, that is, emerge as twinned truths of the self, each requiring a regime of assiduous cultivation and expert management, and each subject to occult perversions.) The becoming-hegemonic, across the postdisestablishment American nineteenth century, of both secularism and a newly constellated "modern" sexuality (complete with homo- and heterosexual versions, for instance) is for McGarry not some curious historical happenstance. Rather, it is the mark of an inextricable mutuality. Hegemonic secularism, we might say, was *always* a biopolitics; biopolitics was, likewise, always a component of secularism.

Of course, every year torn off the calendar of the twenty-first century seems to make this insight at once more important and easier to believe. The torrential Islamophobia of the new millennium, and the violent racialization of Muslims of every conceivable variety in the register of fully civilizational threats, might induce us to imagine that the biopoliticization of secularism is something of a new tactic, as novel as "travel" bans or American statutes staking out firm stances in opposition to the creeping emergence—in, say, Oklahoma—of "Sharia law." There are ugly novelties in the Trumpian moment, to be sure. And yet biopoliticized secularism is not one of them. To the contrary, such braidings of erotic hygiene, devotional propriety, and racial status, all of them tuned to a loosely framed "Christianity"—to religion made seamless with secularism—have been the very stuff of American imperial ambitions for centuries.

Consider only one especially vivid milestone from the archive, which in later chapters will be crucial to our considerations of the fate of the Mormons in the American West. Consider the "Code of Indian Offenses," or

"Code of Religious Offenses," ratified in 1883 by the Bureau of Indian Affairs, a government agency that after the Civil War had been given over to a variety of Christian missionaries as a part of Grant's ambitious 1868 "Peace Policy."[48] It is worth quoting at length, if only for the clarity with which it broadcasts biopoliticized secularism as a strategy of imperial power. Here are some of the Native "crimes" the BIA sought to curtail: *interesting + disturbing*

> 4th. The "sun-dance," the "scalp-dance," the "war-dance," and all other so-called feasts assimilating thereto, shall be considered "Indian offenses," and any Indian found guilty of being a participant in any one or more of these "offenses" shall, for the first offense committed, be punished by withholding from the person or persons so found guilty by the court his or their rations for a period not exceeding ten days. . . .

> 5th. Any plural marriage hereafter contracted or entered into by any member of an Indian tribe under the supervision of a United States Indian agent shall be considered an "Indian offense," cognizable by the Court of Indian Offenses. . . .

> 6th. The usual practices of so-called "medicine-men" shall be considered "Indian offenses" cognizable by the Court of Indian Offenses, and whenever it shall be proven to the satisfaction of the court that the influence or practice of a so-called "medicine-man" operates as a hindrance to the civilization of a tribe, or that said "medicine-man" resorts to any artifice or device to keep the Indians under his influence, or shall adopt any means to prevent the attendance of children at the agency schools, or shall use any of the arts of a conjurer to prevent the Indians from abandoning their heathenish rites and customs, he shall be adjudged guilty of an Indian offense.[49]

In subsequent chapters we will dwell more closely with the proscriptions laid out here, and their relevance to the Mormons (who were from the perspective of the settler state still another Western sect threatening the health of the greater republic with its fantastic rites and rituals, its arational behaviors, its promotion of nonmonogamous marriage). For now it is enough to observe that racial redemption, erotic propriety, and religious correction take shape here as part of a single, fused strategy of disciplinary intervention. (It unfolds on the terrain of what Scott Lauria Morgensen names "the biopolitics of settler colonialism.")[50] The state's target, in its actions, is a misfiring form of life, an embodied heathenishness that travels along an unbroken circuit conjoining race and sex and devotion—a circuitry that, in essence, *is* the biopolitical life of the subpopulation its authors mark out as "Indian." Here, though, Native racialization is not solely a matter of erring religiosity, Native perversity not solely a matter of racial degeneracy, and Native zealotry not solely a matter of some primal carnal backwardness. The machinery of disciplinary secularism feeds each into the other, materializing *as life* their conjunction and mutual ratification, and calculating that life according to metrics of conformity and threat, viability and expendability. The "Code of Indian Offenses" is a brief document, authored by representatives of a state that had taken back, *from* the emissaries of religion, the tasks of civilizing rule. And yet it is a pristine snapshot of the biopolitics of secularism, made functional for American settler-colonial policy, circa 1888.

Axiom 6: "Secularization" is a not a fantasy—change in the conditions of belief is real—but the secularization thesis is a distorting, partisan way of telling the story of that change.

If the work of postsecular critique has made any one point incontestably clear it is that (as Jared Hickman and I put it, some years ago) the secularization thesis is dead. Few, that is, are by now persuaded by accounts of modernity as a victorious lurch toward self-emancipation: a swing from credulity to enlightened skepticism, superstition to rationality, orthodoxy to tolerance, atavism to civilization, and all the rest of it.[51] But this is not to say that the secularization thesis has had done with us. Hickman and I contended, to the contrary, that many of even our most incisive critical languages, our most necessary tools of critique, bear the marks of their germination *within* the secularization thesis. As we have just observed via McGarry, for instance, critical languages about "sexuality," inasmuch as they map out its emergence in the still-indispensable terms Foucault forged for us, nevertheless carry within them a vision of sex as a kind of secularization, a disenchantment of the flesh. This is part of what is at stake for Mahmood when she launches her critique of secularism with the proviso that "liberal assumptions about what constitutes human nature and human agency have become integral to our humanist intellectual traditions," in ways she wishes to interrupt.[52] The terms of critique with which we address race, with which we grapple with sex, with which we understand something of their cross-wiring: these are themselves freighted with the premises of secularism. The genealogical imperative for postsecular critique has not been to abandon our categories—or not quite—but to try to see clearly how the ideology of secularism brought them into being, and to disentangle them in turn from secularist presumption.[53]

In the name of such disentanglement, we might usefully frame the matter like this: "secularism" names the ideology that, in an occluded way, *operates* the secularization thesis. It marks, as Asad shows us, the governing interlinked conceptual premises and grounding-points that make plausible, in the first instance, the story of modernity as a swing from credulity to enlightenment. But that occlusion is especially important. For "secularization" functions ongoingly less as an especially plausible historical narrative—again, it is not—than an ideologically specific way of telling the story of modernity itself: it is, in short, the way certain of the victors of modernity's many seasons of domination and slaughter (Christians, liberals, secularists) collaborate to tell the story of their victory. It is a triumphalist narrative in precisely this sense.

Among the most salient matters to be obscured—and it is here that the work of Charles Taylor, with which we began, most *contributes* to secularization ideologies—is the structuring force of Christianity itself within the transformations later assembled under the sign of "secularization" and bundled into the condition of belief called "secularism." Thus, when we speak of the distinctively Christian inflection of secularism itself, we refer not only, pace Taylor, to the church whose internal self-transformations themselves helped to launch a wide alteration in the available conditions of belief. We speak as well of Christianity as agent in, and authorizing authority for, global imperialism. "The process by which Latin Christendom got to be secular," the editors of *Varieties of Secularism in a Secular Age* note, "was in large part the same as the process by which it got to be colonial."[54] Or as Casanova himself observes, in an otherwise fulsomely praising account of *A Secular Age*, "one could argue with Peter van der Veer that the very pattern of Western secularization cannot be fully understood if one ignores the crucial significance of the colonial encounter in European developments."[55] A more polemical way to turn the point would be to say, with Gil Anidjar, that "secularism is a name Christianity gave itself when it invented religion, when it named its other or others as religions"—that, in brief, "Orientalism *is* secularism"—and that any account of secularism that leaves out what Tomoko Masuzawa calls "the sacralizing character of Orientalism" will, of necessity, lapse into a kind of imperial apologism. For Christianity, in Anidjar's framing, "*reincarnated* itself as secular . . . spreading its gentle

and loving white wings ever further in a world unsuspecting of enchantment or disenchantment, on the efficient heels of earlier missionaries and
merchants[,] . . . its industrious foot soldiers, and its imaginative and unique
scientific achievements."[56]

Masuzawa's work in *The Invention of World Religions* is especially telling
here. She charts the emergence of "world religions" in a set of nascent comparative sciences: comparative philology, comparative religion, comparative
theology. This comparativist "modern discourse on religions," she argues,
"was from the first—that is to say, inherently, if also ironically—a discourse
of secularization; at the same time, it was clearly a discourse of othering."
It made religions comparable by first inventing an *essence*, called "religion"
or "religiosity," that could then be found in variable but fundamentally like
iterations across the increasingly territorialized globe. "Religion," as essence,
became in these discourses putatively universal, while Christianity itself
emerged in curiously doubled form: as at once *"uniquely universal"*—the
center from which all other religious enterprises radiated—and, distinctively, as "the religion of Europe." In this layered way, Masuzawa shows, comparativist discourses enabled "the vital work of churning the stuff of Europe's
ever-expanding epistemic domain, and of forging from that ferment an
enormous apparition: the essential identity of the West."[57] This essentializ-
ing formation of what Masuzawa calls the "singularity of Christianity," and
the subsequent "Christian-monopolistic use of the term 'world religion,'"
worked to bring Christianity into accord with that *other* colonial export, that
grounding-point of the essential identity of the West and authorizing figure
for the placing of enormous swaths of planetary life in subjection: this, of
course, was whiteness.[58]

We arrive, precisely here, at what is perhaps the gravest inbuilt misapprehension of Taylor's monumental work: its commitment to tracking the
emergence of a densely invested secular modernity, and its fragilized condition of belief, in the absence of a live sense that secular modernity *has been
made and sustained in colonial violence*. What comes of this is a marring
disregard for the resultant ways that the categories most precious to secular
self-understanding (freedom, agency, reason, autonomy) come down to us
bloodied, steeped in the history of their use as tools for racialized subjugation.
That is the secularism, as established through Christian domination, made
available to us in the archive of anticolonial and antiracist critique, in works
by Walter Mignolo, Édouard Glissant, Edward Said, and Hortense Spillers,
as well as in more recent scholarship by Asad, Mahmood, Anidjar, Masuzawa, Joseph Massad, and Puar. It is made perhaps most vivid in the work of

Sylvia Wynter, whose "1492: A New World View," for instance, provides an indispensable road map for the world-shattering force of contact. For Wynter, this moment of encounter, where radically divergent cosmologies and incommensurate orders of gods come into violent contact, effectively initiates a conception of a species-wide *nonhomogeneity*, an ontologization of sociocultural variety that metastasizes, in the machinery of colonial expansion, *as* race.[59] In a global world newly traversed, and so newly available to itself *as* planetary and immanent, the disclosure of what Jared Hickman, in the Wynterian key, calls "a radically unforeseen heterogeneity" among its inhabitants precipitates a crisis at once cosmic and, explicitly, racial: a battle between rival gods, mapped onto the flesh.[60] Hence, for Hickman as for Anidjar, "secularism" is finally a pale and misapprehending name for racialized Christian domination. It names, more properly, "the Euro-Christian shaping of global immanence as an eschatological stage for becoming god by dishing out salvation or damnation to non-Euro-Christian heathens." (Secularization, in this framing, is "a mythic narrative of Euro-Christian ascendancy in the finite theo-geopolitical space of the globe.") For Hickman, what moderns have taken up rather blithely as the humanist triumph over the brutal rule of gods, and have with great self-satisfaction named "secularism," speaks much more potently to "a genuine effect of godlike being-in-the-world" available to the victors of colonial domination. It codifies "the blasé stance," in Hickman's killing phrase, "of the complacently divinized."[61]

In these senses, then, secularism is a *theodicy*: a sacralized vindication of the world—colonial, racially stratified, authorizing itself in the exclusions it pledges one day to redeem—as it is. Here, too, is the point of contact between Latin Christendom's obscure but broadly consequential internal reforms and what Spillers calls "the synonymity struck between Africanness and enslavement."[62] What emerges, finally, is a vision in which the much-celebrated de-absolutization of the power of God or the gods reappears as a human capacity for explicitly racial domination, which can then be misrecognized as, precisely, godlikeness. Secular moderns *become gods*, and know that divinization in nothing so much as the exercise of planetary dominion.

Axiom 7: Secularism is a theodicy: the racialized theodicy of hegemonic liberalism.

We can now, I think, venture some summary propositions. We have seen, first of all, that secularism names not the climate of belief that results from a historical process called "secularization," that much-advertised swing from benighted credulity to disenchanted skepticism, fanaticism to rationality, orthodoxy to tolerance. Secularism names instead the ideological compound that makes the secularization thesis go, undergirding it with a series of binarized distinctions that circulate against a universalizing background. Secularism thus is not the condition of life and belief proper to a world that has accomplished the diminishment of religion in public life, or the vanquishing of unreasoning orthodoxy. Irreducible to state tolerance or official neutrality, it is not the cure for the benightedness of orthodoxy; as envisioned by postsecular critique, it is orthodoxy in other clothes. Or rather, in the phrases we have seen, it is a normative sociality, an immanent frame, the set of inaugural cleavings—of reason from unreason, skepticism from credulity, belief from fanaticism—that allows us to know anything at all as "religious" and to know the "secular" as the thing that it is not. Secularism is, in other words, a *discipline*, one that points less to the dissolution of religion in modern public life than to the disciplined accommodation of patterns of belief and devotion to the premises of liberal rationality, its polities, its arrangements of life, its *bodies*. It gives name to the *enforced accommodation of practices of belief to the order of a hegemonic liberalism*, such that the salient division, under conditions of secularism, is not between the religious and the nonreligious but between religion and *bad belief*: a divide between those styles of spirit-practice that comport themselves in accordance with the dictates of liberalism (and so get to count *as* religion) and those that, because they do not, figure instead as species of zealotry, fanaticism, backwardness, or (in the au courant idioms of racialization) *fundamentalism* or *radical fundamentalism*.

In the most compressed of terms, then, secularism might best be apprehended as *the racialized theodicy of hegemonic liberalism*. That, ultimately, is the object of postsecular critique, or at least of the postsecular critique to which I am most committed in the work that follows, and whose intellectual origins I have tried to sketch out. It is in these terms that we can, I think, best mark the dense simultaneity of the operations of secularism—as disciplinary sociality, biopolitical machinery, imperial liberalism's environing atmosphere. And we can begin to mark out, too, something of secularism's dynamic and self-replicating systematicity, that adaptive recursivity that, as we have seen, is stitched into the many redemption-stories secular projects most like to tell about themselves. In these stories, the very legitimacy of secularism appears again and again, with paradoxical insistence, in how much it has *excluded*, how much it will not countenance. For those are the very elements (the story goes) that shall *now*, at last, through the expanding grace of secular inclusivity, enjoy the benefits of what Puar calls "an innocuous inclusion into life."[63] In good time, they too will burnish the glory of secularism (the story goes) by bringing nearer to culmination the perpetually "incomplete project of human emancipation."[64] Such are the different dimensions of recursivity and authority, of critique and its remaking as legitimacy, that make up the tangled inner grammars of secularism.

MAKE YOURSELVES GODS

My shorthand for this encompassing structure is, again, the racialized theodicy of hegemonic liberalism, and it is the burden of this book to give that conceptualization of secularism its maximal historical and analytic heft. The story of the Mormons of the nineteenth century—which is the story of how the exemplars of bad belief came to be transformed, over a handful of vibrant and violent decades, into paragons of good religion—throws that structure, and the processes of its hegemonic solidification, into extraordinarily detailed relief. And it reminds us, too, how saturated by distorting secularist premises even our most cherished languages of critique yet remain. Our familiar stories of sex, of gender liberation, of racialization: to the degree that they speak in unwitting accord with an only *seemingly* routed secularization thesis, they require reattunement, elasticization, renovation. That, at any rate, is the wager of *Make Yourselves Gods*.

JOY

ENDLESS FELICITY

The Radiant Body of Early Mormon Theology

THE CEREMONY

ON 5 APRIL 1841, A YOUNG woman stood beneath an elm tree in far western Illinois. This was Louisa Beaman, twenty-six, and at this point in her life an orphan. Her father had died in Kirtland, Ohio, in 1837; her mother, only a few months before, in 1840. In the aftermath of that latter calamity, Beaman had gone to live with her sister, Mary, and with Mary's husband, and it was that man, Joseph Bates Noble, who now stood before her. But not only him.

Noble was a devout Mormon. He had moved from New York to Kirtland in 1834, with the earliest Mormon émigrés, and had suffered the reversals and disappointments—indeed the terrors—of Mormon displacement. But then, in 1840, something extraordinary happened to Joseph Noble. As if in recognition of this long-standing devotion, the prophet himself had shared with him a momentous secret. None other than Joseph Smith had instructed him, Noble was to report years later, in "the principle of celestial or plural marriage, or a plurality of wives."[1] Smith's startling request was that Noble perform the sealing between Smith and Noble's orphaned sister-in-law, Louisa. This would be, according to later testimony, "the first Marriage Ceremony according to the Patriarchal order of Marriage ever performed in this dispensation."[2] (The first marriage ever *performed*, though not the first plural marriage: Smith appears to have been married polygamously to two other women by this time.)[3] The honor of the request could not have been lost on Noble. "In revealing this to you," Smith is reported to have said to Noble, "I have placed my life in your hands, therefore do not betray me."[4]

Noble did not betray the prophet, though his treatment of his orphaned sister-in-law is a matter considerably more equivocal. As Todd Compton observes in *In Sacred Loneliness*, we do not know if Smith himself announced the doctrine of plural marriage to Beaman, or if this explication, along with the task of persuasion, was left to Noble, in whose home she resided. Nor is it easy to reconstruct the degree to which Beaman herself would have been overawed, or enthused, or honored, or more plainly terrified, by the prospect of such a union. We know she had met Smith before. When living in Avon, New York, her family—also among the earliest converts to Mormonism— had housed Smith, along with a number of early missionaries and apostles, for several days. This was in 1834, when Louisa Beaman was nineteen. In what Compton calls the "family tradition" of her future husband, Brigham Young, Beaman is said to have "asked the Lord in fervent prayer for a testimony concerning the principle."[5] In this version, such testimony was given to her, and she accepted it.

And so she found herself under an elm tree, standing before her brother-in-law and the prophet Joseph himself, on a day in early April. The scene is bucolic and, somewhat strikingly given what Compton calls the "cloak-and-dagger" atmosphere of early polygamy, semipublic. Yet this was to be a queerer than ordinary wedding, and not only because it was by design a rebuke to, and a supersession of, any merely civil rite, or even because the groom was himself already a married man. In part as a measure of the severity of these disruptions of the normative frame of antebellum social and sexual life, there were peculiarities to the ceremony. Chief among them was that the bride, Louisa Beaman, attended her marriage *in disguise*. In a journal entry decades later, Franklin D. Richards would write, "Br. Joseph B. Noble being the master of ceremonies was present and During the visit related that he performed the first sealing ceremony in this Dispensation in which he united Sister Louisa Beaman to the prophet Joseph in May—I think the 5th day in 1841 during the evening under the Elm tree in Nauvoo. The Bride disguised in a coat and hat."[6] Louisa Beaman—who would go on to be a figure much recalled by later Mormons—was married to the prophet, in "the first Marriage Ceremony according to the Patriarchal order," disguised as a man.[7]

HISTORICITY

To trace out the trajectories of early Mormon theology, ritual, and practice is to be confronted at virtually every turn with meanings and countermeanings so extravagant and overripe, and also so strangely telegraphed in their density of signification, that we seem to err in calling them merely "ironies." Mormonism is in this respect one of those historical phenomena that seems always to be overperforming itself, disturbing the parameters that separate the fictive from the putatively real—recalling to us, that is, the historicity of our categories. Famously, near the end of his life, Smith would weigh in on exactly this point: "No man knows my history," he would say. "I don't blame you for not believing my history. If I had not experienced what I have, I could not have believed it myself."[8] What hobbles historical knowledge here is not obscurity or opacity but something nearer to abundance, excess, an *actual* that outstrips the conceptual frameworks we bring to it.

It is part of the endeavor of this book to show that one of the most salient of these frameworks is the complex orchestration of proper belief and dangerous unreality, of saving faith and malign delusion, called "secularism." In his offhand self-description, Smith draws our attention to the ways Mormonism fractures the coordinates of secular belonging and knowledge, those grounding-points for the collective Real of an antebellum America. (We might think again of Talal Asad's short list of stacked conceptual divisions at the center of "the shifting web of concepts making up the secular": "*belief* and *knowledge, reason* and *imagination, history* and *fiction, symbol* and *allegory, natural* and *supernatural, sacred* and *profane*.")[9] But if early Mormonism confounds these familiar oppositions, it shows us something else as well about the very domain of secular distinction, its zones of operation and effectivity. For if Smith is correct, we do well to think of secularism as a matter not merely conceptual or epistemological but *intimate*, adhering closely to the life of the flesh. As Louisa Beaman's idiosyncratic marriage ceremony renders for us especially vividly, the cleavings of secularism extend into divisions between credible and incredible embodiment, sanctioned and deviant desire, flourishing and dangerous carnality. Nothing in the whole of nineteenth-century Mormonism makes this clearer than the theory and practice of polygamy, or so condenses the early Mormon disruption of the grounding oppositions of the secular. It is, I want to argue, Smith's exemplary fabulation, the gemstone in the ornate architecture of his sweeping cosmological vision. And, as Beaman's marriage suggests, it was to be the most unassimilable of Mormon practices.

Think again of the details of that initial ceremony. In the most immediate senses, Beaman's disguise is hardly inexplicable. The doctrine of plural marriage had begun in secret, and would remain so—at least to the public world beyond the Mormon fold—until several years after Smith's death. It could hardly have been otherwise, at least for a faith aiming to expand and flourish. By 1841, the Mormons had already been uprooted, persecuted, and massacred, with murmurs of sexual impropriety an always-near-to-hand pretext for violence. The 1838 massacre of Mormons at Haun's Mill, in Missouri, was only the bloodiest of such confrontations. All this, too, was *before* Smith's assassination at the hands of a mob, in 1844. When Smith asked Noble, as he would later recall, not to betray him to bloodthirsty antagonists, he was not being paranoid, or not only. Secrecy—again, what Compton aptly calls the "cloak-and-dagger atmosphere" of Nauvoo polygamy, and what I would call its queer sociability[10]—was to be expected.

And yet none of this fully obviates the strangeness of Louisa Beaman's appearance on the day of her marriage, or puts to rest its galloping suggestiveness. So many of what were to be the governing, intractable paradoxes of Mormon polygamy are gathered in the figure of the polygamous bride, conducting secret rituals, done up in the guise of a man. They present themselves to us, one by one. We might read out, in the first place, a great depth of commitment to all that is patriarchal in "patriarchal plural marriage"—as though any ritual or ceremony, of any degree of ecclesiastical importance, must of necessity be the purview solely of men, transacting among themselves. This is polygamy as something like a hypertrophied version of patriarchy, a doubling-down on gender difference and the exalted sacrality of maleness itself, all in the name of an eternalized familialism. And yet, as with so many other Mormon efforts to inhabit a kind of normalcy *more normal* than the merely normative—a sort of hypernormativity—the gesture lists inevitably toward its own undoing: toward the possibility of transgression, deviance, perversity. It is as if, in the gathering for obscure purposes of a cluster of persons gendering themselves male, one occluded scandal—the rupture of sanctioned intimacy in polygamy—finds itself replaced by a rival scandal, this one taking form as the specter of suspect male camaraderie: the torquing of same-sex intimacy, via the derangements of some occult religiosity, into something nearer to perverse desire. A residue of transgression is everywhere we look in the riverside tableau, and is unchastened by explications keyed solely to the need for secrecy. A queer devotionality—a perversity of gender, of sex, and of proper belief—invests the whole of the scene. And with it is a central question: What *is* the proper body of polygamy? What kind of flesh is presumed by it? What kind of body does the theory of polygamy imagine for its subjects? What are its forms, its traits, its capacities?

These are the orienting questions of the section that follows, and I want to use them to pursue a series of linked claims about early Mormonism as, at its core, *a radical theory of embodied life.* This is my central contention, and the anchor-point for much of what I will have to say about Mormonism in its relation to the becoming-hegemonic of secularism in nineteenth-century America. In this reading of Mormonism, polygamy is not some inessential temple rite, a merely notional appendage to the more pressing theological insights and doctrinal imperatives that define the faith in its earliest years. It is not incidental to Smith's cosmology, though, as we shall see, a tremendous range of accounts, both contemporaneous and contemporary, labor to make it appear so. Rather, I will argue, plural marriage is at the defining center of Smith's vision of exaltation. It cements his radically anti-Calvinist, fantastically heretical conviction that mortal persons are not merely not fallen away from God—not merely capable of conversing with God, precisely as the ancient saints of the Old Testament had—but are themselves gods in embryo. Exaltation, in the idioms of early Mormonism, names the expansion of the human out toward the divinity, the celestialized timelessness, that is its destiny. This is the radical vision of embodied life that shapes polygamy so definitively—and that is also, in the most familiar stories of early Mormon theology, so frequently deemphasized or displaced, subject to what I will call a kind of secularizing normalization.

Inasmuch as the conceptual project of the book hinges on this counter-secularizing account of the carnality of early Mormon theology, the work of this chapter will hew especially closely to Smith's writings, dwelling with polygamy and the formulations proximate to it with an unhurrying deliberateness and allowing these conceptualizations what Samuel Morris Brown, in a trenchant moment of methodological self-consciousness, describes as "a freer rein."[11] In this—in adhering so closely to Smith's own self-accounting—the chapter risks what for some may seem a worrying sort of credulity, an extended suspension of the protocols of skepticism that might appear to be called for in relation to Smith's propositions for, say, the body and its divinization, or for that matter in relation to what I will describe as the glancing but genuinely counternormative *gendered* possibilities implicit even in Mormonism's patriarchal plural marriage. I take these risks seriously. I am willing to hazard them here, though, insofar as they seem to me a component part of the hard labor of countersecularizing critique: the labor, that is, of reaching toward formulations that unsettle the forms of secularist presumption woven into even our most incisive paradigms. In any case, in the matter before us it is precisely the solidification of the normative framework that *produces* the categories of the credulous and the critical, the unwary and the properly skeptical, that is at stake in the inquiry itself, and so ought not be hastily presumed. The methodological ambition in what follows is thus to sustain a kind of undebunking critical dwelling with Smith.[12] The wager is that this might move us, in turn, toward a vision of Smith's theology that is committed neither to uncritical heroicization nor to some sweeping anticredulity but that aims instead to materialize some of the possibilities occluded by critical frameworks both explicitly and implicitly secularizing, held in the thrall of the layered conceptual divisions whose concretization we are hoping to trace—toward, we might say, an inside narrative of early Mormon polygamy.

EQUAL PRIVILEGE

"Joseph Smith did not merely wish to set his saints apart," Harold Bloom contends, in the midst of an extended consideration of Mormonism in *The American Religion*. "He wished them to become gods, and he decided polygamy was necessary for that apotheosis."[13] Bloom is not wrong in this, though his framing, as Henry James might have it, starts more hares than it follows. Questions cluster in obscuring density around the matter. It is the case that Smith makes explicit the linking of polygamy to exaltation—to the enlargement of the human toward its bright destiny in godliness—and that he does so in nothing other than the polygamy revelation itself. Dictated in 1843 though not made public until 1852, the text delineates the fate of those who "receive" the Lord's commandments, those men—here, explicitly, they are *men*—who "marry a wife by my word." Smith is very clear on this point:

> Then shall they be Gods, because they have no end; therefore shall they be from everlasting to everlasting, because they continue; then shall they be above all, because all things are subject unto them. Then shall they be Gods, because they have all power, and the angels are subject to them. (*EJS*, 194)

By the time the revelation was published, some eight years after Smith's death, these words would have rhymed with those of Smith's great statement on exaltation, the sermon from 1844 known as the King Follett Discourse. There, in terms we will return to shortly, he had told the Saints, in a mixture of entreaty and command, *You have got to learn how to make yourselves Gods*:

> You have got to learn how to make yourselves Gods in order to save yourselves and be kings and priests to God, the same as all Gods have done—by going from a small capacity to a great capacity, from a small degree to another, from grace to grace, until the resurrection of the dead from exaltation to exaltation. (*EJS*, 235–36)

In the polygamy revelation, Smith had noted that this expansion is *arduous*, demanding of its followers nothing less than a comprehensive undoing of the codes and strictures according to which they had lived, strived, become legible to themselves in the most basic ways. "Except ye abide my law," Smith had written, "ye cannot attain to this glory; for strait is the gate, and narrow the way, that leadeth unto the exaltation and the continuation of the lives, and few there be that find it, because ye receive me not in the world, neither do ye know me" (*EJS*, 194).[14] Narrow and forbidding is the way to celestial enlargement and a becoming-divine of the human. In Smith, that narrow and treacherous path leads, without question, through polygamy.

But why should this be so? How, and according to what prophetic logics, does it follow that an expansion of the human into godliness should be mapped so closely upon, of all possible things, the practice of plural patriarchal marriage? The pairing of polygamy with incipient godliness is not, that is, an especially inevitable conjuncture. What in Smith's prophetic imagination makes it happen? In one of the most common answers to these questions, as heralded in the nineteenth century as in the twentieth, the matter is not terribly complicated, whatever outblown cosmologies, whatever shifting hierarchies of angels and gods in various degrees of enlargement, the Mormons labored to append to the practice of plural marriage. In such accounts, the putative "theology" of polygamy emerges, contrarily, as in essence a set of notions reverse-engineered from its founder's plainly earthly desire to break the rigid bonds of the monogamous couple. Since its appearance, that is, it has been easy to presume that polygamy follows no dictate other than the promptings of Smith's own ungovernable carnality, his hunger for a field of erotic possibility unconstrained by social sanction or doctrinal ban. Precisely this case, in iterations more and less hysterical, would be made about Smith, and the polygamous leaders who followed him, for decades, often as one of a tightly linked set of pretexts for violence. "Under the guise of a religion," Vermont representative Justin S. Morrill would intone in 1857, in a densely freighted set of terms we have already encountered and to which we will return, "this people has established, and seek to maintain and perpetuate, a Mohammedan barbarism revolting to the civilized world."[15] That racializing "barbarism" was, of course, polygamy, which would indeed emerge as one of the Mormon practices best suited to the scripting of the Saints as apart from any embracing national public and as in fact a threat to its flourishing continuation.

For all this fulmination, it is worth remembering that although it was read then (and sometimes now) as merely the expression of the carnal avariciousness of its monomaniacal and perhaps sociopathic founders, plural marriage emerges in Smith as part of a dense and burgeoning *theology*, an intricate cosmology tuned especially closely to the matter of the body, and of pleasure, and of their worldly import. A striking revelation only weeks prior to the polygamy text gives us some initial purchase on plural marriage as an invention with which Smith might manage to materialize—in a real way, *give flesh to*—a number of that cosmology's most essential features. In this text, transcribed by Wilford Woodruff in June of 1843, Smith considers the lives of gods and of angels. It finds him fully inside the prophetic mode that would characterize so much of his later writing—a mode, we might say, of unbelabored heresy, of vernacular playfulness and casual overturning. Here, he is thinking directly about the relation between "Godliness" and the fact of bodiliness:

> Their is much said concerning God the Godhead &. The scripture says their is Gods many & Lords many. The teachers of the day say that the father is God the Son is God & the Holy Ghost is God & that they are all in one body & one God. Jesus says or prays that those that the father had given him out of the world might be made one in us as we are one. But if they were to be stuffed into one person they would make a great God.
>
> If I was to testify that the world was wrong on this point it would be true. (*EJS*, 194–95)

It is in relation to passages like this that Bushman writes of Smith, "The record of his revelations and sermons gives no sense of him arguing against received beliefs. He does not refer to other thinkers as foils for his views. . . . His storytelling was oracular rather than argumentative. He made pro-

nouncements on the authority of his own inspiration."[16] If this overstates the
case somewhat in respect to Smith's inattention to the doctrinal prejudices
of the world, it nevertheless gets us nearer to the beguiling offhandedness of
Smith's heresies. To the "teachers of the day," to "the world," to all the manu-
facturers of an uncontested Protestant orthodoxy, Smith offers the simplest
of words: every one of you, he declares, is wrong. In sentences that so much
strike the note of his later prophetic career, where he habitually weds an
escalatingly unorthodox theological vision to a barbed plainspokenness,
Smith here performs a vernacular debunking of some ground-level tenets
of Protestant theology. "If I was to testify that *the world was wrong,*" he says,
as with a sort of countertheologizing shrug, "it would be true."

The world's mistake in this instance is, however, striking. For Smith, the
familiar theology of the three-personed God misapprehends not merely the
structure of the heavens, its orderly distributions of grace and power. More
grievously, it mistakes what it is to be a god. Of God the father he says,
"He has a bo[d]y of his own." As does God the son. "Each has his own body,"
Smith declares, in rebuke to the fanciful notion that "*if they were to be stuffed
into one person they would make a great God.*" His is a point, that is, about
the divinity of the flesh. For what he is insisting upon here is that to be a
god is, of necessity, to have a body. *That* is his point of polemical insistence.
A god of three persons reduced to one body is, for Smith, a god intolerably
diminished.

That there can be no divinity without a body makes, at this moment, for
a disarming and assertively counternormative sort of theologizing. With all
the expository nonchalance Bushman points us toward, Smith insists on the
plurality of gods, their individuated embodiment, the apostasizing misguid-
edness of Christian presumption. And yet, as radically contrary to Trinitarian Protestantism as this theologizing from 1843 may be, it is not new-
grown, appearing in a sudden rush here in this late-dawning prophetic moment. Such nested countertheories of heaven and earth, each and all of
them, in fact follow from notions that had been percolating within Mormonism from the first. It is as if, in this late moment of prophetic hyperpro-
ductivity, we find Smith chasing out to their broadest consequences some
of the first premises of Mormon theology. Taken separately, these grounding premises can seem remote from matters of embodiment. But they lead
Smith recurrently, and with an inexorable directedness, straight to the per-
plexities and promises of life in the flesh.

Perhaps the first of these premises is that direct revelation, the in-the-
flesh encountering of agents of divinity by mortal persons, has not passed

out of the world. This is broadcast as much in Smith's spiritual biography as in the theology he comes to articulate. Famously, Smith himself claims as his moment of spiritual transformation an encounter with an angel, Moroni, in upstate New York, and it is from the series of visitations that follow that he learns how to create his first great work, his new American bible, the Book of Mormon. In an 1832 account he notes that "in the 16th year of my age a pillar of light above the brightness of the sun at noon day come down from above and rested upon me. I was filled with the spirit of the God" (*EJS*, 28).[17] And then later, "on the 22nd day of Sept[ember] AD 1822"—Smith notes the day—"I called again upon the Lord and he shewed unto me a heavenly vision. For behold an angel of the Lord came and stood before me. It was by night and he called me by name." But the meaning of all this youthful mingling with divinity, for Smith, was not merely that he was, by virtue of such visitations, authorized to speak of the "many things concerning the inhabitants of the earth" that would fill up the Book of Mormon. The lesson is related, but different; the visitation rather ratified, in the register of experience, what the young Smith had already read but not wholly grasped: "For I learned in the scriptures," he writes,

> that God was the same yesterday, to day, and forever. That he was no respecter to [of] persons, for he was God. For I looked upon the sun, the glorious luminary of the earth. And also the moon rolling in their magesty through the heavens. Also the stars, shining in their courses. And the earth upon which I stood. . . . And also man walking forth upon the face of the earth in magesty and in the strength of beauty whose power and intelligence in governing things which are so exceding great and marvilous even in the likeness of him who created them. (*EJS*, 27–28)

If the passage shades off toward what would become a bedrock convention of secularized spirituality—the divinity of the world in its majesty and beauty—it manages, too, to strike notes significantly less familiar. In a foretaste of the demotic mode of prophecy that would become his mainstay, Smith tell us God is *"no respecter to persons,"* which for him means that God offers his revelations with democratic generosity, to persons of low birth as readily as to the highborn. Further, He does so *even still*—"yesterday, to day, and forever"—long past the days of the ancient revelators. To these latter points, far more than to the rote pantheism that follows it, Smith would insistently return.

In *The Viper on the Hearth*, Terryl L. Givens argues that one of the most striking of Smith's theological impulses, and perhaps the most fundamental to Mormonism's coding as "heresy," consists in "the disintegration of that distance that separates the sacred and the profane, that defines religious experience as unfathomable mystery, that constitutes religious feeling as the presence of the ineffable, that renders such terms as holiness, worshipfulness, and reverence as constituting the very essence of religion."[18] That collapse of difference unfolds for Smith in the first instance as a live human openness to, and perhaps even a *susceptibility* to, the direct experience of the divine, here within the quotidian doings of earthly life. Explicitly, Smith intends this as a corrective account both of the mortal world and, as we have already begun to see, of the character of divinity. On this latter point, Mormonism's is not the remote and untranslatable God of Calvinism, a force of implacable, occasionally malign, elementally "unfathomable" Otherness, as Givens has it. The Mormon God by contrast is familiar, approachable, *garrulous*. "Our God shall come," Smith says in an 1835 lecture in Kirtland, "and shall not keep silence" (*EJS*, 51).

When this familiar God speaks, moreover, it is not from the whirlwind. Consider Smith's elaborate reading of the Gospel of Matthew, also from 1835, where he makes a point of objecting to the habit of cloaking divinity in a sort of inapprehensible Otherness by insisting on the wrought *mystery* of revelation, on the impenetrability of divine utterance: "Men are in the habit, when the truth is exhibited by the servants of God, of saying, all is mystery, they are spoken in parables, and, therefore, are not to be understood, it is true they have no eyes to see, and see not; but none are so blind as those who will not see." Smith will have none of this labored mystification of the immediacy of God. His rejoinder is as follows: "And although the Savior spoke this parable to such characters, yet unto his disciples he expounded it plainly; and we have reason to be truly humble before the God of our fathers, that he has left these things on record for us, so plain that, notwithstanding the exertions and combined influence of the priests of Baal, they have not power to blind our eyes and darken our understanding, if we will but open our eyes and read with candor, for a moment" (*EJS*, 71–72).[19] To produce divinity as though it required translation into the common terms of human comprehension is, in Smith's accounting, a double blasphemy. It mistakes not only the generosity but the *nearness* of God, even to the ordinary world of human affairs; and it reduces the world itself, with all the mortal creatures in it, to a scene of unavailing striving, a space of haphazard and fugitive grace from which divinity stands majestically apart. To precisely this sequestering of gods and persons, Smith passionately opposes himself, and Mormonism. "The people need not wait for the days of Pentecost to find the king of God," Smith says in 1843. His counterassertion is plain and direct: "Some say the kingdom of God was not set up on earth until the day of the pentecost," he proclaims, "but I say in the name of the Lord that the kingdom of God was set upon earth from the days of Adam to the present time, whenever there has been a righteous man on earth unto whom God revealed his word & gave power & authority to administer in his name" (*EJS*, 168–69).[20] *To the present time*, Smith insists. In another, still pithier pronouncement—one from an 1833 letter in which so much of his prophetic disposition is revealed—he will put it like this: "Have I not an equal privilege with the ancient saints?"[21]

If you wished to describe Mormonism as a variety of "Christian primitivism," this is where you would turn.[22] In all this, Smith's hyperidentification with the "ancient saints" is abundantly clear. And yet the force of such identification, as Smith mobilizes it, is not to set into motion any simple sort of return, or to transform Smith himself into a kind of imitation Abraham. This, after all, is the man who routinely retranslated books of the Bible, tuning them to sacred projects very much his own, and aiming in this not only to enlarge and to clarify but to adapt, amend, *improve*. (The entirety of the Book of Mormon might be grasped as only the most famous, most expansive version of this practice of midrash.)[23] We mistake the matter, then, if we follow too closely Harold Bloom's influential sense of Mormonism as given form and substance chiefly by Smith's "genius" for "restoration," his talent for enacting a species of fundamentalist return-to-lost-origins.[24] In Smith's Mormonism, the present does not revisit the sacred past, or mimic it, or aim to restore it, exactly. Rather, the live mortal present is adjoined to that sacred past and, most crucially for Smith, *continuous* with it, such that the mortal present stands alongside the sacred past in a state of equality. *This* is Smith's, and the Saints', equal privilege. Smith does not look to Abraham, to Isaac, to John as authorizing antecedents, fit to be imitated. (And this agitated nonimitative relation, as we shall see, will be central to the theory and practice of polygamy.) He understands himself instead to live in the world of the here and now *precisely as they lived in theirs*, with divinity not remote but garrulous, familiar, near to hand. Like them, but not in imitation of them, Smith understands himself to live as all mortal creatures do who have eyes to see: that is, in a state of revelation.

THE UNDISENCHANTED WORLD

Another, starker, only slightly more polemical way to say this is that, for Smith, the living, mortal, material world is, in a crucial sense, *unfallen*. So it is that Smith everywhere underscores not the hard separateness of God and the mortal world but an entangled, thrilling intimacy. "Have I not an equal privilege with the ancient saints?" is Smith's interrogative way of insisting that the time of revelation—of direct in-the-flesh encounters with divinity, such as are the mainstay of the Old Testament—has not passed away from the earth. God is not hidden away from the world in Smith, recessed into an inaccessible heaven or an equally remote biblical past. There is, as Givens observes, no "sacred distance" between the human and the divine. Rather, Smith apprehends a thorough interwovenness, one that has been mystified, misplaced in the forms of Christian orthodoxy he sees around him, with their emphases on a fallen humankind, an Other God, a world standing in need of either redemption or—in the idioms of secular religion that were developing around him—reenchantment.[25]

The idea of an unfallen world, in relation to which mortal persons stand primed for exalting revelation, is not, of course, an especially outlandish one, not even to those untrained in nineteenth-century religious esoterica. To the contrary, precisely that notion should sound familiar to students of the highest of high-canonical antebellum literature. A turning-away from Calvinism, an erosion of its stern polarities, a countervailing emphasis on the intrinsic divinity of the natural world and the human soul: these are, in truth, some of the defining movements of thought and belief in the aftermath of disestablishment, as everyone from Perry Miller to Ann Douglas to Mark Noll has made plain. It was none other than Ralph Waldo Emerson who, after resigning his pulpit in Boston's Second Church in 1832, would go on to inaugurate his new career by claiming for himself *an original relation to Nature*, one that transpired not in any primordial past but currently, immediately, in the midst of the accumulating present tense of the American nineteenth century. And there, as if in answer, was Joseph Smith, another child of revivalist New England, claiming for himself and for his followers an equal privilege with Old Testament recipients of God's direct Word.

The temptation to regard Smith as a kind of revivalist Emersonian, taking a vernacular Transcendentalism down *through* the fantastical archive of Christian mythology, rather than around it, is in many respects hard to resist. The resonances between them are real, and telling. But the dissonances may be more revealing still. Consider the resemblance that joins Emerson to Smith: it travels principally along the vein of a shared intuition of a certain already-present divinity in the world. In Emerson, that indwelling divinity comes to life as an instantaneous, flashing impression made upon consciousness, before the cordoning forces of capture (history, society, language and its encoded forms of order) see to its desacralization. Here is Emerson, in 1844, detailing one such triumphant and curative exchange with Nature:

> The incommunicable trees begin to persuade us to live with them, and quit our life of solemn trifles. Here no history, or church, or state, is interpolated on the divine sky and the immortal year. How easily we might walk onward into the opening landscape, absorbed by new pictures, and by thoughts fast succeeding each other, until by degrees the recollection of home was crowded out of the mind, all memory obliterated by the tyranny of the present, and we were led in triumph by nature.

He continues, "*These enchantments are medicinal*, they sober and heal us" (emphasis added)—healing us, in swift Emersonian succession, of the grubby preoccupations of history, church, state, "home," and so forth.[26]

These movements are of course commonplace: they make up the dialectics of enchantment, disenchantment, and reenchantment proper to the epiphanics of post-Romantic nature writing. It's striking to consider, though, how little they accord with what we find in Smith. The matter with the world for Smith, after all, is not that it is in need of redemption, or of the redemptive therapeutics of reenchantment. These, we could say, are procedures that give away the game before the first move. Nothing makes this clearer than the scandal of Smith's practiced offhandedness, his vernacular overturning. The force of it derives, just as Givens asserts, from Smith's refusal to concede a fallenness in the world that must in turn be *redeemed* by a keener consciousness, a piercing insight into a world rendered somehow inaccessible, to be grasped only in its fleeting evanescence. Reenchantment, in other words—like the multiplying kinds of "sacralization" in the nineteenth century, of nation, motherhood, fatherland, and virtually any serviceable abstraction—is the second-phase move proper to a set of previously established distinctions, in which the terms of opposition are at once set and occluded. Or, as Modern puts it, in terms that follow closely from Asad's work on myth, "One must recognize the distinction between enchantment and disenchantment as *integral to the modern secular imaginary* and not as some natural difference between two modes of consciousness."²⁷ To this entire economy, Smith's prophetic idiom is pure frustration. Indeed, from the perspective of Smith's writings, these post-Romantic epiphanies appear rather as distinctively *secular dialectics*, emerging in their clarity only in the aftermath of a prior hardening-into-place of conceptual divisions that are subsequently dematerialized, subsumed under the same bedrock putative real that divides magic from reason, divinity from earth. I have said that in Smith the world is unfallen; it may be more proper to say that what sets him at odds with the secularizing forces emerging around him, and that take up Emerson so differently, is his insistence on a world that is at once unfallen and *undisenchanted*.

In respect to the secular dialectics of enchantment and disenchantment, there is perhaps nothing that sets Smith so definitively apart as his attunement to the world not as scene or as metaphor or as metaphysical staging-ground but as *material*, as fleshy and embodied. That is to say, what most coheres divinity and the extant mortal world in Smith, and what brings about a proximity between them that is forever shading toward identity, is, precisely, matter: the stuff of the earth, the flesh of the world. "There is no such thing as immaterial matter," we are told in Doctrine and Covenants. To the contrary, *"All spirit is matter."*²⁸ It is another unbelabored formulation of wide and upending consequence. Here is a cosmology in which *to be*—to have any conceivable existence, angelic or godly or mortal or otherwise—is to be robed in matter. And it is this, more than anything else, that marks for Smith the crucial juncture between humankind and divinity. The cosmos Smith figures here is, in Jared Hickman's apt phrase, "profoundly monistic": there is, in the heavens and the earth, *one matter*. Everything is composed of it; all partake in it, as the condition of being.²⁹ It is a matter that is, accordingly, *shared*, across the seemingly impassable gulf that separates the human from the divine. There is no unfleshed God for Smith, as we have already seen. (This, for Smith, would be an insupportably diminished God.) But the stunning corollary to this, in the materialist cosmos of early Mormonism, is that to be a person, inhabiting a mortal body, is to be composed of exactly the same elements as God. In the carnal imagination of early Mormonism, that is, the body is not the mark of inevitable mortal corruption, the delivery-system for pain and privation—the "weather-beaten vessel, rack'd with pain," as Anne Bradstreet had it. The world is unfallen, yes. But your nearest encounter with that divinity, in all its unreenchanted glory, is not likely to be via the intercession of some heavenly emissary. You will know of the unfallenness of the world because you live in a body.

Smith's breathtaking funeral oration from 1844, delivered only months before his death, traces out with exemplary clarity his vision of divinity as a property of earthly existence, a trait that *entwines* humankind and gods. Here, in what was later named the King Follett Discourse, Smith endeavors to explain to the Saints "the simple truth of heaven." At the center of the oration is a plain question: "What is the character of God?"[30] From the first, though, the question of the character of God is inseparable from the question of the character of humankind. "If men do not comprehend the character of God, they do not comprehend their own character," he says. Smith promises to reveal to the Saints the character of God because the story of God's character, it turns out, is exemplary and in fact *replicable*. It is a story of exaltation:

> First, God Himself who sits enthroned in yonder heavens is a Man like unto one of yourselves—that is the great secret! If the veil were rent today and the great God that holds this world in its sphere and the planets in their orbit and who upholds all things by His power—if you were to see Him today, you would see Him in all the person, image, fashion, and very form of a man, like yourselves.

God exists, Smith says, in the very *form* of a man. Thus, when Mormonism's enemies speak of the distastefully literal materialism of the faith, of the heretical conjecture that even God's existence is enfleshed, they are not being false. God, for Smith, is made of the muddiness of flesh, even in "His power."[31]

But the greatness of the secret Smith offers to reveal is not that God might be apprehended in the flesh, in the very form of man. Rather, the great secret is that God began as a man and *became* God.

> These things are incomprehensible to some, but they are simple. The first principle of truth and of the Gospel is to know for a certainty the character of God, and that we may converse with Him the same as one man with another, and that He once was a man like one of us and that God Himself, the Father of us all, once dwelled on an earth the same as Jesus Christ himself did in the flesh and like us.

We may converse with God, Smith says, because God is not other to us, an element of inapprehensibility forever beyond the capacities of merely human being, but an enlarged, exemplary *version* of the human. If he is different from us now, it is not because he once lived in the flesh like us but no longer does, but because he has gone, as Smith says, "from exaltation to exaltation," all the while enfleshed. Woven together by a shared materiality, the human and the divine in this way mark out differences of *degree*, though almost the whole of Smith's late prophetic career comes down to an insistence that this difference must not blind us to an elemental *sameness of kind*. To conceive of the relation of divinity and humanity any other way, Smith says, is to do an unpardonable kind of harm to the glory of the world and, especially, to its human inhabitants.

Hence, his next offhand heresy. We might incline to believe, Smith says, that God created humankind, the world, existence. This, however, is incorrect. "All doctors of divinity say that God created [the mind of man] in the beginning, but it is not so," Smith assures the Saints. God is not the sole creator of the world but is, rather, cocreated, *along* with humankind, as part of an "intelligence" that is "eternal and exists on a self-existent principle. . . . There is no creation about it." Of the commonplace but blasphemously misguided notion that God created humankind, Smith will add, "*The very idea lessens the character of man*" (emphasis added). Holding fast to an undiminished vision of the human and its capacities for divinization, Smith exhorts the Saints to endeavor to believe and to receive what is, practically, very nearly inconceivable: that they are, in the very grain of their embodied and mortal lives, embryonic gods.

> You have got to learn how to make yourselves Gods in order to save yourselves and be kings and priests to God, the same as all Gods have done—by going from a small capacity to a great capacity, from a small degree to another, from grace to grace, until the resurrection of the dead from exaltation to exaltation—til you are able to sit in everlasting burnings and everlasting power and glory as those who have gone before, sit enthroned.

Smith maps out an exaltation of the human not *beyond* the flesh but toward a divinity *already present* in the mortal world. Again, there is no redemption here, no corrupt life being transformed, no deadened world being subject to the saving therapeutics of reenchantment. The drama of exaltation is rather one of *receiving* and *believing*, of coming fully into the presence of what is not incomprehensible but "simple." This is what it means to assert that "the great principle of happiness consists in having a body."[32] *The very flesh of the world is the stuff of divinity.*

We are coming nearer to the question of the interwovenness of polygamy with the chief propositions of early Mormon theology. For we have begun to grasp the central, rather than minor, place of polygamy in a cosmology tuned, in these exceptional and persisting ways, to the fate of the flesh. Smith himself draws into tight relation the practice of plural patriarchal marriage and the possibilities for exaltation, as we have seen. ("Then shall they be Gods," Smith says of polygamous husbands, "because they have no end. . . . Then shall they be Gods, because they have all power, and the angels are subject unto them.") And he insists not only upon an "equal privilege" for living persons with the "ancient saints" but upon a proximity between persons and godhead that in the arc of mortal life moves ever closer to equivalence. For Smith, God is no less exalted for having been a person, and even less so for having existence as matter, flesh. And human beings, mantled in a flesh composed of exactly the same matter, are less God's creatures or creations than his kin. Again and again, it is the *shared matter* of gods and persons that makes for Mormonism's all-defining intimacy of gods and persons. The flesh, the material body, vouchsafes to us the divinity of humankind. It is the vehicle not of corruption but exaltation. So to treat that body with a Pauline contempt, to confine and cajole and chastise it, is for Smith not merely a kind of injury but a kind of blaspheming, a calamitous misreading of the generosity, the nearness, the *exemplarity* of God.

There is more to be worked out about plural marriage as an expression of a specific carnal theology. For now we can say that polygamy paves the way for exaltation because, as Smith imagines it, it alone gives form, in the register of intimate life, to the heretical intimation that the body, that great principle of happiness, is in fact the vehicle of an unexpanded divinity, an already-present sacrality that is continually misrepresented and, as a result, unreceived. *Then shall they be gods,* Smith says, and if there are in the revelation elements of a kind of celestial reproductivity—the conventional sense that one's being becomes everlasting through the proliferation of progeny— these in no way blunt the force of its perpetual counterstrain. This is the strain that links godliness and exaltation to the startling capacities of the flesh. Polygamy, we might say—and these terms we will need to specify and finesse—is the fabulation that renders the incipience of divinity in the plain language of daily living, the arrangements of life: it is, for Smith, the intimate form proper to life in the body of a god not yet enlarged.

INTERLUDE: DEFENSE AND PROSECUTION

There are, of course, other ways of accounting for the emergence and signi-fication of Mormon polygamy, and these are worth considering in detail—though, as we will see, much of what's revealed, in defenses not less than scandalized condemnations, is the centrifugal force of secular valuation itself, forming in relation to a practice that is in so many facets, and so nakedly, a rebuke to a secularized ordering of the world. "God Himself," Smith had insisted to the Saints in the King Follett Discourse, "is a Man like unto one of yourselves—that is the great secret!" Yet as fractures and rivalries developed between Smith and other members of the inner circle of the Mormon elite in the volatile 1840s, betrayals of that *other* great secret of early Mormonism—the secret of plural marriage, such as Smith had self-endangeringly confided to Joseph Bates Noble before his marriage to Louisa Beaman—began to appear, in a range of venues. When that secret got out, the responses to it were unsparing. And they were, for the most part, sin-gularly unmystified by the question of the origins of Mormon polygamy. On these accounts, Mormonism had simply invented a theological body—irradiated by an incipient divinity, assembling itself toward godhead—as a species of ruse. That body, antipolygamists would claim, was at base nothing more than a stand-in, a counterfeited double, for the more-than-ordinarily-human flesh of Joseph Smith himself. In the way of despots and scoundrels before him, Smith had rewritten private depravity as spiritual imperative. What resulted was a body not only unrecognizable as Christian but unrec-ognizable as *American*—or, indeed, as anything other than a form of life posing an immediate, potentially existential threat to the health and security of the nation.

Here, for instance, is a man named John C. Bennett, a onetime insider who issued a momentous "exposé" of the Saints in 1842, entitled *The History of the Saints; or, An Exposé of Joe Smith and Mormonism*. The Mormons had, on Bennett's reading, apostasized from whiteness itself, and the Christianity that embodied it. Rather than celestial families, ascending together toward divinity, Bennett found in Mormon sexual sociability the likeness of "licentious Oriental courts, where debauchery has been, for ages, systematized and sanctioned by law and religion on the most extensive scale."[33] He closed on an apocalyptic note, fusing sexual horror and a racialized civilizational peril:

> If this Mormon villain is suffered to carry out his plans, I warn the people of these United States, that less than twenty years will see them involved in a civil war of the most formidable character. They will have to encounter a numerous and ferocious enemy, excited to the utmost by fanaticism and by pretended revelations from God, . . . who will not pause in the execution of their projects, even though to accomplish them they should deluge this fair land with the blood of her sons, and exterminate the results of the toil and the civilization of more than two centuries.[34]

Bushman is right to note that Bennett's book, whatever its distortions and exaggerations, "performed a notable cultural work in antebellum America."[35] *The History of the Saints* sets the terms for so much of the anti-Mormon fulmination that would, over the next five decades, form itself into specialized idioms and subgenres. The eroticized horror, the racialization that extends from it, the slide into visions of a vast bloodletting: all are anticipated in Bennett's pioneering little book.

In subsequent chapters we will scrutinize in further detail this early iteration of Mormonism as a species of expendable life, with an eye to the synthesizing biopolitics that conjoins bad belief to bad sex to racialization. For now I want to note that, as striking as Bennett's strident apocalypticism may be, perhaps stranger still is the uncanny way *The History of the Saints* sets the terms not only for antipolygamy polemicists but for its *defenders*, its partisans and apologists. It does so not least in its commitment to appraising the origins and meanings of plural marriage wholly *apart* from the divinized body, the unfallen flesh, at its center. Both defenders and attackers of Mormon polygamy found it notably expedient, that is, to sidestep the matter of celestial embodiment and its place in a drama of exaltation.

On the partisan, pro-Mormon side, the case is straightforward. Had you wished to defend the righteousness of Mormon plural marriage at midcentury, you would have had at your disposal two strong idioms of response. The first regards Mormonism as, at base, a style of Christian primitivism— or rather, as an attempt to rebuke the fallen state of contemporary Christianity through a revivalist return to misplaced origins. Think again of Harold Bloom's account of Smith's prophetic career. "The religion-making genius of Joseph Smith," Bloom contends, "uniquely restored the Bible's sense of the theomorphic, a restoration that inevitably led the prophet into his most audacious restoration, plural patriarchal marriage."[36] Saying this, though, Bloom does not much more than repeat, as historical assessment, what was in fact one of the commonest defenses of the practice. The polygamy revelation itself articulates something of this in its turn to the Old Testament forefathers of plural patriarchal marriage, each of whom, Smith takes pains to note, takes his place among the range of ancient saints who *appeared* to violate the most immutable moral laws of the world, only to be to exalted in scripture for hewing devoutly to the direct commands of God. ("*In nothing did they sin,*" Smith insists.) Here Smith makes the case plainly: plural marriage is righteous in the sight of the Lord inasmuch as the present is an extension of, continuous with, a sacred past in which polygamy flourished.

Perhaps the first major Mormon defense of polygamy followed out just these terms. Here is Orson Pratt, in 1859, extending the inquiry of Smith's own revelation:

> Let us, therefore, carefully investigate the important question—Is polygamy a crime? Is it condemned in the Bible, either by the Old or New Testament? Has God ever condemned it by his own voice? Have his angels ever been sent forth to inform the nations who have practiced this thing that they were in transgression? Has he ever spoken against it by any inspired writer? Has any Patriarch, Prophet, Apostle, angel, or even the Son of God himself, ever condemned polygamy? We may give a general answer . . . and say to the world, We have no information of that kind on record.[37]

To this he will add, in a familiar counterposing of earthly and divine law:

> Is it not as possible that the sovereign States of this enlightened nation may be misguided in regard to their strict laws which they have passed against polygamy as it was for our forefathers to be misguided in their strict laws against witchcraft in Massachusetts, where every man and woman must be put to death for a witch, if somebody became prejudiced against them? This was a law among our forefathers in enlightened America but a short period back. They thought they were right, and were as sincere in it as the States are in these strict and rigid laws against polygamy. But, thank the Lord, Utah is not in bondage to such bigoted State laws.[38]

Pratt weds what is fundamentally a state's-rights case to an argument he offers not on behalf of the divinity of the flesh, or for that matter of the human trajectory toward exaltation.[39] He anchors his defense, rather, in polygamy's biblically sanctified origins, its freedom from condemnation by any "Patriarch, Prophet, Apostle, angel." For Pratt, Mormon polygamy is a devotional practice that, however authorized by divine revelation, finds its chief legitimacy in, essentially, precedent: as it was for the ancients, so ought it to be in a present tense disburdened of ungodly prejudice.

In "prejudice" we find a link to the second strong, pervasive idiom of polygamy's defense. In this strain of attempted legitimation, what matters is not so much the righteousness of biblical restoration, though that is not discarded. Rather, polygamy emerges most saliently as a direct, needed response to an antebellum world in which varieties of industrial advance had made for a loosening, however uneven and however slight, of the firm comprehensiveness of patriarchal dominion. They hinged, that is, upon a gender-panicked reading of nineteenth-century America. Increasing urbanism, enabled by an escalating move from agrarian to cash economies, the rise of feminist agitation, and in concert with this the emergence of a multifaceted culture of sentiment: all these contributed to that alleged and much-feared loosening of patriarchal authority (to which one notably reactionary Henry James character would memorably refer as "the most damnable feminization!"[40]). As Elizabeth Freeman notes, such conditions enabled the flourishing of many kinds of voluntary "associations" across the era, which modeled lateral, rather than familial-hierarchical, modes of attachment. This was their promise and, for some, their threat: "These early societies," Freeman writes, "threatened to replace parental and marital bonds with affinities between same-sex peers and undermine the patriarchal family and church as means of social control."[41] Mormonism on the one hand expresses precisely this reshifting of the landscape of social attachment, ratifying and in many respects *sanctifying* a widened sort of lateral association; polygamy, in this sense, represents an explosion of the anchoring dyad of familialism and, concomitantly, a sidelong expansion of the field of sanctified social relations. On the other hand, Mormon polygamy—*patriarchal plural marriage*—works assiduously to verticalize those relations, rehierarchizing them along the axis of gender. This is something of what Laurel Thatcher Ulrich means when she writes that "Mormonism reinforced and at the same time transformed patterns of association."[42]

These double-movements, which seem to fold together perversion and normative reaction, could be made to speak in a number of tongues. For instance, Nancy Bentley persuasively argues that renderings of Mormons as polygamy-maddened tyrants, drunk on the terrifying power of an abso-lutized gendered authority, were a mainstay of *anti*-Mormon critique later in the century. In these accounts, she argues, the specter of a kind of hyper-bolized Mormon patriarchy was deployed to mitigate and, in effect, to unwrite the patriarchality of *monogamy*—to produce the binds of monoga-mous marriage as, in the very contrast to the putative enslavement of Mor-mon wives, the image of freedom itself. "Polygamy," Bentley writes, "is the bondage that sanctifies monogamy as freedom."[43] Dip more or less anywhere into the archive of antipolygamy novelizations in the later nineteenth cen-tury, from the stolidly sentimental to the more frankly lascivious, and this is indeed the cohering and elementally conservative logic you will encounter, in which Mormon plural wives figure as in bondage to polygamists, but also to the counterfeit "religion" that propounds it. In this, they are offered in sharp contradistinction to their many American sisters who enjoy the comforts, the veritable liberation, entailed in patriarchal monogamy.

Curiously, though, the notion of Mormonism as a species of hyper-bolized patriarchy—the notion that sends tremors of horror and revul-sion through the sentences of editorialists, pamphleteers, and sentimental novelists—appears no less vividly on the scene of some early *defenses* of polygamy. There, it is prosecuted chiefly in the idiom of an equally scandal-ized and, often, quasi-hysterical counteraction. Here, for instance, is Udney Hay Jacob, writing in *The Peace Maker*, a tract published in Nauvoo in 1842, at precisely the moment the scandal around the Bennett revelations was boiling over.

> Gentlemen, the ladies laugh at your pretended authority. They, many of them hiss, at the idea of your being the lords of the creation. Even in the public prints they have styled you, the would be lords, etc. Nothing is fur-ther from the minds of our wives in general, than the idea of submitting to their husbands in all things, and of reverencing their husbands. They will boldly ridicule the idea of calling them sincerely in their hearts lords and masters. But God' has positively required this of them.[44]

Jacob is also a restorationist—"the momentous question is; *will you now restore the law of God on this important subject, and keep it?*"[45]—but in his tract such revivalist fundamentalism is almost wholly in the service of a this-worldly male authority, understood to be everywhere under siege and everywhere eroding.

A man ought not to be brought under the law of a woman in any wise. But by our law he is in ten thousand instances completely enslaved to an imperious woman whereby confusion and not peace rages in society *at its very root*. And the principle that performs this wicked work, is recognized, and admitted by all, and therefore operates upon all, and disorganizes the universal mind of man throughout Christendom; it being begotten and bred in this disorganizing ruin.[46]

Monogamy, in Jacob's rendering, gives to women a virtually limitless, practically imperial, and broadly ruinous power over men. For Jacob, the putative reciprocality of monogamous marriage makes it a travestying humiliation of men:

> We are placed by our laws under the law of the woman. The word of God saith, for the wife is bound by the law, as long as her husband liveth; but if the husband be dead, she is at liberty to be married to whom she will, (take notice not to marry) but to be married to whom she will, only in the Lord. 1 Cor. 7:39. This text shows what is meant by her being under the law of her husband; that is, she is not at liberty to be married to another, while she has a lawful husband yet living. And if a man is bound to his wife in the same manner, *then is he under the law of his wife*.[47]

The only cure for this ugly state of affairs, in Jacob's account, is the obvious one: the restoration of patriarchal plural marriage.

So here we have twinned explanatory strategies: one emphasizing Mormonism's revivalist ambitions, the other its manic devotion to patriarchy. For all their differences of inflection, though, they cohere around a striking displacement. Absent in both strains is any sustained engagement with what we might take to be among early Mormonism's defining characteristics, Smith's most resonant heresies: exaltation, the world of divinized materiality, the wondrous earthly body, the whole unruly theater of early Mormonism's carnal imaginary. These elisions, like the occasional conceptual overlap of pro- and antipolygamy polemics, are curious. But odder by many powers is how *enduring* they have been, and how well preserved, in and for what are essentially strategies of Mormon legitimation. Indeed, the elision of the divinizing mortal flesh is an indispensable part of the very grammar of post-polygamy legitimation that holds sway today.

Consider in this respect the extended treatment of plural marriage in Richard Bushman's magisterial biography of Smith, *Joseph Smith: Rough*

Stone Rolling, from 2005. Bushman is not a scholar who needs to be reminded of the centrality, or for that matter of the profoundly upending force, of exaltation; he writes about it searchingly, and in detail.[48] Nor is Smith's intricate delight in the corporeal a matter that escapes consideration. ("Joseph had little sense of the flesh being base," Bushman observes. "In contrast to conventional theologies, Joseph saw embodiment as a glorious aspect of human existence.") And yet his account of polygamy turns persistently *away* from that body, from that delight, and indeed from any least whiff of a pleasure-making carnality. Straining against insinuations that Smith could have been a "libertine" in thrall to "his own pleasure," Bushman commits himself instead to a sternly de-eroticized polygamy: "Only slight hints of romance found their way into his proposals," he writes, contending rather that "he understood plural marriage as a religious principle."[49] We might wonder how to make this square with, for instance, Smith's infamous cajoling letter to Nancy Rigdon, in which, after instructing her that "our Heavenly Father is more liberal in his views, and boundless in his mercies and blessings, than we are ready to believe or receive," he concludes that it is surely God's purpose for the creatures of the world that "in the end they shall have joy" (*EJS*, 159). As scholars like Fawn Brodie and, more recently, Samuel Morris Brown recall to us with vivid complexity, one of the principles for which the religion Smith had built would seem quite determinedly to stand is a this-worldly *joyousness*, itself never far from the great gifts of embodied life.

Still, Bushman's anticarnality in respect to polygamy is not in any measure simpleminded, or merely phobic. It speaks rather, with revealing force, to dichotomies *within* polygamy and, especially, to the ways they might be managed and deployed. The fulcrum for Bushman's counterclaim is an insistence on polygamy not as part of an upending theory of embodied life, and even less as a theological exaltation of carnality, but as an expression of what he names "family theology." "The marriage revelation did not overturn the family order," Bushman says, again laboring to rescue Smith from detractors who see in his theory only a brutally patriarchal confinement of women ("Joseph," he writes, "had never tried to demean women") or plain sexual licentiousness. The explication of polygamy's relation to exaltation follows a similar vein. How does celestial enlargement work, in Bushman's account? Persons became gods because, he writes, "they kept bearing children. This capacity to 'enlarge' made them, in effect, gods." Or again: "The marriage revelation culminated in the emergence of family theology. More than any previous revelation, *this one put family first*."[50]

Here, then, is the normalizing strain of Mormon criticism at its most condensed and clarified. Gone is the godliness of embodied life. Gone is the unrelinquished flesh of celestial beings. Gone is the turbulent life of a body composed of the same elements, the same matter, as God. Gone, too, is the arduous labor that is required to believe and receive the news of this divinized embodiment, or for that matter this radical disruption of the normative codes of antebellum intimacy and attachment. And gone are the repeated invocations, in Smith and again in his heirs, of carnality as the vehicle not only for offspring but for joyousness, delight, all the subcategories of pleasure. In its place is a theology that "put family first." To be sure, the binding of the dead to the living down through history often follows out both the routes and the rhetoric of family, though we should note, too, that "sealing" is itself spectacularly more heterogeneous than any such recoding suggests. (To make sealing into family practice steeply misrecognizes, for instance, the sacralization of lateral relation that is so much a part of Smith's theory and practice, made vivid not least in his often gorgeous, quasi-Whitmanian invocations of *friendship*—sociability in a form at once nondyadic *and* extrafamilial—as the sine qua non of the Mormon project.)[51] We might take this for what familialism often is: an attempt to domesticate whatever is unruly in carnality, to subsume it to the tidy orders of reproduction, and, in this instance, to smooth over the committed perversions of the early Mormon carnal imaginary. As we have seen, these are perversions of normative intimacy, perversions of the family form itself, and perhaps above all perversions in the conception of what it is to be *embodied*. Invocations of celestial family, and of the facets of polygamy that seem most in accordance with it, do the work of neutering these perversities, one and all.

Bushman's is an account of Smith that is pointedly not committed to a conventionally secular project of exposure or debunking; this is, in certain respects, one of its most remarkable features. He takes Smith seriously, and at his word, when he says he encounters angels, hears the voice of God, translates ancient plates. So when Bushman says polygamy took shape in early Mormonism as a religious principle, he intends no derogation of either polygamy or religion. And yet what is perhaps most striking in Bushman's rescripting of polygamy is the work it does not only to de-eroticize and so in a manner purify the practice but, in a considerably stranger way, to *secularize* it: to make it a devotional practice one might readily liken to other expressions of *reasonable belief*. A Mormonism that puts family first is a Mormonism so entirely in line with the good religions of secular modernity—so seamless in its folding-together of "religious principle" with that most basic and undergirding unit of liberalism, what Foucault calls the "crystal in the deployment of sexuality," *the bourgeois family*—as to be all but indistinguishable from them, but for some small, if colorful, differences of emphasis.[52] To figure Mormonism in this way is to insist on the untroubled compatibility of Mormonism with the religious life proper to secular modernity, and to do so—more than a little remarkably—without a ballasting sense of the hard-fought, bloodied, decades-long *counterfactuality* of any such claim. This is what it means to say that Bushman's account does not reconstruct an early Mormon conceptual framework, free of the hostile misapprehensions of secular critique, so much as it restages, as argument, the trajectory of nineteenth-century Mormonism itself, away from the perversities of carnal exaltation and toward normative liberal citizenship. It is, we can say, a distinctively postpolygamous way of telling the story of polygamy.[53] This is what makes it as useful, and as revealing, as it is.

Bushman's account displaces the carnality in early Mormon theology, the expansion *through* the materiality of the body out toward an enfleshed divinity, and all the irresolutions and turbulences that go with it. If this makes for a kind of de-perverting misreading—and I think it does—it nevertheless reminds us just how intimately unassimilable that carnal theology was, and in precisely which registers, to the demands of a secular modernity that was bit by bit assembling itself around the scene of Mormonism's contested unfolding. At least in its handling of polygamy, Bushman's account addresses us *from the vantage of* the secularized religion that would, in the end, come to triumph in its struggle with the recalcitrant Mormons. (The Mormons begin their path toward citizenship with nothing other than the church's renunciation of polygamy, and the reassembly of Mormon intimate sociability in forms nearer to those of the liberal nation-state.) Mormonism, that is, recomposes itself, in the name of survival, under a set of pressures—these, too, having everything to do with the unmanageable Mormon body—to which we will turn in subsequent chapters. Bushman's staging of polygamy has the signal virtue of offering us one clear way of measuring what it was in the early Mormon imaginary that, in the name of that recomposition, would have to be expunged.

BELIEVING AND RECEIVING

To return to the workings of polygamy within Mormonism's carnal theology: we have seen already the charge of licentiousness brought against

Smith, and Mormonism generally, with polygamy as its proof-text. It is a note struck early in responses to the new faith, and one that resonates down the decades—a whispering undercurrent, an unquelled suspicion. Here, for instance, is the current official LDS line on polygamy, available online under the telling title "Plural Marriage and Families in Early Utah": "While there was much love, tenderness, and affection within many plural marriages, the practice was generally based more on religious belief than on romantic love."[54] Religious principle, obedience, sacrifice, procreation, family above all: the prioritization of these, at the expense even of an attachment so faintly eroticized as "romantic love," speaks succinctly enough to the postpolygamy imperatives of secularizing normativity and recuperation. The dynamics of exaltation, the ascension of the human into godliness not apart from but *through* embodiment and its piercing pleasures, fall out conspicuously from accounts both damning and defensive, keyed as both are to visions of the body itself as untrustworthy, corrupting, a false grounding-point for the elaboration of "religious belief."

It is a genuine irony of nineteenth-century anti-Mormonism that, though they come down to us from Mormonism's avowed enemies, and though they circumscribe the domain of inquiry dramatically, accusations about Mormon polygamy as an expression of nothing other than its leader's worldly avariciousness are not, for all that, quite as dismissable as one might imagine. In a strange way, they touch directly upon uneasinesses *internal* to nineteenth-century Mormonism. Long, long before the church was to renounce the practice as a matter of political expedience, the question of the provenance of plural marriage, and so of its legitimacy, had run like a tremor through the whole archive of the Mormons' own discourse on polygamy. One need look no further than the polygamy revelation itself, which is preoccupied, beginning to end, with *crime*. "The Principle and Doctrine of Having Many Wives and Concubines" addresses itself, in its concluding moves, directly to Emma Smith herself, Joseph's first wife, whose relation to polygamy was to become famous in the lore of early Mormonism. (There she is in the mythography, playing the cruel mistress to upstart wives in her home, burning the copy of the polygamy revelation in the fireplace in Nauvoo, and eventually breaking with the church over its commitment to the Principle.)[55] "And I command mine handmaid, Emma Smith," one paragraph begins, "to abide and cleave unto my servant Joseph, and to none else" (*EJS*, 197).[56] In this respect, the long detouring through Old Testament figures (Abraham, David, Solomon, Moses) makes a plain kind of sense. These figures function as strategic elements in Smith's effort to badger Emma, through a kind of selective and coercive scripture-mongering, into tolerating what are for her unpardonable crimes against the contract of her marriage. This *seems* like crime, the text insists, but such is often the way with God's commandments. "David also received many wives and concubines, as also Solomon, and Moses my servant; as also many others . . . and in nothing did they sin." Here Smith outlines, as a strategy of persuasion, the defense of polygamy that would ring down through the rest of the century, in forms ever more clarified and insistent: if it is of God, it is no sin. But if that note of anxious defensiveness here tells us anything ("in *nothing* did they sin"), it is that the specter of the illegitimacy of polygamy is conjured not only in the reaches of anti-Mormon fulmination. It haunts Smith's revelation as well, and would cast its shadow, through years and years of practice, over the devotions of even the most ardently faithful Mormons.

Joseph is not quite so effortlessly at one with the word of God, or grounded in unshakeable prophetic conviction, as we might assume, and to miss this is to underread the confoundment that is not merely external to plural marriage but *built into it*, an element of its design and practice. "Confoundment" may in fact be a sanitizing term; though it arrives in starkly different forms to men and to women, and to Saints nearer the inner circles of Mormon hierarchy as opposed to those further from it, in the archive of early Mormonism, that confoundment expresses itself again and again as something nearer to anguish. This is not the pain of self-flagellating abnegation, such as we might associate with conventional spiritual disciplines, or not exactly. The way of exaltation, Smith insists, is *arduous*, though not because it demands elaborate rituals of self-chastisement or mortification. The arduousness of polygamy, like the arduousness of exaltation itself, comes back to a problem of different shape and structure. It is a problem that travels less in the register of an obdurate body, a selfish soul, than in the difficult terrain of *conceivability*. Think again of Smith's famous self-description, which captures something of this difficulty. "No man knows my history," Smith says. "I don't blame you for not believing my history. *If I had not experienced what I have, I could not have believed it myself*" (*EJS*, 245). It is a curious formulation, one in which knowledge and belief struggle to keep pace with the experience of living.

Only a few months before this declaration, in the midst of a scene of multiplying crises—at a moment when scandals around polygamy seemed poised to rend the church and deliver him to his most murderous enemies—

Smith delivered perhaps his most exacting account of the arduousness of Mormon exaltation. "But their has been a great difficulty in getting anything into the heads of this generation," he said in a sermon from January of 1844.

> It has been like splitting hemlock knots with a corndoger for a wedge & a pumpkin for a beetle; even the Saints are slow to understand. I have tried for a number of years to get the minds of the saints prepared to recieve the things of God, but we frequently see some of them after suffering all they have for the work of God will fly to peaces like glass as soon as any thing Comes that is Contrary to their traditions. They cannot stand the fire at all. How many will be able to abide a Celestial law & go through & recieve their exhaltation I am unable to say but many are called & few are Chosen.[57] (*EJS*, 212)

The drama of exaltation in Smith is not, on this account, the familiar one, in which a fallen humanity is laid low and then, from the muck of its descent, uplifted and redeemed. This is not a scene of redemption or even over- turning. Exaltation, rather, is a matter of *receiving*. We might think again of Smith's letter to Nancy Rigdon, in which he assures her that "our Heavenly Father is more liberal in his views, and boundless in his mercies and bless- ings, *than we are ready to believe or receive*." The fire of exaltation demands readiness, which here takes form as a radical reorientation toward the world *such as it already is*.

What disables our capacity to believe and receive, Smith says in 1844, sounding again a quasi-Emersonian note, is "traditions": even the Saints, he says, "will fly to peaces like glass as soon as any thing Comes that is *Con- trary to their traditions*." But of what do these consist? Most immediately, of course, there is the vast and, certainly for Mormon detractors, impreg- nable Western tradition of monogamy. On this point, we need not turn to anti-Mormon screeds for their litany of impassioned eternalizations of monogamous marriage. There is clarity enough, too, in the intimations of a tremendous, corrosive *shame* that weave themselves in and through the documents of early Mormonism itself, including, notably, Smith's own dec- larations. Consider the contrasting tones of Smith's writings to the Whitney family, in the summer of 1842. A revelation from late July speaks in the stately cadence of prophetic utterance:

> If you both agree to covenant and do this then I give you S. A. Whitney my Daughter to Joseph Smith to be his wife. . . . I do it in my own name

and in the name of my wife your mother and in the name of my Holy
Progenitors by the right of birth which is of Preast Hoood vested in me by
revelation and commandment and promise of the living God obtained by
the Holy Melchisedeck Gethrow and other of the Holy Fathers. (*EJS*, 165)

In the letter he writes to the Whitneys on 18 August, however, the voice of
the would-be polygamist speaks like this:

The only thing to be careful of; is to find out when Emma comes then
you cannot be safe, but when she is not here, there is the most perfect
safty: only be careful to escape observation as much as possible, I know
it is a heroick undertakeing; but so much the greater frendship, and the
more Joy, when I see you I will tell you all my plans, I cannot write them
upon paper, burn this letter as soon as you read it; keep all locked up
in your breasts, my life depends upon it . . . you will pardon me for my
earnestness on this subjet when you consider how lonesome I must be,
your good feelings know how to make every allowance for me, I close my
letter, I think Emma wont come tonight if she dont dont fail to come to
night. (*EJS*, 166–67)

There is much to note in the starkness of contrast between the voices here,
those of the revelator and the disobedient spouse. There is the need for
absolute secrecy in a practice that only added to the mortal peril that, by
this time, had become a governing condition of Smith's life; and there is,
contrarily, the bathos of Smith deploying the high-flown language of God
as a kind of sacralizing distraction from the quotidian skullduggery of his
philandering. Then, too, there is his lonesomeness. A generous reading of
the passage might find in it still another expression of the genuineness of
the danger he had put himself in: he is lonely in his exposure to death at the
hands of unmerciful enemies. But even if we find that note of pathos under-
cut by the self-aggrandizing melodrama—the exalting heroicization of,
essentially, *deceiving Emma*—we might be struck, too, by a different sort of
plangency. The Smith who creeps about, who unlooses both biblical cadence
and the melodramatics of the "heroick undertaking," is not a prophet free
from the encroaching sense that what he is endeavoring to undertake is
perhaps something other than holy. We see here, that is, in the rhetorical
labors enjoined to contain it, the afterimage of a great shame. Small wonder
the Saints had been "slow to understand"; Smith himself, the prophet and
architect of plural marriage, knew a good deal of misgiving.

This pair of missives sets other significant patterns for Mormonism as well. Above all, they allow us to trace the lineaments of a drama enacted and reenacted, with great repetitiveness, in the early years of the Mormon entanglement with the practice of plural marriage. Laurel Thatcher Ulrich gives a pointed account of the scene in Nauvoo around 1843: "Years later, many of those who accepted plural marriage in Nauvoo claimed they were horrified by the idea when it was first introduced. John Taylor said it made his flesh crawl.... Brigham Young claimed it was the first time in his life that he ever desired the grave."[58] At its core, this is the drama of a horror-struck misgiving—of an enormity of theological doubt, sinking to the roots of prophetic legitimacy—produced and disclosed in the moment of its heroic overcoming. Polygamy, that is, cannot *not* feel like apostasy, like sinfulness, like crime, even to those practicing it. (This is the moral of the revelation, and of every subsequent account of Mormon polygamy that emphasizes the quality of "sacrifice" entailed, for men and women both, in an obedient commitment to the principle.)[59] The reformulation of that pained misgiving as a sort of epiphanic drama, though, transforms it into a pretext for the staging of a keener piety, a still greater devotion. The grammar of this melodrama is largely static. First, the prophet shocks his disciple with news of the divinity of polygamy; the disciple then recoils in mortified revulsion; there is a period of reconsideration, introspection, and intense prayer; the disciple at last emerges, converted, soldered more securely still to the faith. It is a scene that appears again and again in the documents of the early years of polygamous Mormonism: spectacles of unbelief encountered and then, in rapturous triumph, overcome, often tearfully, and often attended by the melodramatics of male intimacy. ("In these stories," Ulrich notes, "resistance prepared the way for revelation.")[60] As the arrangements around Louisa Beaman's wedding had already displayed with exemplary clarity, patriarchal polygamy was in multiple respects an affair between men, as much in the grain of its promised affective intensities as in its material dispensations.

However they provide a conceptual anchoring-point for hegemonic visions of social coherence and the shape of nationness itself, then, the "traditions" of monogamous marriage might find themselves overturned in moments of fervent piety—and might in fact be figured as still another damning element of the rotted Gentile world. (This, too, in the later years of polygamy, would become a familiar invocation: Gentiles' apostasy expressed in the idiom of their benighted commitment to monogamy.) In these ways the very deep-rooted conventionality of monogamous marriage could be turned to devotional use, its abandonment attesting to a depth of faithful devotion. We see precisely this drama enacted again and again in those scenes of initial resistance at last overcome, and yielding to newborn piety. So when Smith says he has struggled to induce the Mormons to believe and receive the promises of exaltation, he gestures in the direction of some *other* set of compounded forces binding up the Saints, something at once more elusive and more foundational even than socioerotic prohibition.

We return here, I think, directly to the carnal theology at the heart of early Mormonism. For what is difficult to believe and receive—what stands on the edges of the conceivable—is not that intimate life might be organized otherwise; there are, for this, a number of alternate possibilities near to hand, at greater and lesser remove from normative forms. Rather, Smith demands something stranger, *more* arduous, and more difficult to conceive. He asks that the Saints take the measure of the possibility that they are, in the intimate terrain of the body itself, not at all what they supposed. *You have got to* learn *how to make yourselves Gods*, Smith says, and if exaltation is arduous, a standing-in-the-fire few can endure, it is so not least because of the fantastic breadth of counterknowledge that has wrought itself in and through the Saints *and lives in the body*—the accreted knowledge that has left them with so naturalized a sense of the fallenness of the mortal body, the halting grace of the material world, the malignity of flesh. Smith would not have believed the story of his own life, he tells us, had he not lived it, and in his meditations on the rigors of receiving the truth of exaltation he reminds us that merely living, if it is indeed to prompt a new mode of belief, must somehow manage to blast through the accumulated misapprehensions that have territorialized life, bound it into sanctified conjugations of itself, and no other. Exaltation, among other things, is a process of tremendous corporeal denaturalization, an unwriting of the body as nearly two millennia of Christian misperception have overcoded it. Givens suggests Mormonism is at its root a "demystification" of Christianity itself; in a like vein, polygamy— Smith's unwriting of monogamous marriage—might best be grasped as an effort toward the demystification of embodied life.[61]

To learn how to become a God thus involves a vast unlearning, a rescripting of the traditions that make not only the precincts of the spirit legible to the self, and knowable, but the granular composition of the body itself. How do you begin to believe and receive the fact your very flesh is not at all what you have forever conceived it to be? How do you unmake the body imposed by the disciplinary power of sanctioned belief? How, in turn, do you endeavor not merely to grasp but live in, *live out*, the all but inconceivable fact that the body you inhabit is the site of an incipient divinity? These, for Smith, are live theological dilemmas, prophetic crises woven round with the institutional difficulties of political leadership. Polygamy is, in the first instance, the solvent in which these emerge, most frontally, *as* dilemmas, in the grain of their deep intractability. But it is also the solution he devises for them, the prophetic cure.

THEY SHALL HAVE JOY

Polygamy, as we have seen, emerges in Smith as the intimate form proper to protogodly life because it alone grasps the expansiveness, the ever-enlarging multiplicitousness, of the body in its journeying toward divinization. Nothing enacts the early Mormon rebuke to the Pauline contempt for embodied life, the chastisement of the corrupted flesh crystallized over centuries of Protestantism, as much as the breaking of the frame of monogamous marriage, and the sanctification of the intimacies that succeed it. The reach and consequence of that rebuke, and some of the dilemmas that go along with it, have been the subject of our inquiries so far.

Like so much else that upends in early Mormonism, though, polygamy is a practice of divinization that is undertaken securely in the realm of the *quotidian*, whatever the scope of its celestial ambitions. As Brodie, Shipps, Bushman, Givens, Brown, and many others invite us to recall, the divinity of the extant world expresses itself in Smith's revelations chiefly through a startling prophetic attentiveness to the local and the homely, a concerted this-worldliness that can at moments seem strikingly at odds with the sacral contexts in which it unfolds. Scattered amid disquisitions about the origins of the celestial spheres, the life of the gods, the hierarchies of angels, we find revelations concerning plots of land, intrafamilial dispute, all the grubby minutia of workaday Mormon life. At times that combinatory collapsing of sacred distance appears especially strikingly at the level of the sentence, the level of diction. "The people of the Lord," Smith would write in 1833, "those who have complied with the requisitions of the new covenant, have already commenced gathering together in Zion, *which is in the state of Missouri*" (*EJS*, 36, emphasis added).[62] If you want a little primer in Smith's insistent folding-together of the ordinary and the sacred, you could do worse than attend to the punctuation of this piece of heady prophetic utterance with the earthly unexaltedness—the literal indigeneity—of the word "Missouri." Divinity in Smith is undiminished by its yoking to the stuff of mundane life.

We do well to think of plural marriage as another revelation keyed, in a like style, to the quotidian. Polygamy may be a doctrinal dictate, an imperative thundered down from the heavens. But it is also a daily practice, a *form of everyday life*: a moment-to-moment standing-in-the-fire that, if it has consequences of only barely thinkable celestial vastness, unfolds in the punctual rhythm of quotidian living. Think of Brigham Young, who, in a plain echo of Smith, would aver that "our senses, *if properly educated*, are channels of endless felicity to us."[63] Again, this is divinity not achieved through redemption but made available, received, though a kind of training. "If properly trained": Young invokes here a process of education that harkens back to precisely that "learning," which is also an unlearning, demanded in the King Follett Discourse. And this turn toward the educative quality of everyday life, these pedagogics of the workaday, gives us one final framework with which to understand plural marriage, and the willingness of nineteenth-century Mormons to stake so much—to stake their very existence—on its continuance. In this register, we can understand Smith to be offering polygamy as a *method*, a means by which those Saints who can stand in the fire might, in the teeth of the discomposing strangeness of the practice, edge themselves toward that denaturalization of the puritanical body that makes for exaltation. This is polygamy not as revelation, or not only. It is rather a devotional practice that offers everyday life—in this case the realm of the intimate—as a kind of counterdiscipline, a training ground for the unwriting of the orthodoxies of normative Christian, which is also to say secular, embodiment. And at the center of that counterdisciplining, I want to suggest by way of conclusion, are the *erotics* of plural marriage: the central place not only of the body but of its startling, self-surprising capacities.

Religions, like any other social structures, are in the business of imagining the bodies proper to them: of conceiving the parameters, the capacities and liabilities, and the organizing coherences of a body their cosmologies at once solicit, presume, and enact. (Social structures *invent* the objects through and upon which they act, as Foucault is everywhere at pains to remind us.)[64] Part of the scandal of Mormon polygamy, I have tried thus far to suggest, lies in the hard unassimilability of the body it imagines to the flesh as it is conceived in orthodox post-Pauline Christianity. But that atmosphere of scandal draws the greater measure of its energy from Mormonism's stark failure to reproduce the *liberal* body with which such "religious" fashionings of the flesh, over the course of the nineteenth century, were made more and more to comport. One name for that escalating, enforced comportment, I have been arguing, is "secularism"—secularism, in this iteration, marking the styles of adapted compatibility with liberal rationality that allow a given set of belief-practices to come into legibility as "religion" at all, rather than as, say, credulity, fanaticism, superstition, backwardness, or any of the other subvarieties of *bad belief*. Secularism, in this sense, names less the dissolution of religion in modern public life than the disciplined accommodation of patterns of belief and devotion to the premises of liberal rationality, its polities, its arrangements of life, its *bodies*. If for the Mormons polygamy is the fabulation that renders the incipience of divinity in the plain language of daily living, it also conjugates a body so dramatically apart from the normative framework of liberal polity as to appear an affront to it, a violation of the consensual American real, and, of course, a threat. The body ascending in the grain of its materiality toward divinization is a body dramatically ill suited to the tactics and codes of managerial rationalization (however much the *reproductive* body of the liberal subject might, in retrospect, be made coordinate with the dictates of polygamy, as well shall see). It is not a liberal body. This, for the nation's secularizing forces—be they institutionally "religious" or not at all—is its scandal.[65]

Smith thus enjoins the Saints to regard closely the way living ruptures the "traditions" according to which they know themselves, to "believe and receive" in a way that pierces the carapace of accumulated falsity and, in turn, seeds the possibility for new belief. The task is daunting, arduous, and we can see why. The body he is asking them to imagine for themselves is unchristian, unliberal, unsecular. But Smith looks to hearten the Saints by reminding them that, because the world is so much a place of abundance, this piercing, denaturalizing power takes form not as miracle or mystery. Rather, Smith assures the Saints, it is a power that lies very much within their grasp, and is in fact internal to the arrangement of humankind itself. Again and again, with a persistence it would be difficult to overstate, Smith identifies this internal power with that most belittled, least heralded of theological virtues. He identifies it with *pleasure*.

Fawn Brodie long ago described Smith's theological disposition with acute precision. "Joseph was no hair-shirt prophet," she wrote. "He believed in the good life, with moderate self-indulgence in food and drink, occasional sport, and good entertainment. . . . 'Man is that he might have joy' had been one of his first significant pronouncements in the Book of Mormon, and from that belief he had never deviated."[66] This attentiveness to earthly pleasure expresses itself in a great range of asides and small declaration. (We could think of Young's riff on the body's "channels of endless felicity," or Smith's references to God's liberality.) But the underscoring of this-worldly sensation is no less vivid in passages of enormous theological consequence. Here, for instance, is the astonishing conclusion Smith appends to his description of God's biography, his vastly heretical revelation that God was a man and that humankind itself is a collection of ungrown gods, whose futures are divinity. "This is good doctrine," Smith says. "*It tastes good.*" And then:

> You say honey is sweet and so do I. I can also taste the spirit and principles of eternal life, and so can you. I know it is good and that when I tell you of these words of eternal life that are given to me by the inspiration of the Holy Spirit and the revelations of Jesus Christ, you are bound to receive them as sweet. *You taste them and I know you believe them.* I rejoice more and more. (*EJS*, 240, emphasis added)

It is pleasure, here—the sweetness of honey, knowledge *as* delight—that redoubles itself, and makes for precisely the receiving and believing that, for Smith, are the pathways to exaltation.

Brodie goes on, "To every man in love with life—with the tantalizing richness of learning, the sweaty satisfaction of hard work, the luxury of sensual pleasure—Joseph's heaven had profound meaning." What's more, she continues, "it is no accident that his theology in the end discarded all traces of Calvinism and became an ingenuous blend of supernaturalism and materialism, which promised in heaven a continuation of all earthly pleasures—work, wealth, sex, power."[67] We glimpse here, I think, an almost protopsychoanalytic Smith: a theologian in love with life, certainly, but also a man who apprehends in the very intensities of carnal life a power that, in an entirely heartening way, *deranges* us, attunes us to possibilities for living otherwise, apart from the strictures and codes that govern our daylight hours, that comfort and confine us, that offer back to us legible versions of ourselves.[68] (For Freud, of course, sex is where we are most irreducibly strange to ourselves; it is where the errancies locked up in our workaday lives go to flourish.) In this register of Smith's cosmology, the body is both a revelation and a constant surprise. And it is also (as it is for Freud) a challenge: a scene of potential undoing. But what it promises to undo, in those passages of disorienting delight that are proper to it, is precisely those traditions that discipline the body, that induce us to misrecognize the *sweetnesses* of embodied living as temptations, deceitful prompts in the direction of sin and crime. In Smith, the disordering delights of the body are nothing of the kind. They are rather the harbingers of an order apart from the orthodoxies of sanctified religion, and for that matter from the deflat-ing managerial rationalizations of the body to which these, in the sweep of secularizing disciplines, were increasingly conjoined. They are foretastes of godliness: intimations of an immortality not premised on the transcendence of the flesh. God offers us these revelations of grace, Smith insists, "in the view of no eternal dissolution of our earthly tabernacles." This is the largest resonance of Smith's injunction to Nancy Rigdon, his cajoling assurance that "our Heavenly Father is more liberal in his views, and boundless in his mercies and blessings, than we are ready to believe or receive": it is God's purpose, he insists, that "in the end they shall have joy" (*EJS*, 159).

Polygamy works, then, across all these registers, in simultaneity. It is a doctrine making legible a counter-Calvinist vision of the divinity of the mortal body; it is a training ground, anchored in dailiness, for the denatural-ization of the secularizing body; and it is an intimate form built explicitly to recognize, rather than rebuke, the pleasures of carnality, inasmuch as those pleasures deliver back to us the good—if only glancingly conceivable—news that not only does life transpire in a world not fallen away from divinity, we ourselves inhabit *unfallen flesh*, bodies insusceptible to the secular mechan-ics of disenchantment or reenchantment because from the first coterminous with the flesh of God. These are premises at the center of early Mormonism, and polygamy—a daily practice, reinvented in each scene of its unfolding—gives them expression in a form that, as it proved, set the Mormon faithful at odds with local communities, states, public opinion, the federal govern-ment, and, in wrought ways, the regime of secular modernity that was edg-ing toward hegemony over the course of the first decades of its existence. (Accounts that understress the body, that lean on polygamy's familialism as a way of displacing the central place of the carnal, can be seen as efforts to fix Mormonism within precisely those solidifying, contested frameworks that its practices so concertedly disrupted.) This is what it means to say Mormonism took form as a radical theory of embodied life. At the center of early Mormon unassimilability, and integral to the making of Mormon-ism into an orthodoxy direly at odds with the putative antiorthodoxies of secularized liberalism, is the body it imagines: unfallen, fired by undoing pleasures, tracing out a trajectory, *through* its materiality, toward expansion and eternality. There, in the recesses of the body and in its startling capaci-ties, was much of what the Saints needed to learn, on the way to making themselves gods.

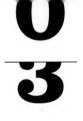

GODS IN SUBJECTION

Women, Polygamy, and the Eternity of Sex

A PERFECTLY INEXTRICABLE KNOT

IN THE MIDST OF *The Blithedale Romance*, Nathaniel Hawthorne's 1852 novel of utopian aspiration, gender disruption, and sex panic, a character named Zenobia makes a striking declaration. It is she, the imperiously beautiful Zenobia, who has until this point in the book embodied for its narrator an especially robust and to his eyes an especially *carnal* style of feminist protest. "Not that I would convey the idea of especial gentleness, grace, modesty, and shyness," Miles Coverdale tells us, "but of a certain warm and rich characteristic, which seems, for the most part, to have been refined away out of the feminine system."[1] Warmly and richly female without being normatively "feminine," Zenobia fascinates Coverdale not least for the ways her very body seems to overspill the confinements of gender propriety, though *fascinates* is perhaps too neutered a term. She prompts in him, rather, a peculiar, delectating kind of admiration. "Deficient in softness and delicacy" though she may be, Zenobia nevertheless puts to rout the whole of the conventionalized "feminine system"; this she does, we are told, with her "bloom, health, and vigor, which she possessed in such overflow that a man might well have fallen in love with her for their sake only" (15–16). Some hypothetical "man" might do so, Coverdale says, though he declines, somewhat coyly, to implicate himself.

Deviance, at any rate, is much on his mind. And well it might be: by the middle of the novel, just this overflowing and counternormative vivacity has helped propel Zenobia into an erotic entanglement of shifting intensities and, to our narrator, dismaying complexity. A "perfectly inextricable knot of polygamy" is the phrase that comes up, though Coverdale, with characteristic duplicity, will not apply it to any erotic community he is a part of, using it rather to describe the branches of the tree in which he sits (90). (Later in the novel he will observe in a Boston lyceum a display of wax figures "illustrating the wide catholicism of earthly renown by mixing up heroes and statesmen, the Pope and the Mormon prophet, kings, queens, murderers, and beautiful ladies" [196].) And yet it is the queenly and unconventional Zenobia, and not Miles, who at a moment of great crisis makes the most striking declaration of allegiance to, it would appear, gendered and erotic normativity.

In the climactic passage, all four of the main players in the novel's great erotic tangle are gathered together, and the domineering man at its center, Zenobia's erstwhile lover Hollingsworth, speaks of the hierarchies of gender. "Man is a wretch without woman," Hollingsworth declares, "but woman is a monster—and, thank Heaven, an almost impossible and hitherto imaginary monster—without man, as her acknowledged principal!" (122–23). Coverdale turns immediately to Zenobia, to watch her response to these bilious assaults on feminism and feminists, "these petticoated monstrosities," as Hollingsworth names them. But what he sees disorients and disappoints him. "'Well; be it so,' was all [Zenobia] said. 'I, at least, have deep cause to think you are right. Let man be but manly and godlike, and woman is only to ready to become to him what you say!'" (124). Let men be not merely masculine but godlike, the once-imperious Zenobia concedes, and a requisite feminine subjection will follow.

Early Mormonism, as we know, was indeed premised upon a crucial but hitherto suppressed *godlikeness of man*: upon the divinization of the human, achieved through a more and more cultivated embrace of the enlarging pleasures of the body itself, mantled in its unfallen flesh. "Then shall they be Gods," Smith had written in the polygamy revelation of 1843—though made public in 1852, the year of the publication of *The Blithedale Romance*—which then went on to map out the trajectory of Mormon exaltation in and through the practice of plural marriage. Or rather, through the practice of plural *patriarchal* marriage, and in that difference, that toggle between the human and its subdivision into genders, lies a tangle of problems for early Mormonism. For if early Mormonism rested its claims for an exalted and divinized humanity on a body presumed as universal—the flesh of mortal humankind—it also *deuniversalized* that body, in a number of overlapping, unsystematized, fantastically incoherent ways. To take only the nearest, greatest unparsed dilemma: Do women *also* inhabit the bodies of gods unenlarged? In their exaltation, are women a like, an equivalent, species of god? Or something other? Is the celestial sphere itself not only hierarchized—it surely is that—but gendered?

Zenobia, in her colliding encounter with Hollingsworth, recoils into something nearing subservience. That, at least, is what Coverdale sees, though it is a great grace of Hawthorne's novel that it arms us to mistrust, at every moment, the standards of measure he brings to bear on his world. *The Blithedale Romance* in fact goes to great lengths to remind us that certain kinds of men, and certain kinds of power, enjoy little as much as declaring women to be dupes and captives, the victims of some malign enchantment. Indeed, it is no exaggeration to say that, in his eager presumption about female susceptibility and the dire need for male rescue, Coverdale reveals himself to be something of a paradigmatic secular liberal. For secularism is not solely a story of, say, the triumph of rationality over superstition and dogma; it is also, and everywhere, a triumphant narrative *as against* styles of contrastingly bad belief that are themselves, inevitably, woven into the very bodies, the very flesh, of erring believers. As Joan Wallach Scott concisely argues, one of the chief structuring oppositions that a discourse of secularism propagates is that "between reason and sex," whereby women *as women*—as the bearers of sex—are consigned to the status of those permanently in need of secular redemption.[2] "The secularization narrative," as Linell E. Cady and Tracy Fessenden observe in their introduction to *Religion, the Secular, and the Politics of Sexual Difference*, "threads the narrative of gender and sexual emancipation into its own triumphal plotline."[3] Cady and Fessenden, as well as Scott, Molly McGarry, Saba Mahmood, Lila Abu-Lughod, and many others, have made especially clear how such redemptive narratives offer up an implicit ratification of the order of the secular itself, no matter its imperial or, for that matter, patriarchal commitments.[4]

For the women of early Mormonism, especially the polygamous wives, absolutely nothing about such dynamics would have been unfamiliar. To the contrary, among the most commonplace arguments about polygamy, repeated with dogged invariance from the moment of its public declaration (and continuing into the present), was that the women ensnared in it were, as a result, consigned to a uniquely abasing subservience, made subject to the authority of one man with whom they were not entitled to share even the equivalent promise of marital exclusiveness. This vision of the special subjection of *religious* women is, of course, a story secularism very much likes to tell about itself, and we can see why. In the first instance, the pleased apprehension of *polygamous* women as subjects of a singularly debasing power—rather than, say, *all women under conditions of patriarchy*—turns plural marriage into an elegant kind of alibi, a counterexample to the contrastive beneficence of a more properly tolerant, liberal, patriarchal order. No one turns this point more exactly than Nancy Bentley, who surveys the genre of sentimental antipolygamy novels that flourished later in the century, noting particularly the figuring of polygamous brides as *slaves* to their husbands (as opposed to those contrastingly *free* women who were married, according to sentimental convention, monogamously). Those antipolygamy novels, Bentley argues, were elementally conservative, and what they conserve is the legitimacy of patriarchy itself, so long as it is geared toward domestic monogamy, and the liberal state it neatly metaphorizes. "Polygamy," she writes, in a potent phrase, "is the bondage that sanctifies monogamy as freedom."[5]

The matter is not, of course, that there is, resultantly, nothing useful to be said about the kinds of longing and loneliness and pain to which the polygamous wives of early Mormonism do indeed give vivid testament. "There is no such thing as happiness known where a man has more than one wife," Mary Richards wrote to her husband in 1846, from the Winter Quarters, where plural marriage had begun to lead a more public and avowed life among the Mormon faithful. She went on, "It realy seems to me that this is a day in which Woman is destined to misery."[6] We have before us, rather, a specifically methodological challenge: the challenge of telling a critical story, keyed to punitive gendered hierarchy, apart from the tidal pull of secularization narratives. How do we tell the story of devoted women who were self-consciously *not* hungering for or in need of secular redemption, while also keeping in focus how their own celestial aspirations came to be thwarted and diminished (as, I will argue, they did)? How do we best keep on guard against the impulse to route our considerations of early Mormon women through an understanding of their pains—which were many, and real—as the expression of a failure to find safe harbor for themselves in a putatively gentler world of secular tolerance, presumed to be brimming with rights and restitutions? How, in all, do we pursue a critical genealogy of the sex in divinization without defaulting to secularizing presumption?[7]

The aim of my work in the chapter that follows, then, is not to spectacularize the sufferings of women like Mary Richards, or Louisa Beaman, or Eliza Snow, or Zina Diantha Huntington Jacobs Smith Young—so that we

might, as it were, play Coverdale to these abased Zenobias. Instead, following the lead of feminist scholars of secularism like Scott and Mahmood, as
well as historians of Mormon feminism from Linda P. Wilcox and Linda
King Newell to Martha Sonntag Bradley, Mary Brown Firmage Woodward,
and especially Laurel Thatcher Ulrich, I mean to track closely the question
of *female power*, especially in its relation to the question of female exaltation
and the divinization of women.[8] Mormon women, I want to suggest, were
themselves fantastically acute readers of the evolving doctrines of the early
church, and many of them found there the promises of an extraordinary
breadth of authority, undiminished by distinctions of gender. "*Not all are
capacitated alike*," Zina Diantha would write in her diary at Winter Quarters,
in the conviction that though there are indeed differences in mortal capacities to believe and receive Smith's breathtaking news of divinization and
a god-vibrant world, they were not the differences of gender.[9]

    Much can and has been made of these counterpossibilities—what I have
elsewhere called "the lost futures of the early Mormon social and sexual
imaginary"[10]—as might be made, too, of the fact that there were, briefly,
polygamous women, married to several living men.[11] But the story I wish
to tell here, however much it speaks to ungrown potentialities, is largely
one of foreclosure. I want to suggest that in the lives and writings of early
polygamous women we find an especially vivid testament to an undersystematized theology of the flesh working itself out negotiation by negotiation, and doing so not least through the bodies of women—through the
capacities afforded them, the permissions granted them, their arrangement
in codified social space, their deployment as figures in disputes less and
less local. The lives of polygamous women made in all for a kind of staging-
ground, on which the irresolutions of Mormon theology, of its vision of
exaltation and the possibilities of celestial carnality, could be managed. But
what this meant, in practice, was that these generative irresolutions, these
habitable counterpossibilities, were brought under the sway of an increasing systematization, forged in the heat of anti-Mormon fervor: a patterning
and, especially after the rise to power of Brigham Young, a style of rigidly gendered normalization. The story I mean to tell here is, in this sense,
somewhat paradoxical: it is of the *solidifying patriarchality* of patriarchal
plural marriage, wherein the larger, looser, ampler possibilities intuited by
women like Zina Diantha came under a more regulated, and more definitively hierarchical, species of centralized control. The early Mormons were
rarely more secular, I will argue, than in their concerted curtailments of
female power.

THE KEYS OF THIS POWER

Do women, like men, inhabit the bodies of gods not yet enlarged? Is exaltation—the trajectory toward godhead inscribed at the heart of early Mormon theology—available equally, *equivalently*, to women? To peruse the polygamy revelation itself is to encounter what seems, on the face of it, to be an incontestable rejoinder, a NO breathed out in the implacable voice of God. As many who came after Smith would note, his detractors and his defenders both, the exemplary figures summoned in the polygamy revelation all are men. Indeed, in the revelation Smith clusters around him, as if in needed defense, an entire phalanx of Old Testament patriarchs: David, Solomon, Moses. ("David also received many wives and concubines, as also Solomon, and Moses my servant; as also many others of my servants from the beginning of creation until this time; and in nothing did they sin" [*EJS*, 196].)[12] More than this, the revelation lays out a distinction between women and men, and between their separate and starkly gendered faculties and responsibilities, that appears to leave little room for vagrant interpretation:

> And again, as pertaining to the law of the Priesthood;—if any man espouse a virgin, and desire to espouse another, and the first give her consent; and if he espouse the second, and they are virgins, and have vowed to no other man, then is he justified; for he cannot commit adultery, for they are given unto him; for he cannot commit adultery with that, that belongeth unto him, and to none else; and if he have ten virgins given unto him by this law, he cannot commit adultery; for they belong to him; and they are given unto him;—therefore is he justified. But if one, or either of the ten virgins, after she is espoused, shall be with another man, she has committed adultery, and shall be destroyed; for they are given unto him to multiply and replenish the earth. (*EJS*, 198)

"She has committed adultery," Smith writes of any woman daring to claim for herself an unburdening from monogamy, "and shall be destroyed." Or, still more directly: "*They belong to him.*"

We might not wonder, then, at those accounts of Mormon polygamy that sought to frame it as a righteous restoration, not solely of an apostasized Christendom, but of a blasphemed patriarchy: a male authority beleaguered, and finally undermined, by a multitude of political-economic forces converging at midcentury. (These included urbanization, the industrialization of labor, and the fractured emergence of a range of feminist counterpublics.)[13] Udney Hay Jacob's *The Peace Maker* is only the most hyperinvested in this version of polygamy's patriarchal restoration, as we have seen, though others would follow suit across the century. And yet that vision of polygamous men laboring to restore a belittled patriarchy was equally commonplace, too, among the sentimental *detractors* of Mormon polygamy, who sought to fashion Mormon patriarchs as cruel, enslaving tyrants. Fanny Stenhouse's *Tell It All: A Woman's Life in Polygamy* (which was introduced by none other than Harriet Beecher Stowe) exemplifies the genre, and at least part of what's striking is how much her account of what polygamy aims to do—restore to incontestable authority the power of patriarchs—accords with Jacob's ardent defense. ("It is painful to witness among the rising generation of boys in Utah the contempt which many evince for every thing that a woman says or does, looking upon her as an inferior being," Stenhouse writes. "The sermons abound with allusions to woman's dependence upon men.")[14] The polygamy revelation would seem to have given, to both varieties of gender-scrutinizing exegetes of Mormon polygamy, plentiful resources to press their point.

But we do well to move deliberately through the terms of the revelation itself. For even here, in a revelation keyed so totally to patriarchal authority, are fissures and gaps, unrationalized contradictions: openings—to those with ears to hear them—for fugitive counterpossibility. It is striking, first, that in a document evidently devoted to the sacralization of male authority we should find that domination subject to a countermanding *female* authority. Take the passage quoted above. The opening subjunctive phrase hinges on female *consent*; it is, indeed, the very phrase Smith uses: "if any man espouse a virgin, and desire to espouse another, *and the first give her consent.*" Both Ulrich and Kathryn M. Daynes underscore one of the long aftereffects of this early framing of the necessity of female consent: the wider accessibility, to Mormon women, of divorce, as a legal remedy for which women themselves might petition. "In sharp contrast to divorces granted elsewhere in the United States," Ulrich observes, "plural marriages were dissolved by 'mutual consent' rather than by civil authority and did not require a judgment of guilt." She goes on, "Marriages broke up because wives as well as husbands ran away, and because increased mobility and multiple jurisdictions allowed them to do so. The Mormon system brought such practices within a system of church law. . . . Divorce," she concludes, "was perhaps the safety valve that made polygamy work" (280).[15] Here, for Ulrich, is just one of the ways so seemingly impregnable an edifice as patriarchal plural marriage might be larger in its affordances, and more habitable to women, than would at first appear likely.

But more is at stake here than earthly law and its relation to church protocols. The polygamy revelation broaches, after all, the matter of exaltation: *then shall they be Gods* is, in many respects, its most crucial declaration. Here, too, the text strikes surprising, if mixed, notes. In the passage subsequent to the one quoted above, Smith observes the following:

> And again, verily, verily I say unto you, if any man have a wife who holds the keys of this power, and he teaches unto her, the law of my Priesthood, as pertaining to these things; then shall she believe, and administer unto him, or she shall be destroyed, saith the Lord your God; for I will destroy her; for I will magnify my name upon all those who receive and abide in my law. (*EJS*, 198)

Smith offers a paean to God's willingness not merely to chastise but, again, to destroy any woman who interposes between His will and the wishes of His chosen men. Nested within even this proclamation, though, is a strange, provoking gesture toward the power of the wife: "if any man have *a wife who holds the keys of this power.*" The phrase is striking, and resonant. A flat reading of the line might remind us of the prominence of the key in early Mormonism as a symbol of secret knowledge, Masonic in origin and especially pertinent to the whispering and skullduggery that surrounded polygamy in its earliest days in Nauvoo, where avowals and denials circulated with ungovernable velocity. On this account, the "wife" is the one who *knows*.[16]

And yet such a reading hardly exhausts the passage, whose implications point toward a different reckoning of the possibilities for female power. In fact, Smith himself, in propria persona, would invoke such ampler possibilities, in ways that spoke vividly to what we might think of as an unforeclosed elasticity in early imaginings of the intimate life of Mormon divinization. This had happened in the spring of 1842, when he informed a gathering of Mormon women that "you may be an ornament unto those to whom you belong, and rise up and crown them with honors, & by so doing you shall be crown'd with honor in heav'n and shall sit upon thrones."[17] Here was indeed a special species of power. For to invoke thrones and crowns in heaven is, in the idiom of early Mormonism, to conjure, precisely, exaltation: the achievement of the largest destiny for human embodiment in its celestialization, its becoming-god. There is equivocation in these remarks, to be sure. (Smith figures woman as mere "ornament," dependent upon "those to whom you belong.") But the countering notes are there as well, and it is in respect to these that we can say that the matter of the incipient godliness of women, even at the moment of polygamy's conception, was not quite forgone. To the contrary, the matter was alive, inviting, and as yet locked into no authorized consensus.

QUEENS OF THE EARTH

In no one institution of early Mormonism did the generative uncertainty about female divinization play itself out quite as vividly, or as consequentially, as it did than at the very venue in which Smith was speaking, that spring day in 1842: this was the Female Relief Society. Created by Mormon women in the heady days in Nauvoo, the Female Relief Society was where Smith, again in 1842, would offer his most capacious vision of the celestial status of gender, and of the divinizing capacities of women. And as Laurel Thatcher Ulrich observes throughout *A House Full of Females*, it was also where Mormon women worked out, *for themselves*, a wealth of strategies for living within the shifting entailments of a Mormon theology in an almost constant state of upheaval, transition, and incomplete codification. Indeed, for many of the women who moved through it, the Female Relief Society provided a venue for testing out ways of being in relation to polygamy in all its cosmic and quotidian multifacetedness: as an arrangement of intimate life; a gendered sociality; a doctrine of faith that was also, escalatingly, a political allegiance, and a radical one at that; and, along with all these, an implicit account of *what the body was*, of its peculiarities, its promises, and its fate.

There is some curiosity in this, inasmuch as the Female Relief Society came into authorized being as something of a bulwark *against* polygamy—or, at least, against the scandal of polygamy, as it was beginning to engulf the Mormons in Nauvoo and beyond. The society, founded in 1842, met first on 17 March, and it was then that the gathered—some twenty Mormon women, along with Smith and two of his male apostles—elected Emma Smith as president. (It had been the "brainchild," in Ulrich's phrase, of Sarah Granger Kimball, then twenty-three years old [62].) It was at this meeting, too, that Smith offered his inaugural sense of the purpose of the organization, imploring the gathered "to good works in looking after the wants of the poor" and—rather more stridently—to set about "correcting the morals and strengthening the virtues of the female community."[18] As Ulrich glosses this, "The goal of correcting morals may have taken some of the women by surprise. They had imagined a charitable society, not a moral-reform society" (65). But a disciplining corrective to possible dissent was, by this time, needed. For 1842 was the year in which the murmurings against the prophet, whispered accusations of sexual errancy and predation, grew too insistent to be ignored, or waved away with blithe dismissal. They had become, in fact, a scandal, national in scale.

In the summer of 1842, shortly after being excommunicated from the church in Nauvoo in what may or may not have been a jointly projective and preventative measure, John C. Bennett went public with accusations against Smith that would take shape as *The History of the Saints; or, An Exposé of Joe Smith and Mormonism*, whose racializations of polygamous patriarchy we observed in the previous chapter. (Bennett had initially launched his accusations in six letters to the *Sangamo Journal*, published in Springfield.) Bennett would soon begin a lecture tour promoting his book, and his accusations, but even before his tour other accusations, and other accusers, had emerged. The atmosphere of sexualized scandal was, just then, everywhere. Turmoil internal to Mormonism would reach a boil in August, when Orson and Parley Pratt, two stalwart Mormon apostles, were excommunicated for their disobedience.[19] It was in this context that Smith, in a meeting on 31 August, thanked the Female Relief Society for having "taken the . . . most active part in my welfare against my enemies." "Altho' I do wrong," Smith said, "I do not the wrongs that I am charg'd with doing"[20]—itself a vexing declaration, inasmuch as he was by this time married polygamously to several women in the room. (Eliza Snow, the secretary of the society whose recording notes we rely upon, had married Smith on 29 January.) We might read this testimony of Smith's as bald falsehood or, less censoriously, as Jesuitical parsings of a truth in dispute. As far as the truly faithful were concerned, Smith had broken no eternal laws; rather, he had labored, against misgiving and incomprehension, to live *according* to God's newly established doctrine. These distinctions were not much present, at any rate, when the Relief Society, as Ulrich recounts, "gathered more than a thousand names attesting to Joseph Smith's virtue, honesty, and integrity" (74–75), and delivered them to the governor of Illinois at the end of July. All of which has led to an understanding of the Female Relief Society, in its early phase, as at least in part a screen organization, employed to discipline dissent, reassure the potentially scandalized, and counteract anti-Mormon propaganda.

None of this is unfair. But the local deployments of the Female Relief

Society do not give us full purchase on what was transacted there, and Ulrich's detailed account of the interwoven lives of several Mormon women works, in the first instance, as a rebuke to any sense that the organizers of the Female Relief Society were quite so docile, or quite so easily manipulated. We will return to Ulrich's way of telling this story shortly, but for the moment we can note that, whatever the uses to which it may have been put in 1842, the Relief Society proved to be the scene of enormously consequential theological speculation, of the airing of ideas that were to ring down through decades of Mormon life. It was there, for instance, that on 30 March 1842, Smith had remarked (as Eliza Snow transcribed him) that "he was going to make of this Society a kingdom of priests as in Enoch's day—as in Pauls day."[21] This was provocative theologizing, intimating as it did a specific and pivotal role for women in Smith's restorationist cosmic imagination. But all the richest provocation was yet to come.

In a meeting on 24 April Smith gave a momentous address. His topic that day was seemingly narrow. He spoke to the society in respect to the disquiet that had evidently attended the proposition that Mormon women might partake in "laying on hands" to heal the sick. Eliza Snow transcribed Smith's comments thus:

> Respecting the females laying on hands, he further remark'd, there could be no devil in it if God gave his sanction by healing that there could be no more sin in any female laying hands on the sick than in wetting the face with water. It is no sin for any body to do it that has faith, or if the sick has faith to be heal'd by the administration.
>
> He reproved those that were dispos'd to find fault with the management of concern saying that if he undertook to lead the church he would lead it right.[22] (*EJS*, 161)

If this point was not sufficiently clear, Smith would amplify it moments later: "Females," Smith continued, "if they are pure and innocent, can come into the presence of God" (*EJS*, 162). The phrase itself—*can come into the presence of God*—is all rich suggestiveness, connotative implications multiplying faster than denotation can contain them. Does it simply imply, as Richard Bushman argues, that women, capable just as much as men of encountering God "while still on earth," were in this way brought "into the circle of the endowed who would be cleansed and purified in the temple"?[23] This would indeed prove to be the case. (Several of Smith's polygamous wives would, after his death, receive their endowments and "join the Anointed Quorum.")²⁴ But might Smith's phrases imply something larger, more upending even than this sanctification of female power in endowment? A gesture, perhaps, toward the incipient, *equivalent* divinity of women?

To be sure, the phrase itself is one note struck within a whole series of orchestrated conventionalities, all of which tilt toward the saving power of *submission to established order*. This—knowing one's place—is the central theme of Smith's remarks on the day, which commence with Smith giving "instructions respecting the different offices, and the necessity of every individual acting in the sphere allotted him or her" (*EJS*, 160), return to the point that "every person should stand and act in the place appointed" (*EJS*, 161), and conclude with Smith insisting on an especially conventional set of female virtues: "Let this Society teach how to act towards husbands, to treat them with mildness and affection," Smith says, adding, "When you go home never give a cross word, but let kindness, charity and love, crown your works henceforward" (*EJS*, 163–64). Charity, mildness, love, confinement to local offices: these are the wholly familiar coordinates. Smith could well be speaking in colloquy with Hawthorne's Miles Coverdale and his association of conventional femininity with "gentleness, grace, modesty."

And yet none of these gendered conventionalities can quite erase the contrary suggestions that animate Smith's remarks, in which we once more find that striking and characteristic cross-wiring of the seemingly normative and the counternormative in Smith's prophetic thought. Watch, for instance, as Smith's comments on the necessity of female "innocence" and placation ascend swiftly into an altogether different terrain of possibility:

> You need not be teasing men for their deeds, but let the weight of innocence be felt which is more mighty than a millstone hung about the neck. Not war, not jangle, not contradiction, but meekness, love purity, these are the things that should magnify us. Action must be brough[t] to light—iniquity must be purged out—then the vail will be rent and the blessings of heaven flow down—they will roll down like the Mississippi river. This Society shall have power to command Queens in their midst—I now deliver it as prophecy that before ten years shall roll around, the queens of the earth shall come and pay their respects to this Society—they shall come with their millions and shall contribute of their abundance for the relief of the poor—If you will be pure, nothing can hinder. (*EJS*, 163)

From a panegyric on female meekness and purity, Smith rises to prophesy a power higher than that of nearly every earthly dominion. He envisions, in fact, a future in which the queens of the earth "shall come and pay their respects" to Mormon women, so exalted will they have become. Then, too, there is the great breadth of the declaration that "these are the things that *should magnify us*," which suggests, however fleetingly, a conjoined, a *mutual* trajectory, via magnification, toward a shared destiny in divinization. Picking up all the scattered invocations of a female exaltation not notably distinct from that of men—a godliness made evident by its transcendence of the highest earthly authorities—Smith here sets about coordinating and, after a fashion, amplifying them.

There is more than this. By this point in his remarks Smith had already made clear that the truly bedeviling facet of Mormon life was not feminine assertiveness but, quite to the contrary, grasping male ambition. "President Smith continued," Eliza Snow would write, with what may well have been deep satisfaction, "by speaking of the difficulties he had to surmount ever since the commencement of the work in consequence of aspiring men, 'great big Elders' as he called them who had caused him much trouble" (*EJS*, 161). Here, too, is the intimation of something more than enlargement through subservience, of something indeed better than mere equality. But more telling still—and more acutely promising to those women in the room whose attentions were tuned toward such directions—was Smith's seemingly thrown-off aside, offered as part of his declaration that "if the sisters should have faith to heal the sick, let all hold their tongues, and let every thing roll on." What followed was a sentence that would echo across the length and breadth of his remarks, charging the whole of it with a current of expansive theological possibility. "Who knows the mind of God?" Smith said. "*Does he not reveal things differently from what we expect?*" (*EJS*, 161, emphasis added).

Here, then, is the early Mormon theological imagination figured as breezy heresy. For Smith, prophetic power gathers its authority not through precedent—the precedent of Old Testament patriarchs, say—but through an aliveness to the possibility of overturning established orthodoxy, of conceiving of past "traditions" as interwoven aspects of an accreting apostasy that any good Mormon is obliged to resist. In this respect the very patriarchality of biblical polygamists might take its place among the other established orthodoxies that Mormonism sets out not to imitate but to *renovate*, to outstrip and undo. Taken together with Smith's remarks on the sharing of magnification, his special opprobrium for aspiring men, and his invocation of the humbled queens of the earth, this insistence on the surprisingness of God's order gives the sharpest point to the question we have been tracking all along: Do women inhabit equally, equivalently, the bodies of gods not yet enlarged? Is it possible that *patriarchy itself* was among the apostasies of a fallen Christendom?

In Smith's remarks to the Female Relief Society, an auditor hungering for just such possibilities, and just such promises of grace, might well have found reason to take heart.

A BRIEF BIOGRAPHY OF ZINA DIANTHA HUNTINGTON
JACOBS SMITH YOUNG (PART 1)

Zina Diantha Jacobs was one such auditor. She was to become among the most formidable women in early Mormonism, though her story, as we shall see, is not entirely typical. When, for instance, at the age of twenty-one, Zina Diantha was "sealed" to Joseph Smith, on 27 October 1841, she was no inexperienced girl. She was by then already, and ongoingly, married. In March of 1841, Zina Diantha Huntington had become Zina Diantha *Jacobs*, the wife of a young man named Henry Jacobs. (They were married, as it happened, by John C. Bennett, who was soon to bring such trouble to Smith and the Mormons with his insider exposé of polygamy.) On the day of her sealing to Smith, Zina Diantha was nearly six months pregnant with her and John's first son. And *then*, in 1846, during another pregnancy, she was once more at the center of Mormon ritual. As Van Wagoner puts it, "On 2 February 1846, pregnant with Henry's second son, Zina was resealed by proxy to the murdered Joseph Smith and in that same session was 'sealed for time' to Brigham Young. Faithful Henry B. Jacobs stood as an official witness to both ceremonies." And these were, in truth, the least of her departures.[25] For what is perhaps most remarkable about Zina Diantha is that, in and through all of this volatility and historical turbulence, she nurtured an intense, long-unforsworn identification with *prophetic power*, and with the spiritual authority it bestowed. In the complex fate of that identification, we can, I think, begin to read out a knottier story of women and polygamy.

In the flattest terms, Zina Diantha's story roils one of the easiest, always-to-hand dismissals of Mormonism on the grounds of its putatively backward, its indeed barbaric arrangements of sex and gender. This is the claim that it inscribes its wild misogyny in the spectacular inequity of the permissions of marriage, as they are distributed to men and to women. Whereas the yoke of marital exclusiveness was to be lifted from men (and this unboundedness account them as virtue, as *righteousness*), for women it would be unaltered. But Zina Diantha knew what it was to be married, as a living woman in one given moment in the mortal world, to more husbands than one. On the one hand, this seeming disruption can be made to appear, with just a little conceptual reframing, not so much an exception or violation as a confirmation of the specifically celestial aspect of plural patriarchal marriage. According to the fast-forming taxonomy of early Mormonism, that is, Zina Diantha was understood to be married to Henry Jacobs *for time*, and sealed to Joseph Smith *for eternity*, made his partner in exaltation, and thus taking her place alongside the other women who would join the prophet in a shared (if pointedly nonequivalent, because gendered) divinization. Precisely this framing was and continues to be a major through-line in appraisals of Mormon polygamy, its divinizing imagination, its entanglements of embodiment and gender and sex. Daynes gives perhaps the most exacting account of these inner categories of early Mormon polygamy. "Mormons recognized several types of marriage with various rights and obligations," she writes, including most saliently those "for time and eternity." "Such marriages," she continues,

> now as well as in the nineteenth century, involve full conjugal rights and obligations on earth, and Mormons believe the marriage will continue in force after both husband and wife have died. Some women in the nineteenth century, however, were sealed to husbands for eternity only. Such sealings entailed few or no marital rights or obligations on earth. In addition, some women were sealed to their husbands for eternity only but used their husbands' surnames. These marriages appear to have conferred no right to sexual access but may have carried some responsibility for husbands to provide some financial assistance and protection to the women.[26]

According to this gridded taxonomy, Zina Diantha's marriage makes a straightforward kind of sense. Her temporal marriage, which involved her mortal life and her mortal flesh with Henry Jacobs, would be superseded in eternity by her celestial marriage to Joseph Smith.

But this framing, clarifying though it is, can also be misapprehending. For one of the great uses of Zina Diantha's story lies in the swift way it unsettles the organized tidiness of any such renderings. From the perspective of her involvement with men both living and dead, anointed and not, these neat divisions come into focus rather as a kind of back-formation, a retrospective reassessing of processes considerably more improvisatory, volatile, and undersystematized. And with Zina Diantha as our guide, we can begin to see, too, how that retrospective systematization accompanied, *participated in*, a certain style of late-century normalization, whereby the underformulated messiness of plural marriage came under an increasingly centralized ecclesiastical control.[27]

Zina Diantha's marriage to Henry Jacobs took place in March of 1841, and one of its notable aspects was that Joseph Smith did not perform the ceremony. As we noted earlier, the task fell to John C. Bennett. Asked about the curious absence of the prophet from this role, Smith is reported to have answered that "the Lord had made it known to him that she was to be his Celestial wife."[28] And so, pregnant with her first child, in the autumn of 1841, Zina Diantha acquiesced to what had been, on Smith's part, a long and assiduous courtship. (As Bradley and Woodward note, "Joseph pressed Zina for an answer to his marriage proposal on at least three occasions in 1840, but she avoided answering him" [*4 Zinas*, 108].) Much has been made of what Bradley and Woodward call Henry Jacobs's "tacit approval" (113); by virtue of his anomalous status—a man consenting to the marriage of his wife to another man—he is a figure familiar to virtually all histories of early polygamy. But I think we might find something more remarkable still in Zina Diantha's own explanation, offered later in life. We know that, after her marriage to Jacobs, Smith presented to Zina Diantha what amounted to an ultimatum. Smith is reported to have said, "Tell Zina I have put it off and put it off until an angel with a drawn sword has stood before me and told me if I did not establish that principle and live it, I would lose my position and my life and the Church could progress no further."[29] Here is Zina Diantha's account of her response:

> When I heard that God had revealed the law of Celestial marriage that we would have the privilege of associating in family relationships in the worlds to come I searched the scriptures and by my humble prayer to my Heavenly Father I obtained a testimony for myself that God had required that order to be established in his Church. I made a greater sacrifice than to give my life for I never anticipated again to be looked upon as an honorable woman by those I dearly loved. (*4 Zinas*, 114)

Zina Diantha does not enter into polygamy with anything like naïveté. The self she styles here is conspicuously not that of the guileless, blinkered ingénue. Rather, she understands herself to be surrendering, irrevocably, one especially precious kind of respectability, and to be making herself subject to the enmity not only of the world at large but of "those I dearly loved." She marries Smith nevertheless, making "a greater sacrifice than to give my life," and does so, she says, after having "obtained a testimony *for myself* that God had required" it.

In this compressed, arresting bit of self-portraiture, we might be struck, in the first instance, by how seamlessly Zina Diantha's response repeats that of the polygamous men Joseph invites into the secret of plurality, whose wrestling with what feels unassimilable to them issues finally in a greater achieved closeness to Smith, to Mormon righteousness, and to God Himself. (Recall Ulrich's canny remarks on how initial resistances "prepared the way for revelation" [85].) Precisely as those devoted Saints one after another reported themselves to have been jolted by polygamy, only to cycle back toward its God-ordained necessity, so too does Zina Diantha map her own trajectory. And if her acceptance is a "sacrifice," it is not, she insists, one she makes out of anything like easy compliance. Indeed, Zina Diantha speaks firmly in the conviction of her own righteousness and, with this, in the conviction of her own access to the ordering wishes of God. This conviction arrives in concert with the dictates from the prophet, but also apart from them: *I obtained a testimony for myself.* Of course, one of the great promises of Mormonism involved the ongoingness of God's presence in the moral world, His aliveness in the present tense, and the concomitant availability of revelation. In her self-accounting, Zina Diantha plainly understands that promise of grace, and its special style of authority, to extend equally to her. That conviction, we might say, lay at the heart of her devotion.

Zina Diantha had come into Mormonism with her family; her parents, who encountered the Book of Mormon in 1833, were baptized into the faith in April of 1835, when she was fourteen. By October of 1836, the family had sold their farm in upstate New York and journeyed with the Saints to Ohio. As early as these Kirtland years, Zina Diantha had shown an altogether remarkable facility in matters of the spirit. There, as Bradley and Woodward note, both Zina Diantha and her sister Presendia came to be "known among the Saints for their spiritual endowments and their piety" (*4 Zinas*, 64). But these gifts, at least as they expressed themselves through Zina Diantha, were not quite those of meekness, love, and purity that Smith would later commend to the women gathered at the Female Relief Society. They were, in tenor, markedly distinct. In a recollection of Zina Diantha written in 1881, Emmeline B. Wells observed that she possessed "a perfect gift of interpretation of tongues as any person in the Church, for although her opportunities for education in language have been limited, and she is not a learned woman, yet she gives the interpretation of hymns, psalms, and sacred songs in the most happy manner, without thought or hesitation. There is something divinely beautiful in thus rendering, by the gift of inspiration, words uttered in an unknown tongue." Zina Diantha's brother Oliver would offer his own recollection of the Kirtland days of piety and prayer: "I used to delight in religious conversation in and among the family; and we finally obtained the gift of tongues, all of us, and Zina the gift of Interpretations" (*4 Zinas*, 64). Zina Diantha, that is, possessed both the gift of tongues and that of what Wells and Oliver describe as "interpretation": a capacity for making legible to others the blazing word of God. She found for herself, we might say, a role much storied in early Mormonism: she performed as a special sort of *translator*, taking sacred text and rendering it available to her contemporaries, regardless of how little formal education they (or she) could claim.

These gifts and the striking identifications they suggest—I think most immediately of Bushman's work on Joseph Smith as translator[30]—did not expire with the peaceable familial days of Kirtland. In the years following, Zina Diantha traveled with the Saints from Ohio to Missouri, endured the violence there, and married and began her family in the hothouse atmosphere of Nauvoo, where she would grieve for the death of the prophet after his murder in 1844. She migrated with the Mormons to Winter Quarters, and there suffered an estrangement from Henry—the father of her children—precipitated by her union with Brigham Young. (We will return to the terms of that parting, and that joining, shortly.) And then, with the rest of the Mormons, and with her two sons—then six and two and a half—she journeyed west. Of that journey, she would write: "Many ware the peculiar incidents that occurred on our journey a cross the planes, toils and hardships cooking with buffalow-chips, stampedes occasionally laying a loved one by the way side, every sabath we had meetings much good instruction was imparted to the saints" (*4 Zinas*, 168). In September of 1848, she arrived at last in what she would call the "vally of the great salt lake," and her gifts soon evolved in a new direction.[31]

For 16 June 1849, she wrote to her diary:

> Just as the sun had set I sat singing to my children and rocking Chariton I commenced singing in tongs and as I arose the speret said go and bless Clarry Decker or young. I done as the impression bid. After I had blest her I blest Lucy B and elizabeth and Sally (the lamanites that Charles Decker bought) was setting by. I lade my hands uppon her hed and my language changed in a moment and when I finished she said she understood every word. I had talked in her mother tongue. The speret bore

testimony but there was positive proof that could not be denied. I told her that her mother and sisters ware coming, and She must be a good girl. It was to her understanding it was a great cross but the Lord crowed it with joy for which I fee(l) to praise his name. ("Diary," 109–10)

I had talked in her mother tongue, Zina Diantha writes of her encounter with "Sally," the Native slave purchased, in an infamous moment of Mormon-Native encounter, by Charles Decker from a Ute named Batiste. (The story goes that when Decker declined to purchase the two captive youths shown to him, Batiste killed the first on the spot. Decker, who was Young's son-in-law, purchased the second and "gave the young woman to his sister, Young's wife Clarissa [Clara], presumably as a servant.")[32] What, we might ask, does Zina Diantha imagine herself to be doing here, as she extends into new precincts her role as a translator and speaker of tongues? What office is she assuming? In a gesture that compounds what might have been an earnest effort at consolation with the most telegraphic white-settler expropriation—"Sally's" misery becoming an occasion for white spiritual renewal—Zina Diantha finds herself suddenly fluent in what she understands to be an ancient language, whereupon she deploys it for purposes hovering between the disciplinary and the evangelical. ("I told her that her mother and sisters ware coming, and She *must be a good girl*.") That those blended purposes accorded quite evenly with, say, colonizing brutality is in this instance quite beyond dispute. But even in and through that colonizing zeal, that conviction of Lamanite convertability, are the clear lineaments of a startling set of identifications. Unschooled, but by a sudden visitation of God's power made adept at translation, and tuning that fluency to the task of proselytizing—of converting the Lamanites—Zina Diantha does more than give proof of the continued presence of God in the world. More pointedly, and with an eerie exactness, *she reinhabits the prophetic role of Joseph Smith himself*, duplicating its patterns and seizing for herself a modicum of its authority. She follows Smith directly not only in his zeal for racial conversion but in what Bushman calls his "liberation from the learned's claims to a monopoly on translation," whereby he transformed himself into a visionary with prophetic power: "a seer with interpretations rather than a scholar trained in languages."[33]

Consider, in the context of these startling identifications, her diary entry from earlier in the year. In January she had described the textures of her day:

In the morning I washed some & charles Hide [Charles Walker Hyde] called in the afternoon. Oliver & I went to Sister Twists. BY & br Bullock

took supper there. She lives with Phines Cook [Phineas Wolcott Cook].
Sister Cobb was there. We had the best supper I have eaten in the vally
the mince pie and gooseberry tarts in particular. In the evening Oliver &
I went down to Adison Prats there connexion [cousins?] ware invited in.
Had some music singing and relating events of past life. Truly interesting. I felt it a duty as the speret rested uppon me in obedience there unto
agreeable to my former covenants with God to obey him. I arose and sung
some and spoke in tongs Leaving the event in the hands of him who bad
me speak. Enjoyed the evening much. ("Diary," 97)

Here, in a single entry, is exactly the untroubled interweaving of the quotidian and the divine, that inflooding of ordinariness with the live presence of
God, that had been so much a hallmark of Joseph's own prophetic career. In
Zina Diantha's diary, mince pies and gooseberry tarts hold space equably,
and in unbroken continuity, with spiritual endowment, covenants with God.
I arose, Zina Diantha writes, *and sung some and spoke in tongs*: it is difficult
to imagine a more precise restatement of the Smithian prophetic idiom, its
confounding of the sacred and the workaday, than this pairing of the gran-
diosity of a scene of divine visitation with the deflating plainspokenness
of *sung some*. It reads in all like the testament of someone who has done
more than comprehend or even identify with Smith, or with the early Mormon prophetic disposition he cultivated. Zina Diantha, with her own equal
privilege, is, rather, actively embodying it. In the dailiness of her encounters
with language, with the ordinary mortal world, and—not incidentally—in
her experiences of a carnality cut free of the confinements of those traditions that most structure it, Zina Diantha might in fact be read as *living out*
Smith's prophetic disposition, annexing its authority to herself. I take this
to be part of what Ulrich means when she writes of Zina Diantha that "she
relished earthly pleasures" (224)—which might recall to us in turn Fawn
Brodie's depiction of Joseph as "no hair-shirt prophet" but a man captivated
by pleasure, and finding there the intimations of larger, divinized destiny
for the human. "Enjoyed the evening much," Zina Diantha writes, with the
assurance of one who knows not only that in the end she shall have joy, but
that such joy is a pathway to exaltation.

Small wonder, then, that Joseph Smith felt he needed to speak to the
Female Relief Society back in April of 1842, when there had been so much
disquieted talk going round about women, and their unsettling pretenses to
priestly power. To the degree that we recognize Zina Diantha to be annexing
something of the power of God-inspired prophecy and even implicitly to

be claiming, for herself, an equal privilege with the ancient saints, Joseph's address begins to appear a countermanding gesture in the direction of disciplinary control. The logic of that circulating male disquiet to which Smith feels called to respond is perfectly clear: as women began to lay hands on the sick, speak in tongues, claim revelation—as, in short, they inserted themselves into what Amy Hollywood and others help us to see as a long tradition of women accruing worldly power through an identification with the rupturing force of the divine[34]—Mormon men recoiled, as Smith reports, in anger and aggrieved discontent. And Joseph's response in his remarks of April 1842 *is* to clarify the nature of priesthood authority, which even in these early commentaries begins to take form as an institution built to corral the less governable intimations of power that attend, as a matter of course, so committedly democratic a version of God's penchant for addressing Himself to persons regardless of status or standing. From the first, that is, priesthood authority *codifies* the accessibility, if not of grace, then of the forms of authority that might be believed to reside in it, making it amenable to verticalization, hierarchy, ecclesiastic control. Hence, Smith's constant return, in his remarks to the Relief Society, on clarified hierarchy, established places, order in authority. Precisely this, especially in respect to the hierarchies of gender, was the role a centralized priesthood was to take more and more in the West, under Young's guidance, as we soon shall see.

But in this context it is once again Smith's *disinclination* to take up any of the ready-to-hand gestures of reaction, his sustained refusal of delegitimation, that sounds most loudly in his remarks. To be sure, we find him insisting on ordered hierarchy, and invoking as well that roster of conventional female virtues: meekness, purity, innocence, and the rest. But with these there is the great counterallowance: *"Does he not reveal things differently from what we expect?"* The force of the line now comes into sharper focus. Again, to the degree that we recognize Zina Diantha to be annexing the power of God-inspired prophecy and claiming for herself an equal privilege with the ancient saints, we can see something of the upending promise she found in early Mormonism. For perhaps the startling thing God revealed was an equal privilege with the ancient saints that was not at all what was expected, inasmuch as it was as unbroken by the distinctions of *gender* as it was by the distinctions of education, wealth, and worldly standing. And perhaps just this uncanceled possibility fomented Zina Diantha's already-burgeoning sense of authority in relation to an accessible divinity, the nearness of God in her world. And perhaps this in turn amplified her sense that the fate of her body lay not inside the parameters of respectability, or reproduction, or meekness and compliance. Perhaps it solidified an intimation that hers was a destiny considerably grander.

A LONE RETREAT (A BRIEF BIOGRAPHY, PART 2)

What Zina Diantha was allowed, we might say, was and was not such grandeur. I want to turn now to a consideration of what happened to her identification with prophetic authority as her life came to be swept up in the restructuring and pivotal clarification of early polygamy. Zina Diantha had spent the initial season of her arrival in the valley of the Great Salt Lake in "what might have been an attempt to recapture the emotional intensity of the female world of Winter Quarters," a world characterized by gifts of spirit, speaking in tongues, and especially by the cohering sociability that these blessings helped to solidify (*4 Zinas*, 179). The years leading up to Utah had indeed been tumultuous, and in many respects rending, but also shot through with intimations of power. The great trouble had begun for Zina Diantha after Smith's death; it was then that Brigham Young began his overtures toward her, which appear to have been different in tenor than Smith's. In May of 1845, she confided to her diary: "Never to be forgotten at 11 o clock, O then what shall I say. At or after 4 I went to sleep." She went on, "Comfort us, yes Henry in his trouble, for he has not repined a word. Accept our thanks for life, forgive the weakness of my heart, and let me do nothing but what shall be to thy honour and Glory and my soles salvation" (*4 Zinas*, 129). Though Young himself is not mentioned here, not long after this she *did* record a visit between her husband and the president. The issue of these encounters was exactly what Zina Diantha, as well as the unrepining Henry, seems to have feared. And so, with Henry as witness, Zina Diantha was sealed for time to Brigham Young, on 2 February 1846. Not three months later, while still at Winter Quarters, Young exercised his authority by sending Henry away on a mission to England, effectively laying to rest any doubt about the nullified status of his marriage to Zina Diantha.

Something of the anguish of this period of Zina Diantha's life is captured in the astounding letter Henry wrote to her on 25 June 1846:

> Whether in time or Eternity Zina my mind never will change from worlds without End no never the same affection is there and never can be moved. I do not murmur nor complain at the Handlings of god no veryly no . . .

I do not blaime any person or persons no may the Lord our Father Bless
Brother Brigham . . . tell him for me I have no feelings against him nor
never had; all is right according to the Law of Celestial Kingdom of our
god and Joseph. Zina be comforted be of good cheer and the god of our
fathers bless you. I know your mind has been troubled about menny
things but fear not all things will work together for good and for them
that Love God.[35] (*4 Zinas*, 153)

"I know your mind has been troubled about menny things," Henry writes,
in a phrase that gestures toward the pain not only of his own but of Zina
Diantha's position, with its divided loyalties, its grief for a lost past, its dread
for an uncertain future.[36]

But there is an inner drama to this marital turmoil, the details of which
suggest that we might err in reading in Zina Diantha's grief as, at root, the
outward sign of an enforced compliance to a religious authority that had
begun to list, just then, toward the monomaniacal. (Young himself does not
do much to disarm such a narrative, it should be said. Here is how, in 1861,
he rationalized the rupture of the marriage of the Jacobses: "If a woman
can find a man holding the keys of the preisthood [*sic*] with higher power
and authority than her husband, and he is disposed to take her he can do
so," adding that in such cases, "there is no need for a bill of divorcement.")[37]
Bradley and Woodward give us an apt framing:

Three days before her sealing to Brigham, Zina and Henry received their
endowments. Zina also received the second anointing, or "fullness of the
priesthood" ordinance, and was admitted into the Holy Order, a circle of
faithful and trusted Mormon elite. Originally, the endowment was performed only for men. When women were included in 1843, they became
participants in the "privileges, blessings and gifts of the priesthood."[38]
(*4 Zinas*, 132)

It's worth noting this turn toward the "gifts of the priesthood." For if Zina
Diantha's parting in anguish from Henry entailed a species of obedience, an
acquiescence to ever more striated distributions of intra-Mormon authority,
it carried with it, just as certainly, an unmistakable endowment of power:
once again, something like an amplification, rather than a sharp curtailment, of precisely those prophet-like postures of authority Zina Diantha
had already begun to explore. She gives up Henry, the father of two of her
children; she receives, in turn, priesthood endowment. (We are perhaps

not unjustified in hearing in this a species of exchange, or blackmail.) There is sorrow for Zina Diantha in her loss of Henry; but there is also, in the wake of that loss, a great flourishing of her gifts—and, perhaps more consequentially, an understanding of herself as progressing along an arc that looks very much like that of divinization, a going from a smaller to a larger capacity.

Listen, for instance, to her account of the earliest days as a member of Brigham Young's home:

> Arrived in Winter Quarters all safe and was welcomed into my new home lived with the President's Family some 6 or 7 of us in a tent. Log cabins were erected, a meeting house also had now and then a dance to cheer us, good meetings, friendly visits kind associations in this our new life, knowing we ware here because God had commanded. The sun shone in the midst of all these temporary inconveniences. Some of the Girls it was the first time they had ever left there parents, but the Pres was so kind to us all, nothing but God could have taught him and others how to be so kindly to these large Families. This order not being on the Earth for 1800 years with all our traditions like garments woven around us, some could act uppon principles with better justice than others, not all are capacitated alike in any respect. (*4 Zinas*, 158)

Not all are capacitated alike: here is Zina Diantha shedding those "traditions like garments woven around us" and, exactly as Smith had dreamed in his riffs on the arduousness of exaltation, bringing herself to a larger capacity.

But divinizing capacitation was not all that would disclose itself to Zina Diantha in these later years. For whatever these intimations of a tradition-confounding endowment of power, in her subsequent life in the West she was to find, as well, a great quantity of sorrow. The poignancy of these transitional years for Zina Diantha lay less in the revocation of this sense of antitraditional expansiveness than it did in its rescripting and, we could say, confinement. And that rescripting had everything to do with transformations to, and newly emerging forms of systematized order within, Mormonism itself. Fresh upon arrival, Brigham Young began to clarify the layered hierarchies of Mormon authority; doing so necessitated, in turn, a more fully realized systematization of the explicitly gendered dictates of plural patriarchal marriage. This meant, in practice, bringing the seeming social chaos of polygamy into stricter order. Such order took many forms. It was written, for instance, into the very structures of the new city. Of Young's "family compound" Bradley and Woodward write, "His own version of a temporal kingdom, the compound included a gristmill, barns and corrals, a family store, a schoolhouse, and even a private cemetery. When the Lion House was completed in 1856, Young had eleven connubial wives with whom he lived from time to time, thirty-five children, and numerous other wives and foster children for whom he took responsibility. . . . Brigham encouraged order in all family business" (*4 Zinas*, 195). Where there had been unsynthesized dictates, powers blended and overlapping, Young would bring clarity, regularity, and a will to order that would radiate out *from* the home to encompass Mormon sociality more broadly.

For Young's wife Zina Diantha, such orderliness had real cost; most immediately, it came at the expense of that mixed sociability, with family and extended family, that had so sustained her and her spiritual gifts in earlier years. Shortly after arriving in the fall of 1848, Zina took up small rooms of her own, purchased by her brother, where for several months her pregnant sister Presendia resided with her. (She turned another of her rooms into a school.) When Presendia was at last to be moved into the row housing for plural wives provided by her husband, Heber Kimball, Zina Diantha noted their separation with pained misgiving. "This morning my sister Presendia moved," she wrote in her diary for 11 December. "How pleasantly have the hours and days passed since we ware bles with the privilege of enjoying each others society but again we are to be separated. O God our heavenly Father wilt thou be mindful of us continually" ("Diary," 92–93). But this burden of isolation would grow worse. After a visit from Brigham Young on 15 March, she commenced preparing, the next day, to move house; by 16 April she found herself removed from her family and, after a brief delay, installed in a log row house nearer to Brigham. The transition was painful. Her entry from 16 April 1849 framed that pain in exacting terms:

> As I sat in my wagon with a hart tender as if berieved of a dear friend meditating I was aroused by a knock on the wagon. BY came to inform me a room was finished &c., &c, &c. O did I not seek a lone retreat beside a murmering [rill oer?] the water rolled over a fall of about 3 feet whare the sound of my voice would not be herd there. I from a heavy hart wept yes wept bitterness of Soul y[e]a a sorrow and tears that wore rung from a heavy hart. Sadness for a while took her seat in my hart and reigned. Predominent for a short time. I could exclaim O Lord have mercy on me.

Yes I did say it with all my heart & I believe he will hear me in his own
time and answer me. About 4PM I moved into the room. ("Diary," 105)

I did not seek a lone retreat, she writes, reminding us of the generative force
of *sociability* in her life, and of the scenes and contests in which her powers
of spirit found most use. As vividly as she would in any of her many other
pieces of writing, Zina Diantha announces herself grief-stricken, grappling
with a sorrow whose impiety she senses but cannot, for that, overcome.
"Predominent," she says, "for a short time."

It is in respect to this new experience of isolation that Bradley and
Woodward write of Zina Diantha that the "next stage of her life" transpired in the "context of bereavement" (*4 Zinas*, 187). She is introduced, we
might say, to what Todd Compton would call the "sacred loneliness" that
marks the lives of early Mormon polygamous women. Her experience was
perhaps not as dire, or not the same variety of wrenching, as that of some
of her sister wives. Augusta Cobb, whose struggles with Young come into
vivid relief in Ulrich's narrative, provides an illustrative counterexample. "Is
there any such thing as an independent woman in the economy of God?"
Augusta had written to Brigham Young in 1850. "If there is, I want to be
that woman." Later, with less circumspection, she would write, "I would
like to be a Mother of Mother's and a Queen of Queen's! I do not like to call
Mary Ann Young Mother or Queen; neither do I like to call Emma Smith or
Eliza R Snow either" (212, 217). Here is a polygamous woman coming hard
up against the constraints of, precisely, *patriarchal* plural marriage. In the
reflected light of these articulate protests, Zina Diantha can indeed seem
docile, accepting her lot with pious resignation.

But Zina Diantha knew those feelings well, even if their most acute expression for her took the form of "sadness" rather than an unreconciled
anger. She had known, after all, what it was to enjoy an equal privilege with
ancient saints. And she had caught there, in what she thought of as her
capacitation, glimpses of an exaltation not conspicuously marked by diminishment or confinement. Her sorrow, though not barbed like Augusta
Cobb's, was nevertheless real. And it was soon to shape itself around a newly
configured set of spiritual expectations. These would be stamped, definitively, by her last husband.

NO MORE THAN THE BUZZING OF A FLY'S WING
(A BRIEF BIOGRAPHY, PART 3)

That Brigham Young's organization of Mormon life came at the expense of the more errant and uncoded possibilities for Mormon women is evident in more than the arrangement of homes, or Augusta Cobb's fury, or Zina Diantha's sorrow. Young's first administrative moves toward a concretization of the patriarchal authority of plural marriage might be dated to 1846, when, under his guidance, the Quorum of Twelve Apostles declared that "no man has a right to attend to the ordinance of sealing except the President of the Church or those who are directed by him to do so," as Wilford Woodruff recorded in his journal on 24 July 1846. (As John G. Turner glosses this development: "In other words, only Young or those he directed could authorize marriages; in numerous instances, Young disciplines followers for performing sealings without his blessing.")[39] In truth, though, the impulses toward centralization, especially as directed at expression of women's authority, had come even earlier.

The Female Relief Society, which had been founded in 1842, did not survive for long under Young's newly established leadership. In March of 1845, still in Nauvoo, while addressing a quorum of elect Mormon men, Young effectively disbanded the Relief Society. In his remarks, he did a good deal more than this, specifying for the assembled men the proper, properly *gendered* order of the whole of Mormon sociality, as he sought to lead it into the future. Here are the clerk's notes of his remarks from the evening of 9 March 1846:

> When I want Sisters or the Wives of the members of this church to get up Relief Society I will summon them to my aid but until that time let them stay at home & if you see Females huddling together veto the concern and if they say Joseph started it tell them it is a damned lie for I know he never encouraged it.[40]

Of the meetings of the Female Relief Society, he continued:

> I say I will curse every man that lets his wife or daughters meet again— until I tell them—What are relief societies for? To relieve us of our best men—They relieved us of Joseph and Hyrum—that is what they will lead

> to—I dont want the advice or counsel of any woman—they would lead
> us down to hell.

The moral he spun was clear:

> There is no woman on the face of the earth that can save herself—but if
> she ever comes into the Celestial Kingdom, she must be led in by some
> man—God knew what Eve was. He was acquainted with woman thou-
> sands and millions of years before—
> He made a few remarks in relation to the revival of the Female Relief
> Society, and disapprobated it.[41]

There is no woman that can save herself, Young insisted, noting that the pathway to the celestial kingdom had, for women, exactly one avenue: *"she must
be led in by some man."*

President's Young's "disapprobation" of the activities of the Female Relief
Society, and of what he contends were the scurrilous rumors of Smith's
approval of them ("if they say Joseph started it tell them it is a damned lie"),
was plain and stark. And nothing about these remarks, or for that matter
about the masculinity pretending itself embattled to better justify its flights
of misogyny, would be refuted by his subsequent disquisitions on women's
honesty, integrity, or the necessity of their sexual availability. "A woman is
the distirist [dirtiest] creature," he would observe; "if a woman won't lie, she
is a miracle." Further, at Winter Quarters (where he wed Zina Diantha and
sent Henry Jacobs away), he argued that it was altogether proper "that you
enjoy a woman all you can to overflowing & tell her to keep all about her
clean and neat."[42] In all this, Joseph Smith's suggestive, ambiguous, considerably more equivocal remarks on female duties and virtues found themselves
transformed into something much more definitive—transformed, in fact,
into something startlingly akin to the defensive, retrenching, hyperpatriar-
chal visions of restoration we find in celebrations of polygamy like Udney
Hay Jacob's in *The Peace Maker.* Or, to put this from the other side: polemi-
cally anti-Mormon accounts of the hyperbolized patriarchy of Mormon
plural marriage—fictions and exposés featuring tyrannical men with ill-
concealed contempt for women—*converge* with Young's own remarks, quite
as much as they might distort Mormon sociability. If Brigham Young's God
revealed anything differently than expected, it was that He thought women
"degraded," even creaturely, with no place in the scheme of exaltation except
standing beside, and subordinate to, some righteous patriarch.

A number of sorts of explanation look to resituate, and at least partially mitigate, remarks like these. Beyond the crude psychological accounts— which would emphasize a merely personal distaste for women, a private misogyny metastasized as celestial orthodoxy—there are local political pressures worth considering. As Young's comments about the murders of Smith made plain ("What are relief societies for? To relieve us of our best men— They relieved us of Joseph and Hyrum"), he understood Emma Smith's avowed disquiet over polygamy, and her use of the Female Relief Society as a venue for that disapprobation, to have fomented the anti-Mormon hysteria that led to the killings. At this moment, too, the church itself was fracturing around the question of polygamy, with Emma Smith disputing the church's claim to Joseph's estate and Sidney Rigdon and William Smith adding their voices in opposition to plural marriage. In this framing, Young's vehemence in defense of polygamy, and his concomitant denunciation of the Female Relief Society, were meant to counter the claims to authority of a set of political rivals.

All of this is true. And yet the salient facts here are neither reducible to Young's psychology nor isolable to this one especially fraught moment of contention in Mormon intrapolitical life. Young was indeed seeking in the mid-1840s to solidify and centralize his authority as the leader of the Mormon church, but this was a task that did not end in Winter Quarters, or with the arrival in the Salt Lake Basin, or for that matter with the return to Salt Lake after the Utah War of 1857–58 had failed, mercifully, to materialize. It was, rather, the *condition* of his presidency. In certain ways, Young was the ideal man to follow Smith. Whereas Joseph's genius lay in prophecy, the on-the-fly unfolding of heavenly mysteries of such compounding intricacy that the structures built to house them could seem always to be lagging behind the protean reach of his vision, Young's deepest gifts were that of an organizer. This is by now a Mormon commonplace, in part because it was a distinction evident across so many registers, visible even at the level of rhetorical self-presentation. ("Smith, while sometimes lapsing into frontier vernacular, could also employ soaring rhetoric to match the heavenly mysteries he described. Young's speech was simpler, more forceful, often humorous, and sometimes coarse.")[43] This is at least part of what is at stake in Turner's claim that we do well to reckon Young "the greatest colonizer in American history."[44] What Young's remarks from the 1840s reveal most significantly—and what would certainly be the largest consequence to Zina Diantha and the other women of the Female Relief Society—was that from the first "organization" and "centralization" depended intimately, for President Young, upon a clarified reestablishment of *patriarchal* authority. "The influence of my women over me," Young had proclaimed, "is no more than the buzzing of a fly's wing in winter," as though in response to some intimation that his authority *had* been compromised, that the fact of the presence of so many women in proximity to his life had resulted somehow in an unmanning acquiescence to them.[45] For a leader without the prophetic gifts of his martyred predecessor, and who began his office in contest with rival claimants to Smith's legacy, the starkness of the authority of men over women provided a touchstone premise, an everyday sort of regrounding, for a power that understood itself to need constant proof against undermining. To be a credible leader, for Young, was of necessity to be a patriarch. And to be a patriarch was to demand with clarity and with force that women— whatever the local forms of social or spiritual power according to them—be ultimately in subjection to men.

We might call what Young begins to institute here the *patriarchalization of plural marriage*—though to say as much misstates the case a bit, inasmuch as Mormon plural marriage was, as we have seen in detail, invented as patriarchal. We do better to say, rather, that Young moves, quickly and decisively, toward the collapsing of those spaces for counterpossibility that might be heard in Smith's own speeches and remarks, and that had so galvanized in women like Zina Diantha the sense of an equal privilege defined with a different capaciousness. That the erasure of just these gendered counterpossibilities was not the haphazard effect, but was in fact the intent of these later tactics and revisions, is not a matter of conjecture. Nothing makes the matter clearer than the story of the 1855 publication, in the *Deseret News*, of some of Smith's remarks from the Female Relief Society. As Ulrich recounts the episode, the minutes for those early meetings of the Relief Society, which had been taken down at the time by Eliza Snow—her transcriptions providing the texts we have been quoting so far—were from the perspective of Young's assistants "not good enough." They required, that is, some pointed revision. The new version, published "with Brigham's approval," did more than clean up the prose; the alterations effectively "reversed [Smith's] cherished promises." "In Eliza's version," Ulrich writes,

> Joseph said "he was going to make the Society a Kingdom of priests as in Enoch's day—as in Paul's Day." George A. Smith and his clerks changed that to "The Lord was going to make of the Church of Jesus Christ a kingdom of priests, of holy people, a chosen people, as in Enoch's day . . ." In

Eliza's version, Joseph "spoke of delivering the keys to this Society and to the church." In the revised version, he "spoke of delivering the keys of the Priesthood to the church, and said that the faithful members of the Relief Society should receive them in connection with their husbands."[46] (309)

The 1855 text suggested as well that, rather than trust to the wisdom of the leaders of the society, the women there did best to "place confidence in their husbands, whom God has appointed for them to honor, and in those faithful men whom God has placed at the head of the Church to lead his people" (310). Where once had been Queens of Queens, now were women enjoined, in that most familiar of frameworks, to honor and to obey.

These consolidations of an authority more and more explicitly patriarchal are telling. They remind us, first, that the counterintimations we have been tracking in Smith's remarks, and in the responses they generated among Mormon women, were hardly the stuff of idle fancy, let alone a matter of wishful retrospective imposition. To the contrary, they were live and vibrant possibilities, real enough in their portended consequence to induce this series of reactive responses, which ranged from Young's caustically misogynist sermonizing, to his dissolution of the Female Relief Society, to those calibrated retractions of even the *implied* promises of Smith's remarks. And these patriarchal consolidations are especially clarifying, too, in respect to Zina Diantha's sorrow, that bereaved loneliness she expresses in the privacy of her diary from the late 1840s. Bradley and Woodward treat the scene of her arrival at Young's home with exemplary generosity. Underscoring her determined fidelity both to the Saints and to her family, they note nevertheless that she enters into life in Utah, as Young's polygamous wife, in the "context of bereavement": "Although much of her grief stemmed from the departure of both brothers and the distance of her sister, at least some must have been over that part of her past represented by Henry Jacobs and Joseph Smith. Moving into Brigham Young's house meant moving away from them psychologically in a way that she had not yet confronted" (*4 Zinas*, 187). What she mourns, Bradley and Woodward suggest, is the compounding loss of those intimates who together made up the sociality that had been so inspiriting to Zina Diantha, in which her gifts had developed and extended themselves.

But this, too, may be to circumscribe her grief—and to do so in ways that repeat, rather than diagnose, its causes. Bradley and Woodward observe that in her transition from Missouri to Illinois, and then west, her life "underwent a fundamental paradigm shift—from a monogamous world to one of plurality. . . . That shift," they continue, "would complete itself in Utah. She had to alter her thinking about family, assumptions about gender roles, and use of social networks, blending the elements of her life and thought into the new social framework of Brigham Young's complicated households" (4 Zinas, 177). That she had to alter her thinking is beyond dispute. But at least part of what that alteration consists in is *a rescripting of her vision of female power*—not of her sense of the fact of female power, but of its scope, its proper extension, and its domain. A too private rendering of her grief, a reading of it as the effect of the loss of a subset of given intimates, can misrecognize this. Again, the matter is not that Zina Diantha ceased to understand herself as gifted in spirit, as capable of revelation or interpretation or of power. (The flourishing rest of her life suggests she continued to understand herself exactly so.) It is rather that these gifts would come to be fitted into a new economy of spiritual authority, in which the differences between the genders had been, in real senses, absolutized. Bradley and Woodward as much as grant the point when they remark that Zina Diantha "succeeded" in the test of self-reconstitution "by becoming central in a female support network of sister wives that functioned like family" (4 Zinas, 177). It is no derogation of that female world, and even less a denial of its efficacies and powers, to say that this was a sphere of action dramatically more confined than might have been dreamed by a woman who imagined her access to God's revelatory power made her higher than the queens of the earth.

But the world of possibility glimpsed in Smith's remarks—a world made so vivid in Zina Diantha's identification with prophetic power—had changed. "I am not guided by revelations coming through any woman," Young would write in a missive of 1857, which answers directly enough to Smith's comments about the mutuality of spiritual magnification, the treachery of aspiring men, a dominion over the queens of the earth.[47] The difference between President Young's later vision of the terrain of female power and Smith's invocation of queenliness, his heralding of a God full of surprising revelation, would not have been lost on the early participants in the Female Relief Society. It was certainly not lost on August Cobb, Zina Diantha's sister-wife, who in 1850 demanded of Young, "Is there any such thing as an independent woman in the economy of God?"[48] With escalating clarity, the answer came back: no, in thunder.

Beside a lonely river in Utah, early in her next new life, Zina Diantha shed tears of bitterness. We can see why.

GODS IN SUBJECTION

There are multiple and varying ways to tell the story of the evolution of polygamy, and of the gendering of Mormon life, in relation to the claims I have been pursuing about, in essence, the patriarchalization of an *already* patriarchal plural marriage—that steady and deliberate cancellation of so many of the larger possibilities for women Smith's prophesying had seemed to imply. My own has taken pains to emphasize not the veritably mesmerized subservience of polygamous women, and not their need of secular redemption, so much as the upending, visionary possibilities for women nested *within* early Mormon theology, which would in subsequent years come to be sharply curtailed. Only one of the hazards in taking up this line of explication is that the evidence of loss, grief, and pain left behind by polygamous women—which is plentiful—can do the work of a kind of exceptionalization of polygamy. We risk, that is, merely repeating the notes struck by anti-Mormon and antipolygamy polemicists, who insisted upon the singular oppressiveness of the institution of plural patriarchal marriage, and did so quite as if patriarchal *monogamy* were itself a haven for women, the scene of a great and abiding female flourishing. Mary Richards's letter to her husband, who had broached the possibility of plurality, was unequivocal, to be sure. "If you had seen what I have seen you would not wonder why I thus wrote for there is no such thing as happiness known here where a man has more than one [wife]." She went on: "*It realy seems to me that this is a day in which Woman is destined to misery.*"[49] And yet the claim about the miserable destiny of nineteenth-century women hardly requires polygamy as a proof-text. However much a style of sentimentalism would make a virtue of domestic monogamy—or, just as often, strive against misgivings and counterindications to make such a case—we have to hand nothing less than the *entire archive* of nineteenth-century feminist critique, from Margaret Fuller to Harriet Jacobs to Elizabeth Cady Stanton to Charlotte Perkins Gilman to countless more, to dissuade us against using the unhappiness of polygamous wives to, in effect, exonerate a form of patriarchy that better conforms to the dictates of a liberal-secular polity. Nancy Bentley, again, delivers this point about the effects of the exceptionalization of polygamy with maximal clarity. "Polygamy," she writes, surveying the sentimental antipolygamy novels of the later century, "is the bondage that sanctifies monogamy as freedom."[50]

And yet the contractions of polygamy, these evacuations of the ampler counterpossibilities of plurality and exaltation for women, were real, and of lasting importance to nineteenth-century Mormonism. In the rush to defend the early Mormons against many varieties of slander, and Mormon women particularly, we can misplace this fact, losing sight of the alterations to the theology of plural marriage—of their causes and their consequences—in the effort to render the women who participated in it as something other than the enthralled subjects of a malign orthodoxy. Think again of Zina Diantha's sorrow: inasmuch as we understand it to register something larger and less enclosed than domestic unhappiness and familial loss, her grief must give us a kind of pause. Her tears enjoin us to worry over those accounts of polygamy that dwell too credulously, or too eagerly, on its special affordances for the women within it. It is not the case that there are no affordances (as we have seen, there are), nor that we need to accede to the familiar secular-redemptive accounts of women as mystified by religious devotion. Zina Diantha's tears speak rather to the competing *domains* in which women's claims to power might be made, and heard. They speak, perhaps most broadly, to the knotty tasks of critique—and especially feminist critique—under conditions of secularism.

Consider Ulrich's exemplary work in *A House Full of Females*. Her narrative, woven around the lives of dozens of early Mormon women, aims above all to counteract the reading of these early Saints as, in essence, dupes: as women too enchanted by the authority of patriarchs cloaking themselves in pretended holiness to recognize the grievousness of their own oppression. "During the long fight over plural marriage," she writes, "nothing outraged Mormon women more than the notion that they were simply pawns of the patriarchy" (385). The force of her book, which itself gathers and follows from the assiduous scholarship of generations of Mormon feminism, is to refute this premise, strongly and finally. That premise should be familiar to us: it consists in a commitment to reading certain styles of religiosity as by their nature illiberal, deficient in the forms of rationality required of citizenship; in making women the chief carriers of such deficiency; and in recognizing women as, concomitantly, the objects most in need of rescue. This is, again, one of secularism's favorite stories about itself, that paradoxically salvific version of good disenchantment that Saba Mahmood, Tracy Fessenden, Joan Wallach Scott, and many others have made subject to thoroughgoing critique.[51] The scandal around Mormon polygamy offers one especially vivid early iteration of exactly this redemptive story, with reformers speaking from within the many and disparate *good religions* of secularism with earnest offers to save Mormon women from their captors and, if needed, from themselves. In prompt retort to all this, Ulrich gives us a composite portrait of religious women not pining for rescue but constructing vibrant and habitable worlds, for themselves and for their families, and doing so often in purposeful fellowship with one another. She underscores throughout what I have been calling the dense sociability of early Mormonism, which she figures as the impulse toward "gathering." "If plural wives stood up for their Church in the 1870s," she writes, "it was not just because pioneering had made them strong but because the concept of gathering that was at the heart of Mormon theology taught them that retreating into a private haven was neither possible nor righteous. *They wanted to change the world*, and they believed God had shown them a way to do it" (xxiv, emphasis added). The story Ulrich looks to tell in *A House Full of Females* is one of women finding in early Mormonism not a retreat into privacy but the vehicle for claims upon, and collective action directed toward, "the world."

And yet, for our purposes, it's telling to consider what ultimately counts for Ulrich as testament to such concertedly public orientation for the women of early Mormonism. Her book concludes where it begins, which is at an "indignation meeting" sponsored by the newly reestablished Female Relief Society, where there had gathered (in the words of a San Francisco newspaper) "a mass of between 3,000 and 4,000 women . . . meeting together to advocate the claims of polygamy and defend the men who practice it" (xii). The women had convened in opposition to the Cullom Bill, which looked to devastate Mormon political power, and perhaps Mormonism itself, by criminalizing polygamy and thus allowing the state the right to seize Mormon property and arrest its many practitioners. The most momentous result to follow from this meeting, and the one that most interests Ulrich, was the enfranchisement of Utah women—momentous not least because at the time, women voted in no states and only one other territory, Wyoming. (Following this, in another momentous turn, Elizabeth Cady Stanton and Susan B. Anthony paid a much-publicized visit to Utah, in 1871.) This, for *A House Full of Females*, is the moment of pivot and culmination. When Sarah Kimball stands up at a meeting about the suffrage bill to say that "she would openly declare herself a womans rights woman," Ulrich's argument achieves a kind of apotheosis (379). The women who had fomented the creation of the Female Relief Society, who had made it a vibrant politico-theological venue, who had reformulated a sociality proper to polygamy, who had kept alive the flame of relief efforts, and who had insisted upon the rebuilding of a new Female Relief Society—these women here unapologetically avow "womans rights," crystallized at this moment in the form of the ballot. It is without

question a moving passage in Ulrich's telling, one that effectively invests all
the previous scenes of struggle, large scale and small, with a sense of hard-
won, explicitly *historical* achievement. Mormon women get their place at the
table of nineteenth-century feminist protest, which Ulrich works diligently
to refigure such that there is no sharp division between certain enabling
kinds of religion—Stowe's evangelical Protestantism, say—and that of the
early Mormons.

But *is* this the sort of consequence to which early Mormons most ardently
aspired? Is that paradigmatically liberal, secular attainment what Mormon
women themselves went looking for? What aspects of early Mormon life
do we misperceive by believing so? We can set partially aside—though not
entirely—the opportunism that surrounded the events Ulrich narrates.
Briefly: the reinstituting of the Female Relief Society came at a moment
when, because of the national battle over polygamy, Young had newly urgent
need of the public support of Mormon women, who had become a coin
of currency in the debate, figured typically as self-deluding victims who
required redemption via the machinery of benevolent government. (Orson
Pratt remarked frankly that extending suffrage to women would "increase
our votes one Hundred percent.")[52] Then, too, the revivification of "relief
societies" had everything to do with the Mormon effort to consolidate their
status as citizens by underscoring the work they had done as *colonizers*,
civilizing the West. (The rebooting of the Female Relief Society originated in
the various "Indian Relief Societies" started by Young in the 1860s, following
the familiar template of colonial charity—*biophilanthropy*, in Kyla Schuller's
excellent phrase, of which we will hear more in subsequent chapters.)[53] This
barefaced instrumentalization of Mormon women by church leaders does
not lessen, in any measure, the bravery or tenacity of these figures.

But Ulrich's turn to suffrage does accomplish a drastic shifting of the
terrain of female authority and power, and it is on that point that I wish
to linger. For to grant too eagerly the possibility that what early Mormon
women aspired to was civic enfranchisement under the sign of legislative
power is to tell a curiously partial sort of story. It is, for instance, to displace
all those *other* transformations in Mormon sociability that do not track
quite so neatly along an arc of progress or widening entitlement. After all,
the forms of enfranchisement extended to Mormon women accorded quite
easily with the all the less liberatory trajectories that we have been tracing,
and that Ulrich's book also describes: the assertive winnowing-down of the
powers Smith had intimated, the isolation of polygamous women in the
home, the greater and greater emphasis on bioreproductivity and family as

the sine qua non of polygamy and its theology. The Mormon women who got the vote had, in other words, also *lost* a great deal. We need think only of what becomes of exaltation in the West.

Listen, for instance, to Heber Kimball, writing to his wife Vilate in 1849 about the children he has had with other wives: "Let me say unto you V. K. every son and daughter that is brought forth by the wives that are given to me will add to your glory as much as it will to them. They are given to me for this purpose and for no other. I am a Father of lives to give lives to those that wish to receive. Woman is to receive from Man" (231). Kimball's is an especially straightforward statement, which echoes the many countersexualizing explanations of polygamy we have already seen, accounts that refer all of polygamy's seeming disruptions of normative social and sexual life back to the glorified purposes of reproduction. Ulrich glosses his remarks by noting, "Sexuality was not about personal pleasure or even about creating a bond between husbands and wives. It was about bringing spirits to earth and raising them to inherit the Kingdom of God" (231). Ulrich speaks through Kimball here in a kind of free-indirect discourse, but the vision of the relation of gendered reproduction to the promised exaltation of polygamy goes uncontradicted—and, indeed, comes to stand in as *the* rendition of the matter, a default setting that critics get wrong by *sexualizing*, making polygamy over into a matter of lechery. But what goes unmarked in such counterpolemical accounts of polygamy is the starkness of its gendering. Turner, in his biography of Young, gives us perhaps the most unvarnished version of an exaltation following out precisely those premises Kimball invokes. "Exaltation," he writes, "began with patriarchal leadership of families, in which a faithful man governed his 'innumerable posterity' as 'their ruler, savior, dictator, & governor.'"[54] (Such a rendering of biologized polygamy, and its attendant distributions of gendered authority, would flourish in postmigration Mormon theologizing, as the writing of a figure like Orson Pratt makes clear: "Let no woman unite herself in marriage with any man unless she has fully resolved to submit herself wholly to his counsel and to let him govern as the head," for such are "sacred bonds of eternal union," and such is "the divine order of family government.")[55] By 1914, Mormon theologian James E. Talmage would give an equally direct framing to the matter, in an essay entitled "The Eternity of Sex": "The distinction between male and female is no condition peculiar to the relatively brief period of mortal life; it was an essential characteristic of our pre-existent state, even as it shall continue after death, in both the disembodied and resurrected states."[56] This is what the celestial sphere looks like according to a polygamous exaltation so rooted in reproduction, and in that way so anchored to gender difference and gender hierarchy.

We do well to mark how little such increasingly hegemonic visions of polygamy comport with the intimations of embodied divinization we have found in Smith. And they comport no less poorly with *Ulrich's own* vision of exaltation, as she expresses it elsewhere in her work. "Enlargement," she writes early on, "included but was by no means reducible to biological reproduction" (xvii). But by the time Mormon women came to defend polygamy in public meetings through Utah, bioreproductive familialism was precisely the note struck. It had become the lingua franca of an exaltation that was steeply gendered, and rooted in polygamy. In this version of plural theology, women are not denied exaltation, by any means. As mothers of children, they become gods in their own right. But they are so to the degree that they are adjuncts to men, the patriarchs who "give lives to those that wish to receive." They may become gods—Mothers in Heaven—but they are gods who obey.[57] They emerge, we might say, as gods in subjection.

Ulrich's story, then, is one of great historical achievement; without contesting that story, I would want to say that we can read out, in the very same details, a narrative rather less heartening. It is still not the story of women who are the mesmerized dupes of patriarchal power. Nor yet is it a story of Mormonism transposed into what is, in essence, a liberal progress narrative. It is rather the story of a profound recalibration of theological terms and, with that, a progressive narrowing of the aperture through which female power might be experienced and known.[58] Suffrage is without question an achievement, one of singular historical magnitude; no expedience or opportunism near the scene of that achievement diminishes this fact. But it is less one, surely, when measured against the hope for an *equal status of godhead*, which was a hope that had flared into live possibility for early Mormon women only to be reduced to something explicitly lesser: a queenly accompaniment. What Mormon women get is the ballot; what Mormon women had been given reason to desire was an equivalent divinity, an undiminished godliness. This they do not get. Perversely, it is only a story with its eye on liberal entitlement—a story working to render early Mormonism as in this sense *already secular*—that would understand the one as a replacement for the other.

This is what it means to say that Ulrich's narrative, echoing Bushman's, looks to defend early Mormonism against its most slanderous detractors by presenting the Mormons as in real senses misapprehended liberals, aspirational liberals unjustly maligned. In these accounts Mormons take their place among the other purveyors of legitimate public religion, competing in the Taylorite marketplace of secularized belief. The Saints are made to appear in all as already in tune with the premises of liberal polity, from which we are invited to understand them as having been unjustly excluded. At least part of what is at stake in renderings like Bushman's and Ulrich's is the understandable desire to wrench Mormonism free from its avowed enemies, whose very terms—"patriarchal theocracy," say—cling even still to commonplace understandings of Mormon life. But such accusations, however hyperbolized and exploited for local purposes, are not so easily reduced to the status of slander or malign fabrication. For the Mormons plainly did fail at being "good religion," inasmuch as any such designation indicated no want of faith or conviction but a growing synonymity between the premises of belief and those of liberal polity. In this way, if they failed, *they failed at being secular.* They did so not merely because they were "theocratic," making private religion too much a matter of public life. I have been arguing, to the contrary, that they were understood to have failed at being secular in far larger part because the very body that Smith had set about conjuring—coextensive with the materiality of God, fired by pleasures that unwrite its traditions of legibility, divinizing—could not be made to square with the managed body of liberal rationality. To be a legitimate religion, a religion by the lights of secularism, was to invoke *this* body. The Mormons, as we know, did not.

Or rather, and crucially: they sometimes did not. It is far more accurate to say that the capacities and extensions of that imagined body were, for the Mormons, the scene of vibrant, fraught, decades-long contestation. The systematizing alterations in the practice of polygamy we have been tracking *are* that contestation. The Mormons were again and again accused of perversity and barbarism, of a damning failure to be secular, and they knew well what the consequences of such failure might be. The Utah War, only narrowly averted, had made that clear. Out of just these crossed pressures and imperatives, a kind of strategy began to emerge, which would be of defining importance to the early Mormons. They sought to have it, as it were, both ways: to hold fast to all that was unassimilable in their faith, all their opposition to Gentile fallenness, *and* to appear before the national public as something other than deviant, atavistic, deranged in their unyielding orthodoxies. As it proved, gender was at the heart of this complex double-move, these tense negotiations with the American world.

THE SECULAR ALIBI; OR, MORMON WOMEN

It's tempting, when considering the Mormon leveraging of gender in these nationalized contests around polygamy and sex and secularism—around, ultimately, sovereignty, and the degree to which it would or would not be granted to the Mormons in the West—to make Brigham Young into a kind of villain. He fits himself into the role with disarming ease. There is an oddity to this. Young was not a man who knew nothing of the errant, queerer intensities of attachment brewed up in the eroticized sociability of early Mormon life. One especially delectable example of this comes in his sermon on the tenth anniversary of Smith's death, where he offered testimony that "Joseph is a prophet by revelation." Young knew this beyond doubt, "for I felt him I slept with him I embraced him and kissed him," he assured the assembled, "drank with him walked with him handled him."[59] It was Young, and not Smith, who would follow out the implications of the Book of Mormon, as well as Smith's theologizing, to insist that "our senses, if properly educated, are channels of endless felicity to us."[60] The intimate possibilities of early Mormon theology were hardly lost on Young—the body's grace, extranormative lateral attachment, all of it. Yet he wedded these intimations of an enlargement via carnality to an ordering imagination that was everywhere committed to a *disciplining deuniversalization* of that body, to gendered distinction and to gendered hierarchy: in short, to patriarchy. Those insistences meant, in practice, that the intoxicating possibilities of embodiment beyond and apart from narrow "tradition," however much they may have flourished in men like Young, did so largely on the condition of their curtailment for women.

And yet Young's was not, in any rigorous sense, a betrayal of some purer, ampler, more fundamental Mormon theology. As we began by noting, the polygamy revelation itself spoke with blunt clarity about the righteousness not merely of plural marriage but of plural *patriarchal* marriage. Young certainly labored to solidify the male-supremacist elements of Mormon polygamy, but his systematization depended upon, and grew out of, an originary gendering in the cosmology of early Mormonism that cannot be pretended away. It was not an invented imposition. However much Young moved to consolidate the patriarchality of polygamy, and of early Mormon sociability more generally, this cannot be justly accounted a perversion, a ruinous apostasization from a Mormonism more truly egalitarian. His ordering of the undersystematized prophetic visions of Joseph Smith made for a new rigidity in the hierarchies of gender, certainly (and not only of gender, as we soon shall see); he did not invent the patriarchality of Mormon theology.

More is at stake here than the exoneration of Brigham Young. I have argued thus far that at the core of early Mormon theology is a radical theory of embodied life, one that imagines humankind exalting itself toward divinity, called there by the pleasures of a body understood to partake in, to be compounded of the same *material* as, God Himself. The Mormons are failed secularists, I have suggested, in nothing so much as these fabulations, from which their other seemingly wide departures from the normative frames of midcentury American life—sexual, social, ecclesiastic—follow one after another. So in the specific deuniversalizations of that body that came to be propounded as the century wore on, we see something larger than Smith's theological multiplicitousness or Young's authoritarian misogyny. We begin to see, rather, the conjoined Mormon effort to live at once apart from, *and also in accord with*, the constraints of a national public they understood to be fallen. Such efforts depended intimately upon what Jan Shipps has described as a "fundamental theological tension" in early Mormonism, and what we have adduced as a kind of protean doubleness at the core of Mormon theology itself. It is a doubleness figured across a multitude of forms, taking shape now in the faith's densely interwoven conventionality and disruptive errancy, now its folded-together orthodoxy and heresy, and now its simultaneous obedient normativity and seeming apostasy.[61] With precisely that doubleness to hand, as theological resource and ultimately as strategy, the Saints would labor to position themselves as exemplary citizen-subjects, entitled to the forms of sovereign liberty they understood to be implicit in the American national political compact, *and* as righteous renegades, in flight from a nation that has doomed itself to an apocalyptic collapse.

Gender—or rather, the deuniversalizing agency made available in a commitment to gender *as* distinction—was essential to, and in many respects the backbone of, this double-move. Indeed, the rendering of female exaltation as an ascent to a real, if lesser, godhead gives us, in perfect miniature, the template for precisely these twinned avowals. Think again of Smith's vision of exaltation as enlargement, the attainment of a godlike power of creation. And think, in turn, of the eventual routing of that vision of exaltation into the strict gendered hierarchy of celestial familialism, with women locked into the scene of domestic reproduction. On the one side, we have a celestialized body, with all its potentially ungendered universality, ascending via carnality into exaltation and godhead; on the other, the biologized and hierarchized orders of gendered reproduction, quite as they are found in the mortal patriarchal world. Setting these two imbricated figurings of the flesh side by side, we can begin to grasp, I think, how a theology of divinizing polygamy might anchor a set of claims on behalf of the *normative* quality of Mormon plural marriage. For this pairing allows us to see, with sharpened clarity, how the divinized body of polygamy, with all its unassimilabilities, might, in moments of crisis or need, be switched out for the forcibly disciplined bodies of polygamous *wives*: biologized, reproductive, subject to hierarchy, sequestered in the family. *They* are the face of a normativity fully (and, in some idioms of critique, *too* fully) embraced.

And more: the hard gendering of celestial familialism in the context of polygamous divinization suggests further that early Mormon men accomplished the derogation and marginalization of women by, in a sense, *becoming* them. For this is an early Mormonism that worked essentially to annex all the most miraculous corporeal feats of female embodiment—*enlargement* or *expansion* or the godlikeness entailed in *the creation of life*—to the bodies of Mormon men experiencing exaltation.[62] Here, we might say, is the most elemental, if masked, drama of gender at the heart of the theology of polygamy: this bait-and-switch reclaiming, for men, of all the threatening quotidian power of female embodiment, conventionally figured, accomplished in tandem with the sharp curtailment of any of the intuited larger destinies for the body, those half-glimpsed counterpossibilities, for women. The bodies of women were in these respects hardly afterthoughts to the polygamous imagination, figures haphazardly conjured by an unsystematized theology that required, in turn, a clarifying ordering of terms. The disciplined bodies of Mormon women emerge, rather, as the anchors of polygamous theology, the occluded site of its most prominent self-justifications.

The Mormons were never more normative than in their familialism, which was, of course, a style of gender hierarchy: this, at least, was the version of Mormonism on offer in their defenses of the righteousness of polygamy, and their right to practice it. As we know, though, these normalizing justifications would themselves backfire spectacularly. Critics of Mormonism would take up—in ways that should be unfamiliar to no students of twentieth- and twenty-first-century imperial imaginations—what they represented to be the forcible capture of polygamous wives, their virtual enslavement, as an emblem both of the anticivilizational barbarism of Mormonism and, covertly, of the expansive freedom afforded to women by *proper* patriarchy, unfolded in the contexts of secular-liberal monogamy.[63] The polygamous family was pointedly not the bourgeois family of liberal polity, and to have diverged from it, as the Mormons did in their momentous public avowal of plural marriage in 1852, was to slip in the gradients of secular legitimacy toward something illegitimate, barbarous, menacing, expendable. Again, this expendability was in no way figurative. Already subject to decades of murder and persecution and catastrophic failures of governmental protection, from Ohio to Illinois to Missouri, the polygamous Mormons found themselves on the brink of a very real extinction in 1857, when the "Mormon War" saw fully one-fifth of all federal troops massed outside Salt Lake and, but for some last-minute backroom dealing, quite prepared to lay waste to the Mormon settlements there.

Even before this tremendous mobilization, the stakes of these descents in the scales of legitimacy could hardly have been lost on the Mormons. By this point, they already had to hand a clear emblem of what it meant to be regarded as expendable life. They had been living in anxious proximity to Native peoples for quite some time.

EXTERMINATION

THE POLYGAMIST'S COMPLEXION

or, The Book of Mormon Goes West

HERETICS OF RACE

BUT WHAT OF ORIGINS? WE HAVE watched Joseph Smith develop and refine his prophetic vision, and have seen him arrive at one after another escalatingly heretical counterrendering of the Protestant God. In Smith's fashioning, God is not, finally, the uncreated Creator as much as He is an element copresent with the matter of the creation. "All doctors of divinity say that God created [the soul] in the beginning," Smith had declared near the end of his life, "but it is not so. *The very idea lessens the character of man*" (*EJS*, 239, emphasis added). Doctrine and Covenants refigured the point: "*All spirit is matter,*" it declares, reminding us that whatever "divinity" may in its essence be, it is not separate or separable from the very substance, the inner truth, of life in the embodied world. Divinity in this rendering is not ineffable, unworldly, the property solely of God. Divinity, rather, is the origin, the ongoingness, and the destiny of the human, wrapped as we are in all the glories of the flesh. This much we have seen.

But if God Himself is not uncreated, neither, for that matter, is Mormonism—an enterprise whose initiation left, after all, a great many tracks in time. What might we make, then, of the origin-story of Mormonism itself? I'm thinking not of the origin-story of the origin-story: not of the ancient buried plates, nor of the seer stones, nor even of the labors of transcription and prophetic channeling, intriguing though all these may be.[1] What of the *text* of Mormonism's origins, that outblown and overstuffed epic of Old Testament revisionism—the book that, when seen through the prisming gaze of a regime of secularism forever cutting its hard taxonomic distinctions, tends to hang uncertainly between the generic codings that might make it legible to us in any stable register? (Do we best apprehend it as *literature*? Or as *revealed text*, and in that sense something more, but also less, than "literary"? Or perhaps, as in some iterations of the latter question, as simply *fraud*?)[2] And what is to be made, especially, of the scenes of origins we find there, of which there are not a few? The question of the origin of God Himself presses very little upon the plot of the Book of Mormon, it's true. But other, related questions *are* of lasting doctrinal consequence.

For instance: What ought we to make of the Book of Mormon's accounts of the origins not of the human as such, or even of the body, but rather of *embodiments*, inhabitations of the flesh as they are marked, distinguished, disaggregated? What makes for the differences between and among differentiated materializations of the body in the Book of Mormon, their complex stratification? Or, to put this in a more pointed way: What is race for the text of the Book of Mormon? What is it to be racialized? And what is it, finally, to be an originary inhabitant—indigenous—in Smith's first great cosmological testament?

These questions, when brought to a text whose own origins are as murky and fraught as the Book of Mormon, are at first glimpse surprisingly unmystifying. If you know much at all about Mormonism, you will likely know at least something of the story about race and indigeneity that gets told in the Book of Mormon. And you will know, too, how ugly it is. At its maximally truncated, that story goes like this: the wicked Lamanites, removed from the Holy Land to North America, where they will do battle over millennia with the righteous Nephites, are marked in their ungodliness with, of course, dark skin. Famously, the Lamanites are at a stroke transformed into the indigenous people of North America, into "Indians." ("It has been said by many of the learned, and wise men, or historians," Smith had written in 1835, in what was by then a not unfamiliar formulation, "that the Indians, or aborigines of this continent, are of the scattered tribes of Israel" [*EJS*, 66].) In this way the Book of Mormon adapts itself to a series of drearily familiar racist tropes of the American nineteenth century: about Indians as remnants of the lost tribes of Israel, or, more saliently, about nonwhiteness as a God-ordained and indelible accursedness. The Book of Mormon, we might say, swallows these conventional racist premises whole, and metabolizes them into an intractably racist cosmology, haphazardly wrought round with a white supremacism that will be unfamiliar to few students of settler colonialism or antebellum America. In this context, what Jared Hickman rightly describes as American Mormonism's "deplorable record of theological racism" oughtn't to surprise us much at all. On the contrary, such racism would appear to be stranded through the very DNA of early Mormonism, written indelibly into its foundational theological text.[3]

Perhaps. But we have by now become familiar enough with the elaborate architecture of Smith's thought to glimpse some wider, or at least less flatly normative, possibilities. As dreamed into place by Smith over decades of prophetic labor, Mormon cosmology glories, after all, less in the extension of the conventions of established Christian practice and belief than in their mitigation and, typically, their overturning. Mormonism may be a variety of revivalism, but it is a revivalism characterized chiefly by a steady *derangement* of inherited forms, prosecuted more often than not with a degree of this-worldly jubilation not easily assimilated to Protestant traditions of, say, rigorous asceticism. (Mormonism, with its ancient buried plates uncovered in American soil, is at once an *indigenization* and an *overturning* of modern Christianity.) These facts alone might unsettle our approach to the Book of Mormon, in several ways. We might incline to wonder, for instance, how precisely this prophetic disposition—the persistent leaning toward the breezily heretical—works itself out in the first of Smith's major theological ventures, the sacred epic that is also a sprawling depiction of a premodern America riven by centuries of race war. The Book of Mormon appears in 1830. By the time of Smith's death in 1844 the Mormons were well-established defilers of normative intimacy, as we have seen: heretics of the flesh. But did these revisionary senses of embodiment come to initial life in the Book of Mormon? Are they grounded there? And—most crucially for our purposes—did they extend to the flesh of others among their contemporaries, to the indigenous, the enslaved? Were the Mormons heretics of race?

To some—in fact, to many—the answer was, indisputably, yes. Here is the antipolygamy and anti-Mormon novel of 1855, *Boadicea: The Mormon Wife*, reminding its readers that the Mormons in their treachery are a species apart, viler even than the "Indians": "Even those poor savages," we are told, "were incapable of committing deeds so infamous, so bloodthirsty, and so cruel, as were common practices of the Mormon Elders, *under the name of religion*."[4] Or listen to *Putnam's Monthly*, also in 1855, denouncing the claim of constitutional "religious" protection for the Mormons, because of the sex practices that religion entails, and the racializations they plainly announce: "Monogamy does not only go with the western Caucasian race, the Europeans and their descendants, beyond Christianity, it goes beyond Common Law."[5] Or again, listen to a character from Jack London's *The Star Rover*, who encapsulates the matter with admirable concision: "They ain't whites," he says, "they're Mormons."[6] As scholars like Hickman, Nancy Bentley, J. Spencer Fluhman, and W. Paul Reeve have shown, in meticulous and exhaustive detail, the notes struck here merely recapitulate what was, across the whole of the later nineteenth century, a commonplace of anti-Mormonism, delivered sometimes by scandalized antipolygamists, sometimes by federal authorities worried over the ceding of political authority to a rival and essentially ecclesiastic power, and sometimes in the cooler idioms of race-science.[7] There are the Mormons, with their fanaticism, their weird sex, their suspect—or simply counterfeit—whiteness.

How, then, does this multifaceted outpouring of racial opprobrium square with a sacred text that, on the face of it, seems so much to embody, even to exemplify, settler-colonial whiteness? If, as I have been suggesting, what makes early Mormonism properly heretical is its rupture not of some transhistorical "Christianity" but of *proper belief* as codified under conditions of secularism—of religion as it is made to comport ever more closely with the dictates of liberal rationality—then what can we make of the explicitly racial character of the secular, this conjoining of violations of secular belief with accusations of racial deception, impurity, or treason? How in all to make sense of these strange crossings, these unstable interminglings of carnality and righteousness, divinity and racialization?

By way of opening up these questions, and with the aid of readers and critics who have preceded me, I want to look closely at the workings of the Book of Mormon itself and then at its turbulent afterlives in the American West. I want to suggest, first, that the reading of the Book of Mormon as plainly and conventionally racist is, while not exactly untenable, nevertheless a serious misapprehension of the text, and especially of the ways the singularity of its narrative structure inflects, entangles, and ultimately overwrites its seemingly stark racist polarities. The Book of Mormon is in fact something other, and something stranger, than the reflexive reproduction of nineteenth-century racism for which it is very, very easy to take it. As devout Mormon readers were themselves quick to recognize, the Book of Mormon tells a story, too, about imperial hubris and the steep decline of a once-righteous people overthrown by their own pride. It speaks of the benighted arrogance of the powerful, and the just damnation it provokes from a God who is not deceived by one people's ceaseless proclamations of their own exemplarity. For early Mormons, who had endured a multitude of persecutions and enjoyed very few of the protections of the state for which they might have hoped, the analogies were not hard to read. Complacent white Americans—the "Gentiles" in Mormon terminology—were the self-amplifying imperialists speeding themselves toward violent decline. "I am prophet enough," Brigham Young declaimed in 1849, in a quote to which we will return, "to prophesy the downfall of the Government that has driven us out."[8]

But my second major point runs hard aslant of the first. As I hope to show in the subsequent chapter to this, one of the things that might make it difficult for us to encounter the Book of Mormon as something other than yet one more artifact in the vast archive of white supremacism is, in fact, Mormonism—or, more exactly, is the shape Mormonism was to take over the course of the later nineteenth century, as the Saints ventured into the American West and began to live alongside the peoples they sometimes referred to as "Brother Laman." This, "Brother Laman," was the curiously fraternal term Mormons used for Native peoples, in deference to their status as the Book of Mormon's surviving remnant. But that fraternal fellowship, which so disquieted authorities and editorialists across the nation, was from the first roiled, and roiled not least by the Mormons' powerful and anxious need to distinguish themselves, sharply and unmistakably, from the very Natives they also understood to be their sometimes brethren. Such anxiousness was not unfounded. Given the United States' expressed readiness to lay waste to the Mormons—to subject them, too, to "extermination"— becoming legible as something other than *expendable life* was, for the Saints, a matter of lived urgency. As we shall see, this took form for the Saints as an allegiance to the ordering principles of the racial state. Venturing into the West, the Mormons, who were in compounding ways identified with secular whiteness's dissolution, would strive to identify themselves *with* whiteness and, above all, with the sovereignty it alone secured.

In what follows, then, I want to dwell closely with the fate of the Book of Mormon, of its contrary legibilities and its volatile reception, in the hopes of unpacking some of the largest vexations of Mormonism in its encounter with an American West, and with a broader midcentury national imaginary, fracturing across several lines of stress. I think we can read in that fate the outlines of several interlocking stories we have already begun piecing together: the story of anti-imperial flight transforming into settler violence; the story of a commitment to heretical renderings of Protestant doctrine reaching their hard and, as it will prove, racial limits; and, especially, a story of the inner workings of racialization, as it unfolds in idioms that are conspicuously other than secular. We can begin to lay out an initial sketch of what I have been calling *the biopolitics of secularism*.[9]

THE LAMANITE'S LAMENT; OR, A BRIEF READING OF THE BOOK OF MORMON

If the Book of Mormon could be said to have villains, they would have to be the Lamanites, the descendants of Lehi's unrighteous son Laman—who, as we are first introduced to him, is marked chiefly by his deceitfulness, his treachery, and the constancy of his "murmuring" against his father and brother. These are the Lamanites who, over the course of many many chapters and many many books, do battle with the various Nephites who are charged with writing, recording, editing, and otherwise transmitting the story of an ancient America, and what transpired there.

The cursing of the descendants of Laman with dark skin happens early on in the Book of Mormon, and makes plain enough their Cain-like racialization, whereby nonwhiteness and spiritual malignancy are made into the simplest of figures for one another. The passage comes in 2 Nephi 5:21:

> And he had caused the cursing to come upon them, yea, even a sore cursing, because of their iniquity. For behold, they had hardened their hearts against him, that they had become like unto a flint; wherefore, as they were white, and exceedingly fair and delightsome, that they might not be enticing unto my people the Lord God did cause a skin of blackness to come upon them.[10]

As they were white: thus commences the text's familiar, straightforward Manicheanism, the delightsomeness of whiteness counterposed to this God-imprinted "skin of blackness." Just so, one does not struggle to find a range of accounts of the Lamanites keyed to the note of a characterological malady of soul, expressed in the shorthand of phenotype. To be sure, there is much in the Book of Mormon to mitigate the clarity of this division. We find passages of earnest Lamanite conversion; periods in which Lamanites and their "good" counterparts, the Nephites, are described as virtually indistinguishable in their faltering distance from righteousness; and others still (though rarer) when Lamanites appear notably *more* righteous than their unaccursed enemies and long-ago brethren. We will turn toward some of these shortly. Nevertheless, whatever the blurring force of these doublings and migrations of virtue, the positioning of the Lamanites as the fearsome enemies of the Nephites, distinguished by their "cunning, and lying craftiness" (Mosiah 10:18), is relatively unfaltering. The Lamanites, cursed with their "skin of blackness," play more or less exactly the role nineteenth-century American readers might expect of racial Others—and none of the wild intricacy of the text's plotting much undoes this. They are the treacherous enemy, untrustworthy and accursed.

In this respect, one might reasonably apprehend the Book of Mormon as, at base, an especially expansive variety of midrash, a respinning of conflicts and tropes and figures from the Bible, adapted to the shifting needs of a particular historical moment. (I will forever be grateful to the undergraduate who, in an observation at once funny and faultless, referred to the Book of Mormon as "Old Testament fan-fiction.") There is much one might make of such an approach to Smith's immersive fluency with the idioms, the narrative modes, and the styles of characterization proper to the Bible. But there are consequences as well. For to read the text this way is to welcome into exegesis a kind of racial contextualism, an interpretive practice that approaches the Book of Mormon as a text overspilling with the racial presumptions of its moment of composition. On such an account, the Book of Mormon amounts ultimately to a biblicized, especially baroque recapitulation of nineteenth-century colonizing racism at its most uncontoured. It is, we might say, straightforward imperial colonialism adapted to the idioms of Old Testament prophecy and tricked out with some "New World" flourishes.

And yet and yet. If it's not wrong to say the Book of Mormon makes villains of the accursed dark-skinned Lamanites, neither is it quite right. The Book of Mormon actually does something more elaborate and more strange. This is so not only because it is, finally, the Lamanites who *win* the millennial race war the book depicts, and so survive as the sacred remnant, the carriers of the seed of Lehi into the future. (Though that survivance, as we shall see, is not inconsequential.) Nor is it so because of the scenes of mitigation and reversal we have already marked; nor, I would argue, because of the peculiar narrative of racial redemption it scripts, whereby the Lamanites are afforded the chance to be (as a scholar like Max Perry Mueller has it) redeemed and transformed, via the text's antiessentialist "restorative racial universalism." (Indeed, the chance to *become white* via righteousness—"a change of heart from wicked to righteous," such as Samuel demonstrates, say—might well strike us as less righteous or restorative than an ultimately *genocidal* species of affordance.)[11] More crucially than any of this, the work itself employs a narrative structure, a mode of sacred history-making, that, as many critics have noted, stands the Book of Mormon in vivid contrast to sacred scripture in the Judeo-Christian tradition. And it does so, I think, in large measure to bring into relief the possibilities of a racial counter-narrative.

The Book of Mormon is not like other sacred texts, and not merely because it was written well within the threshold of the modern (or, for that matter, because it comes trailing an origin-story full of modern miracle and necromancy). As critics like Terryl Givens, Grant Hardy, Elizabeth Fenton, and Jared Hickman all remind us, one of the very most striking features of the Book of Mormon is its insistent foregrounding of the conditions of its production, preservation, and transmission.[12] That is, this postbiblical epic is pointedly not unfolded in the voice of narrators who are "anonymous, omniscient, reticent, and unobtrusive," which is how Hardy rightly describes the narrators of the Hebrew Bible. If you go looking to the Book of Mormon for the unmarked and unchallengeable omniscience of sacred texts, you will be frustrated. Instead, you will find narrators who write from what Hardy calls "limited, human perspectives." You will find, in fact, a series of distinctive personages, with rich backstories and complex motives, all of them interwoven with the plots they recite. The narrators of the Book of Mormon are, in a word, *characters*. Nephi, the first of our narrators, "presents his life story with a particular point of view, a theological vision, an agenda," as Hardy writes, though in truth he could be speaking quite as well of Mormon and Moroni, those other historians and scribes who transcode, shelter, recopy, and otherwise transmit the story of the Nephites.[13] But the fact that the book's narrators could be said to have, in Hardy's terms, an "agenda" matters for more than narratological reasons. It makes an especially crucial kind of difference, too, to the emplotments of race and racial salvation the Book of Mormon seems on its surface to endorse.

Whatever else might be ventured about it, the Book of Mormon does not present itself as an omniscient account of God's grace in the world, as dictated by His appointed prophets, through whom God speaks His incontestable Word in propria persona, as it were. It is, to the contrary, a text forever reminding us that it is assembled by editors and scribes, each of whom is marked as a character *within* the racial dramas being played out and elaborately recounted—with, we could crudely say, skin in all of those games. Here is the first crucial point to note in respect to these narrators: they are, each and all of them, Nephites. They belong to a clan, a bloodline, a people. Moreover, they are the spokesmen for a people whose collective self-understanding is that they are both *chosen* and *at war*—and this matters in a multitude of ways. For although they are telling what amounts to a story of their people's decline and decimation, describing in intricate historical detail a tragedy of fallen righteousness, nevertheless this collection of Nephite narrators can readily be seen to have a moment-to-moment investment in Nephite aggrandizement that is, in many passages, nothing if not conspicuous. From the first, this aggrandizement comes directly at the expense of the Lamanites.

Observe, for instance, how Hardy exemplifies his overarching claim about the human situatedness of the text's narrators. He does so by looking closely at the very first story told by the very first narrator we encounter. That narrator is Nephi. It is from no one other than Nephi that we first learn of the wickedness of Laman and Lemuel, Nephi's own brothers. It is Nephi himself who sets out the grounding terms of Lamanite villainousness, establishing the idiom that will adhere to them across the whole of the sacred epic. But the opening story he tells, though important in several senses, is not merely descriptive, not merely an inaugural episode of genealogical historicizing. It is also a bit of *characterizing self-portraiture*—which is a fact that biblical precedent, its inducements to credulous reading, and above all the convention of sacred omniscience all conspire to obscure. And yet it is crucial that we not misrecognize it. As even the most cursory reading of the story that Nephi tells makes clear, the imputed, insisted-upon wickedness of his brothers is not altogether without contour. Read as a part of a narrative, authored in the first person, its complications begin to emerge in new configurations. For it is difficult not to note, in the first place, that the way Nephi regards Laman and Lemuel is markedly different from how they are regarded by *other* characters, other bystanders, there in the drama he unfolds.

No one figure makes this difference clearer than Lehi, the father of all three of them. As narrated in the first and second books of Nephi, Lehi the patriarch produces little of the vehement condemnation that Nephi does, his self-professingly righteous son. Indeed, the first chapter of the second book of Nephi is taken up largely with Lehi's plea to his vagrant sons to follow the path of the righteous—to follow Nephi—so that Lehi himself might keep his covenant with God. This is a covenant that renders "a land which is choice above all other lands . . . for the inheritance of my seed." "Yea the Lord hath covenanted this land unto me," Lehi says, "*and to my children forever*," marking out a covenant that pointedly *includes* Lemuel and Laman (2 Nephi 1:5, emphasis added). Lehi may worry for his erring sons, and wish them to amend their ways, but he does not believe them to be wicked, in some elemental or unalterable fashion. These discordant notes— the inflected differences of perspective between Lehi and Nephi—do more than remind us of the limited, the invested position from which the text is written. They telegraph, too, something of the quality of Nephi's investment in what amounts to racialized derogation. Nephi, after all, has a good deal riding on the diminishment of Laman and Lemuel; though his brothers may indeed be unrighteous, Nephi himself has also, in several senses, usurped them. And this is a fact to which he is in no hurry to draw our attention. (As Hardy astutely frames the matter, "Lehi speaks as a concerned father, Nephi as a condemning brother [and a younger one at that].") So we mis-read those crucial, lasting, originary disparagements of Laman if we divorce them too greatly from Nephi's own investments, and especially from his notable tendency (in Hardy's words) to "minimiz[e] his personal struggles, weaknesses, and mistakes."[14] Hickman calls this, winningly, the "sheer 'me' factor of Nephi's first-person narrative," while Avi Steinberg, striking a similar note, invites us to read the Book of Mormon as transpiring in "the energetically deluded first person."[15] From the outset, these self-invested delusions torque the narrative in particular ways. For whatever it is we learn of Laman's wickedness, we learn not omnisciently—not from the all-seeing perspective of a God who has judged—but from a rival brother who has risen above his station to claim the mantle of righteousness.

Such involutions are not isolated to the opening of the text. Consider, too, the book of Mosiah, where we encounter "The Record of Zeniff." Here is an embedded narrator who, unlike Mormon and Moroni, actually pauses amid his accounts of Lamanite-Nephite warfare to offer us something of the Lamanite sense of the war's inciting causes. We are told

> they were a strong people, as to the strength of men; they were a wild, and ferocious, and a blood-thirsty people, believing in the tradition of their fathers, which is this: Believing that they were driven out of the land of Jerusalem because of the iniquities of their fathers, and that they were wronged in the wilderness by their brethren, and they were also wronged while crossing the sea; and again, that they were wronged while in the land of their inheritance, after they had crossed the sea. (Mosiah 10:11–13)

Here as much as anywhere in the text, we encounter a relatively uncon-toured version of the Lamanite's lament.[16] According to Zeniff, the Laman-ites persist in their bloody antagonisms not because of any ingrained moral wretchedness, signified phenotypically or otherwise. Startlingly, Zeniff offers an account not of Lamanite wickedness but of Lamanite *grievance*: of a people precipitated into sustained warfare by a sense of usurpation, harm, and lasting injustice. This, we are told of the Lamanites, is *"the tradition of their fathers."* Indeed, that the Lamanites object to being punished in the name of "the iniquities of their fathers" gives point to their understanding of the Nephites as persecutors who use the idea of bloodlines, of inherited sins, to authorize their depredations. It is, we might say, a glancing indictment of the Nephite's racialization of righteousness. Hardy suggests that "there is no comparable passage in the rest of the Book of Mormon," though in his thoroughgoing attention to embedded counternarratives Hickman turns our attention to the other voices (Ammoron in Alma 54; Samuel, especially in Helaman 15) that ratify Zeniff's, and echo his sense of grievance.[17] In a work as intricate and vast as the Book of Mormon, even this litany of irruptions may indeed be small. But their consequences are not. They clarify for us the workings, as well as the racial and theological stakes, of what Hickman calls the Book of Mormon's strategies of "self-deconstruction."[18]

We know that the Book of Mormon is, in its largest movements, a tragedy. It tells the story of a people especially chosen by God who fail, catastrophically, to live up to that God's word. In what precisely, then, does that failure consist? Of what is it made? Faithlessness and avarice surely rank among the Nephites' most dire failings, and the text returns to them repeatedly. But the arrangement of the Book of Mormon as the work of *historians*, of scribes and editors who have taken part in the dramas they depict, and indeed taken sides, gives us another way of measuring Nephite declension, one legible at the level of form if not, or if only glancingly, at the level of narrative. Hickman avers that once we begin to take the situatedness of its narrators with the seriousness it warrants, the Book of Mormon "comes into view as an ethnocentric document, the governing cultural myth of the Nephite people." Nephi and Mormon and Moroni, he argues, write "to prop up Nephite cultural identity."[19] Another way of saying this is to suggest that the racism of the Book of Mormon is not some underthought cultural effect, some reflex of Smith's embeddedness in an antebellum world inescapably ordered by settler-colonial logics he cannot help but reproduce. Instead, that racism—that guiding, distorting ethnocentric narrative framing, in the terms of which the Lamanites can only ever appear in the guise of "a dark and loathsome, and a filthy people, full of idleness and all manner of abominations" (1 Nephi 12:23)—emerges as an essential element of the Nephites' undoing. It marks the failure of righteousness for which they are most chastised, and that they are *least capable of narrating*.[20] The text overturns the expectation of a naturalized omniscience in sacred history-making to remind us of the falsity, the literally *damning* falsity, of imperial historiography. Read against the grain not of its narrative but of its narrators, this sacred and authorizing epic is secretly the story of a vilified people triumphing over enemies who, though they cannot conceive of themselves as anything other than the very pattern of exemplary and God-sanctioned virtue, are actually hubristic, backsliding, unself-knowing, and, finally, wicked. More than this, the Nephites, for all their self-heroization, are in fact damned, speeding toward a just and God-authored annihilation. In this way, the Book of Mormon may be less an exemplification of colonizing racism (and racist historiography) than a sustained performed critique of it, in which it is exactly the Nephites' imperiousness, their incapacity to recognize themselves as anything other than chosen and holy and their foes as anything other than benighted and racially degraded, that dooms them. At the very origins of Mormonism, we could say, is a vast chastisement of the self-blindedness of imperial arrogance.

APOSTATES FROM WHITENESS

There is still more to say about the Book of Mormon as a species of fraught anti-imperial critique, and more to say particularly about the different frameworks and, especially, different scales at which we might understand that critique to transpire. The refusal of omniscience in the Book of Mormon, I have suggested, is the strategy by which the text foregrounds the embeddedness, what Hardy and Hickman and Fenton all encourage us to see as the human situatedness, of its narrators. The Book of Mormon makes use of these formal strategies to stage the cosmological vision of the book, with its explicitly racialized hierarchy of judgment and value, as nonencompassing, delimited, belonging to the Nephites. It is *their* story of originary righteousness, *their* story of adversity, *their* story of destruction at the hands of an ultimately unplaced God. But just this dethroning of omniscience suggests, additionally, a different, larger context for the work. Here, the leaning toward heresy we tracked so closely in previous chapters comes into meaning as, in effect, *a heretical dethroning of a God that has been racialized.* This is a point I want to unpack in some detail. For to the degree that this "addition" to the canon of Christianity pushes toward a species of critique, an intimation of the final inadequacy of established Christian doctrine, the Book of Mormon necessarily inserts itself into a high-stakes terrain of racial contestation. In that effort toward exposure, I want to suggest, the text insinuates an upending of nothing less than the Absolute God that by the nineteenth century had become irreducibly the God of whiteness. Think of Pip, crying out to the heavens in the midst of that other midcentury religious epic and proto-Western: "Oh, thou big white God aloft there somewhere in yon darkness, have mercy on this small black boy down here; preserve him from all men that have no bowels to feel fear!" Pip's God is, at base, the figurehead of a world-spanning imperial theodicy, of a fully racialized Christian cosmos, and he was hardly alone in his turn to Him in the midst of a scene of racial terror.[21] This, I think, is the scene of action in which the Book of Mormon's greatest heresies, its amplest strains of critique, come into sharpest focus.

Consider Paul C. Gutjahr's trenchant remarks, in his "biography" of the text, on what we might think of as the doctrinal multifacetedness of the Book of Mormon, the puzzling simultaneity of its heresies and, with these, its seeming conformities. The Book of Mormon, Gutjahr argues, "differed little on central doctrinal issues from the country's other Protestant denominations." The book, he reminds us, is "Trinitarian in nature and a strong proponent of monogamy" to boot, marking a good deal of distance between it and the more irruptive heresies to come in Smith's prophetic career.[22] We might usefully push this point a bit, I think, even though it largely accords with the case I have been making thus far, which is that the Mormons were marked out as heretics, and racialized in that heresy, to the extent that they departed from the presumptions of a secularism not yet hardened but on its way toward becoming hegemonic, whose solidification was expressed predominantly as a steady closing of the gap between the dictates of a rationalized liberalism and the tenets of *good religion*. On Gutjahr's account, which rhymes nicely with Jan Shipps's reading of the "fundamental theological tension" at the heart of early Mormonism, the Book of Mormon is indeed in some measures upending—it relativizes, we might say, the omniscience of biblical omniscience—though not, finally, so much so as to amount to a sharp break with, an abandonment of, normative antebellum Protestantism.[23] This would come later, with the insistence on polygamy (which as many would note the Book of Mormon goes out of its way to reject) and on the plurality of gods.

Certainly, this story of an inherent doubleness within the Book of Mormon had a lot of appeal to nineteenth-century Mormons, for reasons that require careful parsing. Here we encounter not only Shipps's point about the internal multiplicitousness of early Mormon theology, its as-yet-undersystematized possibilities. We encounter, too, another iteration of the Mormon struggle to, as it were, have it both ways: to rebuke imperial America in its declension from righteousness *and* to be counted among the legitimate agents of and heirs to imperial nationality. (The Mormons labored, that is, both to revile an America putatively fallen into villainy *and*, at moments, to figure themselves as exemplary bearers of some originary American promise.) As we have already seen, it was above all polygamy, an insistence on its holiness and necessity, that posed the greatest challenge to this ambition.

And yet, in his persuasive account of the straining but finally unruptured Protestant normativity of the Book of Mormon, Gutjahr may be ceding too much. His reading, that is, may grant the text a normativity it does not quite achieve. In this vein, we might recall Egbert B. Grandin's reluctance to take the job of printing the initial text, inasmuch as it was a book that, as Gutjahr ventriloquizes Grandin, "promised to significantly challenge the beliefs of those who revered the Bible with its claim to be a revelation that was every bit as divinely inspired and authoritative as their treasured sacred text." Grandin, of course, would only be affirmed in his disquiet by the early New York readers who, again as Gutjahr notes, "shunned *The Book of Mormon* as the worst type of blasphemy."[24] And I think we can see why. For the Book of Mormon, as we have begun to explore, had ventured blasphemies keyed not only to (and against) Protestant orthodoxies. Though published well in advance of the major heresies of plural marriage and plural godhead, the text had undertaken a dispossessive satire not merely of Christianity, and not merely of white imperialism, but—and here was the rub—of *the historical collapse of the one wholly into the terrain of the other*. It had broached the unnerving possibility of the irreducible and unrighteous racism of *any* "God" apprehended too complacently in and through the frameworks of secular Christianity.

What happens to the Book of Mormon when we read it in immediate colloquy not only with the proliferating prophetic testimonies of its loquaciously devoted era but with the many contemporaneous critiques of American Christianity, and particularly of its complicity in, as well as apologies for, antebellum white supremacy? The flourishing of chattel slavery in a nation of fantastic and ever-escalating piety had of course already made such critique especially vivid, in everything from Frederick Douglass's lacerating and oft-reiterated denunciations of proslavery piety to Harriet

Jacobs's searing Book of Revelation reference, in *Incidents in the Life of a Slave Girl*, to the "cage of obscene birds" that is slavery's intimate life (to take the two maximally canonical examples).[25] Douglass turned the point, in 1852, with ringing force and clarity. Under the heading "THE CHURCH RESPONSIBLE" he declared:

> But the church of this country is not only indifferent to the wrongs of the slave, it actually takes sides with the oppressors. It has made itself the bulwark of American slavery, and the shield of American slave-hunters. Many of its most eloquent Divines, who stand as the very lights of the church, have shamelessly given the sanction of religion, and the bible, to the whole slave system.

He went on:

> For my part, I would say, welcome infidelity! welcome Atheism! welcome anything! in preference to the gospel, *as preached by those Divines!* They convert the very name of religion into an engine of tyranny.[26]

Here, then, was the very most compressed version one might hope for of a contra-Christian commitment to *heresy itself*—"welcome infidelity! welcome Atheism!"—as a necessity of antiracist insurgency.

But there were other, nearer configurations of antiracist heresy. Consider the figures that animate Henry Highland Garnet's crucial "Address to the Slaves of the United States," from the 1843 African American National Convention, which turns upon not merely Christian complicity but the status of God Himself in a racialized world. Garnet, who was an advocate for violent revolution for the enslaved—as opposed to Garrisonianism's moral suasion—prosecuted his insurrectionary argument in terms that were unabstractably theological. He set the revelatory scene as one of an ultimate confrontation between racialized suffering and the allegedly redeeming edifice of Christianity. "The propagators of the system," Garnet asserts,

> or their immediate ancestors very soon discovered its growing evil, and its tremendous wickedness, and secret promises were made to destroy it. The gross inconsistency of a people holding slaves, who had themselves "ferried o'er the wave," for freedom's sake, was too apparent to be entirely overlooked. The voice of Freedom cried, "emancipate your Slaves." Humanity supplicated with tears, for the deliverance of the children of

Africa. Wisdom urged her solemn plea. The bleeding captive plead his innocence and pointed to Christianity who stood weeping at the cross. Jehovah frowned upon the nefarious institution, and thunderbolts, red with vengeance, struggled to leap forth to blast the guilty wretches who maintained it. But all was vain. Slavery had stretched its dark wings of death over the land, the Church stood silently by—the priests prophesied falsely, and the people loved to have it so. *Its throne is established, and now it reigns triumphant.*[27] (emphasis added)

Garnet here envisions a God-authored and rending opposition to slavery—*thunderbolts, red with vengeance*—and he imagines, in turn, the shattering *failure* of that divine vengeance, pointing us toward those shafts of retribution that "struggled to leap forth." His stinging address thus hangs between an indictment of Christian complicity in racial brutality and, rather less familiarly, a chilling indictment of the impotence of God Himself, the Christian God of righteousness and redemption, to intervene on behalf of the racially despised and trampled under: *all was vain.* The throne of God, in this vision, has been usurped; slavery sits in His place. As both Eddie Glaude Jr. and Hickman suggest, with differing inflections, Garnet's address in these respects flirts with a kind of apocalypticism, an antiracist eschatology that Glaude calls "radical" and Hickman "Promethean."[28] Notable for our purposes is above all the intimation that a certain kind of theodicy, a belief in the God-sanctioned benignity of the extant Real, might be laid bare, seen with maximal clarity in the grain of its racial triumphalism, through a counterinsistence on the failed, the *false* omniscience of the Christian God.

The resonances here with the Book of Mormon are many and clarifying, and we will turn to them presently. But I want to draw them out into sharper detail by setting them alongside still another antebellum text with its eyes on, precisely, imperial violence, racialized theodicy, and false omniscience. Think of Herman Melville's "Benito Cereno," which delivers what is among the era's most vengeful rebukes to sentimental Northern piety, skewering its easy pretenses and occluded brutalities in the person of the guileless ship's captain Amasa Delano.[29] But like the Book of Mormon itself, "Benito Cereno" aims its critique toward other targets as well. This it does by constellating into a dense unit one character's benighted sentimental racism, the style of religiosity that undergirds it, *and* a staged narrative omniscience in which readers of the shifting and elusive tale are invited again and again to place their trust. The ultimate fraudulence of omniscience is, for our purposes, a key movement in the text: a central element, I want to argue, in how Melville asks us to conceptualize the whole terrain of racialization in an imperial world grounded in domination not only by enslavement but by slavery's Christianization. In this, it makes for a revelatory pairing with the Book of Mormon.

The story and even the narrative metastory of "Benito Cereno" are in certain respects simple enough. It is the tale of a slave revolt told almost entirely through the eyes of an unperceiving Northern sea captain, Amasa Delano, who encounters a distressed ship in remote seas and climbs aboard endeavoring to aid the faltering Spanish captain he finds there—and who, despite the persistence of his suspicions and uneasy surmises, fails and fails and fails to see into the nature of the scene of violence unfolding in front of him. When Captain Delano boards the *San Dominick*, he finds himself beset by a queer array of signs and portents—unexplained breaches of shipboard decorum, unruly slaves, misbehaving sailors: "All of this is very queer now, thought Captain Delano"—the whole of which he cannot quite manage to narrate back to himself in composed, coherent order.[30] For most of the eerie, tranced, slow-unfolding tale, we watch him try. His efforts follow a basic pattern. As Melville depicts it, Delano's consciousness rocks pendulum-like between gothic suspicion, in which he fancies himself at the center of some diabolical Spaniard's plot ("the very word Spaniard has a curious, conspirator, Guy-Fawkish twang to it," he thinks [93]), and a recurring style of self-reassurance in which, like the sentimental man he avows himself to be, he recalls to himself the elemental beneficence of human nature, the benignity of the God-ordered world, and the folly of imagining himself as anything other than a grateful recipient of God's special grace. In this way Delano succeeds in "drowning criticism in compassion" (69) and keeps at bay his more uncharitable or alarmist intuitions.

But these self-soothing stories, however they buttress his faith in "the ever-watchful Providence above" (113), do not by themselves do the work of putting Delano's suspicions to rest. He must join them to others, to stories that, though they differ in tenor, in fact attend every stage in the unfolding of what the narrative calls not Delano's trustfulness but his "undistrustful good nature" (55). These are stories about slaves. They are stories about their docility, their faithfulness, their good cheer, about "the peculiar love in negroes of uniting industry with pastime" (60) and all the winning characteristics "arising," as the narrative puts it, "from the unaspiring contentment of a limited mind" (98). Delano swathes the slaves he sees in figures: Babo is like "a shepherd's dog" (60), the chained Atufal a "bull of the Nile" (92), the slave mothers "leopardesses" (86). Indeed, "like most men of a good, blithe heart," we are told, "Captain Delano took to negroes, not philanthropically, but genially, just as other men to Newfoundland dogs" (99).

By the end of the story we learn the nature of the mystery: the slaves are in revolt and have enslaved the Spaniards, forcing them at the threat of death to perform their assigned roles, their counterfeited authority, for an insufficiently perceptive Delano. Like so many other of the nested ironies of Delano's portion of the tale, the rancorousness of that blank-faced reference to the Newfoundland dog, and the narrative's moral revulsion at Delano, come most to light in this clarifying retrospect. But by withholding this revelation and by mystifying it, the story does something else. "Benito Cereno" compels us to watch, in grinding slow motion, the intricate inner workings of a vast misrecognition. What Delano looks at is enslavement: subjection and horror, violence and desperation. Everywhere the captive Cereno turns is the threat of death; Babo's knife is never far from his heart. But what Delano sees is remarkable. He understands the enslaved as faithful companions, bestial but hearteningly devoted in their loves, not *quite* a different species of being than himself and Cereno but certainly a part of a different, lesser order of creation. What other conviction could permit Delano to do so intimate a business with the unconscionable commerce of transatlantic slavery and to assure himself, all the while, his "conscience is clean"? "Benito Cereno" is in these respects the account of a man who cannot see what is happening directly in front of him, and of the specific narrative machinery with which he transposes subjection into devotion, a rage for freedom into cheery docility, cruel exploitation into God's plan. It tracks, down to their grammar and syntax, the stories with which the pious American beguiles himself into tranquility.

There is more than this. For these many notes of racial self-assurance, these confident presumptions of inborn black inferiority, come to us again and again in a narrative voice not only unclearly marked as Delano's but, typically, bearing all the marks of *determined omniscience*. "There is something in the negro which, in a peculiar way, fits him for avocations about one's person," we are told (98), in a voice that seems to belong less to the befuddled and credulous Delano than to the very omniscient voice that at the outset pointedly *distinguished* itself from Delano, mocking him, in fact. In its very first pages, and with a beguiling directness, the story tells us that that Delano is a bit dimwitted. Here are the sentences in question:

> Considering the lawlessness and loneliness of the spot, and the sort of stories, at that day, associated with those seas, Captain Delano's surprise might have deepened into some uneasiness had he not been a person of a singularly undistrustful good nature, not liable, except on extraordinary and repeated incentives, and hardly then, to indulge in personal alarms, any way involving the imputation of malign evil in man. Whether, in view of what humanity is capable, such a trait implies, along with a benevolent heart, more than ordinary quickness and accuracy of intellectual perception, may be left to the wise to determine. (55–56)

Delano, we are told in this knowing voice, is a bad reader, not good at navigating the "sorts of stories" associated with his scene of action and, for that matter, not possessed of a "more than ordinary quickness and accuracy of intellectual perception." With that small aside, the story extends us the promise of a kind of collusion with the omniscient perspective, inviting our affiliation, our readerly faithfulness, our allegiance to its authority over and against the good if unworldly captain. So when, later, the narrative speaks, again blank-facedly, of "that affectionate zeal which transmutes into something filial or fraternal acts in themselves but menial; and which has gained the negro the repute of making the most pleasing body servant in the world," we have only our own perspicacity to mark it as anything but credible omniscient narration (62).[31] If we do not at once recognize this for what it is, a burlesque of Delano's racist fantasies of innate black servility, then we too have been the insufficiently curious victims of an elaborate ruse. Like Delano—*precisely* like Delano—we are in this way shown to believe rather too readily in the soothing dictates of an omniscience we had understood to be, as it were, on our side.

This is what it means to say that "Benito Cereno" *punishes* its readers for their undistrustful regard for the authority of omniscience. (One moral of the story, for readers in the nineteenth century and after, might be articulated concisely: Herman Melville hates you.)[32] In "Benito Cereno," omniscience is a ruse, "a literary man-trap," what Hickman understands to amount to a sort of "desperado heckling" at the grounding presumptions of Delano's cheery white supremacism.[33] Here, too, we arrive at another consequence of the tight ligaturing between readers and Delano the story accomplishes. Melville makes it clear: though Delano has his queasy moments, *he too believes in omniscience.* And for him, "omniscience" comes mantled in an explicitly theological significance. Witness this astonishment of a paragraph, which unfolds in the bare moments after Delano has passed through what he had convinced himself was the direst threat to his life:

> The next moment, with clenched jaw and hand, he passed Atufal, and stood unharmed in the light. As he saw his trim ship lying peacefully at anchor, and almost within ordinary call; as he saw his household boat, with familiar faces in it, patiently rising and falling, on the short waves by the San Dominick's side; and then, glancing about the decks where he stood, saw the oakum-pickers still gravely plying their fingers; and heard the low, buzzing whistle and industrious hum of the hatchet-polishers, still bestirring themselves over their endless occupation; and more than all, as he saw the benign aspect of nature, taking her innocent repose in the evening; the screened sun in the quiet camp of the west shining out like the mild light from Abraham's tent; as charmed eye and ear took in all these, with the chained figure of the black, clenched jaw and hand relaxed. Once again he smiled at the phantoms which had mocked him, and felt something like a tinge of remorse, that, by harboring them even for a moment, he should, by implication, have betrayed an almost atheist doubt of the ever-watchful Providence above (113).

Melville presents us here with as pure a version of racialized theodicy as we find anywhere in antebellum fiction. "As charmed eye and ear took in all these, *with the chained figure of the black*": for Delano, black enslavement does not disorder but, to the contrary, *expresses* the benignity of God's creation. The cosmos is a God-ordered scene of racial subjection and—as far as Delano is concerned—selective racial exaltation. Not long before, in his flurry of suspicion, Delano had imagined the possibility of Cereno being league with the slaves in precisely such theologico-racializing terms: "Besides," he thinks, "who ever heard of a white so far a renegade as to *apostatize* from his very species almost, by leaguing in against it with negroes?" (89, emphasis added). To deny this imperial order, this fully racialized theodicy, is, Delano concludes, *atheistic*. (Think again of Douglass: "welcome infidelity! *welcome Atheism!*") To throw into doubt the pure omniscience of God, in this imperial dispensation, is as Melville stages it to *apostatize from whiteness.*

"Benito Cereno," like Garnet's address, anatomizes imperial whiteness as a category whose content is theologically supercharged. In the person of Amasa Delano, that whiteness nourishes itself in a seeming deference to God's will—an undistrustful faith in ever-watchful Providence—although what such Providential obedience actually expresses, as Melville sees it, is nothing other than the relishing enjoyment of an in-the-world authority of *omniscience*: a godlike reposing in the power to order and rescue the world, to punish or redeem, as one sees fit. The novella identifies Delano's comfort in whiteness, from which he will not "apostatize," with the divine racial order in which, with great sentimental self-satisfaction, he all but literally plays God. "Whiteanity" is William Jones's pungent phrase for the tuning of Christian theodicy to the imperatives of an enslaving white supremacism, a designation Hickman usefully amplifies when he contends that the proper name for this exercise, for the unself-acknowledging gathering into the human of the powers of divinized omniscience, is in fact *secularism*. It is secularism not as the ideology that sees to the routing of "religion" in the lived world but rather as "the blasé stance of the complacently divinized." This, in effect, is Hickman's great intervention into the conversation about secularism and (for Hickman, *as*) globality. Within a planetary modernity shocked into new being by 1492 and the fragilizing of religion in the immanent sphere of the globe, "secularism" acquires a kind of phenomenological descriptiveness, and what it names best, Hickman argues, is "the luxury of imperialists in the ascendancy to deify themselves so absolutely as to enjoy a sense of command that can make the world seem entirely subject" to their unbroken authority.[34] This is what Hickman means when, with the accumulated force of his century-spanning argument, he describes secularity as "a genuine effect of the experience of godlike being-in-the-world—a disenchantment of the world by virtue of its seeming responsiveness to one's creative will."[35] In this potent framing, what we have been calling heresy—the defiance of a secularized cosmological order—necessarily carries within it a volatile racial charge. It emerges, in fact—just as Douglass had suggested—as a crucial tool in the repertoire of anti-imperial strategies.

We will return shortly to Mormonism's own divinization of the human, and its conflicting, contrary significations in a global modernity framed out in these eschatologically racialized terms. For now we might simply note that the Book of Mormon, for its part, is a text explicitly *about* racialized eschatology—and, if our reading is correct, a text invested in the unraveling, and stinging critique, of racialized claims to omniscient authority. In the Book of Mormon, little is rebuked so decisively as Nephite self-aggrandizement, and rebuked in the most countereschatological terms available. The Nephites' benightedness—their willingness to believe their own self-mythologization—eventuates in nothing less than their annihilation. In this respect we might apprehend the Book of Mormon as something like a countersecular epic, where secularism comes into meaning in the context of a postcontact racialized globalization. "From the standpoint of globalization as I've defined it," Hickman writes, "secularization narratives can be shown in fact to be divinization narratives—*self-cloaking accounts of Euro-Christians at the expense of non-Euro-Christians*, the making of Europe the sacred center of the modern globe" (emphasis added).[36] Though there is nothing to mark this sentence, which comes early in Hickman's capacious volume on the political theology of Atlantic radicalism, as explicitly *about* the grand self-cloaking Nephite myth that is the Book of Mormon—or nothing beyond Hickman's own work elsewhere on the text—still we might take it to point toward exactly those strivings toward apotheosis, toward benignity, toward racialized self-exaltation, that the narrative structure of the Book of Mormon seeks point by point to detonate. By these lights, the Book of Mormon appears as something other than blandly conventional racist midrash. In its damning of Nephite racial self-aggrandizement and of the racializing falsity of imperial omniscience, it takes shape, rather, as one of the more narratologically intricate texts in the great archive of heretical, antiracist Atlantic radicalism.

LION AMONG SHEEP

Were the Mormons, accordingly, heretics of race, apostates of whiteness? By the time the Mormons headed into the Wasatch Range, these dramas around racial imperialism, heresy, and eschatology were far from abstract. And their morals, as unfolded in the sacred epic of Mormon and Moroni, were far from clear. But the matter is hardly that the Mormons themselves, as they ventured west, had ceased to understand the Book of Mormon as an indicting document of imperial hubris and decline, especially pertinent to a nineteenth-century America racing toward crisis and soon to founder on its own wild hypocrisies. On the contrary, exactly that reading of the Book of Mormon—as the story of a people who fall, and whose decline follows from its self-blinded imperial arrogance—animated the rhetoric of postmigration Mormonism. Our reading of the counterimperial implications of the Book of Mormon were, in effect, the conventional *Mormon* readings of the Book of Mormon. When, for instance, Brigham Young declared in 1849, in a quote we have seen already, "I am prophet enough to prophesy the downfall of the Government that has driven us out," he outlined something of the clarity of Mormon identifications with and around the defining trajectories of their sacred epic.

In this moment, Young was decrying the federal government's refusal to let the Mormons continue to use the incorporated land they called the Winter Quarters as a gathering place for their westward migrations. And Winter Quarters, as we saw earlier, is an especially revealing vantage from which to encounter some of the most fraught dilemmas of postmigration Mormonism, fired by the anti-imperialist intimations of its sacred epic. Consider the scene once more: it's the winter of 1846, and Young and the Saints are beginning the great migration. "In 1846," the environmental historian Jared Farmer writes,

> Young needed a wintering place to prepare for the migration. He could have set up camp in Western Iowa, but the Mormon persecution complex propelled him across the Missouri River to unorganized territory. Better to live among the red men than among whites. Young knowingly violated a federal law that forbade contact with Indians on reserved land. He went ahead and negotiated his own extralegal treaties with Omahas and Otoes, both of whom claimed the land at Winter Quarters.[37]

These are the very Winter Quarters of which Young's biographer John G. Turner writes, "One of the unusual aspects of life [there] was the partial emergence of the church's altered and expanded family structures."[38] Here we find in one place Mormons and Omaha and Otoe, with their adjacent histories of violent displacement, their like yearnings for landed spaces of self-rule, their familial forms that from the perspective of the white secular nation could only read as derangements of normative intimacy. The scene of layered colonial contact would be arresting in itself—two very different displaced people reaching accords over the sharing of land—but is only made more densely and strangely so by the fact that the Mormons were encountering those fellow refugees through the prism of a dense system of beliefs, indeed an entire *cosmology*, in which the indigenous people of North America played an immeasurably important part. The Book of Mormon had, in a sense, endeavored to tell their story. They are the sacred remnant. They are Brother Laman. And here they were, with the Mormons, suffering at the hands of the imperious Gentiles, whose "downfall" Young prophesied with an eager certainty.

The fraught, multiple cross-identifications here are worth disentangling element by element. First, if the note Young had struck in his prophetic denunciation, in which white America played the role of the self-vanquished Nephites, was vehement, it was not, for the Mormons, new. Decades of persecution, violence, contempt, and many, many failed promises of protection had left the Mormons not just suspicious of federal authority but, rather more broadly, convinced of the spiritual malignity of the Gentiles. All this, too, was *before* a full-scale federal annihilation of the Mormons seemed imminent, as it very much did in the run-up to the nearly cataclysmic Utah War of 1857–58. Back in 1845, with the pre–Civil War saber-rattling beginning in earnest, Young had declared, "This nation is doomed to destruction," but in truth this merely echoed Smith's own dire prophecies about the fate of a nation so given over to wickedness, and so divided as well.[39] This was not, however, a position without shifting and intricate complications, both geopolitical and scriptural. For instance, as the scene at Winter Quarters begins to suggest, the Mormon disidentification from the imperiousness of the midcentury United States could only prompt a special relation with those Native Americans, those latter-day Lamanites, who, quite plainly, suffered grievously federal betrayals and depredations. Again, this was an affinity—call it, for the moment, an *identification*—that would rise to the level of explicitness, as when Young, in virtually the same breath as he foresaw the doom of the American nation, declared, "The nation has severed us from them in every respect and made us a distinct nation *just as much as the Lamanites*."[40] The Mormons figure in this proclamation as a people attuned especially keenly to the violences of colonial hubris, and as a result inclining to regard the Natives as, in the words of one historian of Winter Quarters, "common sufferers in exile."[41]

In theological terms, there is nothing at all startling about this provoking cross-identification: How could it be otherwise, inasmuch as the Mormons had been equipped by their scripture with the rudiments of anti-imperial critique? Indeed, for scripture-minded Mormons newly arrived in the West, an identification with the "Indians" was, in a way, compulsory. The Lamanites, after all, are the surviving descendants of Lehi, who carry the promise of his line into the future. As Farmer concisely writes, appraising the eschatological visions of the Book of Mormon that were to shadow the Mormon ventures in the West so decisively, "In addition to earthquakes and floods, Mormons anticipated an army of Lamanites—the 'strong arm of Jehovah,' the 'battle-ax of the Lord'—crushing their enemies like a lion among sheep. *The United States would be destroyed in the process*."[42] Just so, outbursts of "Lamanism" among the transplanted faithful—spasms of fervent, pious interest in the welfare and spiritual education of the indigenous people

among whom the Mormons now lived—would convulse settlers periodi-
cally, each one intimating the possibility of an encounter tuned less to racial
difference than to something (from the Mormon side, at least) nearer to
cohesion, a unanimity traveling along the vein of a shared *disidentification*
from imperious "American" injustice and exploitation.

An especially strong revival of Lamanism picked up in earnest around
1856, when the US Congress rebuked Utah's initial bid for statehood, in what
Farmer calls "a repudiation of veiled theocracy and unveiled polygamy."[43]
This was, of course, precisely the rebuke to foment the disidentificatory
strain in Mormon relations to the government of the Gentiles, and to the
whole of America itself, both of which would appear to the Mormons at this
moment more menacing than worth the labor of redeeming. In the glow
of this new rejection, Farmer writes, "many Mormons anticipated an alternative scenario—an independent LDS nation that would flourish even as
the iniquitous United States burned to ashes. As foreseen by Joseph Smith,"
Farmer continues, "*the Mormon apocalypse included a prominent role for
the 'remnant of Jacob'*" (emphasis added).[44] The text of the Book of Mormon itself gave point to such dreams of destruction. The prophet Micah
says there, in what would become a famous set of locutions, "The remnant
of Jacob shall be among the Gentiles . . . as a young lion among the flocks
of sheep, who if he go through, both treadeth down and teareth in pieces"
(Micah 5:8). Apostle Parley Pratt reminded the faithful that scripture, on
this point, was not hard to decipher: "Not only does this page set the time
for the overthrow of our government and all other Gentile governments on
the American continent," he had written back in 1838, "but the way and
means of this utter destruction are clearly foretold, namely, *the remnant of
Jacob will go through among the Gentiles and tear them in pieces like a lion
among the flocks of sheep.*" And more: "This destruction includes an utter
overthrow, and desolation of all our Cities, Forts, and Strong Holds—an
entire annihilation of our race, except such as embrace the Covenant, and
are numbered with Israel."[45]

Here, then, was precisely the apocalyptic anti-imperial vision of the
Book of Mormon, come to vivid new life in the Mountain West and routed
through a redoubled commitment to the Lamanites. It is a scenario in
which Mormons refuse the Nephite-like fate of America, over whom, as
scripture dictates, the Lamanites will surely triumph. Strikingly, in these
passages of Mormon crisis and precarity, anti-Americanism trumps the
hierarchies of racial distinction, under the authorizing sign of scriptural
and prophetic decree. Indeed, at a conference in Provo in 1855, designed

by Mormon leaders to incite a solidifying Mormon revivalism among the backsliding faithful, future president Wilford Woodruff struck a note that reminded his auditors in no uncertain terms where their allegiances, spiritually speaking, must lie. Mormon declension, he suggested, made itself visible not least as an unsavory *likeness* to white America. "You will eat their fish," Woodruff told the Saints of the Utes among whom they were then living, "on which they depend for a living one part of the year, and every service berry that you can find in the mountains, and still you grumble to let them have a little with them. . . . Before the whites came, there was plenty of fish and antelope, plenty of game of almost every description; but now the whites have killed off these things, and there is scarcely anything left for the poor natives to live upon."[46] Backsliding Mormons, Woodruff insisted, look like Americans: the Gentiles, whose destruction the Book of Mormon foretells, and whose imperiousness it warns against through the example of the Nephites and their terrible fall. The thrust of Woodruff's preaching, in fact, was to encourage among the faithful a sharper, more genuinely demanding sense of Mormon-Native indistinction. In this iteration of devout Mormonism, to believe in the remnant of Jacob was explicitly to identify with them: to recognize the colonial violence with which they, too, had been treated by the Gentiles—by Americans—and to refuse to replicate it. Good Mormons, under such a dispensation, could only be anti-American Mormons. This is why the backsliding faithful appear in Woodruff's account not as "Mormons" or as "Saints" but, strikingly, as "*the whites*"—a designation, in this moment, remarkably equivocal. The anti-imperial heresies of the Book of Mormon would seem not to have been lost on Woodruff.

Nor was such equivocality lost on Native peoples themselves, forced into increasingly dire negotiations with these various, varying white people. Listen to Kanosh, a leader of the Pahvant band of Utes, speaking of the disastrous treaty signed in 1865, relinquishing indigenous "possessory right of occupation." "If the Americans buy the land," he wondered, "where would the Mormons, who live here go to?"[47] It is a striking, biting turn, especially coming from Kanosh. Among the Native leaders most well-disposed toward the Mormons, and toward Brigham Young in particular, Kanosh had married Young's "adopted" Paiute daughter, Sally (to whom Zina Diantha had spoken in tongues). He was, as Farmer observes, "one of the first Indians to receive the endowment" that would lead to exaltation, eclipsed in importance perhaps only by Sowiette, whom Kanosh himself would call "the father of all the Utes."[48] All of this had helped make his own Pahvant band "the most favorable to Mormon settlement of all the Indians associated with the Northern Ute Tribe," and an important ally in Mormon conflicts with Wakara, in what is often referred to as the "Walker War."[49]

Of course, that "favor" is easy to overstate and misperceive. As Native studies scholarship reminds us with exemplary clarity, we do well to regard Native "favor," no less than Native "conversion," not in the self-heroizing frameworks of imperial religion but as *tactics*, elements within broader and shifting strategies of survivance undertaken in the teeth of annihilating violence.[50] In the greater Southwest, for instance, one major effect of Euro-imperial incursion was both the domination of equestrian tribes (Utes, Apaches, Navajos, Comanches) and, with that domination, a flourishing market in slaves culled from nonequestrian bands—bands such as the Paiutes. "For many," Ned Blackhawk writes, in his meticulous history of the region's nineteenth-century conflicts, "Mormons brought a reprieve from Ute domination, and Paiute bands often allied themselves with the Mormons in the region's conflicts." Or again: "During the first decade of colonization . . . Mormon newcomers were the Paiutes' only potential allies"—though as Blackhawk clarifyingly observes, "Alliance conveys a semblance of shared interest and power that Paiutes never achieved."[51] The Mormons, opposed to the Native slave trade and in rivalrous relation to Ute-Timpanogo groups such as those led by Wakara, were thus a strong tactical ally for Kanosh, whose Paiute band were otherwise extremely vulnerable in the intra-Native geopolitics of the region.

And yet even Kanosh, as committed a tactical loyalist to the Mormons as could be wished for, *even Kanosh* would call upon the Mormons to recognize the imperial violence of their treaties. He did so in the canny distinctions he cut: "If the *Americans* buy the land, where would the *Mormons*, who live here go to?" Kanosh gave back to the Mormons in this moment a stark reading of their own oft-stated, if fluctuating, commitments. In the high throes of Lamanism at least, the Mormons might be many things—difficult interlocutors, changeable politicians, unsteady allies—but they could not be mistaken for Americans. And yet as Kanosh pointedly reminds them, the Mormons were never *less* anti-American, never more cohered with their supposed enemies, than in their treatment of Native peoples.

THE BIOPOLITICS OF SECULARISM

We have been interested to explore just how it is that a people armed by their very scripture with the tools of anti-imperial critique—a critique, we might say, of the racialized theodicy of Christianity in the scene of a secularizing globality—would comport itself as it ventured into the American West, and into a necessarily more intimate contact with the Native peoples there, the Lamanites of scriptural lore. One answer is to be found in those periodic fits of Lamanism we have seen, and in the larger affiliative possibilities that flicker into view there. We have dwelled in those possibilities here, enlarging and amplifying them, for the sake of tracing out in close detail the ways the encoded and, I have suggested, heretical anti-imperialism of the Book of Mormon found traction for itself in the immediately colonial context of the Mormons' midcentury migration. Here we need to underscore: those possibilities were, as praxis, decidedly short-lived. Indeed, what happened in the aftermath of that migration was less any living-out of the anti-imperialist, counterracialist, autocritical narrative insinuations of the Book of Mormon than it was, give or take some few details, more or less exactly what you would expect: hesitant and self-interested alliances crossed almost immediately with catastrophic outbreaks of disease, violence, resource expropriation, the dubiously legal seizure of land, all of it culminating in a seizure of sovereignty offered in the name of white charity—what Kyla Schuller, in her work on the racializing civilizational biopolitics of postbellum America, calls "biophilanthropy."[52] It was, that is to say, the conventional story, writ large, and in the next chapter we will look more closely at the inner workings of the Mormon commitment to settler-colonial imperialism, as it worked itself out across the uneasy terrain of a secularity the Saints were always, in these years, failing to achieve.[53]

I want to hold these counterpossibilities in focus a bit longer, though, those impulses toward identification, indistinction, allegiance in many keys. For however truncated these intimations proved to be, or ultimately oblique to the emerging conventionalities of Mormon life in the West, they did not go unremarked. More particularly, they did not go unremarked *by the Gentiles*, those ranks of Euro-Christians whose destruction Young was eager to prophesy. The doomed and backsliding Gentiles, it proved, were more than ready to regard the Mormons as still another species of heretic—as, precisely, apostates of whiteness.

Their commitment to polygamy had given to a secularizing America the nearest-to-hand way to excise the Mormons from any embracing conception of the national public, so strongly did it violate both the foundational fantasy of national familialism and, with it, the codes of secular-liberal embodiment that fantasy did so much to solidify. But this was not the only manner of rebuke the Mormons were to encounter. We do well to recall that, with the exception of charges of moral degeneracy related to polygamy, there were few accusations lobbed at the Mormons with more frequency in the late nineteenth century than that they were collaborating, against America, with the treacherous Indians. Here, for instance, is Garland Hurt, writing to the commissioner of Indian affairs in Washington, DC, in May of 1855: the Mormons, he warned, have "created a distinction in the minds of the Indian tribes of this territory between the Mormons and the people of the United States." For Kanosh, as we have observed, this would prove to be absolutely the case. But matters were more dire even than this: "I suspect their first object will be to teach these savages that they are the rightful owners of the American soil, and that it has been wrongly taken from them by the whites."[54] Hurt's is a vision of the Mormons not as conventional midcentury racists or even loosely affiliated sympathizers. Rather, he apprehends in them a people determined to live out, even unto its apocalyptic ends, a strange kind of colonial critique—to live out, in fact, the very anti-imperial critique we have found woven through the pages of its sacred epic, and animating the more fervently anti-American passages of postmigration Lamanism. Small wonder, then, that, in Reeve's words, "when President James Buchanan sent federal forces to Utah in 1857 he used the threat of Mormon-Indian conspiracy as one justification."[55]

Bracket for a moment the salient fact that the agents of federal authority were not, in these elaborate conspiratorial fantasies, *wrong*. (Reeve: "Further complicating matters, Mormon leaders did attempt to forge Indian alliances in the face of an impending federal invasion.")[56] At stake here was something larger than an accusation of collusion, potent as that was. Buchanan's brewed-up sense of dangerous proximity between Mormons and Indians had been some time in the making. Long before the dire troubles of 1857, Mormons had already been appearing in the American imagination as strangely ligatured to Native peoples—to their practices, their ambitions, their fates—and not simply because of any momentary paramilitary expedience. Such comparisons proceeded, of course, on grounds other than a shared oppression at the hands of colonizing powers. Rather, Mormons were more frequently described as "Indians" by their most committed *enemies*, those most devoted to the erasure of the possibility of Mormon self-rule,

if not of Mormonism itself. As scholars like Bentley and Reeve and Fluhman have made especially clear, readings of the Mormons as colonial civilization's unassimilable Others were altogether commonplace in the later
nineteenth century, especially in the vibrant pseudo-pornographic genre of
anti-Mormon novels, but not only there.[57] In these documents, we find the
Mormons being read again and again as "Mohammedan," "Muslim," and,
most pervasively, as menacingly *Indian-like*—Indians, as it were, in other
skins. It is as though the anti-imperialist counterpossibilities of the Book of
Mormon had found their greatest traction, their most vivid realization, in
the tract-pages of a flourishing anti-Mormonism.

No one has made this case more forcefully than Reeve, whose excellent
book *Religion of a Different Color* portrays in plentiful detail the strategies
by which Mormons were cast, by what he calls "the Protestant majority,"
as degenerating and unassimilable racial Others, closer not merely in their
political allegiances but in their racial character to "Indians," to "Blacks,"
and to "Orientals," than to the white Americans whose rightful hold on the
spaces of national authority was being threatened from without by these and
other mongrel upstarts. As Reeve's book makes inarguably clear, the specter
of Mormon-Native likeness was not only a tale told by attentive Mormon
readers, fiery sermonizers, and eager apocalypticists. It was not, as it was for
the Mormons, a revivalist story. For the Mormons' enemies, it was something far more uncanny: an attack on the legitimacy of Mormonism that
proceeded very much as if the countersupremacist critique we have teased
out of the Book of Mormon, its indictment of a racialized Christian theodicy, *defined* the faith, and defined it not merely ecclesiastically or socially
but beneath the skin, in the indelible grain of the flesh.

To say this in another idiom: the anti-Mormon narrative of a troubling
Mormon Indian-likeness was a story of biopolitical delegitimation—one
in which, given their previous decades' experience, the Mormons could
hardly be blamed for hearing a pretext for annihilating violence. It had
come before. The Saints would long remember the 1838 massacre at Haun's
Mill, in which seventeen Mormon men and boys were slaughtered only days
after Missouri governor Lilburn Boggs issued his infamous "extermination
order," which read in part, "The Mormons must now be treated as enemies,
and must be exterminated or driven from the state." Reeve offers an apt
summary of the violence of 1837: "In essence," he writes, "the Missouri-
ans appropriated the rhetoric of Indian hating in an effort to eliminate the
moral compunction of exterminating and removing white people form
their land"—in this case, Mormons—"in the same way that Americans had

been exterminating and removing Native Americans for over two hundred years."⁵⁸ The Utah War of 1857 and its prospect of federal invasion gave point to these old narratives of Mormon nonwhiteness, and to their purposes. These were, again, appraisals of Mormonism keyed directly to the calculus of life: narratives, in all, of Mormon expendability.

We will consider the biopoliticization of early Mormonism more closely in the next chapter. For now, and if only in respect to intricate cross-wirings like these, we might demur a bit from Turner's account of Brigham Young's style of racism—his lasting horror of "amalgamation," his alternating exterminatory violence toward and paternalist seizure of Native persons—as, essentially, normative: an expression of the times. ("Ecclesiastical discrimination was the norm among white American Protestants," he writes, "and it is no surprise that the Latter-day Saints followed suit.")⁵⁹ Such racial contextualism, which echoes the racially normativizing readings of the Book of Mormon we saw earlier, leaves us ill equipped to describe the density and peculiarity of the Mormon place in the racial imaginary of nineteenth-century America. It forgets, perhaps above all, the exquisite pressure postbellum Mormons found themselves under, in their shifting proximities to an indigeneity they both expropriated and, as Book of Mormon readers, revered, *but from which they labored also to distinguish themselves*—at least insofar as they wished to be established as something other than expendable life. Little of this density, this multiplicity of investment, can find room for itself in renderings of the Mormons as just another among the ordinarily racist subjects of the American nineteenth century, awash in garden-variety settler-colonial visions of nonwhite degradation and therefore eager to deploy, rather than be targeted by, such fantasies.

This much, I think, is clear. But neither do we best grasp the intricacies of the scene surrounding the Mormons in the West by understanding the Saints as Reeve's book encourages us to do, which is as the victims of a kind of category mistake—a people persistently *misapprehended* as nonwhite despite being, in fact, "overwhelmingly white." "Protestant America," Reeve writes at the outset of the work, "constructed elaborate illogical arguments that struck at the morals, intellect, and the heart of a fabricated Mormon body," which is a startling sort of formulation, implying as it does that readings of the Indians as, say, racially Other were the issue of some *proper* deployment of logic. Or again, considering representations of Mormons as "a racial threat to democracy": "The irony, of course, was that nineteenth-century Mormons were overwhelmingly white and should have easily blended into the racial mainstream."⁶⁰ Reeve takes whiteness to mean, essentially, "Anglo-

European lineage," and this, on its own terms, is not a wholly unreasonable premise from which to proceed. But it is also a delimiting and distorting one, on several accounts. It neatly transforms racializations of the Mormons into a matter of "illogical accounts," quite as if, again, the figuring of Native peoples as cosmically, unassimilably Other expressed a truer, more genuine exercise of "logic," from the ambit of which the Mormons had been singularly and unjustly excluded. More than this, it erases the fraught and contested *emergence* of these categories, the policing of their closely watched borders, the management of their internal coherences, as this unfolds over a period of decades. Reeve refers back to whiteness as though it possessed an altogether taken-for-granted clarity; in the era in question, it emphatically did not. As Tavia Nyong'o astutely observes, "Race was mobilized in this period as itself a mutable and even volatile category." This is what Kyla Schuller, in her intervention as against weakly "social constructionist" visions of racial formation, calls "the dynamic ontology of race."[61] By taking up the putative mistaking of an actually white populace for some other, somehow properly racialized populace, Reeve's work misses above all the story of the *invention* of these taxonomies, their extraction and implantation, their manufacture, circulation, and enforcement. He misses the story not so much of how the Mormons became white as of how whiteness itself came into being in nineteenth-century America, and came into being in part through its elaboration as against the form and arrangement of life called "Mormonism."

Nothing makes this clearer than the vexed terrain of Mormon-Native likeness. As we have seen, this was a likeness the Mormons themselves underscored and, at moments, insisted upon, as when they figured themselves not as rivals but as *fellow refugees* from a violent imperial nation. ("The nation has severed us from them in every respect," Brigham Young would assert, "and made us a distinct nation *just as much as the Lamanites*.")[62] Their allegiance was also, as we know, scriptural, a matter of devotional obligation, Native people figuring for the Mormons not only as Omaha, Otoe, and Utes but as "Lamanites." Falling hard aslant of these affinities, too, were other and, for the Mormons, considerably more difficult likenesses. These we can count off one by one. In the register of politics, both Mormons and Natives believed themselves to be sovereign people—each a "distinct nation," as Young has it—possessed of a right to self-governance that exceeds the secular powers of the United States. (It is not for nothing that Bigler and Bagley refer to Young's rebellious confrontations with federal authority in the 1850s as part of his "*crusade for sovereignty*.")[63] Both assembled themselves into social forms that were conspicuously unstructured by dyadic monogamy and its arrangements of genders, sex, and property, making them both, in the eyes of the nation, *sexual deviants*. And both, from the perspective of the Protestant America Reeve invokes, figured less as nonbelievers or even heretics than as populations marred—intellectually, socially, sexually—by the deranging zealotry they chose to name "religion." Precisely these interwoven derangements, this fused religio-erotic deviance, fueled the racialization of Mormons and Natives both, in a way not usefully divisible into practices of logic and illogic.

On the Native side, of course, this is a very old and a very violent story. At least from Jefferson's speculations about Native impotence onward, indigenous people in North America had suffered a style of racialization anchored by and sustained in accusations of sexual errancy. Here, to take only one salient example from a vast archive, is Lewis Henry Morgan, in his *Ancient Society* of 1877, giving point to the racial content of sexual propriety: "Modern society," he writes, "reposes upon the monogamian family. The whole previous experience and progress of mankind culminated and crystallized in this preeminent institution."[64] The "Indians," however admirable as preservers of an ancient quality of "spirit," have no place in this progress narrative, this civilizational history of sexuality. As queer critics like Bethany Schneider, Deborah Miranda, Mark Rifkin, Scott Morgensen, and J. Kehaulani Kauanui have made splendidly clear, it was precisely Native arrangements of gender, property, and intimate life—the way (to quote Schneider) "the kinship structures of . . . tribal relation stood directly against the heteronormative structures of private property ownership and inheritance"—that rendered "Indians" the object of an immensely punitive kind of racialization, one substantiated *through* imputations of failed monogamousness.[65] We will return to these dynamics in the next chapter. To the insights of this tradition of queer critique we might now add only that the subsequent distillation of "Indian" life and ritual to a laudable practice of "spirit" effectively transformed Native religiosity into an emblem of atavistic backwardness—but one that, once purified of its deviance as well as its credulities, might replenish a parched imperial rationalism with a saving measure of secular spirituality. These are the secular mechanics of disenchantment and reenchantment proper to the American nineteenth century, deployed in this case to produce a racialized indigeneity made tolerable in its extirpation.

The nineteenth-century Mormons were subject to a related racialization (though one appended by differently redemptive secular mechanics).

Reeve's most consistent claim is that the Mormons, as a rival strain of main-stream Protestantism, were cast as racial outsiders. "Religion" figures, in this reading, chiefly as an element of distortion: something that incites a mis-reading of the Mormons' actual, biologically substantiated whiteness. But in the persistent casting of Mormons as Indian-like, we see something conse-quentially different. We encounter, rather, a set of figures racialized both by extremities of doctrinal devotion that violated the putatively secular codes of liberal Protestant polity *and* by the forms of specifically sexual deviancy that could be read alternatingly as cause and effect of these deranging ortho-doxies of belief.[66] *This* is the multilayered and, as it were, multidirectional shape of racialization in the American nineteenth century. That editorial from the pages of *Putnam's*, which we have seen already, comes now into its fullest clarity: "Monogamy is sanctioned by our religion," we are told, but "goes beyond our religion. . . . Monogamy does not only go with the western Caucasian race, the Europeans and their descendants, beyond Christianity, it goes beyond Common Law":

> It is one of the elementary distinctions—historical and actual—between European and Asiatic humanity. It is one of the frames of our thoughts, and molds of our feelings; it is a psychological condition of our jural consciousness, of our liberty, of our literature, of our aspirations, of our religious convictions, and of our domestic being and family relation, the foundation of all that is called polity. It is one of the pre-existing condi-tions of our existence as civilized white men. . . . Strike it out, and you destroy our very being; and when we say *our*, we mean our race.

Here is the sexual project of a racialized secularism written out in its plainest terms. Whatever we might incline to call "religion" and "sex" are not sepa-rate or separable integers here. They are not distorting mirrors in which the hard facts of lineage or phenotype reappear in "illogical" combination. They are, rather, *what race is*: the conceptual grounding-points through which expendability and nonexpendability are materialized, and the degrees of dis-tinction between them are given substance in and through the flesh. So when a Jack London character declares, "They ain't whites . . . they're Mormons"—when he insists, in essence, that the devotional practice of polygamy is *racial-izing*—we are not in the presence of any failure of logic or reason.[67] We are bearing witness, rather, to the biopolitics of secularism: to the fused, disci-plinary calibration of sex, racial status, and religiosity that would shape itself into hegemonic coherence around and through the Mormons.

SOVEREIGN WHITENESS

These failures of the Mormons to comport themselves in respect to the nor-malizing secular codes of devotional practice, along with their failure to live within the normative codes of intimate life, were not all that entangled them with Native peoples in the midcentury American imaginary. Woven across all these likenesses, and drawing gravity from their coordination, was something else as well: both Mormons and "Indians" imagined them-selves to be peoples whose rights to authority, land, and self-determination exceeded those of any rival governmental power. They considered them-selves, as we noted above, *sovereign people*.[68] In the next chapter we will unfold some of the paradoxes of these like, but rival, claims to sovereignty, but for now we can consult the *Salt Lake Tribune* for the sharpest statement of the problem. It was there, in an 1885 editorial, that the matter was put most concisely: "The essential principle of Mormonism is not polygamy at all," the editorial read, "but the ambition of an ecclesiastical hierarchy to wield sovereignty."[69] It is that rare editorial that can claim for itself the vir-tue of being absolutely correct. For this *was* the Mormon ambition, where we understand "sovereignty" to suggest a freedom from the enactment of a liberal biopolitics of expendability—though precisely that longing, to the degree that it was undertaken in the name of a theology that ran counter to the normative frames of secular nationality, could only be read back as an exercise of "theocratic" ambition.[70] In the Mormon story we do indeed find the case of a group of "faithful" adherents devoted to practices that set them so at odds with the secularizing parameters of belief that they fail to appear as practitioners of religion at all—a people who in this way make political secularism, which understands itself as the cure to all orthodoxies, visible *as* orthodoxy. And we find, too, that very group of believers claiming for them-selves nevertheless the right to political authority and sovereign self-rule.

Given all this, there is little enough to surprise us in the desperate urgency of Mormon avowals of a normativity scaling toward a kind of *hypernormalcy*—defenses of polygamy as not perversity but familialism, not rupture but deep tradition, not anchored in divinized embodiment but in bioreproduction. Nor, for that matter, is there much to surprise us in the extravagances of Mormon racism under Young, and their afterlives in what Hickman calls Mormonism's "deplorable record of theological racism."[71] In all this, we can hear a familiar trope of fragilized American whiteness: a straining disidentificatory effort not to be mistaken for nonwhite, misap-

prehended as the Indians they resemble, with their perversities, their backwardness, their acivilizational arrangements of life. It is part of the long
labor of shoring up the everywhere-contested whiteness of the Mormons
themselves, a labor undertaken in the belief—the *correct* belief—that without whiteness there could be no hope for sovereignty, in whatever meager or
compromised form. The fate of the Lamanites—those Native peoples with
whom they were sometimes aligned, and through whose violent exploitation the Mormons strove also to secure for themselves the vaunted status of
pioneering colonizers[72]—gave especially vivid testament to the cataclysm of
failed sovereignty in the imperial United States. And yet, as the Mormons
were to learn, settler-colonial whiteness was in secularizing postbellum
America a matter larger than phenotype and a willingness to indulge in
racist disidentification and violence. Such whiteness was compounded as
well of comportments of gender, orderings in the sphere of sex, and dispositions toward secularity. On this shifting terrain, the Mormons were to find
for themselves a great deal of trouble.

Much of the vexed ambition of the Mormons after their journey west
was thus not only to establish outposts of the faithful at a saving distance
from the reach of federal authority, though Young did indeed take to this
task with the industriousness and vigor for which he is known. It was also to
undo these multivalent racializations, and to reset the Mormon place in the
biopolitics of nineteenth-century America. As we will see in the next chapter, this would require becoming in certain senses other than themselves,
or at the very least new versions of themselves. It would require, as nearly
as they could manage it, harnessing all the errancies of Mormon ritual and
practice—all the departures from the codes and strictures of liberal rationality and its interwoven norms of embodiment, organization, and belief—and
rerouting them, rechanneling them, subjecting them to a clarified regime of
order and systematicity.

Another way to say this: it would require becoming secular.

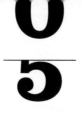

WARDS AND SOVEREIGNS

Deviance and Dominion in the Biopolitics of Secularism

NITS MAKE LICE

EVERY DECADE OR SO IN THE mid- to late nineteenth century the United States, or some nonnegligible subset of its population, went to war with the Mormons. Perhaps earliest among this series of bloody misadventures was the 1838 "Mormon War" in Missouri, which saw a number of skirmishes between local anti-Mormon militia and the "Danites"—a battalion of militarized Mormon defenders—and which culminated in the infamous "extermination order" issued by Governor Lilburn Boggs on 27 October 1838. That order read, in part, "The Mormons must now be treated as enemies, and must be exterminated or driven from the state if necessary for the public peace."[1] In the familiar terms of securitization via *extermination*, the governor had decided, in essence, that non-Mormon society must be defended. And so it was. At Haun's Mill, in Caldwell County, three days after the extermination order, a mob attacked a group of Mormon settlers, killing seventeen, and generating the probably apocryphal story of William Reynolds, a Missourian who is said to have murdered ten-year-old Sardius Smith in cold blood while declaiming, "*Nits will make lice, and if he had lived he would have become a Mormon.*"[2] That pungent phrase, as W. Paul Reeve notes, itself led a migratory life in nineteenth-century America, coming into its greatest fame some years later when, after the Sand Creek massacre of 1864, it became a byword for Indian-killing.[3] The Missouri Mormons, for their part, were disarmed and expelled from the state, taking flight back east to Illinois, and settling eventually in the haven that was Nauvoo.

Nauvoo would be the scene of enormously generative theological foment. It was there that Joseph Smith would expand his vision of divinizing flesh, prophesy about polygamy, invent new echelons of church organization— and there, too, that the Female Relief Society would begin its work, in 1842. It was also to be the scene of Joseph's murder—once again by an anti-Mormon mob—at a jailhouse in nearby Carthage, Illinois, on 27 June 1844. Consequently, in 1845, the state of Illinois revoked the Mormon charter to Nauvoo, though it did so only after declining to consider seriously the proposition of one William P. Richards, of Macomb, Illinois, who had called for the creation of a section of land to be parceled off and "forever set apart and known and designated as the *Mormon Reserve*."[4] (The Indian Removal Act had been signed into law more than a decade earlier, in 1830, though the Second Seminole War had only recently come to its uneasy conclusion, in 1842.) After some further mob skirmishes, sometimes referred to as the Illinois War, the Mormons began their great exodus westward in 1846, pausing at Winter Quarters, and negotiating extralegal treaties with the Omaha and Otoe they found there.

Removal, resettlement, reservation, mob violence, land seizure, forced migration, *nits* who make *lice*: these are the recurrent tropes of early anti-Mormonism. We can say, at the very least, that the Mormons' persistent and multivalent departures from the codes of secular liberalism that we have been tracing—ruptures of the interimplicating orders of normative intimacy, nationalized whiteness, and secular embodiment writ large—were not lost on their countrymen. They were, to the contrary, registered again and again in the shifting idioms of *racialization*, whereby the Mormons were made over into a racially dubious populace, poisoned in body by orthodoxy and erring belief, figured by alternating turns as Indian, as Mohammedan, as African or Asiatic despots, as slave-like sycophants to domineering theological masters. That these scattered denunciations, emerging from scenes of intense and often intensely local contestation, would gather the systematized coherence of state policy—the coordinate gravity of a *biopolitics*—would be made inarguably clear by the events of 1857 and '58, or, as they would come to be known, the Utah War. In 1857, with Mormon opposition to the perceived imposition of hostile federal authorities ascending toward its saber-rattling peaks, President James Buchanan decided to remove Brigham Young as territorial governor and sent more than 2,500 troops to Utah to reestablish federal control. In this already overheating atmosphere, a group of Mormons murdered a party of migrants in the infamous Mountain Meadows Massacre (the Saints recruited Southern Paiutes for this attack and then, with extraordinary clumsiness, endeavored to attribute it to them).[5] Buchanan was convinced that "the Mormons were now in armed rebellion against the government," while Young understood the government to be preparing what he called a "war of extermination."[6] Both of them were, in effect, correct.

The great bloodletting both men foresaw did not, however, come to pass. Chiefly through some deft back-channel negotiations by Thomas Leiper Kane, full-blown war was averted, and the Mormons, having fled Salt Lake in fear of annihilation, returned in triumph, there to resume their fractured quasi-allegiance to the United States. Such was the uneasy state of peace, at least until the coming of the Civil War, which, of course, gave new gravity to questions of popular sovereignty, federal power, and the racial constitution of American liberty.

"Peace," however, is a distorting term. For even in "the smallest of its cogs," as Foucault reminds us, "peace is waging a secret war," and "beneath the law, war continues to rage in all the mechanisms of power, even in the most regular."[7] Foucault's cautionary methodological note about the submerged warlikeness of *law* certainly holds true for the Mormons, whose longings for what they described as liberty, and what others recognized as unchecked political sovereignty, were eroded and eroded over the next decades, with the largest blows coming not by mob or army but via a multitude of acts of law designed, one and all, to criminalize plural marriage. With the Morrill Anti-Bigamy Act of 1862, the Cullom Bill of 1869, the Poland Bill of 1874, the *Reynolds v. United States* decision of 1879, the Edmunds Act of 1882, and finally the Edmunds-Tucker Act of 1887, the polygamous Mormons became a curious species of sexual outlaw, committing crimes against monogamy and the sanctified national order for which it stood.[8] Thus, after President Chester A. Arthur invoked the "odious crime" of polygamy in his 1881 address to Congress, there followed, as Reeve notes, "no fewer than twenty-three bills or constitutional amendments aimed at solving the Mormon problem."[9] As pro-Mormon lobbyist George T. Curtis put it bluntly in 1887, "You are a mere handful of people: 150,000 against 50 or 60 millions, and those millions have made up their minds that polygamy shall be exterminated."[10] Here it was again, all those years later: the promise of Mormon extermination. From a certain perspective, the eventual Mormon surrender of the practice of polygamy—Mormon president Wilford Woodruff issued his epoch-making declaration in 1890—is surprising mostly for having taken as long as it did.

One quite reasonable historiographical response to this litany of assaults

on Mormonism has been to regard them as the shifting indices of an unvarying persecution, a maligning misapprehension of the Mormons calculated
to denigrate their faith, delegitimate their social authority, and cheapen their
very lives—to expel the Mormons as, in all, a seditious intranational population, at odds in all the ways that might be said to matter with the norms
of which national coherence was made. Indeed, just such a reading makes
for an undercurrent in what I have described as the liberalizing strain of
appraisals of nineteenth-century Mormonism, accounts that, whatever their
object of historical pursuit, do not always resist the temptation to stand a bit
aghast at the Mormons' countrymen for having so often failed to recognize
the Saints as the good religionists, and the vexed patriots, they were.[11] And
these are not wholly implausible accounts of the period in question. That
the Mormons were the targets of decades of violent persecution is, as even
this capsule recitation suggests, beyond dispute.

And yet and yet. It will not quite do to regard these many episodes as, at
base, spasms of vengeful reaction, fueled by the purposeful misrecognition
of essentially righteous, essentially citizenly, essentially *American* Mormonism. This is so not only because the Mormons *did* eagerly prophesy the
destruction of the United States, *did* seek to employ Native peoples in the
West as against invading armies, *did* seek to override federal authority, and
did understand Gentile America as fallen, imperialist, doomed. More even
than any of this—and this has been the cumulative argument of the previous chapters—early Mormonism was in a multitude of its aspects unassimilable to the solidifying codes of an explicitly secular legitimacy that
had grown around them into a new sort of postdisestablishment hegemony
(a hegemonicization achieved in part through the violent expulsion of the
Mormons). *They were not secular liberals*, even if they could, on occasion,
as needed, figure themselves as such. If these attacks show us nothing else—
attacks on Mormon theology, the milieu of Mormon sociality, the Mormon
body itself—it is that to fail at being secular, as the Mormons were so often
found to do, was to emerge into racialization: to slip in the gradients of
American worth to the status of expendable life. This is, again, the racialized
theodicy of a liberalism speeding its way toward hegemony.

The work of this chapter is, in large part, to map out the trajectories of
this seizure of the Mormons, with an eye toward the emergence, and internal constitution, of what I have been calling the biopolitics of secularism.
At stake in this insistence on biopolitics is, most broadly, a genealogical
counterclaim about "secularism" as something other than we have become
accustomed to recognizing: as something other than a climate of pluralistic

fragilized belief; or a scene of fair play among theological options; or a sociality anchored in a capacity for adjudication and free choice among the multiplying possibilities for belief in a rationalizing and therefore disenchanted world. The unceasing attacks on Mormonism, and the specific terms in which they were prosecuted, bring into exceptional focus a contrary rendering of secularism as, rather, a normative and disciplinary force, one intimately involved in the harnessing of the terrain of ritual, practice, belief, and spirit to the imperatives of a settler-colonial empire coming to understand itself more and more entirely in the framework of a redemptive liberalism. Those interlocking religio-carnal disciplines, and their biopolitical optimization of populations along the axis of life, achieve a virtually diagrammatic vividness in the story of late-century Mormonism, its persecution, and its eventual transformation. To put it compactly: the Saints are a people disciplined out of their devotionally charged carnality, into monogamy, and eventually into the secular American whiteness for which that disciplined sexual comportment was, all along, a neat metonymy.

And yet to say that the Mormons found themselves, as it were, persecuted into a suitably secular version of themselves—this, perhaps, is itself a distorting way of framing the matter. For however coerced the Mormon turn toward secular whiteness may have been, it was not involuntary, or not quite. The pressures of these arrayed disciplinary forces propelled the Mormons into particular styles of self-accounting, and these did more than lay bare the elemental fractures—the "fundamental theological tension"—upon which Mormon theology had itself been built (which we might identify with its toggle between the perverse and the hypernormative, the orthodox and the heretical, the obedient and the dissident).[12] More consequentially, in the teeth of these hazardous passages of Mormon life, the Saints professed a growing allegiance to those versions of themselves *most* identified not only with the promises of "liberty," nor of "sovereignty," but with their nineteenth-century avatar. We can read out of the texts of this era, that is, the solidification of a Mormon identification with *imperial whiteness*—an identification of sovereignty and liberty *with* whiteness, and not its overcoming, its rebuke, its undoing. Absolutely integral to this identification, as we shall see, was an escalating suppression of all the countervailing possibilities that Mormon theology, in its wildness and extravagance and nonrationalized multiplicitousness, had also set into circulation, especially as they involved its theology of the divinizing flesh. Through these steady suppressions, the Mormons would find their clearest path back to the charmed realm of tolerably normative belief, with all the civic entitlements found there.

These ironies, if we may call them that, have large-scale theological consequences. It is Jan Shipps's point that early Mormons were, so to speak,
metaphysical literalists: they understood themselves not to be some figurative Israel but to be living their lives, day by quotidian nineteenth-century
day, *inside sacred time*. But it is Shipps's further point that as Mormons
emerged into a more viable status, and into a less nominal national citizenship, the Saints began their transition, too, out of sacred time. In the
subsequent casting of the Mormon past as *having been* sacred history, and
in the turn toward what we might call the sacralization of Mormon historiography, something dramatic happens. For that identification with the
whiteness of secular imperialism, newly figured as a *culmination*, installs a
particular theological narrative into the core of Mormon self-conception,
fastening onto Mormonism a trajectory, a fixed directionality, whose effect
is to stabilize its vagrant, deeply divided legacy. Those unruly counterpossibilities we have been tracing become in turn fugitive echoes, the trace
marks where something had been cut off. And the Mormons themselves
begin what was perhaps their greatest metamorphosis: a shift not only into
a religion by the lights of secularism—a striking enough transformation, to
be sure—but into a people who had always been modern, liberal, family-
friendly. They emerge, rather astonishingly, as a people who had always been
patriots, to God *and* country.

HERESY, BARBARISM, ETC.

Perhaps the most greatly bedeviling fact for accounts of nineteenth-century
America keyed to an unvarying Mormon persecution is one we have already
noted. The Mormons, as we began to see in the previous chapter, were only
too ready to avow themselves enemies of the state. Or, at the least, they
were quite happy to describe agents of that state as their blood-enemies, villains who, in their determination to destroy them, had made themselves fit
objects for violence. This was especially true of Brigham Young's first years
in Utah, when the parameters of Mormon and federal authority were yet in
dispute. "We shall rid ourselves of as many such white livered, blackhearted,
sycophantic Demagogues, as the Administration shall send," Young wrote
to John Bernhisel, a territorial delegate, in response to the possibility that
Franklin Pierce would appoint non-Mormons to the territorial judiciary.[13]
In 1854–55, Lieutenant Colonel Edward Steptoe, commanding some 325 sol-

diers, was tasked with investigating the death of John Gunnison (author of
The Mormons, who had been killed by Pahvant Utes, of whom we shall hear
more shortly). It was Steptoe who would inform Pierce, in John Turner's
words, that the problem in the territories "was not just polygamy." Rather,
the Mormons "were also thoroughly alienated from the national government."[14] Young, in 1855, offered a discourse that did little to counter this
vision of an "alienation" that was quite ready to turn violent. "*We ought to
have slain them in the middle of the day*," Young offered, "and hung up their
bodies or thrown them to the wolves" (emphasis added).[15] Suffice to say that
those visitors, investigating officials, and sundry Gentile informants who
returned east with stories of an anti-American and even seditious Mormonism did not do so without reason, or very ample evidence.

This does not mean that the stories they told about the Mormons were
not themselves easily fitted into a growing web of essentially delegitimating discourses, inflected by varying degrees of violent intent, all of which
coalesced around a kaleidoscopic array of racializing analogies and examples. To be sure, they did, and these dynamics—persecuting delegitimation, followed by antistate Mormon avowals, followed by more eschatologically racialized portraits of the Mormon menace—made for a kind
of self-enlarging feedback loop. In a real sense, nineteenth-century anti-
Mormonism *is* that feedback loop. J. Spencer Fluhman's *"A Peculiar People":
Anti-Mormonism and the Making of Religion in Nineteenth-Century America*
helps us see this especially clearly. Fluhman maps the convulsions of anti-
Mormon sentiment into divided stages, in which the Mormons appear, in
order, as imposters, deluded fools, fanatics, barbarians, and heretics. Fluhman's pursuit of these terms, and of a trajectory between them, is both ana-
lytically and historiographically useful, though this plotting of categories
across a kind of narrative arc ought not to distract us from the *coherence*
of these idioms of disparagement, all of them, as subsidiary elements of
what I have been calling *bad belief*. As Fluhman himself notes, the divisions
between them—between the imposter and the fanatic and the barbarian—
are themselves quite porous, with the seasons of each overlapping as much
as progressing in smooth linearity. Heresy, barbarism, etc.: these categories
mark out less a series of proper stages, I would argue, than the flexible and
interwoven terms of a condemnation proper to a failure to live to the dictates of a liberal-secular order on its way to becoming hegemonic. This is
the backdrop—what John Modern would describe as the unacknowledged
metaphysics—*against* which those local terms emerge into their shifting,
operationalized synthesis. That backdrop, I have been arguing, might be

called "secularism," and it is under its ambit that these local terms of dele-gitimation come into contact, lean against and connect up with and speak through one another, become materialized *as* a biopolitics.[16]

Consider, in this vein, the many-voiced iterations of Mormon *deprav-ity*. John C. Bennett's scandal-making *History of the Saints* is exemplary here, in part because, as one of the very earliest articulations of an already hyperbolized and fully eschatological anti-Mormonism—the text works essentially as an aggregator of all previously existing condemnations of the Mormons, up to 1842—Bennett's work did much to establish a kind of genre-precedent, one that would live itself out, with changing inflections, across the subsequent decades. Notably, all of Fluhman's categories get stage time in Bennett's breathless jeremiad. Some we have seen. For Bennett, for instance, polygamy outstrips "the most luxurious and corrupt empires of pagan antiquity."[17] This makes for Smith's perverse "Mohammedanism" (8). But these are hardly the only notes Bennett strikes in the effort to expose Mormon impiety, zealotry, savagery, and scheming malignity. Indeed, Ben-nett's little book plays up and down the keyboard of an explicitly racialized sexual depravity. As Bennett renders them, the Mormons are a menace, to be understood quite precisely on the model of a "large, powerful, and increas-ing tribe of savage Indians," intending only "evil to the whites" (8). Like dreaded slave rebels, storing up arms and planning in secret for overpow-ering attack, they merely pretend to peaceable coexistence as, meanwhile, they build up fearsome armies for the destruction of the republic (5).[18] They are popish in ecclesiastic order ("The Roman pontiff never exercised the dominion over the minds and property of the Catholic church, as Joe" [217]); "Oriental," "Persian," "Moorish," and "African" in their countenancing of polygamy (following, as a like instance, those "Oriental and African mon-archs, both in ancient and modern times," where "we find the most glaring examples of the practice of polygamy and concubinage" [219]). For Bennett, all of this depravity, all of this *racially indicating erotico-religious errancy*, makes the Mormons villains of outsized destructive power, lying in wait "to exterminate, or convert forcibly, all those, whether Christians or Heathens, whom they style Gentiles" (302). They are, that is, an existential menace, carrying within them an imminent threat of civilizational ruin.

Each of these substrains of anti-Mormonism would prove its own sort of enduring. We might think, for instance, of how Bennett's scattershot denun-ciations would be echoed, with note-perfect compression, in the 1855 edito-rial from *Putnam's* we have already seen, which had insisted that "monog-amy is sanctioned by our religion, but goes beyond our religion. . . . It is one of the elementary distinctions—historical and actual—between European and Asiatic humanity. . . . It is one of the pre-existing conditions of our existence as civilized white men."[19] Here was religion and its disciplinary "beyond" mapped out exactingly, wherein the norms of intimate life and proper belief fused in the elaboration of a rigidly hierarchized order of racial life, named "civilization." We might add to this, in turn, the transposition of such terms into the idiom of domestic sentimentality, which looked to expose the depravity that made of men tyrants and exacted from women an explicitly *slave-like* docility. Speaking directly to "American women," and invoking exactly the rhetoric of the unrepresentability of the slave woman's trauma, Fanny Stenhouse writes,

> What can you know—you, American women, who are petted and in- dulged to such an extent that you really do not know what sorrow is? How can you possibly judge what the feelings of a Mormon woman are, who has been taught to believe that "her desire shall be unto her husband, *and he shall rule over her.*"
>
> This is no imaginary "rule," but a stern fact. Woman in Utah is only a chattel![20]

In Stenhouse we find one of the very most concise versions of polygamous women as white slaves, whose subjection ratifies, as a veritably indulgent haven of pleasure, the lives of women living in submission to *monogamous* patriarchy.

Gather all this together, and the skeletal outlines of an entire discursive order begin to come into bright clarity. At its center is this flexible, adaptive, mutual ratification of sexual perversity and racial status, underwritten by a species of zealotry merely posing as "religion." With their public avowal of polygamy in 1852 the Mormons had of course made themselves known, unmistakably, as deviants, where such deviation could be read as both cause and effect of misfiring belief, and so could authorize in turn a panoply of overlapping racializations of Mormon practice and Mormon life. Thus, Ben- nett's closing peroration: "The Mormons, strong already in their number and their zeal, are increasing like the rolling snowball, and will eventually fall with the force of an avalanche upon the fair fabric of our institutions, unless the people, roused to resist their villainy, quit the forum for the field, and, meeting the Mormons with their own arms, crush the reptile before it has grown powerful enough to sting them to the death" (307). When Bennett strikes this apocalyptic note—rallying his somnolent countrymen to ready

themselves for what he ominously calls the *"final suppression"* of the Mormon menace to home, church, nation, civilization (307)—we are confronted
with a fully exterminatory vision of the Mormon menace, with its fusing of
racial status, sex practice, and religious zealotry wired into the order of *life
itself*. It is a vision in which a risk to "the people," and to "our institutions,"
authorizes a wider and wider willingness to kill. We are in the presence, I
think, of secularism's biopolitics, beginning to find its voice.[21]

HYPERNORMATIVITY; OR,
THE PATRIARCHAL SUBLIME

The Mormons themselves were hardly silent in response to these conjoined
imaginings, and to the terms of legitimation and delegitimation that circulated within them. Indeed, the Mormons' own fast-accumulating statements about the proper ordering of Mormon sociality—their efforts toward
a newly systematized set of hierarchies for gender, for sex, and for race—
ought not to be approached apart from this networked array of delegitimating racializations. On the contrary, as a set of indirect rebuttals, self-
clarifying avowals, and oblique countermeasures, such remappings of the
milieus of Mormon life emerged from directly within them—from within
the turning gears, we might say, of the biopolitical machinery of Mormon
derogation. Those countermeasures, varied and paradoxical as they were,
nevertheless offered one avenue toward the solidification of the Saints' precarious standing in the metrics of national life.

The Mormons had, after all, confessed themselves to be living in flagrant
disregard for the erotic-familial norms of nineteenth-century American life
(norms which, for good measure, they themselves had spent a good deal of
time claiming to uphold[22]). And they had set about disrupting the sanctity
of that cherished centerpiece of liberal polity, monogamous marriage, with
the impassioned conviction of the newly converted. To this deliberate disruption they soon appended a number of explanatory frameworks, some of
which we have already seen. There was, for instance, Orson Pratt's defense,
sketched out in several discourses, which the Mormons were meant not
only to ponder but to carry out into the world with them, as an article of
faith. ("The newly culled missionaries," Laurel Thatcher Ulrich writes, "were
going into the world not only to preach repentance but to defend the argu-
ably least defensible aspect of the faith—plural marriage.")[23] Pratt contested

head-on the accusations of Mormon lustfulness and portrayed polygamy, by sharp contrast, as the great preservator of sexual decency. His defense *presumed* an impulse toward lustfulness—it is the divine spark of procreativeness, overspilling the channels of the permissible and in that way making for a great wealth of human miseries—and proffered polygamy as its solution, an intimate form in which to honor all that was godlike in sex (i.e., its reproductivity) by setting around it the perimeter of a wider sanction. *It is better to be polygamous than to burn* would be one way of summarizing Pratt's contention, which he offered in supplement to a more straightforward argument about the righteousness of reproduction. Among the chief beneficiaries, in Pratt's account, were women: "We believe that woman is just as good as man, if she does as well," he wrote. "If a good man is entitled to a kingdom of glory . . . a good woman is entitled to the same, and should be placed by his side."[24]

Then, too, there was Udney Hay Jacob's more extravagant account of the necessity of polygamy, *The Peace Maker*, where plural marriage served above all as a required corrective to the precipitate and, to Jacob, horrifying disintegration of male control in a world gone mad with claims to female entitlement and equality. *The Peace Maker*, too, understood itself to be intervening in a civilizational debate keyed to gender. "Many husbands," Jacob fretted, "are induced by the unnatural and intolerable nature of female tyranny and usurpation, to even abandon their families to the mercy of a heartless world. Such unnatural crimes never did exist under the ancient law of God. All law or government of a woman over a man, except it be the law of kindness, is an usurpation of power destructive of the order, peace, and well being of society." He would go on to observe that "our ladies have long possessed a power, which the very nature of things, the nature of women, and the law of God utterly forbid; it must and does produce misery, vanity, confusion, and sorrow both to them and us." Only polygamy, and with it the restoration of a properly indomitable patriarchal hierarchy, could rectify this misery and confusion: "This ruinous, disorganizing, debasing principle," Jacob wrote, "cannot be eradicated but by the strong arm of the law."[25] Though the stories told by Pratt's account—about polygamy as a curative kind of celestial familialism—would indeed come to be the most dominant form of Mormon self-accounting, *The Peace Maker*, for all its extravagance, had its own gravity as well. Brigham Young's barbed remarks about the Female Relief Society, and the intolerable absurdity of female authority—"There is no woman on the face of the earth that can save herself—but if she ever comes into the Celestial Kingdom, she must be led in by some man—God knew what Eve was. He was acquainted with woman thousands and millions of years before"[26]—would make this more than clear.

And yet Young's strong leaning, in such moments, toward the more Jacobian line with respect to polygamy, and toward the urgency of something like patriarchal restoration, was not a merely incidental piece of Mormon self-conception, propounded in the crisis-ridden aftermath of the expulsion from Illinois. What could make sense of such flights of bilious misogyny? On first blush, after all, the turn to an ever more self-amplifying patriarchal ordering of the world of the Saints would seem among the *least* cagey responses to accusations of Mormon despotism: to accounts of Mormon depravity focalized around the tyranny of Mormon men, holding in subjection Mormon women, and in this way racializing them (turning them into slaves) and themselves (inasmuch as they become Asiatic, Oriental, Mohammedan, and African despots). This had been a through-line of anti-Mormon novels especially—Stenhouse's perhaps most famously, though vivid as well in *Boadicea: The Mormon Wife*, attributed to Alfreda Eva Bell[27]—and if one effect of it was to render polygamy as the unique female bondage that, by force of contrast, sanctifies monogamy as a scene of great female flourishing, another was to amplify the crossed, paradoxical racialization of the polygamous Mormons. (Paradoxical because, in this iteration, the practice of enslaving women rendered Mormon men not *hyperwhite* but racially dubious.) Precisely this folding-together animates the intricate plotting of *Boadicea*, where tyrannical Mormon elders cover over their murderousness by "*disguising themselves in Indian costume*, and waylaying such persons as are obnoxious to them, and putting them to death" (emphasis added). (The novel will qualify such racial pairing thus: "Even those poor savages were incapable of committing deeds so infamous, so bloodthirsty, and so cruel, as were common practices of the Mormon elders, under the name of religion.")[28] Such turns are the mainstay of Stenhouse's book, itself built in rhetoric and in conception as if in precise imitation of the female slave narrative, and coalescing around the enslavement of Mormon women to treacherous polygamous patriarchs, all of whom violate the most sacrosanct forms of respect owed to white womanhood. In the context of these visions, where male despotism and racialization twist around one another, Brigham Young can indeed begin to seem a ready-made villain, a man who, however sagacious and indomitable a religious leader, appears more nearly as if sprung directly from the fever dream of some especially outraged anti-Mormon sensationalist. No amount of noting how varyingly and contradictorily Young spoke of so many things, and especially of women, can obviate just how easily, with what little resistance, he fitted himself to the role of hyperdomineering patriarch.

But the ordering of Mormon sociality along the lines of a stricter and stricter patriarchal dispensation was not without a contrary set of cogencies. We have noted already that Young propounded an emphatic and starkly hierarchized difference between the genders as a figure with which to clarify the hierarchy of church leadership, at moments of flux, rivalry, and contestation. For a man looking to solidify his disputed authority, the clarified hierarchy of gender difference provided a convenient, because always to hand, set of usable terms. (We might think here with Joan Wallach Scott: "Gender," she writes, "is the implementation of the always imperfect attempt at discipline.")[29] In Young's rendering, as the genders were ordered in a rigid and unchallengeable hierarchy, so too would be Mormon structures of sociality and of authority. "The influence of my women over me," Young had declaimed, "is no more than the buzzing of a fly's wing in winter."[30] The radicalized patriarchality of plural marriage that followed hard upon the move to Utah—the leaning more and more toward Udney Hay Jacob's conception of polygamy, with Pratt's account as rationale—we have already seen up close, in our tracing of Young's steady suppression of the gendered counterpossibilities nested in early Mormon theology.

The Mormons, though, were at war on more fronts than one. And so the hyperbolization of gender difference and gender hierarchy under Young, that committed patriarchalization of an already-patriarchal ordering in the sphere of intimate life, comes into meaning in other registers as well, and not merely as a confirmation of the worst, most sensationalist fears about Mormon male tyranny. For the story of Mormon male authority is, inevitably, also a story about race. It takes form, I mean, as part of a Mormon effort toward the leveraging of a certain style of gender distinction for the purposes of a clarified *racial* distinction. Precisely that cross-wiring of gender to race, under the sign of a threatened authority, had in fact animated Jacob's polemic in *The Peace Maker*. Quoting Leviticus, Jacob attacked the notion that God ever intended there to be *equality* among persons, noting in particular the very different punishments proscribed for a man who would "lie carnally" with a "bond woman," as opposed to with a woman who was free. "O ye miserable fanatics of New England," he exclaimed, in the midst of a meditation on the divine necessity of female subjection. "How certain is it that God has *never made all men equal*, neither has he intended to make them equal in this world, nor in that which is to come." For Jacob, the foolishness of antislavery ("Teaching an endless torment of some of your fellow men; while you strain at the idea of negro slaves not being made equal with the chosen people of God") matched, point for point, the pernicious misappraisal of women as the equal of men. Gender hierarchy and racial hierarchy fitted together: the mutually ratifying signs of an authority properly ordered.

Such conjoining figures entangled the Mormons in intricate ways. Consider, in this respect, one of the most steeply complicating strains of Mormon racialization, which was their rendering as *Indian-like*, and therefore uncitizenly, unfit for self-governance, menacing, expendable. (Think once more of the invocation with which we began, from the massacre at Haun's Mill: *Nits make lice.*) We observed in the previous chapter how the Mormons themselves complicated this iteration of racialization through their own shifting allegiance to, and faltering identification with, the Native peoples of North America. As we saw, those fractured affiliations spoke in several tongues: through the pursuit of Mormonism as an indigenization of Christianity; through a regard for Native peoples as *fellow refugees*; through the claim, for themselves, of an intranational sovereignty, in relation to a federal authority seen through the scrim of the Book of Mormon's racialized geopolitics as cruelly imperial. Then, too, with their arrival in the West had come a series of fraught allegiances (with Wakara, Kanosh, and others) framed explicitly as against the possibility of Gentile invasion. (As Young wrote of the "Indians" in 1857, "They must learn that they have either got to help us or the United States will kill us both.")[31] In all this, as in their own gestures in the direction of anti-imperial critique, the Mormons made themselves available for racialization in relation to the fearful Indians they too closely resembled.

But not *only* in these ways. Another sort of commonality adjoined the Mormons to the Native peoples they also, explicitly, sought to colonize. That was nonmonogamy. Or rather, it was nonmonogamy deployed, from without, as a key element in a racialization played out across a terrain of intimate life and proper religiosity. We need only think back once more to *Putnam's*, which set about reminding its readers at midcentury that monogamy "is one of the pre-existing conditions of our existence as civilized white men. . . . Strike it out, and you destroy our very being; and when we say *our*, we mean our race." Such fulmination would itself rhyme with, be *repeated* by, similarly quasi-anthropological accounts of Native erotic sociality, and its purported acivilizational atavism. (Lewis Henry Morgan, whose evaluation of the "ancient society" of Native peoples concluded that they had *failed* at monogamy, was only the most prominent among the many proponents of what Tisa Wenger calls "social evolutionary theories.")[32] As these anti-Mormon jeremiads and the concomitant scientized appraisal of the Mormon body made vivid, the Saints were Indian-like not least in having been racialized as deviants, living outside the strictures of the civilizational bedrock that is monogamy. Across their many and ineradicable differences, Mormons and Indians shared in the racialization proper to the perversely nonmonogamous.[33]

The racializing crimes of Native people were not, however, *only* crimes against monogamy—and this, as it proved, was crucial. Failed monogamousness was indeed at the heart of Native racialization, or rather the way "the kinship structures of . . . tribal relation stood directly against the heteronormative structures of private property ownership and inheritance."[34] But a constitutive element of that racialization, and certainly of state responses to Native authority, was an equally frightful disordering of the proper relations between women and men. The Native crime against monogamy, that is, was part of a simultaneous crime against *gender*. Indeed, if the work of queer Native critique of nineteenth-century American settler colonialism makes anything incontestably clear, it is that one of the foremost Native violations of normative national intimacy involved a commitment to arrangements of erotic-familial life that, whatever else they were, *could not be read as patriarchal*. "Gendercide" is Deborah A. Miranda's term for the enormous coordinated effort, undertaken by the state and a variety of what Kyla Schuller terms "biophilanthropic" nonstate actors, toward the erosion, erasure, or violent rearrangement of vast structures of gender and sex among Native peoples.[35] Miranda is thinking of "adoption," of Native schools, of forced migration and its environing conditions, of the "gentle genocide" of Christianization in the aftermath of Grant's "Peace Policy," of the Dawes Allotment Act of 1887, and of the immense systems of bureaucratized biopolitical investment designed to discipline the array of extant Native social forms, to cinch them up, and to route them—at the cost of *survival*—back into the narrow channel of heteropatriarchy. She is thinking of what Robert H. Keller Jr. calls "the theology of American manufacturing and the gospel of ploughs and shoes, of knives, forks, and spoons, of balloon-frame houses and rising real estate values"—a theology undergirded at every point by "exclusive monogamy."[36] She is thinking, in all, of the intricate biopolitical machinery keyed to liberalized forms of private property and grounded in a private nuclear family, itself under the benevolent sway of one man (though shaped, too, by the improving influence of one woman). Indeed, this is what Schuller means when she argues that, in the solidifying biopolitics of nineteenth-century America, gender difference itself—"sexual differentiation"—was understood as the *attainment* of uniquely civilized populations: one of the foremost markers, that is, of racial advancement.[37] *To fail at gender differentiation was to fail at civilization*—and vice versa. In this sense we may say that the ideology of Native depravity held at its very core an imputed departure not merely from monogamy but from the exalting, civilization-bearing righteousness of indomitable male authority.

And these Native crimes, whatever they may have been understood to consist in, were in simultaneity *religious*: both cause and effect of a disordered devotion that, in the eyes of the state and its deputized agents (many of them Christian missionaries), ought not to be distinguished with designation *as* religion. Nothing makes the interwovenness of these infractions clearer than the 1883 "Religious Crimes Code," authorized by Secretary of the Interior Henry M. Teller (who had jurisdiction over the Bureau of Indian Affairs) and codified as a "Code of Indian Offenses." Among the rules drawn up by Hiram Price, the commissioner of Indian affairs, were the following:

> 4th. The "sun-dance," the "scalp-dance," the "war-dance," and all other so-called feasts assimilating thereto, shall be considered "Indian offenses." . . .

> 5th. Any plural marriage hereafter contracted or entered into by any member of an Indian tribe under the supervision of a United States Indian agent shall be considered an "Indian offense," cognizable by the Court of Indian Offenses. . . .

> 6th. The usual practices of so-called "medicine-men" shall be considered "Indian offenses" cognizable by the Court of Indian Offenses, and whenever it shall be proven to the satisfaction of the court that the influence or practice of a so-called "medicine-man" operates as a hindrance to the civilization of a tribe, or that said "medicine-man" resorts to any artifice or device to keep the Indians under his influence, or shall adopt any means to prevent the attendance of children at the agency schools, or shall use any of the arts of a conjurer to prevent the Indians from abandoning their heathenish rites and customs, he shall be adjudged guilty of an Indian offense.[38]

From the perspective of the state, Native "offenses" to civilization were not solely about property or sex or "so-called" dances and feasts, in and of themselves. They were rather, and quite explicitly, a fused compound of erotic depravity, disordered intimate and economic life (disempowering to the man who would be "head of a family"), and committed *heathenishness*, with each element coming into salience as it ratified the others. That inextricably mutual constitution is the cumulative moral of the document.

In the reflected light of these disciplinary seizures and investments, these reiterated tunings of settler-colonial state policy toward propertied hetero-patriarchy, we might wonder rather less at the Mormon drive to turn their own alternative kinship structures not only toward patriarchy but into a species of *hyperpatriarchy*. The Udney Hay Jacob line, which at many angles can seem little more than a reflex of something like male hysteria, acquires an altogether different gravity in these contexts, where sexual differentia-tion *confirms* a given population's civilizational attainment. Recall again Brigham Young's concerted suppression of the more errant gendered possi-bilities of Mormon embodiment—those possibilities for female power unto godhead—and his doubling-down on the already-patriarchal aspects of polygamy, in the effort to articulate a clarified, newly systematized hierarchy of permissible authority. That turning of plural marriage into hypertrophied patriarchy, that embrace of what I have called *the patriarchal sublime*, now comes into its clearest meaning as a gambit of invidious distinction, fueled by all these dangerous proximities: a bid to shore up the nondeviance of the Mormons through the cutting of a hard, clarifying distinction between those intimacies that are degenerate, because nonpatriarchal, and those that, because they are hyperbolically patriarchal, are not merely normative but, as it were, hypernormal.[39] The Natives have their loose, heathenish ways, where men are denied their proper station as uncontested head of the household and so (according to a further dictate in the Code) "become[] discouraged," unable to actualize themselves as against their atavistic "rites and customs." *Not the Mormons*, whatever their sharing with the Indians in the stigmatized practice of "plural marriage" and extravagant religiosity. "Let no woman unite herself in marriage with any man," Orson Pratt had written, "unless she has fully resolved to submit herself wholly to his counsel and to let him govern as the head," for such are "sacred bonds of eternal union" and such is "the divine order of family government."[40]

These avowals and stacked distinctions, the disquisitions of Jacob, and of Pratt, and of Young himself—they speak, as it were, in a clear voice. Yes, the patriarchalizing Mormons say, *yes*. Like the Indians, we make claims for an intranational sovereignty. Like the Indians, we understand ourselves as refugees from imperial America. Like the Indians, we are indeed nonmo-nogamous, and non-Protestant religionists as well. But unlike the Indians, we are in possession of a righteous sense of gendered order and hierarchy in the sphere of authority. *We have our patriarchy.* This is what distinguishes us. This is what testifies to our civilizational advancement. This is what makes us white.

NEGROS SHALL NOT RULE US

If the performed hypernormativity of an escalatingly patriarchal practice of plural marriage worked in this way toward the shoring up of a broadly contested Mormon whiteness, its effects, in the national uptake of Mormon life, were considerably more varied. The predictable recoil from the inflated patriarchality of the Mormons in Utah would come from many quarters, and speak in many voices. We find it, in its protean form, even before Young takes control of the church. It was there, for instance, as far back as Bennett's "exposé" of the Saints, where Mormon depravity figured most prominently as the malign outgrowth of a lascivious "Eastern" decadence, a pagan sensual indulgence freighted with Orientalist visions that run together "Mohammedan," "Oriental," "Asiatic," and "African" excess. It spoke as well in John Cradlebaugh's splendidly scandalized "Utah and the Mormons" speech of 1863, in which he reserved an entire horror-struck section for crimes under the heading "CONDITION OF THE WOMEN."[41] Reeve quotes a minister visiting Salt Lake in 1870, who conjoined racialized paganism and patriarchal-cum-ecclesiastical excess in all the ways Bennett's and Cradlebaugh's work had foreseen: "It would be hard to find a tribe of savages in the interior of Africa," he observed, "who are more completely subject to a despotic power than the Mormons of Utah."[42] Curiously, for Bennett, back in the 1840s, Mormon women were themselves *part* of the ambient malice, happily serving the lusts of Mormon men by helping to ensnare more and younger women into the varied cabals of iniquity taxonomized in his book. ("The Mormon seraglio is very strictly and systematically organized," Bennett wrote, before listing the three major subdivisions of polygamous women: the "*Cyprian Saints,*" the "*Chambered Sisters of Charity,*" and the "*Consecratees of the Cloister*" [229].) In later constructions, those women would largely be figured very differently. They would be mesmerized victims, captives of a fraudulent religious authority. More resonantly, they would be slaves, whose enchantment by those pretended religionists left them in dire need of secular redemption (typically by Anglo-Protestantism and the virtuous monogamy to be found there). And thus, in a peculiar formulation in which Orientalist fantasies seeped into the more nakedly Manichean racisms of midcentury America, that cruel indulgence in the enslavement of women made the Mormons themselves not more but less white, the violators of a racial order upon which they had no real purchase.[43]

On this discursive front, in which the vague Africanicity of a sultan-like indulgence in plural marriage met the racializations played out in the vicinity of enslavement, the Mormons were, once again, far from silent. In their retorts, as they ranged from the explicit to the more oblique, the Saints would return again and again to a single point, expressed in disquisitions on social order or racialized theology, or merely in the language of condemnation and praise that circulated around scenes of political dispute. This was, across all these occasions, a reiterated insistence on the reclamation of a distorted, denied, unjustly misapprehended yet *always fully present* quality of Mormon whiteness. And it was a whiteness, the Saints would insist, that *aligned* them with settler-colonial imperialism and its many imperatives and entitlements—or should, if the Gentiles would only stop misreading them.

Perhaps most famous among these iterations are Young's florid discourses and speeches concerning a piece of legislation entitled "An Act in Relation to Service," which Young signed into law in February of 1852. This act took up the matter of enslavement, its conditions and legalities, in the Utah Territory, though in his speeches on the matter Young addressed the broader question of race in its relation to Mormon theology and Mormon sociability. Here, the tropes of racialization via accursedness that played such a complicated part of the Book of Mormon, with respect to the Lamanites and indigeneity, spoke, by contrast, with the disentangled simplicity of declarative policy. "If there never was a prophet or apostle of Jesus Christ spoke it before," Young asserted, "I tell you, this people that are commonly called Negroes are the children of old Cain. I know they are, *I know they cannot bear rule in the priesthood*" (emphasis added).[44] Black authority was impossible, Young argued, in light of the markedness, the accursedness, of African Americans. That curse, Young opined, had left ineradicable effects. As he put it in a sermon from 1859: "You see some classes of the human family that are black, uncouth, uncomely, disagreeable and low in their habits, wild, and seemingly deprived of nearly all the blessings of the intelligence that is generally bestowed upon mankind."[45] That God-authored mark fostered in Young, too, a lasting horror not merely of black rule but of black *sex*, in any conceivable relation to whites. "The moment we consent to mingle with the seed of Cain," Young insisted in his remarks on service, "the Church must go to desstruction,—we should receive the curse which has been placed upon the seed of Cain, and never more be numbered with the children of Adam who are heirs to the priesthood untill that curse be removed." Though Young offered equivocal and deflating remarks as well, the direction of his com- ments was altogether plain: "In the kingdom of God on the earth, a man who has the Affrican blood in him cannot hold one jot nor tittle of priesthood"; and, further, "In the kingdom of God on the earth the Affricans cannot hold one partical of power in Government. . . . Therefore," Young makes clear, "I will not consent for one moment to have an african dictate me or any Bren. with regard to Church or State Government."[46] Or, more concisely still (in Wilford Woodruff's rendering of Young's remarks), "*Negros shall not rule us*" (emphasis added).[47] Young did not require sententious lectures from the Gentiles on the racial necessity of sexual propriety nor on the cumulative benevolence of white rule. These he wrote into law.

Clear as Young had made it in 1852, this strain of Mormon self-accounting found other articulations as well, all of them tending toward a rendering of the proper ordering of power in the key of a properly hierarchized racial world. Listen, for instance, to Young's account of his reluctance, in 1858, to embrace the offer of peace by which the Mormons would, very narrowly, avert the cataclysm of federal invasion and likely destruction in the Utah War. "I would rather live in those rocks and eat roots," he wrote, "than be a miserable slave to their whims." John G. Turner glosses these lines by say- ing, "Young feared political subordination and equated it with a state of slavery,"[48] which is, of course, correct. But it neglects to explain as fully as it might the concomitant point, which is less about enslavement as such than its putative opposite. It is a point, that is, about whiteness: about the Mormon claim upon it, about the misrecognition of that claim, and about its presumed purchase upon civic entitlement. That is the matter at the heart of all the language of *enslavement* (in their case, to federal authority), which animated the discourses internal to postmigration Mormonism every bit as vibrantly as it did anti-Mormon fulmination, with its array of stock- character charlatans and sexual despots. In these discourses, the Mormons figured themselves again and again as subjects of a power they wished to mark as tyrannical less because it was, say, imperial in its racial designs than because, as far as the Mormons were concerned, it *propounded racial misrecognition*. The *Deseret News*, for example, thundered its objection to the 1870 Cullom Bill by noting that "the slavery from which the blacks of the South have been emancipated would be delightful compared with the crushing bondage which this Bill would bring."[49] Such commonplace post- migration rhetoric as this is not difficult to parse. To the degree that the

Mormons understood themselves as white, and to the degree they understood whiteness quite precisely in the key of the settler-colonial imperialism they sometimes pursued and sometimes suffered—whiteness, here, as *the* property conferring an inborn and inviolable sovereignty—federal checks on polygamy could only read as their own species of racial crime: crimes against Mormon whiteness, and all the permissions it conferred. This is what made the possibility of submission to federal edict not citizenship, say, or obedience to law, but *enslavement*.

Young's seemingly abrupt turn toward a church policy built up around newly cut racial distinctions thus makes a rhyming kind of sense alongside his reiterative insistence on the boundless and sacrosanct authority, within a social order already structured around patriarchal plural marriage, of men. Both policies had internal coherences and local applications, to be sure, but they emerged, too, as countermeasures: ways of asserting, as clarified properties of the Mormon body itself, a conjoined gendered and racial constitution it was increasingly understood to lack, having been distorted in the grain of the very flesh by the practices attending to misbegotten belief. Recalling this, we can better approach what are too often misframed as Young's merely personal dislikes and private biases, or—correlatively—as his too-great acquiescence to a generalized midcentury racism. Considerably more than this is, I think, at stake. For instance, in the midst of still another territorial crisis of authority, this one in 1863, Young excoriated territorial governor Stephen Selwyn Harding. He was, Young claimed in a typically unsparing March discourse, among the "Republicans, rabid abolitionists, or negro worshippers" conspiring to bring destruction to the Mormons in Utah. In a version of Young's remarks prepared by US representatives in Utah and sent back east, Young was said to have called Harding a "nigger worshiper," while enthusiastically fomenting Mormon violence against him.[50] (Harding would be removed from office in 1863.) The matter is not merely that Young, in this and like moments, was expressing some characteristic prejudice or, for that matter, indulging in a conventional bit of anti-Republican derogation. In such turns as these Young was insisting, too, that the Mormons be understood within—and *not* in opposition to—a fully racialized order of political authority. With his characteristic directness, he made it as plain as possible that a hierarchy in racial distinction, as rigid and stark as that between the genders, was for him the measure of the proper distribution of political authority, with the consequence that anyone who would violate those orders, who would dissemble the proper taxonomies of authority, could only be a race-traitor. This was Harding's crime. He had disregarded not only Mormon claims to autonomy and political sovereignty but, with these, the very whiteness that authorized them. This is what made him something more, and other, than an ineffectual leader, a party hack, a demagogue. This is what made him a *nigger-lover*.

Once again, a composite portrait begins to emerge. Tyrannized by "nigger-worshipping" authorities who threatened nevertheless to enslave them, condemned as deviants despite laboring to secure the imperiled righteousness of patriarchal civilization, persecuted as though not entitled to the protections of sovereign whiteness: these were some of the interior grammars of Mormon self-defense across the decades of escalating anti-Mormonism, wherein a biopoliticization of Mormonism as a species of declined and backward-turning life marked them out as a fearsome variety of menace, threatening the civilizational health of the nation. For Young there was no dispute about the *correctness*, the probity and righteousness and necessity, of a fully racialized political order of American life. There was great contention, rather, about its application.[51] For with Young at their head the Mormons were eager to position themselves not in any sort of dis-identification from the imperial state and its ordering of political authority, not at all—very much in spite of their own multiply inflected anti-imperial leanings, visible in their scriptures as much as in their tenuous allegiances with their Lamanite brethren and fellow refugees. *They did not object to the racialization of political authority.* They objected, rather, to their expulsion from protected status *within* the logics of settler-colonial racialization.

This is what I mean when I say that Mormonism itself, as it was to take shape in the later nineteenth century, is one of the things that can make it difficult to encounter the Book of Mormon as the dispossessive satire, the anti-imperial critique, that I think it is. Despite their own prophecies of doom for benighted imperialists, and despite their own plainly faltering status within a discourse of race-hierarchy crosshatched to sexual propriety—despite their persistently losing place in the secular biopolitics of American empire—the Mormons again and again sought to anchor their contestatory self-accounts in a clarified, reiterated identification with imperial whiteness, and with the ordering of the flesh for which it stood. As against the accursed "Africans" in their midst, as against the Indians, as against imputations of racial fraudulence, the Mormons gave account of themselves. "I will not consent for one moment," Young insisted in 1852, laying claim to that particular idiom of American sovereignty that would find only its most crystalline statement in law in the Dred Scott decision of 1857, "to have an african dictate me or any Bren." And so he would not.

DIVINIZATION AND DOMINION

_____

The Mormon identification with the racialized order of imperial whiteness is, and is not, a surprise. It is a surprise for the reasons we've remarked: within the patterned logics that bound racial status together with erotic deviance, gender stricture, and a conformity to proper belief, the Mormons could only fail and fail. Whatever the elemental doubleness of Mormon theology, however resolutely the Mormons might seek to trade upon some especially normative or Protestant-seeming aspect of belief or practice as a kind of cover story for any of its more forceful heresies, polygamy— undisavowed polygamy—forever gave the game away. It was a ready-made tool for delegitimation, a stark emblem of all that was lastingly unassimi- lable in Mormonism: a condensation, in all, of the Mormons' ill-fittedness to the hegemonicizing liberalism that, streaking across the terrain of bad sex and racial declension, provided the biopolitical grounding-points for "religion" as such under the aegis of secularism. (Think again of the neat folding-together, in the "Code of Indian Offenses," of "plural marriage" and dances, ritual, "heathenishness.") Inasmuch as whiteness in postbellum America was a matter greater than phenotype and lineage and geography, but extended as well to calibrations of gender, of sex, and of secularity, the proudly polygamous Mormons were bound for no glory whatsoever in the metrics of racialized imperialism. *Nits make lice*, the assassin at Haun's Mill had said, in a phrase whose afterlives remind us starkly enough of the Mor- mons' vulnerability within the settler state's national imaginary, and with what ease the Mormons could be slotted in among the other varieties of expendable life.

And yet the Mormon embrace of that very imaginary, if not the par- ticularities of its enactment—the Mormon identification with the racialized order of settler colonialism, often as a mode of protest *against* Mormons' treatment by federal authorities—is in other respects understandable. In the first place, one strong line of defense for the Mormons, as against claims of a seditious anti-Americanism running wild among them, had long been that they were in fact the truest of patriots, and had proved this in nothing so much as their willingness to act, with exemplary venturesomeness, as *colo- nizers*. This had been the substance of John Gunnison's praise for the Saints in his important book from 1852, *The Mormons*. Gunnison was an army surveyor and explorer who had done extensive work mapping the Great Lakes region in the 1840s. In 1849, he was sent west as part of the Stansbury

Expedition, whose charge was to sight vast areas of land in advance of the possibility of a transcontinental railway. (Gunnison was to be killed in 1853, in a raid by Pahvant Utes, which in turn prompted federal investigations that brought unfriendly reports of the Mormons back east.)[52] The book he wrote about the Mormons, "derived from personal observation during a residence among them" according to its subtitle, was no jeremiad. It is matter-of-fact and, given the anti-Mormon genres flourishing around him, notably unemphatic.

But Gunnison does speak especially warmly of an admirable Mormon fortitude, be it in the face of "savage" Indians or a more general American persecution. Mormons have, Gunnison suggests, *earned* what he calls their "right of sovereignty": "Smarting under a bitter recollection of violence, that people could easily be goaded into rebellion, or rather into warfare. A small force would be a vain insult among them. Protection they ask not, nor do they need it. They are a mighty moral force among the threatening cloud of savages on our frontiers." That mighty moral force, Gunnison observes, has come at high cost. Indeed, the Mormons have in his estimation been martyrs, their colonizing efforts among the "savage" Natives sanctified by the spilling of Mormon blood: "And there they are, bidding defiance to their persecutors and readying to fight for the land that has been fertilized by their labors, and made valuable by their perseverance and almost superhuman exertions. It has been made sacred to them by the blood of their sons, which has flowed in its defense against hostile Indians. It is holy ground, set apart to their use by the rights of their conscience-loved religion."[53] Gunnison adds, "They feel well entitled to the land, *as already well paid for*" (emphasis added)—and with that gives us a concise version of an American settler colonialism in which the Mormons are, rather than degenerate outsiders, exemplars. That belief in an entitlement to land not their own would invest not only Mormon deliberations with the Timpanogos and Utes and Paiutes in their immediate surround; it would shape, too, those many tenuous, faltering allegiances with federal authorities, with whom they could at least broadly agree on the necessity of Native containment. (The United States had not annulled Native title to the land in the time of Gunnison's writing, which is part of what made Young such a key player in what were for the Natives largely disastrous treaties struck in the following years.) Gunnison figures the Mormons as patiently defiant, superhuman in labors, devout in their commitment to land reclamation, and fired by an indomitable righteousness. All of which might remind us of John Turner's summary estima-

tion of Young as "the greatest colonizer in American history"—a proposition to which it is not difficult to imagine Gunnison's assent.[54]

If their heralded role as a vanguard colonizer of the West explains something of the Mormons' seemingly self-defeating allegiance to the settler
imaginary and an imperial order of racialized political authority, it does
not, however, *exhaust* that allegiance. For such allegiances had roots apart
from, if necessarily entangled with, geopolitical expedience; those roots
were, more precisely, theological, and they went deep. Some we have seen, in
different configurations, already, and we must return to them now, though at
a different angle. Over the course of these last chapters we have been pursuing a claim about the body, and the fate of the flesh, as conjured in Smith's
cosmological vision. A steady polemical contention has been that it was not
polygamy, in itself, that made for the Mormon departure from the norms of
liberal personhood. The claim has been instead that polygamy expressed—
was the chief vehicle for—a radical theology of embodied life, a vision of
the mortal flesh in its arc toward divinization. That dream of the body, I
have argued, was the bedrock of the early Mormon theological imagination,
and one of its chief effects was to build into the edifice of Mormonism itself
a hard kernel of unassimilability. Whatever else we might say of the radiant body of early Mormonism, I have tried to suggest, it was not a liberal
body; it was not amenable to the managerial rationalism, calculable systematization, and optimized circulation and deployment proper to a mode of
power emerging over the century into a more and more granular seizure of
individuals, as particularized subjects *and* subsets of the extraindividual life
of populations. The Mormons were forever failing at being secular, I have
argued, because what was increasingly demanded of "religion," if it wished
to be legible as religion, and not atavism, zealotry, backwardness, and all the
rest, was conformity to the premises of liberalism, and to its stacked forms
of order, including the carnal. Polygamy, in other words, articulated what
was most inexpungeably heretical in Mormonism, what made it the least
convertible to the terms of secular legitimacy, because it gave form to the
celestialized carnality upon which early Mormon theology had been built.
As Smith dreamed that radiant body into being over a series of increasingly
daring prophetic visions, it advertised all the aspects of early Mormonism
that would not yield to the secular order of things, anchored as it had come
to be not only in monogamy but in the body it presumed. ("The origin of
secular politics, its very possibility," Joan Wallach Scott writes, invoking a
tradition that ran from Locke and Rousseau and into its critical assessment

by a figure like Carole Pateman, "*rested on monogamy.*")⁵⁵ For their stubborn
ill-fittedness, the Mormons were rewarded in all the ways we have seen:
they emerged in public discourse as *Mohammedan*, as *African*, as *Indian-
like* and *savage*, degenerates whose zealotry, styled deceptively as "religion,"
deranged them sexually, socially, racially.

Nothing we have seen in Mormons' responses to their own racialization,
so many of which were taken in up in those multipronged efforts toward
the suppression of the more unruly possibilities broached by Smith's own
fabulations of embodied life, unsettles this reading of early Mormon theology as performing, in its most basic theological structures, a rupturing
sort of departure from the growing orthodoxies of the secular. That drive
toward suppression was surely fomented, *induced*, by the racialized violence
directed at them more or less continuously across the century. Nevertheless,
it would, I think, make for a flattening, exonerating sort of misreading to
say that the Mormon embrace of a settler-colonial whiteness, however compelled, was a species of rebuke, the betrayal of some hardwired originary
truth of Mormonism. This is not quite the case, and, once again, the fractured multiplicitousness of early Mormon theology itself—Shipps's "fundamental theological tension"—matters here especially. For the Mormon turn
toward imperial whiteness did not require any sort of wholesale rewiring of
Mormonism. It had the effect, rather, of potentiating *other* interior strains
of Mormon theology, of materializing those possibilities in particular directions, and in particular ways. Most strikingly, the Mormon identification
with whiteness would make plain that within the theory of divinizing flesh
itself, there had always been inflections that led not away from the premises
of the secular but toward them. Within divinization, that is, there had been
movements toward a formulation of "secularism" as, in its essence, the self-
ratifying theology proper to a white Christendom in its ascendancy.

In some respects, such supremacist inflections of divinization, as we
might call them, are not at all difficult to grasp. One easy irony to note
in Mormon racialization, for instance, is that its vision of men-become-
gods, attaining an unchecked and irresistible power, set the Mormons in
identification with no antebellum figure so much as the slave master. That
identification was a mainstay of a strand of anti-Mormon thought we have
already noted: in and through anti-Mormon sentimentality, the wives and
even the deceived followers of polygamous men figured as *slaves*, in need of
secular rescue and a saving reimmersion in the redemptive machinery of
patriarchal monogamy. Stenhouse, in *Exposé of Polygamy*, writes of her husband and the "foreshadowing of doubt creeping over him" that she "rejoiced

to think that at last there was a probability that he would yet use his own brains and experience, upon which I placed great reliance, and be no longer a slave to others."[56]

Beyond the discursive terrain of committed anti-Mormonism, though, were other testaments to the crossings between enslavement and not merely white power but white *deification*. We might think most immediately, for instance, of William Lloyd Garrison's seemingly offhand comment in his preface to Frederick Douglass's 1845 *Narrative*, wherein he remarks on slavery's blunting disregard for what he calls, in a thick bit of phrasing, "*the god-like nature of its victims*" (emphasis added).[57] If there is a familiar Christian humanism echoing in Garrison's observation, which would take as its target chattel slavery as a practice of opportunistic dehumanization, there is also, a bit more obliquely, a trenchant, stinging irony. Garrison's transposition of *godlikeness* into the persons of the enslaved gives back to slaveholders a version of *their own* self-conception, inverted and racialized; he offers slavery's calculated semierasures of black humanness as the expressions of a malignant pretension to godlikeness. This is slavery as, at its root, a scene of *ceaseless white male self-deification*, such as would come to be detailed, in all its gothic sexualized terror, in the genre of the slave narrative. It is not for nothing that among the chief objects of horrors for Harriet Beecher Stowe, in the Christian sentimental antislavery epic that is *Uncle Tom's Cabin*, is the prospect, vivified in the character of George, that slaves in their hopelessness might *cease to believe in the goodness of God*. What godlike powers appear on the horizon of enslavement do so, more often than not, in the guise of masters.[58]

Then, too, the archive of Mormonism itself speaks volubly of divinization as a style of radical self-hyperbolization that tracks quite neatly alongside the deified whiteness of the slaveholder. These notes, once we go looking for them, are plentiful. The polygamy revelation itself positively abounds in them. Celestialization, there, is a matter not only of living to the furthest edges of the self's embryonic divinity, and thereby attaining the status of godhead. It is also, explicitly, about hierarchy and power: about the achievement of dominion, not in any general sense, but *over others*. "Then shall they be Gods," Smith had written in "The Principle and Doctrine of Having Many Wives and Concubines," "because they have no end." He continued, "Therefore shall they be from everlasting to everlasting, because they continue; then shall they be above all, because all things are subject unto them. Then shall they be Gods, because they have all power, and the angels are subject unto them" (*EJS*, 194). *Because all things are subject unto them*: to be a god on this account is not merely to achieve eternity but, as the revelation states and restates, to enjoy the capacity to place others *in subjection*. And this is not all. More direct even than these invocations of divinization as dominion is Smith's account of the divinized polygamous man and his bearing within a lived world that includes women. Here again is Smith thinking through the salience of gender difference in the context of plurality: "If any man espouse a virgin . . . he cannot commit adultery, for they are given unto him; for he cannot commit adultery with that, that belongeth unto him, and to none else: and if he have ten virgins given unto him by this law, he cannot commit adultery; for they belong to him" (*EJS*, 198). *Given unto him, belongeth unto him, belong to him*: Smith's reiterative insistence telegraphs, as concisely as one could wish, an in-practice yoking of divinization to a will to subjection, a dominion unto possession. As Young, Jacob, Pratt and others would not leave unremarked, such dominion was thus written into the scriptural life of early Mormonism. In the light of such passages, little seems especially untenable in the claim that a Mormon theology of divinization contained within it from the outset, and in fact propounded, elements of the possessive deification proper to slaveholding whiteness.

It might be objected that to say as much is to argue, as it were, by analogy. But the mutuality we are tracing here is a matter considerably larger than analogy and, I want to suggest, more intimately consequential. Such mutuality returns us to still another turning element in the confounding paradoxicality of early Mormon theology, the jarring simultaneity of its apparent orthodoxies and heresies. We have taken the measure already of Mormonism as an apostasizing counter-Christianity—or rather, as Terryl Givens argues, following from the insights of James Talmage, as a theological project that figures Christianity itself *as* apostasy, a centuries-long falling-off from a set of originary propositions that, once retranslated and reassembled under the sign of Mormonism, might be restored at last in all their millennial glory and power.[59] Following such premises as these, one might accordingly expend a good deal of energy chasing down those elements of Mormonism that do, and that do not, accord with what then must appear as "orthodox" Christianity.[60] (This exercise takes up an abundance of nineteenth- and twentieth-century speculation about the nature of Mormonism, most especially that inflected by Protestant skepticism.) That is not my intention here, in part because the work of this book has been to make such contrastingly *legitimate* Christianities legible in other terms, and at other scales. I have not been concerned to fix Mormonism's place within, or for that matter as among, the range of legitimized belief-practices, of "good religions," in nineteenth-century America. I have aimed above all to bring them into relief as component parts of a disciplining biopolitical force I have been calling, as a kind of shorthand, "secularism."[61]

But I think that we might now come at the matter from, as it were, both sides. For we are now in a position to see that what marks Mormonism as most deeply, we might even say most ineradicably, "Christian" in its orientation is not its Trinitarianism, not its revivalist primitivism, not even its invocations of the figure of Christ himself. To conceive of "Christianity" at other scales and within other genealogies, and especially within racial genealogies, is to vivify other possibilities. In these frameworks, the most ineradicable impress of Christianity might rather be found in nothing so much as Mormonism's vision of the divinizing flesh. For precisely that divinization of the human, and that vision of *divinization as dominion*, had been woven into the heart of Christianity, and set the parameters for what it might be, from the moment of its shattering encounter with what Jared Hickman calls the "radically unforeseen plurality" of persons, and cosmologies, and *gods* that attended what is variously named "contact," "discovery," "1492." As we have seen, Hickman's claim in *Black Prometheus* is about the emergence of Christianity itself, from the cataclysm of "contact," as a racial theodicy, a political theology of planetary white domination. What appears in 1492, in Hickman's compact formulation, is "a radically unforeseen heterogeneity within the horizon of a radical homogeneity," the latter conceptualized as "the emergent singularity of the globe." Hickman's "metacosmographic" claim is that within the newly immanent frame of the globe itself, and against a previously undreamt panoply of divergent theologies and rival gods, Christianity absorbs into itself an impulse toward divinization (Hickman considers this in the key of "Euhemerism"), but one materialized in the matrices of historical contact as *the divinization proper to racial domination*. "Christianity," that is, becomes the sign of the plastic, world-shaping, life-giving or death-delivering power of white people colonizing the heathen world, toppling its false idols, laying waste to its counterfeited deities, and carrying with them the promise of redemption. In this thesis we can trace out the defining impress of scholars like Enrique Dussel, Édouard Glissant, Walter Mignolo, Gil Anidjar, and perhaps above all Sylvia Winter—the latter chiefly in her exacting commitment to tracking how racialization is (in the exegetical words of Alex Weheliye) "converted to the stuff of ontogenesis." In conversation with them, and with postsecular critics like Asad and Casanova, Hickman proposes that what we have taken to calling "secularism," with all its implied human triumphing over the reign of gods, might best be understood as the divinization not of the human as such but of those "imperialists in the ascendancy" who "deify themselves so absolutely as to enjoy a sense of command that can make the world seems entirely subject" to their will and their desire. Secularism, he writes, is in this sense "the blasé stance of the complacently divinized."[62]

And there is Joseph Smith, summoned across the centuries, offering prompt reply: "Then shall they be above all, because all things are subject unto them. *Then shall they be Gods, because they have all power.*"

What comes into new focus in the Mormons' more and more vehement identification with imperial whiteness is thus not so much a hardwired, somehow inevitable theological racism. Nor, for that matter, does the steady suppression, under Young especially, of all those many theological counterpossibilities amount to a perversion of some ampler, better, essential Mormonism, toward which there might be enacted some sort of fundamentalist return. It is true that it can be tempting to regard the suppressive Mormon drive toward settler-colonial whiteness as precisely that: a betrayal of all those wilder, unformalized fabulations in which Smith had trafficked. (My own work, you will have noticed, is not free of such impulses.) But the figuring of Christianity as a metacosmology built around what Wynter calls "nonhomogeneity" in the order of life, one that metastasizes as *race*, allows us a different angle of approach.[63] We see rather the Mormons turning toward an aspect of their thought that had *always* been there, a presence susceptible to multiple and contradictory mobilizations, but that might in moments of need bring them into a larger conformity with the very regime of secularism to which they had made themselves, in so many respects, unassimilable. Where secularism signifies in the register of *the divinization of white domination*, early Mormonism, for all its fruitful heresies, had at least one path to legitimacy, or to something like it. "*You have got to learn how to make yourselves Gods*," Smith had said, mapping out a journeying from the human to its divinization that led determinedly through polygamy. But then also, in the many iterations and through the many voices we have been tracking here: "*Negros shall not rule us.*" The Mormon drive toward imperial whiteness was in these respects neither an inevitability nor a betrayal. It unfolded, rather, as part of an effort, not quite voluntarily entered into, to materialize an originary *attunement* to the orders of secular modernity and, especially, to its racialized theodicy.

As Pratt, Jacob, John Taylor, and above all Brigham Young would go on to demonstrate, the Mormons' was a cosmology that provided amply for such attunement.

EXPENDABILITY AND SURRENDER: THE MANIFESTO

None of this insistence and retrenchment and revision, none of these efforts to formalize Mormon sociality toward an aspect not merely normal but hypernormative, would, in the end, make a great deal of difference. Polygamy, undisavowed, remained what it had always been: a rupture of the normative frame of national intimacy that could be figured as both cause and effect of a deranging pseudo-religiosity, a steeply racializing form of sexual deviancy that showed just how irredeemably far the Mormons had strayed from the parameters of tolerable belief-practices. No matter its subterranean conformity to the racialized orders of secular modernity, Mormonism's path to godhead *through* polygamy set it too greatly at odds with the orthodoxies of a solidifying nineteenth-century liberal polity, and that unameliorated ill-fittedness consigned Mormonism, definitively, to the status of *bad belief.* And so, taken up by the biopolitical machinery of secular distinction, the Mormons came to appear in the national imagination as racially dubious and criminally deviant (Mohammedan, African, Asiatic, Indian-like), posing an all but existential threat to the republic. The Saints could embrace and identify with the practices of American settler colonialism as much as they might, out in the West. (There they are in Gunnison, "a mighty moral force among the threatening cloud of savages on our frontiers.") So long as they were polygamous, traducing both federal authority and national intimacy, they would find themselves in alarming proximity to a status they knew well, at least as it had befallen other adjacent populations: the status of expendable life.

For perhaps the clearest articulation of the bitter ironies rebounding here, we need look no further than the words of Wilford Woodruff, the Mormon president during the eventual renunciation of polygamy. Woodruff had become president, after some hard contention among the Quorum of Twelve, following the death, in 1887, of President John Taylor, who had staunchly defended the righteousness of plural marriage and its practice. (Van Wagoner calls him "the longtime champion of plural marriage," and his importance to the post-Manifesto Mormon fundamentalists bears this out.)[64] By the time Woodruff was at last made president, in August of 1889, the political situation for the Mormons was dire, and darkening. In March of 1887 the shattering Edmunds-Tucker Act, which disincorporated the church and shifted local judiciaries from local to federal (i.e., non-Mormon) appointees, while for good measure disenfranchising women (who had voted since 1870), became law. Then came the Cullom-Struble Bill, created on the model of the Idaho Test Oath of 1884 (which the Supreme Court had newly approved as constitutional), under which all Mormons in Utah would have been disenfranchised. George T. Curtis, a member of the church's lobby in Washington, summed up the grim and enclosing circumstances in precise terms. "I have never known anything in the course of my life that presented such a phenomenon," he wrote. "In the ante-bellum period, when the whole country was so much excited about slavery, there were great and powerful States interested in defending it . . . and throughout the North there were at least large masses of people who, before actual war had begun, cordially and heartily stood by the South." Such was conspicuously *not* the case for the Mormons: "You are a mere handful of people; 150,000 against 50 or 60 millions, and those millions have made up their minds that polygamy shall be exterminated."[65] He did not add that should *polygamy* not be exterminated, the United States would be more than ready to see to it that countless *Mormons*, and likely Mormonism itself, would be.

These, then, were the local political conditions. But no one apprehended the exterminatory possibilities more precisely, or in terms more resonant and suggestive, than Woodruff himself, the man who would see to the eventual renunciation of polygamy in 1890. One year before that declaration, he had written to a friend named William Atkin about the desperate straits in which the Mormons found themselves, and of the potentially rescuing power of statehood, should the Mormons contrive to wrangle it from the government: "We are now, politically speaking, a dependent or ward of the United States but in a State capacity we should be freed from such dependency, and would possess the powers and independence of a sovereign State, with authority to make and execute our own laws."[66] *A dependent or ward of the United States*: this is, I want to suggest, an altogether remarkable turn. With swift concision, it gathers up all the fraught, contested racializations we have been tracking, as the Mormons labored to establish their secure place in a biopolitical hierarchy of life, and clarifies them. For in his language of infantilized dependency, Woodruff marked out with an eerie precision how the Mormons had been, in effect, *Indianized*: transformed into "wards," dependent upon the haphazard and often exterminatory "charity" of what Mark Rifkin calls the "adoption nation" of the settler-colonial United States.[67] Such language delivers us promptly back to John Marshall's ruling, in *Cherokee Nation v. Georgia* of 1831, that Native nations were to be understood as, in the court's words, "domestic dependent nations." If this was a definition of indigenous nationality that "allowed for a limited definition of sovereignty for Native nations," as Bethany Schneider writes, "it also insisted on the eternal infantilization of those same nations, 'wards' to the federal government's 'guardian.'"[68] This is "the Indian of white fantasy, in all his dime-store musculature and *eternal infantilized dependence*," a queer subject punitively excluded from the state and marked out, with whatever flourishes of secular melancholy, as declining, or, as Lora Romero has it, *vanishing* life.[69] "Native people," Schneider writes, "forced from their traditional genders and sexualities, were requeered as children, eternally stunted, *the sexualized wards of the state*."[70]

So when Woodruff says the Mormons are, politically speaking, a ward of the state he invokes, with a stunning *directness*, a powerlessness and, most especially, a racialized vulnerability to state violence that is immediate, close-up, and far from imaginary. The examples, had the Mormons any need of them, were many, and acutely near. We could think here once more of the 1883 "Code of Indian Offenses," and its welded rebuke to sexual errancy (named there "plural marriage") and counterfeited religiosity ("heathenish rites and customs"). More nearly still: it was, after all, also in 1889 that the Paiute leader Wovoka had the vision that led to the Ghost Dance Movement in the West, which would culminate in the decimating Wounded Knee Massacre of 1890, all of three months after the Mormons had announced the cessation of plural marriage. Indeed, what Louis S. Warren reminds us was a *religion*—"Ghost Dance religion"—was attributed by many *to the Mormons*, and to their desire to foment some "larger conspiracy" with the Natives, as against the US government. (As General Nelson Miles pronounced: "It is the Mormons who are the prime movers in all this.")[71] That the Mormons might see their own destiny written out in the murders of the Lakota was hardly the stuff of idle fantasy. "I tell you Mormonism will never be destroyed until it is destroyed by the guns of the United States government," preacher DeWitt Talmage had declared in a scandalized sermon of 1880. "If the Mormons submit to the law, all right," he went on. "If not then send out the troops of the United States government. . . . Arbitration, by all means; but if that will not do, peaceful proclamation. If that will not do, then howitzer, and bombshell, and bullets, and cannon-ball."[72] The fate of those religionists living in opposition to federal authority, and to its particular arrangements of life, was perfectly clear. Wounded Knee was but one culmination, the rule rather than the exception.[73]

And so, in response to this descent into expendability, the Mormons made their momentous decision. Woodruff's "Manifesto" took the form of a press release (though it was ratified by the church, and so made binding, on 6 October 1890). First, there is defense: "We are not teaching polygamy or plural marriage, nor permitting any person to enter into its practice, and I deny that either forty or any other number of plural marriages have during that period been solemnized in our Temples or in any other place in the Territory." But then comes the rub: "Inasmuch as laws have been enacted by Congress forbidding plural marriages, which laws have been pronounced constitutional by the court of last resort, I hereby declare my intention to submit to those laws, and to use my influence with the members of the Church over which I preside to have them do likewise."[74] A year later, he would frame the matter more dramatically, observing that "it is not wisdom for us to make war upon sixty-five million people. It is not wisdom for us to go forth and carry out this principle against the laws of the nation *and receive the consequences*" (emphasis added).[75] With this, at last, the Mormons had surrendered.

SACRED HISTORIOGRAPHY, SECULAR REDEMPTION

Mormonism did not, of course, cease at a stroke to be a controversial mode of devotion. (Kathleen Flake, for examples, offers an excellent account of the turbulence of the in-between time that followed the Manifesto, centering her study around the seating of Reed Smoot in the senate in 1903, and the exoneration of Mormonism against charges of secret anti-Americanism, which was a major milestone in the Mormon story of assimilation.)[76] But the Saints had, with the Manifesto, initiated a series of profound self-revisions. They had pledged to adhere at last, and in earnest, to the secular codes of normative intimacy; they had bartered what for many was the righteousness of plural patriarchal marriage, its divinized body and promise of exaltation, for the limited (if saving) sovereignty of statehood; and, in their renewed allegiance with the United States, they had in effect recommitted themselves to the biopolitical project of imperial whiteness—with all the revisionary historicizing, scriptural recalibrating, and (in Hickman's phrase) "deplorable theological racism" that would entail.[77] With this, we could say, Mormonism began its transformation into another of America's exemplary Protestantisms, assuming its rightful place among the other good religions made possible by the secular state and its promise of "toleration" and thereafter competing in the secular marketplace of privatized belief. It had begun, in all, its great metamorphosis into a religion by the lights of secularism.

Such transformations were thick with resistance and disquiet, to be sure. "So intimately interwoven is this precious doctrine with the exaltation of men and women in the great hereafter," George Q. Cannon had editorialized in 1885, "that it cannot be given up without giving up at the same time all hope for immortal glory."[78] Cannon's remarks, which after the Manifesto would be echoed and reinflected by scores of the Mormon faithful, telegraph what for many were the stakes, quite dizzyingly high, of the renunciation of plural patriarchal marriage. As Cannon and President John Taylor had made abundantly clear, as well as those many Mormons willing to contest federal authority even unto imprisonment and death, polygamy was plainly not some minor procedural flourish, of merely notional theological gravity. To the contrary, it came into meaning as an indispensable element within a broad vision of exaltation, that centerpiece of the spectacular labor of imagination that was Smith's Mormonism. In exaltation lay the fullness of Mormonism's promise, where its vision of the radiant body in the God-saturated world expanded into a prophecy of the glorious celestial fate of the flesh: a promise, in all, about the destiny of the human in its divinization. Van Wagoner quotes a plural wife named Lorena Eugenia Washburn Larsen. "I thought that if the Lord and the church authorities had gone back on that principle," she recalled, "there was nothing to any part of the gospel. I fancied I could see myself and my children, and many other splendid women and their families turned adrift, and our only purpose in entering it, had been to more fully serve the Lord. I sank down on [my] bedding and wished in my anguish that the earth would open and take me and my children in. The darkness seemed impenetrable."[79] It is a scene that might recall to us Zina Diantha's lonely anguish, as she came to realize that her own celestial ambitions were to be circumscribed not by the breadth of her piety, or by the strength of her devotion, but by the dictates of mortal men. Larsen's experience, too, was of a desolating spiritual abandonment. To have renounced plural patriarchal marriage as the Mormons were forced to do in 1890— at the point of a sword, as it were—was on her account to revise so greatly the deep structures of Mormon theology, as they had been elaborated over some sixty tumultuous years, as to amount to revocation: *nothing to any part of the gospel.*

With the Manifesto, the Mormons did indeed begin that unlikeliest of metamorphoses, wherein a people once widely reviled, regarded as zealots and frauds and deviants, savages and seditious race-traitors, would emerge first as chastised rebels, reluctant monogamists, and dubious citizens—but then, later, in the slow reach of years, as paradigmatically virtuous national subjects, protected in their citizenship less by statehood or the official "toleration" extended to certified religion than by the wages of a sovereign whiteness, at last attained. (*Negros shall not rule us*, Young had written, and the later Mormons proved to be, on this front, as good as his word.) But as the voices of Mormons like George Q. Cannon and Lorena Eugenia Washburn Larsen suggest, the renunciation of polygamy, if it smoothed the way for these and other surprising conversions, made for a good deal of rupturing turbulence as well. With the Manifesto came not only slow-moving entitlement but a series of elemental fractures, wide and deep, in the very edifice of Mormon life. And these would give shape not only to the trajectory of twentieth-century Mormonism but to the ways Mormons of the *previous* century, early Mormonism, came to be thought, imagined, and reproduced. In curious and revealing ways, they would shape, definitively, post-Manifesto Mormon historiography.

Of all the scholars and explicators of Mormonism's profound reorientation after the abandonment of polygamy (and, it is worth noting, the attainment of Utah statehood, in 1896), few seem to me as far-sighted or as conceptually powerful as Jan Shipps. In *Mormonism: The Story of a New Religious Tradition*, Shipps makes a series of linked claims about the theological dividedness of early Mormonism. Her argument is about how these unresolved internal tensions made for a particular way of being-in-history for the Saints, and ultimately about how the renunciation of polygamy altered, profoundly, the Mormon disposition toward history and history-making. "From the beginning," Shipps writes, summarizing a thesis that has enabled much of my own work here,

> the Mormon movement had held in suspension conceptions of the LDS gospel that were fundamentally contradictory. On the one hand there were Saints who understood the Mormon message [about "the concepts of the Kingdom, being chosen as the elect, the Promised Land, and Zion"] and accepted its substance metaphorically, and on the other there were those Saints who accepted the gospel quite literally. (121)

This division, for Shipps, tracked alongside a like fracture between Mormons and "nineteenth-century evangelical Protestants" more generally.

> While others preached that the New Testament apostolic church was restored and ready to accept new communicants, the Latter-Day Saints spread the "good news" of the beginning of the literal gathering of Israel

and the restoration of the Ten Tribes, as well as the organization of a
church led by a prophet and God's holy priesthood, also restored to the
earth in these latter days. (119–20)

The differing inflections of *being in time* that followed from such divisions,
of the present's relation and access to an ongoing sacrality, came dramatically to the fore, Shipps argues, after Smith's murder and the commencement of the westward exodus, at which point "those whose understanding
of the Mormon message was mainly metaphysical generally stayed behind"
(121). The resulting "millennial idea" invested nineteenth-century Mormonism with a distinctive sort of autohistoriography (124). "While Christ had
not come to earth to reign, nineteenth-century Saints nevertheless lived so
clearly in the kingdom, *in illo tempore*, that the sacred and the not-sacred
cannot be considered separately" (125). That collapsing of sacred distance
Terryl L. Givens makes so essential to the project of Mormonism expressed
itself, in the lives of the postmigration Saints, not as a feeling of return to, or
repetition of, some numinous moment from the scriptural sacred past but
as a vivid sense of *living in sacred time*.[80] This is why polygamy made sense
not as an imitative reinhabiting of the time of the ancient saints but as the
intimate form proper to the sacred time of the present. Smith's "equal privilege with the ancient saints," in other words, was also *temporal*.

   Here, then, is the other great transformation wrought by the renunciation of polygamy. Shipps recognizes what we might call the practical
momentousness of the 1890 decree:

> The Manifesto signaled the beginning of the end of a Mormon world
> in which the practice of plural marriage was not only tolerated but cel-
> ebrated. More than that: it was a part of an unstated bargain which, on
> one side, involved a fundamental alteration in the manner of exercising
> Mormon political and economic power, as well as the discontinuation of
> plural marriage, and on the other, made possible the institutional survival
> of the Church of Jesus Christ of Latter-Day Saints, as well as the en-
> trance of a Mormon state into federal union. Thus, whatever else it did,
> the Manifesto announced that the old order would have to pass away. (115)

But what passed away in that old order was not merely the taking of multiple wives, or the structures of sociality that emerged around that practice.
Shipps contends rather that "when the Manifesto signaled the end of plural
marriage, it also signaled the beginning of the end of the extraordinary situ-

ation wherein the Latter-Day Saints had lived their lives in sacred space and sacred time" (125–26). The momentousness here transpires in a different key. Shipps concludes her chapter by noting that "twentieth-century Latter-day Saints still possess the means of reentering sacred time and space," remarking that temples and tabernacles and ward chapels, and all the rituals to be found there, "permit the regular recovery of a certain kind of sacred time" (129). But to *recover* and to *reenter* sacred time is, definitively, to be exiled from it (as Shipps's hesitating "certain kind" suggests): to be living in quotidian estrangement, and to be searching, like good historians, for paths back to a scene of plenitude.

A more pointed way to turn Shipps's contention is to observe that after polygamy, *Mormon history itself* becomes scriptural: an account not merely of places and personages, conflicts and accommodations, dates and names, but of that passage of Mormon time now consecrated as *having been* sacred, in a singular and now bygone way. (It is no kind of surprise, in this vein, that a distinctive Mormon fundamentalism appears on the scene in the years following the Manifesto.)[81] The Mormons passed gradually out of sacred time—emerging, we might add, into the different orders of sacrality offered by *nation-time*[82]—but also, in this emergence, came into a broadly reconfigured estimation of their own history, and of *its* sacrality. On Shipps's account, contemporary Mormons "reenter sacred space and time" in their engagement with a handful of select "places and events in the everyday world," among which she includes "standing in Temple Square, looking up at Eagle Gate . . . or even simply watching the pioneer parade on 24 July each year" (129). But the method of reentry she lists first among all those she names is telling. It consists, she writes, in the "*reading of the history of the pioneer period*" (129, emphasis added). *That* is how contemporary Mormons might "reenter sacred . . . time." Smith's revelations, the buried plates, the miraculous production of the Book of Mormon, the expansion of the church, the years of dire persecution, the building of temples, assassination, exodus, the handcart disaster, the colonization of the West, the surviving through threats multiple and grave: these are not, or not only, the facts of the matter. They are rather Mormonism's own sacred history, reencountered and resanctified year after year. *Historiography itself becomes an encounter with the sacred.* Where once had been a living in and through sacred time, there is—after polygamy—the "reading of history," and the uncovering there of what Shipps calls "the uniquely sacred time in the Utah Mormon experience" (129).

The consequences of such a shift are, of course, extensive. In certain respects we have been measuring out those consequences all along, and have done so nowhere as much as in our as working-through of those contemporary accounts of the Mormon past tuned to a definitive *liberalism*, misrecognized in its moment but present from the first, at the heart of early Mormonism—accounts tuned, that is, to early Mormonism's tolerance, its merely conventional racism, its basically normative misogyny, and above all its essential Americanness, malignly misperceived over decades of vindictive persecution. My point has not been that such persecution was not real, or lethal. It has been rather that accounts such as these, in Bushman or Turner or Reeves or Ulrich, retroactively manufacture the Mormons as liberal subjects they very much were not—or, at the least, were never capable of being quite convincingly enough, in the racialized metrics of national belonging, until such time as they renounced polygamy. Thus, in such twentieth- and twenty-first-century conjurings, polygamy becomes merely family-friendly after all, Mormon women agitate more for the ballot than equivalent godliness, the Saints find themselves racialized via the illogical turns of an otherwise functional racial order, and so forth. These are, again, the motions of a committedly liberalizing Mormon criticism, in which modern scholars produce a Mormonism that had *always* adhered to the normative frame of good religion. This they do by reading back into Mormonism the shape of a political bearing that the Saints did not quite have and often, in fact, resisted, inasmuch as they understood it to come at the cost of a kind of secularization, a yielding to Gentile fallenness.

What Shipps helps us to see with new precision is that this style of appraisal—what I have been calling the liberalizing strain in Mormon criticism—*extends the transformative historiographical work of the Manifesto itself.* For the turning of early Mormonism into sacred history had itself fitted Mormon sacred time with an extraordinary sort of culmination: that apotheosis arrives, according to the terms of a post-Manifesto narrative, in an achieved comity between the Mormons and those very United States to which, for so long, they were reluctant to belong. The closure of Mormon sacred time in a moment of accommodation to the state effectively consecrates American national belonging as *internal* to early Mormonism, an aspect of its inner truth, the secret destiny that it labored to bring to fulfillment. *The destiny of sacred time is American belonging.* With this destiny installed as an endpoint for the Mormon nineteenth century, those many stark divisions and unreconciled fractures in early Mormonism we have been tracing undergo a profound reorientation themselves. Ruptures and irresolutions around American imperialism, around the gendering of the

celestial spheres, around the racialization of political authority—the contrary pull of errant possibility and its recoding in terms more committedly
normative that we have been observing—all this comes to be elided precisely *here*, in the reading of Mormonism as a belief-practice whose inbuilt
telos, though interrupted by some misfiring turns of history, was forever in
liberal democracy. Or, rather, in a liberal democracy whose occluded other
side was empire, settler-colonial expansion, heteropatriarchy, and a fully
racialized statecraft. In this post-Manifesto iteration of the story of the Mormon nineteenth century, ratified as the sacred history of Mormonism itself,
the Saints become just another peculiar people, finding their place among
the litany of peculiar peoples, *pluribus* and *unum*, embraced by an America
committed to understanding itself as multiplicitous and tolerant, whatever
its internal orthodoxies or the violence required to sustain them.

   We had started by noting that "irony" is a word too bland by far, and too
flattening, to encompass the reversals and revisions and wild involutions
of early Mormonism, as it made its way across the nineteenth century. We
arrive at last at what is perhaps the largest, and strangest, of these more-
than-ironies. For the post-Manifesto fabrication of the nineteenth century
as the sacred history of Mormonism itself, available for reencounter as historiography, etches into early Mormonism a trajectory toward the premises of liberal personhood that its own theology, and its own practices, had
struggled, often bitterly, to dislodge. (Think again of Smith, insisting on how
difficult it was to get even the most devoted Saints to "believe and receive"
the breathtaking news of Mormonism's carnal imagination and cosmology
of exaltation.) In this newly minted historiographic frame, the Mormon
accommodation to those strictures becomes in turn something other than,
say, a collapse, the losing outcome of a bloodied and long-fought campaign,
an acquiescence to the very most self-exonerating stories the Gentiles liked
to tell about themselves and their pluralistic tolerance. All those violent conflicts come to figure instead as a series of misunderstandings, at last righted.
The renunciation of polygamy begins the long, slow process whereby, as
Fluhman puts it, "a seemingly monogamous Mormon people were deemed
just innocuous enough for a seat at the national table." They make themselves ready to emerge at last in the guise Harold Bloom would offer nearly
a century later: as *the* American religion.[83]

   In the bright light of that curious ascent, the array of unruly counterpossibilities we have been at pains to trace out—those strains that had been
anti-imperial, that had suggested a different fate for the body than rationalized familial reproduction, and a different future for women than queenly

accompaniment to godly men—grow fainter and fainter, harder to see, or to see as anything other than curiosities. Rather than the enemies of a biopolitics rooted in the racialized theodicy of a liberalism emerging into hegemony, the Saints become its inheritors, practitioners of a faith soon to boast senators, businessmen, scholars, governors, and all the rest. These are the contours of Mormonism's post-Manifesto backward-birthing into American hegemony. This is their story of secular redemption.

THEODICY

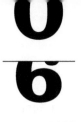

CONCLUSION

Protohomonationalism

TRADITIONS OF A DECLINING WORLD

ON 30 SEPTEMBER 2017, ELDER DALLIN H. OAKS, of the Quorum of Twelve, made an untimely sort of declaration to the general conference of Mormons. He riffed for some time on the guiding Mormon document from 1995, "The Family: A Proclamation to the World," reminding his auditors that the Saints were still a people putting family first—by which he meant, more particularly, that family wherein, "by design, fathers are to preside."[1] And he reminded them, relatedly, of the proclamation's wholesale want of ambiguity on the question of the inborn and immutable nature of gender itself. ("Gender," it reads, "is an essential characteristic of individual premortal, mortal, and eternal identity and purpose.") None of which is especially surprising, given modern Mormonism's ever more seamless identification with American religiosity in its most, as the phrase goes, "traditional" guises. That Elder Oaks felt compelled to soften his orthodoxies by preaching a humane attitude of tolerance toward those who choose the less righteous path, *apostates though they may be*, was marketing, not doctrine.

And yet running like a fault line through all this stolid conventionality were the tremors of a peculiar disquiet. Bemoaning the "rapid and increasing public acceptance of cohabitation without marriage and of same-sex marriage," Elder Oaks found himself wandering into discursive terrain considerably more, let us say, freighted: "Even as we must live with the marriage laws and other traditions of a declining world, those who strive for exaltation must make personal choices in family life according to the Lord's way whenever that differs from the world's way."[2] Speaking in the neutered language of "personal choice"—that signature of tolerable religiosity in a secular age[3]—Elder Oaks managed nevertheless to invoke a whole unruly tradition of dissident Mormonism, mobilized here to fortify the faithful in their resistance to the erosion of a series of sanctified norms and standards. But in that hard turn against the "declining" Gentile world, with its unrighteous sexual mores, Elder Oaks invoked every bit as directly the very tradition that goes hand-in-glove with that of Mormon dissent, which is, of course, a great tradition of Mormon *perversity*—or, at the least, of a committed opposition to the normative framework of marriage as *a* man and *a* woman. The *traditions of a declining world*? Oaks could just as well have been Orson Pratt, anatomizing the benightedness of Gentile adherence to monogamy, or John Taylor, pledging to defend the righteousness of plural marriage against whatever threats of violence the state might offer, because to do otherwise would be to deny the promise of exaltation. "Utah's always had queer marriage," a writer for *Q Salt Lake Magazine* declared in 2014, not at all incorrectly.[4] Think again of that humble originary scene: Louisa Beaman, standing before Joseph Noble and beside Joseph Smith, on the eastern bank of the Mississippi River, disguised as a man. Such queernesses were as good as advertised. In 2017, preaching on retrenchment, Elder Oaks as good as recognized as much.

These ironies are by now, I hope, familiar. Here again we find an insistence on hypernormativity giving way, with clockwork inexorability, to the specter of nonnormativity, perversity, errancy, an aspect unexpurgatedly queer. No one should be startled to find that the politics of respectability are ever thus—that to insist on normativity is, necessarily, to fail at being normative. The much more telling pronouncements from the general conference of 2017 thus came not from Elder Oaks at all, but from Elder M. Russell Ballard, who in his address recalled to the Saints a spiritual imperative somewhat afield of the necessity of erotic propriety. He spoke, rather, of the urgent "need to embrace God's children compassionately and eliminate any prejudice, including racism, sexism, and nationalism."[5] (His remarks echoed those of Elder Quentin L. Cook, who the previous day had called racism "morally wrong.")[6] This was the turn that made the headlines—although these remarks, too, even if seen in the hard light of Elder Oaks's sterner comments, ought not to startle us too greatly. For these are the very voices of an assertively *planetary* Mormonism, of elders speaking beyond the frame of an escalating strain of American illiberality—the shadow of the white violence of Charlottesville, and of a more general Trumpian noxiousness, fell clearly across the conference—to reassert the Mormons' place in the vanguard of a liberalism, of a certain sort, gone global. Where once had been sexism, or racism, or nationalism, the Mormons promise a wider, even a redemptive, tolerance. The idea of this sort of rights-based inclusivity, with its several specifications, might strike us as contemporary. (It is, we could say, the argot of the progressive executive class, a TED Talk tuned to the Mormon gospel.) The grammar of redemption, however—of an insisted-upon erotic normalcy opening out onto vistas of liberal enfranchisement— very much is not.

Whatever else they accomplish, the remarks by these contemporary elders do us the favor of surfacing, in clarifying detail, the set of linked his-torical emergences, the vexed analogies, that have shadowed all this book's investigations into early Mormonism. We might put the matter, at its most frontal, like this: the early Mormons, I have been insisting, were queer. More precisely, the early Mormons were the purveyors of what was all but uni-versally recognized as a *deviant carnality*, and this is so much the case that we profit greatly, both historically and conceptually, by considering them through the terms offered by queer theory, queer historiography, and queer critique. In their counterorthodox imaginings of the body, of its divinizing capacities, of the reach and consequence of carnal pleasure, and in their vigorous disassembly of the sanctity of monogamous marriage, the Saints made themselves legible to their nineteenth-century countrymen as a spe-cies of erotic dissident. Before the advent of homo- and heterosexualities, before the tightening of the ligature of sexual taxonomy, the Mormons mapped out a life for the body that could not be corralled into easy con-formity with the codes of erotic comportment that were even then evolving toward solidity.

Of course, one potent way to describe precisely this evolution toward the bifurcated taxonomic distinctness proper to modern sexuality—as, for instance, Molly McGarry has shown in her pathbreaking work on nineteenth-century Spiritualism—is in the idiom of secularization. Think only of the famous Foucaultian story, wherein modern sexuality issues from the slow, steady migration of ritualized disclosure and its interiority-effects from the Catholic confessional to the psychiatric couch: the history of sexuality, that is, looks a lot like a secularization narrative, a putative disenchanting of the flesh in its movement toward discursive rationalization.[7] In this respect, Joseph Smith might fascinate us for the ways his theology dreamed a body *otherwise*, apart from its capture by the modern sexual imaginary, not yet reduced to its terms, or disciplined into its structuring norms. He exempli-fies, in this, some of the uncanceled possibilities of nonsecular embodiment, proffering for us—as I have put it elsewhere—an account of broken-off or uncreated futures, futures for the body that would not come to be.[8] On the ground of just that audacious imagining, and of the Mormon commitment to the institutionalization of Smith's visions, the Saints came to be figured in the many guises we have seen: as Mohammedan, Asiatic, Indian-like, of a dubious or counterfeit whiteness. The Mormons, I have been insisting, make for a vivid chapter in the racial history of American sexuality.

But the trajectory of early Mormonism *toward* a revised religiosity more tolerable under the disciplinary sign of the secular, which is also for the Mormons a trajectory toward eventual protection by the state itself, has nested within it a number of other stories as well, and it is to these that I wish now to turn. For many, we should note, the arc of early Mormonism toward American enfranchisement is at its heart a happy story, a tale of overcoming, of achieved comity, and of eventual triumph, at scales larger than are easily imagined. This is, in a sense, the official story. The LDS Church has long enjoyed describing itself as among the planet's fastest-growing religions, and without putting pressure on the measures according to which such a claim might be ventured we can surely say that Mormonism's fully global circulation (there are currently approximately *fifteen million* members, speaking some 180 languages) quite matches even the most outblown of Smith's visions for the future of the faith. Far from being stamped out, as seemed more likely than not for much of the nineteenth century, Mormonism has achieved a fully planetary sort of success. However violently induced, Mormon adaptation has led to an extraordinary Mormon flourishing, vast and increasing still. Or so this story goes.

And yet the precise terms of this story might give us some pause. For that narrative, that sequence—*overcoming, comity, flourishing*—is itself fantastically portable. More exactly, *it is the story of liberal enfranchisement itself*: the now-familiar narrative arc of a liberalism made adaptive to multiple minoritized positions, each new habitation doing its part to confirm the broad munificence of those regimes (tolerant, multiplicitous, demonstrably progressive) in which it unfolds. Like the narrative of secularization itself, this is the immobilizing and cruelly optimistic story a hegemonic liberalism most likes to tell about itself—and, of course, we can see why. It is a heartwarming sort of story, cinematic in sweep, broadly sentimental in outline, brimming with occasions for rich affective engagement and microsatisfaction. There are villains and heroes. There are scenes of undeserved persecution and hard-won victory, culminating moments of restitution, mutual comprehension, and respect.[9] It is a story we know well.

And it is a story that *sells*, more broadly than you might guess. For several decades now, in fact, it has been among the preferred narrative frameworks not only for "liberalism" in the abstract but *for queerness itself*—preferred, at least, by national queer organizations, mass media, the more secure and protected among us, and the state itself. Back in 2007, and borrowing from Lisa Duggan's work on the neoliberal rise of "homonormativity," Jasbir Puar gave us an entire conceptual grammar for the adaptation even of queerness, and of queers, to just these kinds of triumphalist narratives, these arias of inclusion into liberalism, law, nation, empire, the whole consecrated order of flourishing life. She called it *homonationalism*.[10]

We arrive here, then, at the principal historical and theoretical analogy that has magnetized all of this book's considerations of the Mormon story, especially in its arc toward an embrace of state normativity that was, if never quite voluntary, eventually avowed with great fulsomeness: I mean, inevitably, the latter-day movement of queer politics toward the marriage plot, toward the imperializing terms of liberal hegemony, and toward its own style of hypernormativity.[11] The claim I wish to unfold, by way of conclusion, is that the Mormons exemplify an early, halting, and especially revealing iteration of homonationalism. They are pioneers, that is, in their efforts to destigmatize their own religio-erotic errancy through the fervent performance of a countervailing normativity (in the dispensation of genders, for instance) and the championing of, precisely, the racial entitlements proper to the white imperial state. Much of their deviance was stamped out, as we have seen, though that allegiance to the racialized liberalism of secular politics would remain, to shift and transform as the complexion of liberal hegemony itself adapted to new iterations, and new terrains. But my cumulative claim is that these conjoined stalemates—avowals of hypernormativity forever announcing the perversity they labor to mask—speak not only to the Pyrrhic victories of respectability, or even to the intimacy of putatively secular political promise with something closer to "liberalism," with all its disavowed orthodoxies, its self-insisting narrowness of vision, its fast and slow violences. They ask us, too, to read the story of postpolygamous Mormonism not as one of a vast and expanding triumph but as something much nearer to cautionary. There are Mormons in every corner of the globe now, and pride flags in almost as great a number as well. We might wonder, though, about the conditions under which they are permitted, to the degree that they are, to flourish. What must happen to a religion, a cosmology, a style of world-making, for it to become tolerable by the lights of liberal secularism? What must it be? What must it *cease* to be?

HOMOSEXUAL PROBLEMS

———————

The yoking of Mormonism and homosexuality can seem, in these latter days, to have about it something less perverse than obvious, and possibly preordained; it has not, at any rate, required anybody's queer counter-genealogies of Smith's cosmology, or of his carnal theology, to find for itself wide and varied articulation. The Romney presidential campaign, the subsequent uptick in national attention to the peculiarities of this peculiar people, and the dawning of what has widely been called "the Mormon moment" all contributed to the naturalization, perhaps even the *inevitabilization*, of this yoking.[12] In truth, it had been in the making even before. From Tony Kushner's queer Mormons in *Angels in America* (1991) to the HBO prestige (polygamous) family drama *Big Love* (2006) to the megahit musical that was *The Book of Mormon* (2011), the drawing-together of the (now) mild scandal of Mormonism with the (increasingly) mild scandal of homosexuality has become a kind of midcult staple, and once again it is not especially difficult to see why. In the era of the gradual achievement of a series of national-level entitlements for queer people, how better to think about what shape *family* might take, or what belonging to America might look like, than by meditating on the Mormons, who after all can boast both a vibrant twentieth-century history of American patriotic exemplarity *and* an early (and, in some fundamentalist scenes, ongoing) history of erotic and familial dissidence? If you have in the last decades wished to think together a series of high-profile mass-cultural conceptual integers—*family, faith, sex, marriage, America*—the Mormons have been there for you, at the ready for your consideration and your use.

But the wedding of queerness and Mormonism has not been solely mass-cultural, and has not wanted for effects in and through Mormonism itself. To the contrary, these unnerving proximities have hardly been lost on the LDS Church—and, once again, the inculcated tactic of invidious distinction has come directly to the fore. Indeed, the strategy of hypernormativity we saw play out so starkly in relation to racial others in the nineteenth century finds itself repeated, today, with an altogether remarkable want of variance. This is evident across several recent Mormon contributions to campaigns pitted against homosexual entitlement, and the erosion of precious norms for which it is understood to stand. Perhaps most infamously, the Mormon church put its heft behind California's Proposition 8 of 2008, which dictated that "only marriage between a man and a woman is valid or recognized in California."[13] Thanks in significant measure to immense Mormon labor, pressure, and money, the measure passed. (It was declared unconstitutional in 2010, in a ruling ultimately affirmed by the Supreme Court in 2013.) The *New York Times* headline was pithy: "Mormons Tipped Scale in Ban on Gay Marriage." The *Times* piece is itself overfilled with delectable ironies, most of them played unblinkingly straight. Of the talking-points issued to Mormon volunteers in their wards, for instance, we learn that "church volunteers were instructed to emphasize that Proposition 8 would restore the definition of marriage God intended."[14] Whether that "definition" included a place for the righteous patriarch's multiplicity of wives, the documents do not say. Add to this the excommunications of 2014, and the 2015 specification of Mormon policy, such that "Mormons who enter into same-sex unions will be considered apostates . . . and their children will be barred from blessing and baptism rituals," and the grammar of anxious proximity coupled with vehement condemnatory distinction comes ringingly clear.[15] Such has been the strategic self-positioning of much of contemporary LDS policy: where there is any perceived errancy around the sanctified order of monogamous reproductive heterosexuality and what Mormon theologian James E. Talmage long ago named the "eternity of sex," the Mormons will be at the front line of its opposition.[16] Or, to put it differently: where there is perversity, so too is there an opportunity to assert, as against it, a normalcy *more normal* than the merely normative. Call it hypernormativity for the twenty-first century.

All of this is straightforward. More revealing than any of these exercises in projective disidentification, though, are some of the Mormons' own imaginings of the fate of queer people, of their place in a cosmology keyed to exaltation, and of the envisioned trajectories of their postmortal lives. Here, I think, we find an even more uncanny set of restagings, where the idioms of race and sex, as they unfold within the carnal theology of Mormon exaltation, come to be puzzlingly entangled. One exemplary text from this archive was issued by Century Publishing, of Salt Lake City, in 1997, and is called *Helping LDS Men Resolve Their Homosexual Problems*. Written by Jason Park, and most deeply indebted to the work of infamous gay-conversion-therapy advocate Charles Socarides—the book is essentially Socarides, gospelized—it is exceptionally depressing reading, perhaps never more so than in its passages of brittle cheeriness.[17] Park makes a good deal of Mormonism's generously humanistic anti-Calvinism. "To believe that God would give us problems that we could not overcome," he writes, "is to deny the power of the atonement and the omnipotence of God." And he

offers the usual frameworks and the usual prognoses: an emphasis on the
gift of choice, and the sovereign agential self; a pragmatist's commitment
to procedure (one does well to *lessen* impulses, rather than be frustrated by
failing attempts to *eliminate* them); a wholesale incapacity to assimilate, *as
masculine*, any conceivable form of male homosexual desire or contact or
sex; and a fixed determination to keep steadily in view the "plan of salvation"
and its promised glories. Park quotes none other than Elder Dallin H. Oaks,
who explains: "By focusing on and living the principles of the Heavenly
Father's plan for our eternal happiness, we can separate ourselves from the
wickedness of the world. . . . If we are determined to live by Heavenly Father's
plan, we will use our God-given moral agency to make decisions based on
revealed truth, not on the opinions of others or on the current thinking of
our world." One ought not to expect to live without struggle—"God may
not take away your friend's homosexual desires," Park writes, "but He will
stand by him as he overcomes the desires of the flesh by learning to control
the homosexual actions"—but exaltation, for the faithful, awaits.[18]

And exaltation, it transpires, promises its own miraculous alterations—
transformations no less astonishing than those the Mormons had promised,
back in the nineteenth century, to the other sorts of heathens, deviants, and
degenerates they looked to rescue and redeem. In a long address from September of 2009 to the Evergreen International annual conference (Evergreen is a gay-conversion group centered in Salt Lake City, cited greatly by
Park), Elder Bruce C. Hafen, while laying out his case against the conjoined
malignities of pornography, homosexual activists, and "the American Psychiatric and Psychological Associations," made a breathtaking declaration.
"Having same-gender attraction is NOT in your DNA, but being a child
of God clearly IS in your spiritual DNA," he assured his listeners. For the
Mormon God is, again, not the God of Calvin: "You are literally God's spirit
child," he said to those struggling with homosexuality. "He knows and loves
you. He wants you to find joy." And the way to this joy? Elder Hafen was
clear: "If you are faithful, on resurrection morning—and maybe even before
then—you will rise with normal attractions for the opposite sex. Some of
you may wonder if that doctrine is too good to be true. But Elder Dallin H.
Oaks has said it MUST be true, because 'there is no fullness of joy in the
next life without a family unit, including a husband and wife, and posterity.'
And 'men (and women) are that they might have joy.'"[19] It is worth marking the claim Elder Hafen was pursuing here. In essence, it is that queer
people—afflicted with homosexual desires and struggling through a world
that wishes only to foment and potentiate them—will rise in exaltation and

find themselves, by the grace of a generous God, no longer queer. They will be transformed in their exaltation, in spirit and in desiring flesh, *into straight people*, no longer burdened with the labor of preventing those misfiring "attractions" from blossoming into the malignity of deeds. *That* is the promise Elder Hafen made: bathed in the grace of achieved exaltation, your body will be made new, purified of its sorrowful maladies. You will be, in the grain of the flesh, heterosexualized.

Elder Hafen's promise of a sort of self-revisory redemption—an enlargement in exaltation that is also, and more directly, a body-wide metamorphosis—is startling, not least in a faith that, as we have seen in some detail, has so notably little to do with conventionally Christian paradigms of fallenness and redemption. It is not, however, unique in the annals of Mormonism. To the contrary, the promise of a metamorphic bodily redemption, *precisely that promise*, is woven into the sinews of Mormonism's foundational text. For this is nothing other than the Nephite promise of redemption to the Lamanites, recoded for a different set of embodied maladies. Recall again Nephi's prophecies in the Book of Mormon. The millenarian assertion at the heart of the text is that in the fullness of time the accursed, dark-skinned, and finally victorious Lamanites—the Lamanites who have destroyed the Nephites, and whose descendants would become the modern-day Native peoples of North America—will themselves arrive at a stunning redemption. 2 Nephi 30:4–6 reads, famously, as follows:

> And then shall the remnant of our seed know concerning us, how that we came out from Jerusalem, and that they are descendants of the Jews.
>
> And the gospel of Jesus Christ shall be declared among them; wherefore, they shall be restored unto the knowledge of their fathers, and also to the knowledge of Jesus Christ, which was had among their fathers.
>
> And then shall they rejoice; for they shall know that it is a blessing unto them from the hand of God; and their scales of darkness shall begin to fall from their eyes; and many generations shall not pass away among them, save they shall be a white and a delightsome people.[20]

As a range of historians observe, exactly this scriptural promise organized the Mormons' colonizing relations to the latter-day Lamanites in their midst, the Utes and Paiutes and Shoshone with whom they hoped, finally, to "covenant." "In Utah," Max Perry Mueller writes, "the Mormon leadership dedicated blood and treasure to build up a Lamanite people with whom they could finally covenant. . . . [They] worked to restore the Indians to their true selves—to make them Lamanites, and then white and delightsome Latter-day Saints."[21] The transformative grammar here, too, is unmistakable. The Mormons, on Mueller's account, were no ordinary racial redemptionists; rather, they "were unique in their belief that the ultimate success of their own covenantal community was incumbent on turning Indians into Lamanites, who would eventually become (literally and figurative) white Mormons."[22]

In his book, *Race and the Making of the Mormon People*, Mueller contends head-on with the language of redemptive metamorphosis proper to the early Mormon racial imaginary. He refers to this tenet of the Book of Mormon as a "vision of restorative racial universalism," and his work is taken up with a strange sort of melancholy about what he calls "the failure of these efforts to create a (relatively) racially inclusive people"—strange because this is (as we have seen) a particularly Nephite universalism, and strange perhaps most of all because the force of violence in these visions of redemptive transformation does not seem especially well hidden. It is not that Mueller does not notice that what he calls the Mormons' "(white) universalism" grades quite seamlessly into something nearer to, for example, genocide. Wakara, whose relation to the Mormons he deftly traces, recognizes quite as much. (In Mueller's words, he recognizes that "the Mormon project of building the Indians into Lamanites *by definition* involved the deconstruction of the Ute [hunting, fishing, and slaving] way of life.") Yet Mueller's work asks us to see something of the redemptive promise of this universalist vision, inasmuch as it seems to him to push against the regrettable *white particularism* that would so possess Mormonism into the twentieth century. And so the book performs a kind of prolonged vacillation among these points, at moments championing the Book of Mormon's "radical new racial hermeneutic" and at others inclining itself a bit more mistrustingly toward the Saints' "divine mandate of paternalistic redemption."[23] That "universalism" might itself be the very mechanism of violence—that, as Asad writes, violence will forever fail to register *as* violence when it is understood as the force required to bring the benighted or unredeemed into a brighter future, enfolded at last into the universalizing secular regime of life[24]—has considerably less conceptual pull in Mueller's account than you might expect.

In the treatises on gay conversion and the prospect of a bright unqueer future for struggling Mormons, the violence of heterosexual presumption carries itself quite without embarrassment, cloaked as it is in a language

CONCLUSION 225

of patience, pity, and pastoral care. *But these are cognate strategies*, and what expresses itself in the fantasy of gay conversion is an old, old violence. Very little conceptual agility is required to make this connection, or to see queer youth being fashioned on the model of the to-be-redeemed Native: Lamanites for the contemporary scene. Indeed, quite as if conjured by some obscure but irresistible force, the colonial precedent for gay redemption, far from being repressed or ignored, comes swimming right to the surface in Elder Hafen's remarks. Here is how he conceptualizes the struggle with erring desires:

> There's an old Native American parable, about a young brave [who] is brought before the tribal elders, who are concerned about his aggressive tendencies. One of the tribal elders is assigned to teach this young man that his anger is understandable, but he needs help. So he tells the young brave all humans have within them two dogs. One dog is good and peaceable. The other dog is angry and evil. The two dogs are in a constant battle with one another, since neither is powerful enough to destroy the other. The young brave asks, "If they are of equal power, which dog will win?" The elder replies, "The dog you *feed* the most."

Elder Hafen goes on to argue that "you feed the angry dog when you cultivate lustful feelings, view pornography, label yourself as gay, or associate with activists who aggressively promote gay lifestyles," whereas "you feed the peaceful dog when you simply stop fighting the angry dog. Don't let your challenge define your entire identity."[25] Native Americans, in this account, are no longer at war with their Lamanite identity, however much queer people be with their own.

Of course, no one much talks anymore about transforming the Lamanites into a white and delightsome people, redeemed in spirit and, in that redemption, purified in body toward the universalized holiness of whiteness—at least not since the shuttering of the Mormons' much-decried "Indian Student Placement Program" in 2000.[26] That would surely be accounted "racism," of just the sort that Elder Cook, in 2017, encouraged the faithful to recognize as morally wrong. The Mormons much prefer to boast about their multiethnic and polyglot inclusivity—note Elder Hafen's eagerness to borrow from the antique wisdom not of the unredeemed Lamanites but of the "Native Americans"—even if that vaunted pluralism is underwritten by a different orthodoxy, this one offering the promise of celestial release from a body suffering not from racial accursedness but from a lamentable erotic dysfunction. In each and every case: the metamorphic redemption is all. For a faith that otherwise comports itself so equably apart from any need or promise of redemption—think again of Smith's multi-faceted refusal of the coding of the world, or persons in it, as fallen away from God—these insistences are surely striking. They remind us that, even in the nonredemptive orders of Mormonism, certain ways of being in the body *do* demand alteration. For a radical theory of embodied life, the fate of the body—crossed by its materialization *as* race and *as* sex—can only be a matter of fantastic urgency, however these materializations might shift, alter, interweave, and revise themselves in the changing climates of liberal hegemony. Queer, Native, Lamanite: the Mormons, we might say, are rarely more normatively Christian than in their regard for those they understand to be suffering maladies of spirit woven ineluctably into the flesh. For *them*, the redemption is all.

PROTOHOMONATIONALISM

The point is not finally that the Mormon were racists but are now homo-phobes (however usefully such a position might be mobilized in local scenes of dispute). Nor is it quite that as racial normativity once was, so now is erotic normativity. Much of the argument we have been pursuing over the course of this book has been about the entangled *coarticulation* of race and sex under a regime of secular liberalism that, if it was achiev-ing hegemony in the late nineteenth century, is very much with us today, finding new extensions, iterations, and scenes of capture. That shifting and long-lived hegemony is, indeed, much of what makes for the challenge of postsecular critique more generally. For we are ineluctably within its terms, subject to the horizoning effects of secularism, its occluded forms of order, its encompassing metaphysics. Those metaphysics, as a host of critics have reminded us, are exquisitely difficult to bring into relief. Given the way secularist presumption has written itself into even the most incisive of our critical paradigms, "secularism" is less our object of thought than *what we have to think with*: the environing condition that lends stability—again, a perhaps falsifying stability—to the categories we presume we know. (On the corollary necessity of immanent critique, I think of Foucault: "I start from the theoretical and methodological decision that consists in saying: *Let's suppose the universals do not exist.*")[27] Two among these tenuously stabilized categories, I have been arguing, are race and sex.

On these grounds, I think we can gain a good deal of new conceptual purchase by thinking carefully through the proposition that the early Mormons, in their dance with state power, foreshadow the structure we have come to know as homonationalism. How, I want to ask, does such a conceptualization give us better hold on some of the categories that have been crucial for queer critique and queer historiography, as well as for postsecular inquiry more generally? In what configurations do we find race and sex and their shifting entanglements with misfiring devotion, bad belief?

I think it's worth considering, in close detail, Puar's deployments of the term in *Terrorist Assemblages*. Puar's first move there is to recognize the multiple, overlapping, and often crossed imperatives found in the repertoire of strategies that circulate through liberal arrangements of power. Accordingly, she asks us to note the curious *variety* of contemporary uses for "homophobia" on the scene of a globalized liberalism: the way it sometimes acts as a tactic of control and delegitimation (deployed as against queer people) and, in other contexts and in the presence of other actors, is itself delegitimating, the sign of backwardness, atavism, illiberality. This is "homophobia cast as properly conservative and traditional when it serves the political right and the state, cast as uncosmopolitan and hopelessly provincial when it can fuel anti-immigrant, counterterrorist, and antiwelfare discourses." What follows, Puar argues, is "a geopolitical mapping of neoliberal power relations in the guise of cultures of sexual expression and sexual repression," wherein racist imperial relations can be imagined, still again, as the labors of the tolerant in their struggle to bring the good news of sexual diversity to the benighted.[28]

We might think of it like this: in Conrad's *Heart of Darkness*, the brutal colonizer Kurtz works for the "International Society for the Suppression of Savage Customs"; "homophobia," in our current geopolitical mapping, offers itself to the West again and again as a *savage custom*, giving authorizing cover to precisely those "secular redemptive politics" Asad observes in imperial liberalism.[29] *That* self-ratifying power—inclusive, liberal, tolerant, secular—finds itself in turn the proper object of a loyalty, even from formerly exploited or excluded populations, that is rooted in its proffering (in Puar's great phrase) of "an innocuous inclusion into life."[30] An assemblage of power that prompts a fealty to the state on the basis of its tolerant inclusion of some minoritized populations (an inclusion "highly mediated by huge realms of exclusion"), that abets white supremacy by anchoring, in certain queer bodies, an alibi for the benignity of a liberal power no matter its imperial reach, and that maps out a collusive circuitry running between homosexuality and American nationalism: this, for Puar, is homonationalism.[31] It is not, then, an accusation, and even less an identity—*the* homonationalist, say—but the name for the entanglements of violence, tolerance, and inclusion within an order of liberal power keyed to the life it fosters, promotes, protects, and optimizes.

"An innocuous inclusion into life": to read that phrase properly is to recall that at the center of Puar's analysis is an invigorating turn to biopolitics. Indeed, Puar begins by taking up Rey Chow's invitation to consider Foucault's work on biopolitics as one potentially promising way into "the ascendancy of whiteness in the modern world," as Chow has it, and much of the subsequent work of *Terrorist Assemblages* is to situate the dynamics of homonationalism within a larger, fully globalized iteration of racializing biopower.[32] As in her more recent work about debility and capacity as chief vectors for the calibration of life under late-capitalist conditions marked by the need to extract value from wider and wider swaths of surplus populations, Puar takes up and renovates Foucault's vision of a regulatory form of power that works in tandem with the individuating ambitions of disciplinary power, takes the life of the population or species as its object, and operationalizes distinctions of race as (in Foucault's phrase) "caesuras within the biological continuum addressed by biopower."[33] *Biopolitics*, on this account, refers to an order of power that optimizes the life of populations, sutures the self-disciplining of individual bodies to larger groupings made coherent through their statistical regularities as projected over gulfs of time larger than the life span. It hinges on making live, more than killing; on securitization, more than punishment; and in stabilizing the conditions for a life that is, as it were, made free to flourish.

Foucault is speaking of European powers in the nineteenth century, though we need not labor overmuch to envision the American nineteenth century as a scene of biopolitical contestation and struggle. Dana Luciano, Kyla Wazana Tompkins, and Kyla Schuller have already produced searching accounts of the frameworks, the strategies and multiple domains, of a power routed through life and its optimizing calculation, fracturing, or refusal.[34] And, at least as I have tried to tell it, the story of the Mormons has made this exceptionally vivid as well. We have seen a dissident group, finding itself figured not merely as deviant but, in that deviancy, a species of *declining life*, propagating a belief-poisoned milieu, threatening the civilizational health of the nation, and thus fit to be exterminated. "I tell you Mormonism will never be destroyed until it is destroyed by the guns of the United States government," DeWitt Talmage declaimed in 1880, though he was doing no more than echoing Lilburn Boggs from 1838 ("The Mormons must now be treated as enemies, and must be exterminated"), *Putnam's* from 1855 (which had editorialized that monogamy "is one of the elementary distinctions—historical and actual—between European and Asiatic humanity.... It is one of the pre-existing conditions of our existence as civilized white men") and many, many others.[35] And we have seen, too, the Mormons' own efforts to countermand their status as racialized expendable life through a vigorous identification with both the norms of patriarchal sociality *and* the racial order of the imperial state itself—as though to wash away the stain of erotic errancy through a distinction-cutting insistence on their own patriarchal purity, their sovereign whiteness. ("Let no woman unite herself in marriage with any man," Orson Pratt wrote, "unless she has fully resolved to submit herself wholly to his counsel and to let him govern as the head." And then there was Young: "Negros shall not rule us.")[36] In these senses, we may say that the Mormons are America's own exemplars of a sort of *protohomonationalism*: a homonationalism in inchoate form and moving toward solidity in tandem with the becoming-hegemonic of a new style of political liberalism. To say as much is to recognize in the first instance that the operative elements of that biopoliticized arrangement of liberal power—deviance, racialization, empire—preceded the ascent of gay marriage, and for that matter hetero- and homosexualities, by some time. Or, to put this another way: homonationalism has a history as long as, and longer than, homosexuality—and the Mormons *are* that history. Theirs are the ghostly presences, the muted and mixed voices, that speak through and across the many scenes Puar's work does so much to anatomize. Sometimes those presences speak in the voice of Elder Quinn, preaching of the moral crime of racism and nationalism; and sometimes it is the voice of Elder Hafen, or of Elder Oaks, reminding us, irony-free, of the definition of marriage that God intended.

And yet the Mormons do more than remind us of the longue durée of homonationalism. More saliently, I wish to suggest, their story affords us as well a powerfully reorienting set of parameters for biopolitical critique, allowing us to begin to align that style of critique not only with sex and racialization, not only with gender and empire. For we cannot so much as begin to read the Mormon story, or read it properly, outside of a framework that tracks the indissociability of biopolitics from what might largely be called "religion," or from its routing through a calculus of suitable devotion and proper belief. This is a biopolitics aligned every bit as consequentially with the ghostly tangibility, the *matter*, of the spirit.

And this, it transpires, returns us with a new and recalibrating gaze to one of the strangest and most vexing stories of the emergence of biopower—in fact, of biopower as a mode of sexualized racial domination—that Michel Foucault would ever tell.

PROPHECY, PROMISE, INDIRECT MURDER

Consider Foucault's lectures at the Collège de France from the winter of 1976, which are among his earliest meditations on the matter of biopolitics. There, in a couple of his lectures from January, Foucault unfolds one of his many compact genealogies, and I want to dwell with it for a moment in the hope of bringing into relief some of what it might offer both for our purchase on the Mormon story itself and, more broadly, for a postsecular critique with its eyes on both queerness and racialization. In this century-spanning genealogy, Foucault is looking to account for what he calls "the discourse of race struggle," and what he most wishes to describe is how this discourse, which in its origins "was essentially an instrument used in the struggles waged by decentered camps," in time came not only to be "recentered" but emerged as well as what Foucault calls *"the discourse of power itself."*[37] He is wondering, in all, how what he will shortly call *racism* became the governing mechanism, the master-trope, through which an entire order of power would come to operate. "It will become the discourse of a battle," he writes, "that has to be waged not between races, but between a race that is portrayed as the one true race, the race that holds power and is entitled to define the norm, and against those who deviate from that norm, against those who pose a threat to the biological heritage" (61). What follows is the famous passage from which the title of this set of posthumously published lectures—*"Society Must Be Defended"*—would be taken:

> At this point, the discourse whose history I would like to trace abandons the initial basic formulation, which was "We have to defend ourselves against our enemies because the State apparatuses, the law, and the power structures not only do not defend us against our enemies; they are the instruments our enemies are using to pursue and subjugate us." That

discourse now disappears. It is no longer: "We have to defend ourselves against society," but "We have to defend society against all the biological threats posed by the other race, the subrace, the counterrace that we are, despite ourselves, bringing into existence." (61–62)

This, then, is at the center of Foucault's sense of biopower, this "internal racism of permanent purification," which will adjoin the techniques of optimization, discipline, and securitization to take hold of life at the level of the population and, through that statisticized figure, the *species* (62).

But the history of the discourse of race struggle is, as Foucault writes it, curious. "Racist discourse," he claims, "was really no more than an episode, a phase, the reversal, or at least the reworking, at the end of the nineteenth century, of the discourse of race war" (65, emphasis added). This latter discourse, not of race but of *race war*, in fact begins for Foucault as an altogether different deployment: as a sort of revolutionizing countermeasure, an insurrectionary mobilization that had proved crucial to the breaking up of sovereign power. And its origins, as irruptive counterdiscourse, are telling. Where once had been the discourse *of* power and its unbroken totality and efficacy, the "dazzling discourse that power uses to fascinate, terrorize, and immobilize," there comes something new, and disquieting (68). Shattering the identification of the people in their totality with sovereignty and its ordering power, there arises what Foucault calls "the discourse of those who have no glory": the "counterhistory of dark servitude and forfeiture." (In the light of this discourse, he writes, sovereignty appears as that which "does not bind [but] *enslaves*" [69, emphasis added].) This, Foucault says, is "the counterhistory of prophecy and promise, the counterhistory of the secret knowledge that has to be rediscovered and deciphered" (70, 73). The striking vocabulary here—servitude, prophecy, the deciphering of secret knowledges—is not accidental. For, as Foucault reminds us, "with this new discourse of race struggle, we see the emergence of something that, basically, is much closer to *the mythico-religious discourse of the Jews* than to the politico-legendary history of the Romans" (71, emphasis added). He locates the insurrectionary discourse of race war firmly in a tradition of religious dissent: in "direct challenge to the history of sovereignty and kings—to Roman history . . . we see a new history that is articulated around the great biblical form of prophecy and promise" (71). ("The Bible," Foucault notes, "was the weapon of poverty and insurrection" [71].) The discourse of race war that would be so crucial to liberal power, Foucault insists, commences elsewhere: as "a biblical, almost Hebraic, history which, ever since the end of the Middle Ages, has been the discourse of rebellion and prophecy, of knowledge and the call for the violent overthrow of the order of things" (72).

But the fate of race discourse, whatever its irruptive and emancipatory "biblical" origins, did not lie in insurrection. And so, having offered the discourse of race war as this kind of God-fired eschatological counterhistory, essential to the dawning of liberal revolutions, Foucault then goes on to narrate its détournement. For over the course of the nineteenth century, in Foucault's telling, precisely this insurgent idiom of counterhegemonic history-making is seized upon, rerouted, biologized, and in essence *reversed*. "The theme of the counterhistory of races," he writes, "was, finally, that the State was necessarily unjust. It is now inverted into its opposite: the State is no longer an instrument that one race uses against another: the State is, and must be, the protector of the integrity, the superiority, the purity of the race" (81). Race discourse at this point "begins to be converted into biological racism" and woven into what he calls "a sort of grand antirevolutionary project": "Racism," he goes on, "is, quite literally, revolutionary discourse in an inverted form" (81). And it is in just these terms that the new mode of sovereignty Foucault wishes to track, the biopolitical state, authorizes itself. Following the shift in race discourse "from the emancipatory project to a concern with purity," the sovereignty of the biopolitical state comes to be identified with "the imperative to *protect the race*" (81, emphasis added). Here, then, is the iteration of "racism" that comes into solidity as an indispensable component of biopower—or, as Foucault puts it in a later lecture, "as the basic mechanism of power, as it is exercised in modern States" (254). Foucault asks us to figure racism as "a way of fragmenting the field of the biological that power controls . . . of separating out the groups that exist within a population" (255). The meaning of this introduction of "a break into the domain of life" is plain: it is "the break between what must live and what must die" (254).

Making live and letting die: these are the basic imperatives of power under the sign of biopolitics. "The enemies who have to be done away with," Foucault writes, "are not adversaries in the political sense of the term; they are threats, either external or internal, to the population and for the population. In the biopower system, in other words, killing or the imperative to kill is acceptable only if it results not in victory over political adversaries, but in the elimination of the biological threat to and improvement of the species or race. There is a direct connection between the two. In a normalizing society, race or racism is the precondition that makes killing acceptable" (256).

Such "elimination," Foucault notes, encompasses more than murder as such, "killing" as such. It encompasses, too—in his inexhaustibly trenchant phrase—"*every form of indirect murder*": "the fact of exposing someone to death, increasing the risk of death for some people, or, quite simply, political death, expulsion, rejection, and so on" (256). Such, then, is his account of racism as made operative by biopolitics, linked for Foucault both with the colonial project, its state-sanctioned exterminatory campaigns, the empires of expropriative neglect it would build, *and* with what he elsewhere calls "the nuclear situation" and its endangerment of planetary existence, its exposure of the whole of the species to death in the struggle to defend and securitize it.[38] And, if we are following his swiftly drawn genealogical maps, that biopolitical racism emerges out of, and finds its origins in, *an eschatological language of religious dissent*, one that features suppressed pasts, race wars, prophecy, "the counterhistory of the secret knowledge that has to be rediscovered and deciphered" (73).

We have dwelled in the details of Foucault's account of biopower, its terms and its trajectories, because they carry within them some remarkable echoes and premonitions. For Foucault, this transformation takes two-plus centuries to unfold, bracketed on one side by what is called "contact" and the emerging of colonial empires and on the other by the ascent of the racial state as a scene of biopolitical securitization. A striking fact to consider: the Mormons walk us through this sequence, *this sequence exactly*, in what amounts to two generations. From a counterhistory of race war to the order of the biopoliticized racial state: the trajectory Foucault maps out *is* the trajectory of early Mormonism. This is the Mormonism whose origins lay in an epic tale of millennial race war, penned by counterhistoricizing scribes, who labored to preserve an esoteric set of knowledges as against their misunderstanding and repression in a doomed putatively Christian empire; the Mormon sacred text, that is, resuscitated what Foucault calls "the great biblical form of prophecy and promise" as a counterdiscourse and delivered it as rebuking judgment upon the fallen nineteenth-century Gentile world. And this is the Mormonism whose terminus was in an initially halting but eventually vehement identification with the racial state, a Mormonism whose leaders came to be convinced in succession of the irredeemability of the "Indians," the necessary servility of African Americans, and the benevolence of an American empire that *included* them. This, again, is the Mormons who come to us trailing their long record of what Hickman names, succinctly, "deplorable theological racism."[39]

From counterhistoricizing prophecy and promise to the order of the

racial state: this is the arc of early Mormonism; and it is also, according to
Foucault, that of the emergence of biopower. We might take such coincident
mappings as only the starkest indication of the force of biopolitical capture
in the postbellum United States, and of the desperate urgency with which
a subpopulation, designated as threatening and expendable, might strive to
secure for itself what Puar calls "an innocuous inclusion into life." For the
Mormons, as we know, that striving for inclusion within life took form as a
multifaceted hypernormativity, expressed as an allegiance to patriarchality,
to the racial state, and eventually to monogamy itself. Or we might take it to
underscore the rapidity with which secular discipline took hold in the postdisestablishment American world, marking out as counterfeit or heretical or
simply dangerous whatever religiosities failed to cohere around the liberalized grounding-points of Anglo-Protestantism. Biopolitical racialization,
disciplinary secularity: the arc of early Mormonism, across precisely the
investments and reversals Foucault sketches out in his compressed genealogy of the emergence of racism as a linchpin of biopolitical sovereignty,
seems to give direct testament to both.

The most salient matter for our purposes, however, is not the one emergence or the other. It is rather the *convergence* of the two: the welding of
exterminatory racism and the disciplinary sociality of secularism into a
generalized politics of life. For this is a politics of life in which belief and
its attendant practices—erring belief, false belief, overzealous belief, *bad
belief*—live like a heritable malady in the flesh of the believer, as we have
seen. But it is also a quality of belief that lives at the scale of the population,
the sodality, the menacing subspecies, such that a given "sect" can appear as
one of those "heterogeneous elements" within the order of life that must be
suppressed.[40] Think again of what we have seen of clergymen, of senators
and congressmen and sundry agents of the state, of novelists, memoirists,
and editorialists of every stripe, weighing in on the Mormon menace. The
Mormons have made precisely this exterminatory biopoliticization of religious deviance spectacularly, diagrammatically clear.

But the Mormon story does more. We remarked earlier that one of the
challenges of postsecular critique involves unlearning certain of the key
categories through which we are required to think. The occluded premises of secularism, its inbuilt teleologies and conceptual divisions, saturate
our analytic vocabularies, even those offered in the register of critique.[41] As
McGarry observes perhaps most pointedly, this is certainly true of many
of the to-hand narratives of conceptual emergence we inherit from Foucault, wherein varieties of power are forever being shown to emerge from

the rationalizing systematization of what had been scenes of religiosity. The implicit secularity of the conventional rendering of the history of sexuality and, indeed, as we have just seen, *the implicit secularity of the genealogy of the emergence of biopower*: it is easy enough, by now, to mark this. It remains harder by far to reconfigure the categories ("sex," "race") those histories have done so much to stabilize. What *is* "sex" if it is not the liberal-secular cynosure of selfhood Foucault suggests? What happens to "race" if we imagine it to be forged as much by rival conceptions of godhead as by the imperatives of settler colonialism? Can there be a secularism apart from whiteness, and its violent aggrandizement? For that matter: How do we inflect—and not merely inherit and reproduce—Foucault's own implicitly secularizing idioms of critique, adapting and expanding them by brushing, as it were, against their own grain?[42]

The chief wager of this book has been that the story of the early Mormons—the Mormons who were forever violating the codes of secular legitimacy foisted upon them—can do expansive work for us exactly here, in this labor. For in order to tell that story at all, and to take hold of its salient terms, we are required at the least to convert the implicit and perhaps underinterrogated secularity of an account like Foucault's, its perhaps too-easy coherence in and as a narrative of secularization, into a critical disposition that folds the disciplinary force of secularism *into* the story of the transformations of liberal power. In the absence of such a move, we are consigned to the types of stories we have seen: either to narratives about the Mormons as misunderstood protoliberals, awaiting their eventual reconciliation, or to narratives about the Mormons as prophecy-maddened "theocrats" running roughshod over the benign constraints of republican governance. In both cases, the supervalent ordering force of a racializing regime of secular discipline remains intact and untroubled.

But the Mormon story has helped us begin to see our way into a different sort of argument. In the light that story throws, we have begun to recognize "sex," for instance, as something other than the disciplinary rationalization of the body's capacities, a scientized coding according to which one's "sexuality" comes to be implanted, incited, mapped and graphed, distributed into a variety of hierarchies, taxonomies, networks of control. "Sexuality" *is* that, but it is no less a condensation of *styles of devotionality*, an instantiation of what we might call the inevitably carnal life of the spirit. That is to say that whatever might in turn be recognized as errant in erotic comportment, or deviant, or dangerous, or simply queer, is the *residue of misfiring devotion* that lives in the body, the trace remains of one or another failure of secular embodiment. (This is part of what it would mean to think, with Saba Mahmood, through "the pernicious symbiosis created between religion and sexuality under modern secularism.")[43] None of this, I suspect, will come as much surprise to the followers (in all senses) of Mormonism. With their ongoing and vividly compensatory pledges of hypernormativity, the Mormons would appear to know as well as anyone what it is be marked out, in whatever period of the devotional past, as *having been* deviant, dangerous, queer. Such queerness adheres to them even now, a tremoring presence beneath all that sunny stolidity. Rifle through the litany of the Saints' strenuous refusals and projective disidentifications and you will see, plainly enough, what a strategy of anxious counternormativity looks like.

In concert with these new angles of appraisal, the Mormon story has helped us, too, in the endeavor to conceive of "race" as not merely the biologization of phenotypic difference or the hierarchized ontologization of sociocultural variety—which, again, *it also is*—but as the conjugation of a set of relations to devotionality: to the forms of embodiment predicated in a given faith-practice, to the norms it observes, to its orientation toward privacy and publicity. Indeed, that conjugation of race in concert with the norms of devotionality functions, we might say, multidirectionally. Nothing is clearer in the Mormon story than that pursuit of belief-practices that deviate from the norms of secular liberalism is, in the most immediate terms, racializing. This we have seen across a multitude of scenes and texts. But the corollary to this is that one *effect* of racialization, among its many others, is *a suspect secularity*. Or, to put it differently, part of the ontologization of variation in life, its materialization *as* race, is *the desecularization of raced bodies*. To be racialized, that is, is to contend with the implantation of an ill-fittedness to the disciplines of secular belonging. So when, in the classic example, Du Bois famously turns from his social-scientific training to fashion a critical analysis of the *souls* of black folk, the implication is doubled. If, for Du Bois, the category of "soul" means to invoke all that falls hard aslant of the comprehensive disciplines of secular liberalism, and that thus, dialectically, heralds a corrective set of counterpossibilities to the racist orthodoxies around which the nation had built itself up, it also tells a grimmer sort of story. *The Souls of Black Folk* might prompt us to wonder if what Du Bois is naming "soul" is not in fact a constitutive element of the disqualification from liberal entitlement, the racial brutality, that is his subject—to wonder if, in all, it is even possible to be both nonwhite *and* properly secular.[44]

There are, just now, an almost infinite number of ways we might instrumentalize this insight, from the subtle to the crude, given how wildly over-stuffed our current moment is with the floating signifiers of racialized religion and desecularized races: the policed beaches of France, American "travel" bans, Breitbartian disquisitions on whether or not "Islam" is actually a religion, and all the grim fucking rest of it. The racializing discipline of secular liberalism is, we could say, among the least occluded governing aspects of our fragmented modernity. Take, then, only one example among the crowded multitude. Think once more of the broad evangelical mistrust of a public figure like President Barack Obama, whose fluency in the idioms of Protestant devotionality exceeded, by many powers, that of any comparable American figure one might name. And yet, from the perspective of a distinctively *white* Protestant religiosity, his practice could only read as a suspect devotionality, whatever its earnestness or political purpose or achieved oracular power.[45] Such is the desecularization of the raced body, where "the secular" figures in the key of sanctified practice, tolerable belief, good religion.

This, then, is what it means to think of secularism as *the racialized theodicy of hegemonic liberalism*. And it is in these terms that I have tried to take hold of the trajectories of early Mormonism as part of a developing biopolitics of secularism. For the Mormons, whose relations to the promises of secular belonging were excruciatingly vexed—marked at once by a strident refusal of its terms of legitimacy *and* a longing for whatever political legitimacy was required for sovereignty—for the Mormons, the answers to the questions posed by secularity, in respect to sexual propriety and racial authority, were not especially hard to decipher. They were written, with all needed clarity, in letters of blood and fire. The queerly infantilized "Indian," whose decimation in the West the Mormons observed closely, and in fact expedited; the "Negro" incapable of the spiritual discipline required to endure a priesthood authority, and so resigned to servility; the "Moham-medan" despot, with his cruel authority and his deviant carnal indulgence: these were only a few of the proximate figures against which the Mormons, with their weird sex and fantastic cosmology, would set out to define themselves, often cutting distinctions only the more insistent for being so vanishingly fine. Disciplined by state and nonstate authorities, figured in biopolitical terms as a veritably existential menace to the nation, the Mormons recalibrated the terms of that very cosmology, routing its promise of a divinizing body back through the narrow channel of dyadic reproductive heterosexuality and neutering its anti-imperial critique in the name of what would at best be paternalism and at worst a dug-in commitment to racist delegitimation. They became Americans.

* * *

Again, this story, and that trajectory, should not sound unfamiliar to us, here in the twenty-first century. I have said the Mormons were, so to say, a prehomosexuality version of queer, early exemplars of homonationalism, and I recognize that from some angles this might seem to be a sort of back-handed *endorsement* of homonationalism. Given the altogether planetary proliferation of a reconciled Mormonism, what could possibly recommend against such metamorphosis, or against that long-fought submission to secular discipline? It appears to have served the postpolygamous Mormons exceptionally well. It is safe to assume that some similarly undimmed faith in the bright futures of liberal enfranchisement stands behind a good deal of new-millennial queer politics, which is, of course, distinguished by its own drive toward dyadic monogamy and its own disquieting tolerance for liberal imperialism.[46]

And yet I would insist that if the long, bloody, paradoxical, and fantastically unlikely story of the early Saints does anything, it dissuades us from any bland enchantment with the many global "successes" of a reconciled Mormonism. I think rather of Joseph Smith, speaking in April of 1842 to the assembled members of the Female Relief Society, in the upper rooms at Nauvoo. I think of the varieties of vehement investment, still unchastened, swirling around his pronouncements there: "Who knows the mind of God?" Smith had said, and then, *"Does he not reveal things differently from what we expect?"* I think of the great breadth of counterpossibility condensed in these phrases and, in 1842, yet circulating around Smith, and the Saints, and the still-kindling project of embodied divinization working itself into new configurations, there on the eastern banks of the Mississippi River. And I think in turn of Zina Diantha Huntington Jacobs Smith Young, weeping by the river in her new home in the West, her unbounded spiritual ambitions having come into colliding contact with the realities of an institutionalized plural patriarchal marriage.

Modern Mormonism, of course, is not unrecognizable, in respect to its origins. Smith had conceived a faith around the premise that God's love for mortal persons exceeded, by many powers, what conventional Christian doctrine had been willing to grant, and that it was the determination of that God—a sibling human Himself—that everything most splendid and joyous about *living in the world* would persist, in still greater glory, in eternity: friendship, family, embodiment, sex (as well as acquisition, dominion). None of this has vanished from Mormonism, not at all.[47] And yet it seems to me nevertheless that we might look back on the story of early Mormonism and find ourselves struck by the many and grievous *losses* inflicted on Mormon life and practice in its transformation into still another of America's exemplary Protestantisms, competing—with whatever planetary "success"—in the secular marketplace of fragilized belief: curtailments, I mean, of its errant beauty, its counterhegemonic power, and of the great discomfiting wildness of its theological imagination.

You can see, I imagine, where this is leading. The world-making cosmologies of queer life have themselves not wanted for wildness, and errant beauty, and power, to be sure. They unfold around us, in an ungovernable multitude of forms, even still.[48] And so I hope that those of us ongoingly invested in what remains unreconciled there can be forgiven for regarding stories of Mormonism's achieved solidity and triumphant expansion with, let's say, a colder eye. We might find reason to apprehend there something nearer to a warning—call it, if you want, a prophecy—about the high costs of liberal success, and the narrow promises of secular belonging.

ACKNOWLEDGMENTS

WRITE A BOOK ABOUT SOMETHING A bit afield of your accumulated intellectual experience—molecular biology, say, or metallurgy, or American dissident religious history—and you too will know what it is to be deeply, mortally indebted to your interlocutors. I'm grateful to the following people for their patience, curiosity, and generosities of mind. Perhaps above all I'm grateful for their steady reminder that thinking in unfamiliar ways is, or can be, a joy.

Thanks first to my new colleagues in the Department of English at the University of Illinois at Chicago, who took a chance on me, and to the adventurous-minded students I have found there. Special thanks to Anna Kornbluh, Walter Benn Michaels, Jennifer Ashton, Madhu Dubey, Nick Brown, Kim O'Neil, Rod Ferguson, Lisa Freeman, Sunil Agnani, Mark Canuel, and the life-brightening Nasser Mufti. Thanks to the Chicago home team: Zach Samalin, Sonali Thakkar, Chris Taylor, Sarah Pierce Taylor, Lauren Berlant, Adrienne Brown, Andy Ferguson, Harris Feinsod, Emily Licht, Benjamin Morgan, Alex Ring, Edgar Garcia, Alexis Chema, Ivy Wilson, Leah Feldman, Ed Koziboski, Kathy Flynn, Jim Arndorfer, Catherine Carrigan, and Liz McCabe. David Diamond and Andi Diamond have departed for other climates, but we all know their spirit remains in Lincoln Square. Deep thanks, too, from coast to coast, to Jennifer Doyle, Heather Lukes, Virginia Jackson, Hester Blum, Reg Kunzel, Gayle Salamon, Mark Rifkin, Katherine Biers, Kyla Tompkins, Tasha Graff, Caleb Smith, Greta LaFleur, Justin Tussing, Brock Clarke, Ann Kibbie, Franklin Burroughs, Stephanie Foote, Kathryn Bond Stockton, Nate Vinton, Ian Balfour, Paul Erickson, Jennifer Mellon, Anne Helen Petersen, Brian Connolly, Pamela Thurschwell, and my beloved Gus Stadler. Sarah Blackwood, Jordan Stein, Jordy Rosenberg, Kyla Schuller, and Jasbir Puar have spent a lot of years making New

York a scene of tremendous happiness for me. So, too, did José Muñoz. Like everybody else, I miss him.

The greater part of this book was written at the Institute for Advanced Study, where Joan Wallach Scott convened a small group of thinkers to talk about, among other things, secularism and its complications. Without them, this book would be a far, far poorer thing, if it'd be a thing at all. To everyone in our SSS cohort, to Didier Fassin, to dining-hall stalwarts Jonathan Sachs, Cecily Hilsdale, Catherine Clark, Shatema Threadcraft, and Will Hedberg, and especially to Joan, Peter Thomas, Sara Farris, Johanna Bockman, Andrew Zimmerman, Julie Orlemanski, and John Modern: my friends, my co-celebrants of all things üseless, I am in your debt.

As ever, my whole wide family was in equal measure forbearing and encouraging, and I am supremely grateful for their unwavering love. No one smoothed my Maine-to-Chicago transition more deftly, or with more grace and heroic care, than Sophie and Eliza, young women I admire so deeply, love so much, and who continue to be standard-bearers, on a global scale, for awesomeness.

And what season of life would be livable without those friends-from-forever, whose ballasting hilarity I've relied on for (good god) nearly three decades? Great love and great gratitude to Karen Gliwa, John Dorr, Ilona Miko, Sandy Zipp, Elisa Tamarkin, and Mark Goble. I've known Dana Luciano just about as long, and she continues to teach me about all the most important things: Melville, red sauce, love. Beth Freeman's presence illuminates every corner of my life, which is a blessing unto me indeed.

One thing to say about this book: only a few years ago it would have seemed to me, in form no less than content, steeply unlikely. I have leaned so much upon the expertise of people who know greatly more than I about religious history in general and Mormonism in particular. Seth Perry, Katie Lofton, Nancy Bentley, and the peerless Molly McGarry have been exemplary in their generosity. At the University of Chicago Press, Alan Thomas has been an astonishingly generative reader, propelling the book at every turn toward stronger versions of itself. And way back in 2001—if the inscription is to be believed—none other than Jared Hickman gave me a book entitled *The Essential Joseph Smith*, effectively setting me on this improbable winding course. I will never manage to thank him enough for all that his wise and patient counsel has enabled. I consider him, as I hope he knows, one of my greatest teachers.

Lastly, during our weird year in Jersey, John Modern and Julie Orlemanski and I made a point of drinking and dining together at least once a week.

And it was there, at our Tuesday Night Conte's Seminars, that the ideas of this book came at last into coherence, lit up by the shining joyousness of their company. In the most literal sense, John made this book possible. ("I don't even know how to begin to write this," I whined to him some years back. To which he responded, memorably: "What you're going to do is, you're gonna sit down and fucking *write it*—that's how.") To say he is an inspiration to me is true, but it leaves off far too much of the delight.

As for Julie, I will just say that everything that's good here, *everything*, comes through her. But that, I promise you, is the least of her formidable magic. So it is with an eye toward all of our worlds still to come, and with a raucous and abounding love, that I dedicate this book to her.

NOTES

PROLOGUE

1 Jared Farmer, *On Zion's Mount: Mormons, Indians, and the American Landscape* (Cambridge: Harvard University Press, 2008), 59.

2 John G. Turner, *Brigham Young: Pioneer Prophet* (Cambridge: Belknap Press of Harvard University Press, 2012), 153. On the Mormons at Winter Quarters, see also Richard E. Bennett, *Mormons at the Missouri, 1846–1852: "And Should We Die . . ."* (Norman: University of Oklahoma Press, 1987). The Mormons had, at Winter Quarters, entered into a volatile intratribal economy. The Omaha and Otoe had had a contentious relation since the Omaha, in the earlier 1840s, fled to the area following attacks by the Dakota Sioux. By 1855 both the Omaha and Otoe would be removed from these lands to reservations located in Nebraska, Missouri, and Oklahoma.

3 Brent M. Rogers, *Unpopular Sovereignty: Mormons and the Federal Management of Early Utah Territory* (Lincoln: University of Nebraska Press, 2017).

4 "The Mormons," *Putnam's Monthly* 5, no. 27 (March 1855): 225–36, 234.

5 The archive of postsecular critique is extensive, and growing. Chapter 1 will provide a small critical genealogy, though here it is worth marking a few of what have been, for me, indispensable interventions: José Casanova, *Public Religions in the Modern World* (Chicago: University of Chicago Press, 1994); Dipesh Chakrabarty, *Provincializing Europe: Postcolonial Thought and Historical Difference* (Princeton: Princeton University Press, 2000); Talal Asad, *Formations of the Secular: Christianity, Islam, Modernity* (Stanford: Stanford University Press, 2003); Saba Mahmood, *Politics of Piety: The Islamic Revival and the Feminist Subject* (Princeton: Princeton University Press, 2005); Tomoko Masuzawa, *The Invention of World Religions; or, How European Universalism Was Preserved in the Language of Pluralism* (Chicago: University of Chicago Press, 2005); Gil Anidjar, "Secularism," *Critical Inquiry* 33, no. 1 (2006): 52–77; Tracy Fessenden, *Culture and Redemption: Religion, the Secular, and American Literature* (Princeton: Princeton University Press, 2006), as well as her "The Problem of the Postsecular," *American Literary History* 26, no. 1 (2014): 154–67; Amardeep Singh, *Literary Secularism: Religion and Modernity in Twentieth-Century Fiction* (Newcastle: Cambridge Scholars Press, 2006); J. Kameron Carter, *Race: A Theological Account* (New York: Oxford University Press,

2008); Molly McGarry, *Ghosts of Futures Past: Spiritualism and the Cultural Politics of Nineteenth-Century America* (Berkeley: University of California Press, 2008); *Secularisms*, ed. Janet R. Jakobsen and Ann Pellegrini (Durham: Duke University Press, 2008); Joan Wallach Scott, *The Politics of the Veil* (Princeton: Princeton University Press, 2010), as well as her more recent *Sex and Secularism* (Princeton: Princeton University Press, 2018); José Casanova, "A Secular Age: Dawn or Twilight?" in *Varieties of Secularism in a Secular Age*, ed. Michael Warner, Jonathan VanAntwerpen, and Craig Calhoun (Cambridge: Harvard University Press, 2010), 265–81; Kathryn Lofton, *Oprah: The Gospel of an Icon* (Berkeley: University of California Press, 2011); John Lardas Modern, *Secularism in Antebellum America* (Chicago: University of Chicago Press, 2011); Hussein Ali Agrama, *Questioning Secularism: Islam, Sovereignty, and the Rule of Law in Modern Egypt* (Chicago: University of Chicago Press, 2012); Talal Asad, Wendy Brown, Judith Butler, and Saba Mahmood, *Is Critique Secular? Blasphemy, Injury, and Free Speech*, 2nd rev. ed. (New York: Fordham University Press, 2013); Linell E. Cady and Tracy Fessenden, eds., *Religion, the Secular, and the Politics of Sexual Difference* (New York: Columbia University Press, 2013); Jared Hickman, *Black Prometheus: Race and Radicalism in the Age of Atlantic Slavery* (New York: Oxford University Press, 2017).

6   See Lauren Berlant, *The Female Complaint: The Unfinished Business of Sentimentality in American Culture* (Durham: Duke University Press, 2008). With its synoptic account of sentimentality as a fundamental grammar of the style of American liberalism proper to racial empire, *The Female Complaint* is, in my reading of it, a companion volume to Berlant's subsequent *Cruel Optimism*, whose terms—especially in relation to the fast and slow violences of liberal self-legitimation—will be crucial for how this book thinks about secularism.

7   I borrow the phrase "the metaphysics of secularism" from Modern, *Secularism in Antebellum America*, 1–47.

8   I am quoting from the "amalgamated text" of the King Follett Discourse, as assembled by Stan Larson and included in *The Essential Joseph Smith* (Salt Lake City: Signature Books, 1995), 232–45, 235–36. As observed by the editors of the Joseph Smith Papers, the discourse was transcribed by several observers—Willard Richards, Wilford Woodruff, Thomas Bullock, and William Clayton among them—and these transcriptions began to be condensed, amalgamated, and published as soon as the summer of 1844. For the reader's ease of reference, and where the texts are not so subject to multiple renditions, I will try throughout to cite from available print editions of Smith's writings, chiefly those collected in *The Essential Joseph Smith*, cited internally throughout the text as *EJS*; in other cases, the material gathered online in the Joseph Smith Papers will be indispensable. For multiple transcriptions, and something of the history of the discourse, see "Accounts of the 'King Follett' Sermon," Joseph Smith Papers, http://www.josephsmithpapers.org/site/accounts-of-the-king-follett-sermon.

9   "There is no such thing as immaterial matter," we are told in Doctrine and Covenants 131. "All spirit is matter, but it is more fine or pure, and can only be discerned by purer eyes." See *The Book of Mormon: Another Testament of Jesus Christ; The Doctrine and Covenants of the Church of Jesus Christ of Latter-day Saints; The Pearl of Great Price* (Salt Lake City: Church of Jesus Christ of Latter-day Saints, 1981), 266.

10 Joseph Smith, "Account of Meeting and Discourse, 5 January 1841, as Reported by William Clayton," Joseph Smith Papers, http://www.josephsmithpapers.org/paper-summary /account-of-meeting-and-discourse-5-january-1841-as-reported-by-william-clayton /4; Smith, "Happiness is the Object and Design of Our Existence," quoted in *EJS*, 159; Book of Mormon, Nephi 2:25.

11 Smith, "The Principle and Doctrine of Having Many Wives and Concubines," quoted in *EJS*, 194, emphasis added.

12 Fawn Brodie, *No Man Knows My History: The Life of Joseph Smith* (New York: Knopf, 1945), 294–95.

13 This was the germinal point of my previous work on Smith, early Mormonism, and the history of sexuality in nineteenth-century America. For a fuller elaboration of what it means to see Smith as a kind of "historian of the body," see *Tomorrow's Parties: Sex and the Untimely in Nineteenth-Century America* (New York: New York University Press, 2013), 104–28.

14 This is from Morrill's "Utah Territory and Its Laws—Polygamy and Its License," quoted in *At Sword's Point, Part I: A Documentary History of the Utah War to 1858*, ed. William P. MacKinnon (Norman: University of Oklahoma Press, 2008), 87.

15 Jack London, *The Star Rover* (1915; New York: Macmillan, 1963), 131.

16 See D. Michael Quinn, *Early Mormonism and the Magic World View* (Salt Lake City: Signature Books, 1987), as well as Quinn's subsequent *The Mormon Hierarchy: Origins of Power* (Salt Lake City: Signature Books, 1994); John L. Brooke, *The Refiner's Fire: The Making of Mormon Cosmology, 1644–1844* (New York: Cambridge University Press, 1994); and Catherine L. Albanese, *A Republic of Mind and Spirit: A Cultural History of American Metaphysical Religion* (New Haven: Yale University Press, 2008). My sense is that the strongest work toward something like a reconciliation of the esoteric tradition with the mainstream body of Mormon studies appears in the capacious scholarship of Terryl Givens, especially his *People of Paradox: A History of Mormon Culture* (New York: Oxford University Press, 2007), as well as *The Viper on the Hearth: Mormons, Myths, and the Construction of Heresy* (New York: Oxford University Press, 1997). A bedeviling work in this matrix is Harold Bloom's *The American Religion*, in which he famously treats Mormonism as both *the* exemplifying American faith and, as Smith initially formulated it, a restorationist religion so telepathically in tune with its Old Testament predecessors as to amount, finally, to an Americanized iteration of Jewish Gnosticism. See Bloom, *The American Religion: The Emergence of the Post-Christian Nation* (New York: Simon and Schuster, 1992).

17 I have been inspired especially, and most directly, by Givens's parsings of Mormon heresy, in *The Viper on the Hearth*, and by Samuel Morris Brown's fantastically persuasive account of Smith as a theologian not only in love with life but, as a result of this, "roaring in the face of death" (*In Heaven as It Is on Earth: Joseph Smith and the Early Mormon Conquest of Death* [New York: Oxford University Press, 2012], 12).

18 I am referring here, in order, to Richard Lyman Bushman, *Joseph Smith: Rough Stone Rolling* (New York: Knopf, 2005), 445; Laurel Thatcher Ulrich, *A House Full of Females: Plural Marriage and Women's Rights in Early Mormonism, 1835–1870* (New York: Knopf, 2017); John G. Turner, *Brigham Young: Pioneer Prophet* (Cambridge: Belknap Press of

Harvard University Press, 2012); and W. Paul Reeve, *Religion of a Different Color: Race and the Mormon Struggle for Whiteness* (New York: Oxford University Press, 2015). These will be, in chapters 2 through 5, the exemplifying cases of what I describe as the liberalizing strain in Mormon criticism, and I choose them not because of their deficiencies but because they are among the strongest, most edifying works about the Mormons I know. My claim is that we can see especially clearly, in these most highly accomplished works, the naturalized presence of secular presumption, and of the coordinates that shape our understanding of "good religion."

That presumption does not, of course, exhaust Mormon studies; it has, indeed, been more and more interestingly attenuated in much agile new work, and I have found a great deal of inspiration there. I am thinking of works ranging from as far back as Kathleen Flake's *The Politics of American Religious Identity: The Seating of Senator Reed Smoot, Mormon Apostle* (Chapel Hill: University of North Carolina Press, 2004) to Taylor G. Petrey, "Toward a Post-Heterosexual Mormon Theology," *Dialogue: A Journal of Mormon Thought* 44, no. 4 (2011): 106–41; J. Spencer Fluhman, *"A Peculiar People": Anti-Mormonism and the Making of Religion in Nineteenth-Century America* (Chapel Hill: University of North Carolina Press, 2012); Matthew Garrett, *Making Lamanites: Mormons, Native Americans, and the Indian Student Placement Program, 1947–2000* (Salt Lake City: University of Utah Press, 2016); and Max Perry Mueller, *Race and the Making of the Mormon People* (Chapel Hill: University of North Carolina Press, 2017). In these latter two the decolonial turn has been especially important. (Its most vigorous expression, to my mind, appears in Jared Farmer's *On Zion's Mount*, cited in note 1 above.) And this is not even to speak of the scholarship that has heartened and made possible this newer work—that of Jan Shipps has been the most important to me, for instance, along with that of Givens and Brown—or of the brave work appearing even now in venues like *Sunstone Magazine* and *Exponent II*.

Nevertheless, it is worth saying frontally: to the degree that Mormon studies is engaged, however directly or obliquely, in a project of legitimation, *Make Yourselves Gods* situates itself apart from it. It is committed to bringing queer theory to the scene of postsecular critique, and to tracking the forces that took hold of early Mormonism and bent it—often violently—toward the disciplinary norms of secular belonging. It is in that sense neither a blandly neutral nor an unsympathetic account of the plight of the early Saints. But it is not interested in producing the early Mormons as, in their moment, misunderstood liberals, or in manufacturing early Mormonism as another, particularized iteration of good religion.

19   There is, of course, good reason to do this, to side against nineteenth-century Mormon detractors and to manufacture a Mormonism more in step with the dictates of acceptable belief under conditions of a solidifying liberal hegemony—to make Mormonism, in all, a good religion by the lights of secularism. Those bygone assaults on Mormonism were not merely figurative in their violence; they brought with them blood and fire. In this respect wrenching early Mormonism free from its enemies, and from the whole conceptual vocabulary they brought to the scene of delegitimation, can seem to have behind it a certain moral-historical imperative. Though one may not be able to rescue Joseph and Hyrum Smith from the Carthage mob, on 27 June 1844, one *can*

contest the derogation, the willful misperception, and the delegitimating incitement that gave that mob its voice. I will speak critically throughout of the inclination to produce nineteenth-century Mormons as, as it were, *misunderstood liberals*, but this is not because it is a malign or discreditable impulse.

20 Michel Foucault, *"Society Must Be Defended": Lectures at the Collège de France, 1975–1976*, trans. David Macey, ed. Mauro Bertani and Alessandro Fontana (New York: Picador, 2003), 256.

21 See, as exemplars of some of these projects, Jacob Rama Berman, *American Arabesques: Arabs, Islam, and the 19th-Century Imaginary* (New York: New York University Press, 2012); T. J. Tallie, "Queering Natal: Settler Logics and the Disruptive Challenge of Zulu Polygamy," *GLQ: A Journal of Lesbian and Gay Studies* 19, no. 2 (2013): 167–89; and John Durham Peters, "Recording beyond the Grave: Joseph Smith's Celestial Bookkeeping," *Critical Inquiry* 42, no. 4 (Summer 2016): 842–64.

22 Jan Shipps, *Mormonism: The Story of a New Religious Tradition* (Urbana: University of Illinois Press, 1981), xii. See also Samuel Morris Brown's related remarks on "allowing Mormonism a freer rein" in scholarly accounting, in the conclusion of his *In Heaven as It Is on Earth* (307). I am heartened here as well by the work (as well as the conversation) of Seth Perry. See his "An Outsider Looks In at Mormonism," *Chronicle of Higher Education*, 3 February 2006, https://www.chronicle.com/article/An-Outsider-Looks-In-at/5520.

CHAPTER ONE

1 See, paradigmatically, Sylvia Wynter, "1492: A New World View," in *Race, Discourse, and the Origin of the Americas*, ed. Vera Lawrence Hyatt and Rex Nettleford (Washington, DC: Smithsonian Institute Scholarly Press, 1995), 5–57.

2 Gil Anidjar, "Secularism," *Critical Inquiry* 33, no. 1 (2006): 52–77, 62. The work of the other critics I mention here will be elaborated more fully over the course of the chapter. There are of course ways of thinking about the racialization of Christianity—or something tellingly akin to it—*before* 1492. For especially patient renderings of this history, and of some of its conceptual intricacies, see David Nirenberg, "Was There Race before Modernity? The Example of 'Jewish' Blood in Late Medieval Spain," in Nirenberg, *Neighboring Faiths: Christianity, Islam, and Judaism in the Middle Ages and Today* (Chicago: University of Chicago Press, 2014), 16–90, as well Nirenberg's more synoptic *Anti-Judaism: The Western Tradition* (New York: Norton, 2013), especially chapter 2; and Ania Loomba, "Periodization, Race, and Global Contact," *Journal of Medieval and Early Modern Studies* 37, no. 3 (2007): 595–620.

3 Hussein Ali Agrama, *Questioning Secularism: Islam, Sovereignty, and the Rule of Law in Modern Egypt* (Chicago: University of Chicago Press, 2012), 27–32. Agrama writes that "secular power works by rendering precarious and even undermining the very categories on which it ostensibly demands and aims to establish" Hence, his work "sees secularism as a set of processes and structures of power wherein the *question* of where

to draw the line between religion and politics continually arises" (26, 27). See also David Scott, *Conscripts of Modernity: The Tragedy of Colonial Enlightenment* (Durham: Duke University Press, 2004).

4 John Lardas Modern, "Conversion Diptych," *The Immanent Frame*, 18 October 2017, https://tif.ssrc.org/2017/10/18/conversion-diptych/. Anidjar, in a similar move (and similarly fortified by Talal Asad), puts it like this: "The two terms, *religious* and *secular*, . . . function together as covers, strategic devices and mechanisms of obfuscation and self-blinding, doing so in such a way that it remains difficult, if not impossible, to extricate them from each other . . . as if by fiat. Ultimately, of course, their separation would be detrimental to an analytics of the power they enable, support, and maintain, an understanding of its strategic and disciplinary operations" ("Secularism," 62).

5 Eve Kosofsky Sedgwick, *Epistemology of the Closet* (Berkeley: University of California Press, 1990), 22. A corollary piece of writing that stands behind the introductory efforts here is to be found in Bruce Lincoln's famous "Theses on Method," with its vigorous defense of "critical inquiry" in the study of religion and its insistence on reflexivity in respect to the "system of ideology" that encompasses the scene of one's own critique. For me, one strong name for that encompassing ideology is "secularism," which requires specific forms of attentiveness and reflexivity, many of which I look to specify here. See Lincoln, "Theses on Method," *Method & Theory in the Study of Religion* 8, no. 3 (1996): 225–27.

6 Among the countless appraisals and reappraisals, the work gathered at *The Immanent Frame*—a venue that originates in consideration of Taylor—has been especially clarifying for me.

7 Charles Taylor, *A Secular Age* (Cambridge: Belknap Press of Harvard University Press, 2007), 1, 3. Taylor's aim, he says at the outset, is to investigate how the change brings us "from a society in which it was virtually impossible not to believe in God, to one in which faith, even for the staunchest believer, is one human possibility among others" (3). For an especially strong interrogation of the first part of this claim—about what Taylor hypothesizes as the medieval inevitability of belief—see Stephen Justice's "Did the Middle Ages Believe in Their Miracles?" *Representations* 103, no. 1 (Summer 2008): 1–29.

8 On the nova effect as "a kind of galloping pluralism on the spiritual plane," see *A Secular Age*, 300, and also 300–313—where, for Taylor, it becomes entangled with the "buffered self" and the "matter of living in a disenchanted world."

9 José Casanova, "A Secular Age: Dawn or Twilight?" in *Varieties of Secularism in a Secular Age*, ed. Michael Warner, Jonathan VanAntwerpen, and Craig Calhoun (Cambridge: Harvard University Press, 2010), 265–81, 67.

10 Warner, VanAntwerpen, and Calhoun, "Editors' Introduction," in *Varieties of Secularism in a Secular Age*, 1–31, 24.

11 Jordan Alexander Stein, "Angels in (Mexican) America," *American Literature* 86, no. 4 (December 2014): 684.

12 See, for instance, Casanova's *Public Religions in the Modern World* (Chicago: University of Chicago Press, 1994).

13 Warner, VanAntwerpen, and Calhoun, "Editors' Introduction," in *Varieties of Secularism in a Secular Age*, xxx. As the editors of this early volume of critical appraisals of

Taylor note, one striking aspect of the thesis of *A Secular Age* is its location of the origins of secularism *within* Latin Christendom itself, and not—pace Weber, for instance—in the imposition of the norms and requirements of a developing capitalist order upon it. "At the center of Taylor's account," they write, "is an epic irony: that secularity in its modern Western sense is significantly a product of the long history of reform movements within Western Christianity" (15). Importantly, then, "the secular as Taylor sees it is not a force that assaulted religion from without; it did not suddenly appear from modernity; it was not contrived by Enlightenment rationalists; it did not entirely happen willy-nilly as the result of capitalism" (16). Later we will consider in more detail the liabilities, as well as the benefits, of this reconceptualization, though we can gesture toward them here. For if Taylor's thesis gives us the tools to begin the crucial work of anatomizing the inextricable mutuality—and not the mere opposition—of the religious and the secular, it also does a great deal to occlude the decisive force of *global colonialism* (also emergent "around 1500") in the remapping of Latin Christendom and its climates of belief.

14 Talal Asad, *Formations of the Secular: Christianity, Islam, Modernity* (Stanford: Stanford University Press, 2003), 191. Cited internally hereafter. See as well his *Genealogies of Religion: Disciplines and Reasons of Power in Christianity and Islam* (Baltimore: Johns Hopkins University Press, 1993). For expansions of the project, see Asad, Wendy Brown, Judith P. Butler, and Saba Mahmood, *Is Critique Secular? Blasphemy, Injury, and Free Speech* (New York: Fordham University Press, 2013), especially Asad's generously chastising response to Butler.

15 Nancy Bentley, "Clannishness: Jewett and Zitkala-Sa," ms. of a talk from C19, March 2016, Penn State University, 4. Another way to say this is that secularism specializes in the propagating of putative universals, which are then subject to hierarchized *deuniversalization*. So, secularism proposes, "family" is something all people have and know, though only some iterations of the familial (monogamous, dyadic, heterosexual) *achieve* full universalization. This is part of what Tomoko Masuzawa means when, in her splendid study of the history of comparative religion, she argues that secularism made "religion" universal and made Christianity itself, in her sharp formulation, "*uniquely universal.*" See Masuzawa, *The Invention of World Religions; or, How European Universalism Was Preserved in the Language of Pluralism* (Chicago: University of Chicago Press, 2005), 29.

16 Asad continues, "Far from having to prove to existing authority that it is no threat to dominant values, a religion that enters political debate *on its own terms* may on the contrary have to threaten the authority of existing assumptions" (185).

17 In this Asad's work follows from, and amplifies, scholarship like Edward Said's *Orientalism* (New York: Vintage, 1979) and Margot Badran's *Feminists, Islam, and Nation: Gender and the Making of Modern Egypt* (Princeton: Princeton University Press, 1995). And its insights speak especially forcefully, as we are soon to see, in the work of Saba Mahmood, particularly her *Politics of Piety*—though it echoes as well through more recent work like Joseph A. Massad, *Desiring Arabs* (Chicago: University of Chicago Press, 2007), Deepa Kumar, *Islamophobia and the Politics of Empire* (Chicago: Haymarket Books, 2012), Lila Abu-Lughod, *Do Muslim Women Need Saving?* (Cambridge:

Harvard University Press, 2013), and Mayanthi L. Fernando, *The Republic Unsettled: Muslim French and the Contradictions of Secularism* (Durham: Duke University Press, 2014). Which is to say that, whatever the shape or direction of postsecular critique as it has come to flourish after Asad, it is marked, indelibly and unabstractably, by its germination in the context of a long-practiced imperial Islamophobia, heightened after 2001, and flourishing evermore virulently since.

18   Joan Wallach Scott, in her recent *Sex and Secularism*, frames her study with the caveat that she will be treating secularism as, precisely, a discourse, which in her usage "is meant to signal that I am not treating secularism as a fixed category of analysis but as a discursive operation of power whose generative effects need to be examined critically in their historical contexts," with attention to "the ways in which the term has been variously deployed and with what effects." As she further argues, in a reflection on both the counterfactuality and *lived efficacy* of the secularization thesis: "Although it may not reflect the realities it claims to describe, the secularism story (secularization, secularity) does have an important influence on the way these realities are perceived. It is a story, moreover, that has served different purposes in different historical moments and contexts in which it is told. In the eighteenth and nineteenth centuries, secularism was deemed the progressive alternative to religion—the sign of the advance of civilization. In our current context, it is portrayed as a practice threatened by the return of religion, specifically Islam, although the Islam it refers to is as much a manifestation of secular politics as it is of the spiritual qualities associated with religion. The point is that *secularism is a political discourse*, not a transcendent set of principles, or an accurate representation of history. Like all discourses, though, it has a purpose and a set of effects that produce a particular vision of the world—a vision that shapes and is accepted as reality, even as it misrepresents history." Joan Wallach Scott, *Sex and Secularism* (Princeton: Princeton University Press, 2018), 4, 9–10, emphasis added.

19   John Lardas Modern, *Secularism in Antebellum America* (Chicago: University of Chicago Press, 2011), 46. His quote about the materiality of discourse comes from Foucault's "Theatrum philosophicum." Cited internally hereafter.

20   Though his attentiveness to a disciplinary metaphysics for secularism is distinctive, Modern is of course hardly alone in his resistance to the use of religion, and a putative religious pluralism, as part of a self-exonerating story about American democracy: an alibi for liberalism. He is enabled in this work by John Corrigan, *Business of the Heart: Religion and Emotion in the Nineteenth Century* (Berkeley: University of California Press, 2002), Tracy Fessenden, *Culture and Redemption: Religion, the Secular, and American Literature* (Princeton: Princeton University Press, 2007), Courtney Bender, *The New Metaphysicals: Spirituality and the American Religious Imagination* (Chicago: University of Chicago Press, 2010), and Kathryn Lofton, *Oprah: The Gospel of an Icon* (Berkeley: University of California Press, 2011).

21   "Disenchantment," Modern writes about antebellum Spiritualist science, "was not the vanquishing of ghosts. Rather, it was a matter of calculating them; a style of living with them, free from the bondage of ignorance, in a kind of egalitarian state" (*Secularism in Antebellum America*, 179). Ghosts, we could say, are forever revealing themselves to be but household spirits after all, until they reemerge as ghosts once again, and on and

on. Salient here as well is Avery Gordon, *Ghostly Matters: Haunting and the Sociological Imagination* (Minneapolis: University of Minnesota Press, 2008). On the simultaneity of ascent and critique in secularism's metaphysics, I'm especially indebted to the conversation of Dana Luciano.

22 On the recursivity of liberal self-legitimation, as it rhymes with the dimensions of self-replicating systematicity Modern lays out in his account of secularism, I am thinking in concert with Lauren Berlant's work on "the unfinished business of sentimentality," in *The Female Complaint: The Unfinished Business of Sentimentality in American Culture* (Durham: Duke University Press, 2008) but also in *Cruel Optimism* (Durham: Duke University Press, 2011); Sara Ahmed's work on unrequited love and the nation, in *The Cultural Politics of Emotion* (London: Routledge, 2005); Asad's treatment of "suffering," within "secular redemptive politics," as a regrettable but necessary entailment of "the unfinished business of universal entitlement" (*Formations of the Secular*, 61); and, in respect to the adaptive plasticity of secularism as an order of power, Agrama's *Questioning Secularism*.

23 Modern, "Conversion Diptych," emphasis added. I am heartened as well in this formulation by Mark Seltzer's work on recursive systematicity and modernity's self-accounting, in *The Official World* (Durham: Duke University Press, 2016).

24 Modern, *Secularism in Antebellum America*, xxxiv.

25 José Casanova, "The Secular, Secularizations, Secularisms," in *Rethinking Secularism*, ed. Craig Calhoun, Mark Juergensmeyer, and Jonathan VanAntwerpen (New York: Oxford University Press, 2011), 55.

26 Ronald Inglehart and Pippa Norris, "The True Clash of Civilizations," *Foreign Policy* 135 (March–April 2003): 62–70, 65. See also Inglehart and Norris, *Rising Tide: Gender Equality and Cultural Change around the World* (Cambridge: Cambridge University Press, 2003). Another high-water mark might be found in Susan Moller Okin's "Is Multiculturalism Bad for Women?" in *Is Multiculturalism Bad for Women? Susan Moller Okin with Respondents*, ed. Joshua Cohen, Matthew Howard, and Martha Nussbaum (Princeton: Princeton University Press, 1999).

27 Sara R. Farris, *In the Name of Women's Rights: The Rise of Femonationalism* (Durham: Duke University Press, 2017). Farris's book is an exacting exploration of the "peculiar encounter between anti-Islam agendas and the emancipatory languages of women's rights" as they are pursued by seemingly disparate political actors: "right-wing nationalists, certain feminists and women's equality agencies, and neoliberals." Following especially closely from Jasbir Puar's work on "homonationalism"—which will be of signal importance to the work of *Make Yourselves Gods*—Farris names this constellation "femonationalism" (2, 3, 4). See also Puar, *Terrorist Assemblages: Homonationalism in Queer Times* (Durham: Duke University Press, 2007).

28 Lila Abu-Lughod, *Do Muslim Women Need Saving?*, 146.

29 See Gayatri Chakravorty Spivak, "Can the Subaltern Speak?" in *Marxism and the Interpretation of Culture*, ed. Cary Nelson and Lawrence Grossberg (Urbana: University of Illinois Press, 1988), 66–111.

30 Saba Mahmood, *Politics of Piety: The Islamic Revival and the Feminist Subject* (Princeton: Princeton University Press, 2005), 7.

31   Asad, *Formations of the Secular*, 25.

32   Mahmood, *Politics of Piety*, 5.

33   Asad, *Formations of the Secular*, 62.

34   Mahmood's work has been enabled and amplified by a range of scholarship on sex
     and secularism in the matrix of colonial domination. See especially Margot Badran's
     Feminists, Islam, and Nation, as well as her *Feminism in Islam: Secular and Religious
     Convergences* (Oxford: Oneworld Press, 2008), and Rajeswari Sunder Rajan, *The Scan-
     dal of the State: Women, Law, and Citizenship in Postcolonial India* (Durham: Duke
     University Press, 2003), as well as *The Crisis of Secularism in India*, ed. Rajeswari Sunder
     Rajan and Anuradha Needham (Durham: Duke University Press, 2007), Abu-Lughod,
     Do Muslim Women Need Saving?, and Fernando, *The Republic Unsettled*.

35   Linell E. Cady and Tracy Fessenden, in their introduction to the volume *Religion, the
     Secular, and the Politics of Sexual Difference*, turn this point precisely: "The privatization
     of religion under the reign of secularism," they write, "leaves religion to find its stron-
     gest articulations in this private domain, the domain not only of legally protected belief
     but also of the regulation of gender and sexuality in the service of religious conviction."
     "Gendering the Divide: Religion, the Secular, and the Politics of Sexual Difference," in
     Religion, the Secular, and the Politics of Sexual Difference, ed. Linell E. Cady and Tracy
     Fessenden (New York: Columbia University Press, 2013), 9. The work of this volume
     follows from, and extends, the work of an earlier important collection, *Secularisms*, ed.
     Janet R. Jakobsen and Ann Pellegrini (Durham: Duke University Press, 2008).

36   Mahmood, *Politics of Piety*, 24, 9, 25.

37   Cady and Fessenden, "Gendering the Divide," 5.

38   Scott, *Sex and Secularism*, 7.

39   Scott, *Sex and Secularism*, 101; Claude Lefort, *Democracy and Political Theory*, trans.
     David Macey (Cambridge: Polity Press, 1988), 17, 19, 102, 120.

40   Charles Hirschkind, "Is There a Secular Body?" *Cultural Anthropology* 26, no. 4 (Octo-
     ber 2011): 633–47. I am inspired here as well by Asad's essay in the same volume of
     Cultural Anthropology, "Thinking about the Secular Body, Pain, and Liberal Politics"
     (657–75), and William E. Connolly's "Some Theses on Secularism" (648–56).

41   "Any power overwrites bodies with the fictions that its mechanisms require" is how
     Mark Jordan elegantly summarizes this central aspect of Foucault. See Jordan's *Con-
     vulsing Bodies: Religion and Resistance in Foucault* (Stanford: Stanford University Press,
     2015), 55.

42   See Berlant, *Cruel Optimism*; Ahmed, *The Cultural Politics of Emotion*; and Puar, *Ter-
     rorist Assemblages*.

43   Asad, *Formations of the Secular*, 59. Agrama's point, in *Questioning Secularism*,
     about what he calls "the deeper intractability" of secular power—its continually self-
     undermining elasticity—is salient here as well (26).

44   Modern, *Secularism in Antebellum America*, 21, emphasis added.

45   Kyla Schuller, *The Biopolitics of Feeling: Race, Sex, and Science in the Nineteenth Century*
     (Durham: Duke University Press, 2017), 14. Schuller is working here, in her elaboration
     of Foucault, with the scholarship of Jemima Repo, *The Biopolitics of Gender* (New York:
     Oxford University Press, 2016), and Ed Cohen, *A Body Worth Defending: Immunity,*

Biopolitics, and the Apotheosis of the Modern Body (Durham: Duke University Press, 2009). On biopower, and especially its relation to expendable life, see Michel Foucault, *Security, Territory, Population: Lectures at the Collège de France, 1977–1978*, trans. Graham Burchell, ed. Michel Senellart (New York: Picador, 2009).

It is worth saying here that one of the absences in this extended account of secularism, postsecular critique, and biopolitics involves the terrain of the inhuman and nonhuman. As Dana Luciano turns the point: "Biopolitics . . . is not only about whose life counts enough to be fostered or maximized, but also fundamentally about what counts as life, and what kinds of 'nonlife' it is counted against. Hence the quite literally foundational activity, even vitality, of rock and water and wind become crucial, both as formative to 'life' as structured by power and as sites for thinking possible shifts in those structures." Here, too, secular discipline is especially salient, not least in its dismissive half-approbation (as "animacy," for instance) of forms of regard for the lithic, the inhuman temporalities of geology, the vital life of matter that does not cohere into easily demarcated person- *or* thinghood. As I am telling it, the Mormon story foments a different story of secularism, one focused perhaps too determinedly upon aspects of regulation keyed to persons and sociability (and thus cued also to *belief* and *devotionality*), though of course Mormonism's fascination with what the earth discloses, with archaeology and history, suggests the salience of secularism in its relation to the non- and inhuman. For excellent work in the tradition of biopolitical critique keyed to the inhuman, see, along with Schuller, Luciano, "Sacred Theories of Earth: Matters of Spirit in *The Soul of Things*," *American Literature* 86, no. 4 (2014): 713–36; Jasbir Puar, "'I Would Rather Be a Cyborg Than a Goddess': Becoming-Intersectional in Assemblage Theory," *philoSOPHIA* 22, no. 1 (Spring 2012): 49–66; Neel Ahuja, *Bioinsecurities: Disease Interventions, Empire, and the Government of Species* (Durham: Duke University Press, 2016). Luciano quoted in "How the Earth Feels: A Conversation with Dana Luciano," *Transatlantica* 1 (2015), http://journals.openedition.org /transatlantica/7362#ftn17.

46 Michel Foucault, *"Society Must Be Defended": Lectures at the Collège de France, 1975–1976*, trans. David Macey, ed. Mauro Bertani and Alessandro Fontana (New York: Picador, 2003), 252; Molly McGarry, *Ghosts of Futures Past: Spiritualism and the Cultural Politics of Nineteenth-Century America* (Berkeley: University of California Press, 2008), 157.

47 McGarry, *Ghosts of Futures Past*, 157. As she puts it, "histories of secularism structurally underwrite histories of sexuality and function to elucidate some forms of sexual subjectivity while occluding others" (155).

48 For a strong account of the Peace Policy, its management of American religions, and its relation to nineteenth-century settler colonialism, see Tisa Wenger, *We Have a Religion: The 1920s Pueblo Indian Dance Controversy and American Religious Freedom* (Chapel Hill: University of North Carolina Press, 2009). See also Ake Hultkrantz, *The Religions of the American Indians* (Berkeley: University of California Press, 1979); Robert H. Keller, *American Protestantism and United States Indian Policy, 1869–82* (Lincoln: University of Nebraska Press, 1983); Frederick E. Hoxie, *A Final Promise: The Campaign to Assimilate the Indians, 1880–1920* (Cambridge: Cambridge University Press, 1989); and

Tom Holm, *The Great Confusion in Indian Affairs* (Austin: University of Texas Press, 2005). On the violence of efforts to suppress Native religions in general, and the Ghost Dance in particular, see Louis S. Warren, *God's Red Son: The Ghost Dance Religion and the Making of Modern America* (New York: Basic Books, 2017).

49 "Code of Indian Offenses," Department of the Interior, Office of Indian Affairs, https://en.wikisource.org/wiki/Code_of_Indian_Offenses.

50 Scott Lauria Morgensen, "The Biopolitics of Settler Colonialism: Right Here, Right Now," *Settler Colonial Studies* 1, no. 1 (2011): 52–76.

51 Peter Coviello and Jared Hickman, "Introduction: After the Postsecular," *American Literature* 86, no. 4 (2014): 645–54.

52 Mahmood, *Politics of Piety*, 5.

53 On the revisionary conceptual work of postsecular critique, see also Tracy Fessenden, "The Problem of the Postsecular," *American Literary History* 26, no. 1 (2014): 154–67.

54 Warner, VanAntwerpen, and Calhoun, "Editors' Introduction," 27.

55 Casanova, "A Secular Age: Dawn or Twilight?" 277. See also Peter van der Veer's *Imperial Encounters: Religion and Modernity in India and Britain* (Princeton: Princeton University Press, 2001).

56 Gil Anidjar, "Secularism," *Critical Inquiry* 33 (Autumn 2006): 52–77, 56, 62, 60. Anidjar's conjoining of an Asadian critique of secular hegemony with the work of Edward Said is enabled especially by work like Peter van der Veer's in *Imperial Encounters*, and speaks resonantly alongside historian Tomoko Masuzawa's splendid work in *The Invention of World Religions*.

57 Masuzawa, *The Invention of World Religions*, 29, 20. The phrase "uniquely universal" captures deftly Bentley's point about "the secularization two-step" and secularism's propagation of universalizing categories that are themselves, in turn, fractured and hierarchized.

58 Masuzawa, *The Invention of World Religions*, 23, 29. Her work ultimately suggests that "the discourse of world religions, . . . when it finally erupted in the early twentieth century, facilitated the conversion of the Eurohegemonic claim from one context to another—that is, from the older discourse of Christian supremacy (now considered bankrupt by many liberal Christians) to the new discourse of world religions, couched in the language of pluralism and diversity" (29).

59 Sylvia Wynter, "1492: A New World View," in *Race, Discourse, and the Origin of the Americas*, ed. Vera Lawrence Hyatt and Rex Nettleford (Washington, DC: Smithsonian Institute Scholarly Press, 1995), 5–57. I'm fortified here by Alexander G. Weheliye's reading of Wynter in *Habeas Viscus: Racializing Assemblages, Biopolitics, and Black Feminist Theories of the Human* (Durham: Duke University Press, 2014), 24–29, as well as by the work gathered by Katherine McKittrick in *Sylvia Wynter: On Being Human as Praxis* (Durham: Duke University Press, 2014). See also Édouard Glissant, *Caribbean Discourse: Selected Essays* (Charlottesville: University Press of Virginia, 1999); Walter D. Mignolo, *Local Histories/Global Designs: Coloniality, Subaltern Knowledges, and Border Thinking* (Princeton: Princeton University Press, 2000); Edward Said, *Orientalism* (New York: Vintage, 1979); Hortense Spillers, "All the Things You Could Be by Now If

Sigmund Freud's Wife Was Your Mother," in Spiller, *Black, White, and in Color* (Chicago: University of Chicago Press, 2003); and Massad, *Desiring Arabs.*

60 Jared Hickman, *Black Prometheus: Race and Radicalism in the Age of Atlantic Slavery* (New York: Oxford University Press, 2017), 39. Hickman writes of the "radically unforeseen heterogeneity within the horizon of a radical homogeneity that constitutes an inescapable network of relation for the foreseeable future—the emergent singularity of the globe." He names what emerges here "the Babel of 1492—the theologically provocative experience of sudden, radical differentiation of the human sphere" (13). Hence his larger claim that race "is *ontological* in a historically qualified sense": for it is "woven into the global cosmos by virtue of its historical role in mapping—not only retrospectively and descriptively but prospectively and prescriptively—that cosmos." His work thus "offers an understanding of race not as abstract metalanguage that for some reason evidently attaches to and engulfs other social relations but as a historically specific metacosmography meant to chart the lived eschatology of global life" (51). We will consider Hickman's work more closely in the chapters ahead. For now it is perhaps worth remarking that Hickman's vision of race as the signal category of globalized modernity gets us, in certain measures, less far than we might wish toward a conceptualization of racialization as a *multiplicitous* carnal investiture—one from which the materializations of sex and gender are no less determining than those forged in the metacosmic drama of colonial misadventure. Nevertheless, it is among the most exhaustive, persuasive, and conceptually rich visions I know of the supersaturation of race with theological force, and of the inescapably racial character of a secularism made in the machinery of Atlantic slavery.

61 Hickman, *Black Prometheus*, 304, 54, 134.

62 Spillers, "All the Things You Could Be," 380.

63 Puar, *Terrorist Assemblages*, 31.

64 Asad, *Formations of the Secular*, 59.

CHAPTER TWO

————————

1 For a full account of the wedding of Louisa Beaman, and its recollection, see Todd Compton, *In Sacred Loneliness: The Plural Wives of Joseph Smith* (Salt Lake City: Signature Books, 1997), 57–60, 59. See also Richard S. Van Wagoner, *Mormon Polygamy: A History* (Salt Lake City: Signature Books, 1989), 6, 23–24.

2 Quoted in Wilford Woodruff's journal, 22 January 1869, cited in Compton, *In Sacred Loneliness*, 653.

3 According to Compton's accounting, Smith had likely married both Fanny Alger and Lucinda Pendleton, in addition to Emma Smith. See Compton, *In Sacred Loneliness*, 25–54.

4 Compton, *In Sacred Loneliness*, 59.

5 Compton, *In Sacred Loneliness*, 59.

6   The entry is from Franklin D. Richards's journal, 22 January 1869. Both Woodruff, quoted above, and Richards, are recounting the conversation of Joseph Noble. See Compton, *In Sacred Loneliness*, 654. For more on Noble, and especially on the multiple and not always coincident recollections of this scene—some putting it under an elm tree, some under an apple tree, and some in Noble's home—see David L. Clark, *Joseph Bates Noble: Polygamy and the Temple Lot Case* (Salt Lake City: University of Utah Press, 2009), 69–87, 74.

7   See also reference to Louisa's disguise in Richard Lyman Bushman, *Joseph Smith: Rough Stone Rolling* (New York: Knopf, 2005), 438.

8   Joseph Smith, *The Essential Joseph Smith* (Salt Lake City: Signature Books, 1995), 245. As noted earlier, the King Follett Discourse comes to us in multiple transcriptions; I am citing here the "amalgamated" text. (It is from Willard Richards's transcription that we get the famous quote about not blaming the Saints for failing to believe his own history. See "Discourse, 7 April 1844, as Reported by Willard Richards," pp. [67–71], Joseph Smith Papers, http://www.josephsmithpapers.org/paper-summary/discourse -7-april-1844-as-reported-by-willard-richards/1.) Where I can, and where the texts are not so subject to multiple and disparate renditions, I will try throughout to cite from available print editions of Smith's writings; in other cases, as I have mentioned, I will rely on the material gathered online in the Joseph Smith Papers.

9   Talal Asad, *Formations of the Secular: Christianity, Islam, Modernity* (Stanford: Stanford University Press, 2003), 23.

10   Compton, *In Sacred Loneliness*, 59. Laurel Thatcher Ulrich puts it like this: "Plural marriage generated conflict and gossip. Some men competed for women. Wives as well as husbands negotiated alliances and dispensed advice. Emotions pivoted from rage to melancholy and from joy to despondency." This stages, in my reading, something of the eroticized sociality proper to scenes in which the norms of sexual propriety are held in abeyance or rebuked: a distinctively queer sociality. See Ulrich's *A House Full of Females: Plural Marriage and Women's Rights in Early Mormonism, 1835–1870* (New York: Knopf, 2017), 99.

11   Samuel Morris Brown, *In Heaven as It Is on Earth: Joseph Smith and the Early Mormon Conquest of Death* (New York: Oxford University Press, 2012), 307. See also Jan Shipps's remarks on method in her preface to *Mormonism: The Story of a New Religious Tradition* (Urbana: University of Illinois Press, 1981).

12   My own sense is that this critical disposition, which is crucial to the labor of immanent critique that secularism demands, is written deeply into the practices of queer close reading in which my own work has long been engaged. As I mentioned earlier, when accounting for Whitman's erotic representations I have not done so in the interest of proving, as if prosecutorially, that he did or did not have the sex he suggests. This is not for me a matter of surface reading, or of some reading pitching itself as against the putative paranoia of "critique," since none of these framings seem to me to do much justice to the actual *labor* of critique—which is to say, the labor of prying apart our naturalized presumptions from the objects we wish to account for. It is the labor, in other words, of taking up our object in such a way that its terms might crack open a little, fissure or reshape—however momentarily—the frames in which thought, however

critical *or* presumptively reparative, necessarily transpires. For two strong, differently inflected accounts of the perils of surface reading and its satellite undertakings, see Julie Orlemanski, "Scales of Reading." *Exemplaria: Medieval, Early Modern Theory* 26, no. 2–3 (2014): 215–33, and Kathryn Bond Stockton, "Reading as Kissing, Sex with Ideas: 'Lesbian' Barebacking?" *Los Angeles Review of Books*, 8 March 2015, https://lareviewofbooks .org/essay/reading-kissing-sex-ideas-lesbian-barebacking.

13 Harold Bloom, *The American Religion: The Emergence of the Post-Christian Nation* (New York: Simon and Schuster, 1992), 106.

14 Doctrine and Covenants 132:21–22.

15 This is from Morrill's "Utah Territory and Its Laws—Polygamy and Its License," quoted in *At Sword's Point, Part I: A Documentary History of the Utah War to 1858*, ed. William P. MacKinnon (Norman: University of Oklahoma Press, 2008), 87. J. Spenser Fluhman's is perhaps the most detailed and persuasive account of the many idioms of anti-Mormonism in the nineteenth century, many of which return to the malignant (and sexually motivated) counterfeiting of religiosity by its leaders. Fluhman, *"A Peculiar People": Anti-Mormonism and the Making of Religion in Nineteenth-Century America* (Chapel Hill: University of North Carolina Press, 2012).

16 Bushman, *Rough Stone Rolling*, 458. See, too, Bushman's remarks on what some take to be a kind of "rhetorical incongruity" in Smith, by which he means his persistent running-together of quotidian detail and "everyday affairs" with the stuff of divine revelation. For Bushman, the creation of a "rhetorical world in which the Lord God and weak and faltering people work together" is one of the chief effects of Smith's vernacular. "The 'Little, Narrow Prison' of Language: The Rhetoric of Revelation," in Bushman, *Believing History: Latter-day Saint Essays*, ed. Reid L. Neilson and Jed Woodworth (New York: Columbia University Press, 2004), 248–61, 257.

17 See also "History, circa Summer 1832," p. 1, Joseph Smith Papers, http://www.joseph smithpapers.org/paper-summary/history-circa-summer-1832/1.

18 Terryl L. Givens, *The Viper on the Hearth: Mormons, Myths, and the Construction of Heresy*, updated ed. (New York: Oxford University Press, 2013), 89–90.

19 See also "Letter to the Elders of the Church, 30 November–1 December 1835," p. 228, Joseph Smith Papers, http://www.josephsmithpapers.org/paper-summary/letter-to-the -elders-of-the-church-30-november-1-december-1835/4.

20 See also "Discourse, 22 January 1843, as Reported by Wilford Woodruff," p. [4], Joseph Smith Papers, http://www.josephsmithpapers.org/paper-summary/discourse-22 -january-1843-as-reported-by-wilford-woodruff/1.

21 "Letter to Silas Smith, 26 September 1833," p. 5, Joseph Smith Papers, http://www .josephsmithpapers.org/paper-summary/letter-to-silas-smith-26-september-1833/4.

22 The idea of "Christian primitivism" is something of a cliché in Mormon appraisals, offered with greater and lesser degrees of incisiveness. Harold Bloom famously works one angle of this (though for him what is restored is, most fundamentally, Jewish theurgy), and Richard Hughes and C. Leonard Allen place Mormonism firmly within a longer history of American Christian Primitivism in their *Illusions of Innocence: Protestant Primitivism in America, 1630–1875*. D. Michael Quinn's is a related, detailed account of "magic," which speaks usefully to the metaphysical readings we find in both

John L. Brooke's *The Refiner's Fire* and Catherine Albanese's *A Republic of Mind and Spirit: A Cultural History of American Metaphysical Religion*, though I think the very strongest parsing of Mormon restoration—of what, precisely, is restored, and in what terms—appears in Jan Shipps's *Mormonism: The Story of a New Religious Tradition*. I have learned a great deal from this scholarship, though my own work follows out different emphases, largely as part of the effort to unloosen the grip of presumptions that *divide* the primitive from the modern, the magic from the real, in the first place. These accounts, in other words, surrender a bit too readily, on the ground of their formulation, to precisely those secular distinctions whose emergence and solidification, alongside the emergence of a Mormon theology in many respects counter to them, I am hoping to trace. See Harold Bloom, *The American Religion: The Emergence of the Post-Christian Nation* (New York: Simon and Schuster, 1992); Richard Hughes and C. Leonard Allen, *Illusions of Innocence: Protestant Primitivism in America, 1630–1875* (Chicago: University of Chicago Press, 1988); D. Michael Quinn, *Early Mormonism and the Magic World View* (Salt Lake City: Signature Books, 1987); John L. Brooke, *The Refiner's Fire: The Making of Mormon Cosmology, 1644–1844* (New York: Cambridge University Press, 1994); Catherine L. Albanese, *A Republic of Mind and Spirit: A Cultural History of American Metaphysical Religion* (New Haven: Yale University Press, 2008); Shipps, *Mormonism*.

23 The details of this claim will emerge more fully in chapter 4. See, on Smith's translations, Richard Bushman, "Joseph Smith as Translator," in *Believing History*, 233–47.

24 Bloom, *The American Religion*, 99.

25 For a vigorous genealogical accounting of these dialectics of disenchantment, see especially Modern, *Secularism in Antebellum America*, 119–24. As we will see, Native "spirituality" would prove crucial to the secular mechanics of reenchantment.

26 Ralph Waldo Emerson, "Nature," from *Essays: Second Series* (1844) in *Ralph Waldo Emerson*, ed. Richard Poirier (New York: Oxford University Press, 1990), 235–36. In my brief descriptions of Emerson's project I am thinking most in concert with Poirier, *The Renewal of Literature: Emersonian Reflections* (New York: Random House, 1987), as well as Barbara Packer, *Emerson's Fall: A New Interpretation of the Major Essays* (New York: Continuum, 1982), Eduardo Cadava, *Emerson and the Climates of History* (Stanford: Stanford University Press, 1997), and Sharon Cameron, *Impersonality: Seven Essays* (Chicago: University of Chicago Press, 2007).

27 Modern, *Secularism in Antebellum America*, xvi, emphasis added.

28 "There is no such thing as immaterial matter," we are told in Doctrine and Covenants 131. "All spirit is matter, but it is more fine or pure, and can only be discerned by purer eyes." See *The Book of Mormon: Another Testament of Jesus Christ; The Doctrine and Covenants of the Church of Jesus Christ of Latter-day Saints; The Pearl of Great Price* (Salt Lake City: Church of Jesus Christ of Latter-day Saints, 1981), 266.

29 Jared Hickman, "'Creative Literalism': The Mormon Imagination," *Books and Culture: A Christian Review*, (May–June 2011), http://www.booksandculture.com/articles/2011/mayjun/creativeliteralism.html.

30 Again, I am quoting from the "amalgamated text" of the King Follett Discourse, as assembled by Stan Larson and included in *The Essential Joseph Smith*, 232–45. The

discourse was transcribed by several observers—Willard Richards, Wilford Woodruff, Thomas Bullock, William Clayton—and these transcriptions began to be condensed, amalgamated, and published as soon as the summer of 1844. For multiple transcriptions, and something of the history of the discourse, see "Accounts of the 'King Follett' Sermon," Joseph Smith Papers, http://www.josephsmithpapers.org/site/accounts-of -the-king-follett-sermon.

31 The charge of "muddy materialism" appears among the annotated horrors in the editorial "The Mormons," *Putnam's Monthly* 5, no. 27 (March 1855): 225–36.

32 See "Discourse, [5 January 1841], as Reported by Unknown Scribe–A," p. [1], Joseph Smith Papers, http://www.josephsmithpapers.org/paper-summary/discourse-5-january -1841-as-reported-by-unknown-scribe-a/1.

33 John C. Bennett, *The History of the Saints; or, An Exposé of Joe Smith and Mormonism* (Boston: Leland and Whiting, 1842), 218.

34 Bennett, *History of the Saints*, 306–7.

35 Bushman, *Rough Stone Rolling*, 465. For a more local reading, and for the claim that the book's "greatest influence was felt in western Illinois, since many eastern papers considered it a blend of conventional charges and outlandish tales that could scarcely be believed," see Fluhman, *"A Peculiar People,"* 97–99, 97. For an account of Bennett keyed to the effects of his revelations within the social world of Nauvoo, see Ulrich, *A House Full of Females*, 70–83.

36 Bloom, *The American Religion*, 99.

37 Orson Pratt, "Polygamy," 24 July 1859, *Journal of Discourses* 6:350, http://jod.mrm .org/6/349. See also Pratt's "Celestial Marriage," from 1852, in *The Essential Orson Pratt* (Salt Lake City: Signature Books, 1991), 256–71.

38 Pratt, "Polygamy," 360–61.

39 On the legalities of polygamy, inside a matrix of antebellum claims about privacy and states' rights, see Sarah Barringer Gordon, *The Mormon Question: Polygamy and Constitutional Conflict in Nineteenth-Century America* (Chapel Hill: University of North Carolina Press, 2002); and Christine Talbot, *A Foreign Kingdom: Mormons and Polygamy in American Political Culture, 1852–1890* (Urbana: University of Illinois Press, 2013).

40 Henry James, *The Bostonians* (New York: Penguin, 2000), 260. The figure speaking is Basil Ransom. Salient here, too, is the work of Ann Douglas, which mixes stinging critique with rage at the delimited options for women excised over two generations from the workings of national power. See Douglas's *The Feminization of American Culture* (New York: Knopf, 1977).

41 Elizabeth Freeman, *The Wedding Complex: Forms of Belonging in Modern American Culture* (Durham: Duke University Press, 2002), 127. She is arguing here in colloquy with Mary Ryan's *Cradle of the Middle Class: The Family in Oneida County, New York, 1790–1865* (New York: Cambridge University Press, 1981).

42 Ulrich, *A House Full of Females*, xix.

43 Nancy Bentley, "Marriage as Treason: Polygamy, Nation, and the Novel," in *The Futures of American Studies*, ed. Donald E. Pease and Robyn Wiegman (Durham: Duke University Press, 2002), 341–70, 350. An important precursor to Bentley's exemplary work appears in Sarah Barringer Gordon's "'Our National Hearthstone': Anti-Polygamy

Fiction and the Sentimental Campaign against Moral Diversity in Antebellum America," *Faculty Scholarship*, paper 1429 (1996), http://scholarship.law.upenn.edu/faculty_scholarship/1429.

44 Udney Hay Jacob, *The Peace Maker* (Nauvoo: J. Smith, 1842), 11.

45 Jacob, *The Peace Maker*, 37, emphasis in the original.

46 Jacob, *The Peace Maker*, 4–5.

47 Jacob, *The Peace Maker*, 4, emphasis added.

48 See especially his reading of "The Vision," an early work of Smith's, in which, as Bushman says, "the workings of heaven were made intelligible" (*Rough Stone Rolling*, 202).

49 Bushman, *Rough Stone Rolling*, 420, 326.

50 Bushman, *Rough Stone Rolling*, 444–45, emphasis added.

51 We might think most immediately of Smith's account, in Doctrine and Covenants 130, of heaven itself, where "that same sociality which exists among us here will exist among us there, only it will be coupled with eternal glory, which glory we do not now enjoy." "Let me be resurrected with the Saints, whether to heaven or hell or any other good place," Smith declared in 1843. "What do we care if the society is good?" To which point he added: "Friendship is the grand fundamental principle of Mormonism, to revolution[ize and] civilize the world, [to] pour forth love" (*EJS*, 200). These are the queerer sociabilities to which, with the aid of scholars like Brodie and Quinn and Taylor G. Petrey, I tried to attend in my previous work on Smith and the history of sexuality. See especially Petrey's "Toward a Post-Heterosexual Mormon Theology," *Dialogue: A Journal of Mormon Thought* 44, no. 4 (Winter 2011): 106–41.

52 Michel Foucault, *History of Sexuality*, vol. 1, *An Introduction*, trans. Robert Hurley (New York: Vintage, 1978), 111. For an especially fine account of family, normativity, and the entailments of liberal subjecthood in nineteenth-century America, see Brian Connolly, *Domestic Intimacies: Incest and the Liberal Subject in Nineteenth-Century America* (Philadelphia: University of Pennsylvania Press, 2014). Connolly's thinking about sex, familialism, and liberal power has been particularly generative to my work here.

53 Orson Pratt surely paved the way for this, inasmuch as his accounts—designed as they often were to justify the ways of Mormonism to Gentiles—also underscored reproductivity and, with this, a stark difference between the genders. In later chapters we will look more closely at the interplay of arguments like Jacob's and Pratt's in the solidifying sociability of Mormonism under Brigham Young.

54 See the LDS homepage, and the article "Plural Marriage and Families in Early Utah," https://www.lds.org/topics/plural-marriage-and-families-in-early-utah?lang=eng.

55 See, for instance, Van Wagoner, who gives us rival versions of the event in question, in *Mormon Polygamy*, 58–60. See also Ulrich, *A House Full of Females*, 89–93.

56 See also "Revelation, 12 July 1843 [D&C 132]," http://www.josephsmithpapers.org/paper-summary/revelation-12-july-1843-dc-132/1.

57 See also "History, 1838–1856, volume E-1 [1 July 1843–30 April 1844]," p. 1866, Joseph Smith Papers, http://www.josephsmithpapers.org/paper-summary/history-1838-1856-volume-e-1-1-july-1843-30-april-1844/238.

58 Ulrich, *A House Full of Females*, 84.

59   The official LDS essay, in its emphasis on sacrifice and obedience, is exemplary in this
     respect, but not unique. "For these early Latter-day Saints," it reads, "plural marriage
     was a religious principle that required personal sacrifice. Accounts left by men and
     women who practiced plural marriage attest to the challenges and difficulties they
     experienced. . . . They believed it was a commandment of God at that time and that
     obedience would bring great blessings to them and their posterity, both on earth and
     in the life to come." My argument is not that these claims are disingenuous. It is that the
     staging of the call to polygamy as an occasion for a performance of piety is, for Smith,
     a refraction of the grander piece of learning and unlearning that the practice supports,
     which is the vast recoding of the body proper to the discipline of exaltation. These latter
     accounts, which stall at the merely social or even moral sacrifice entailed, once again
     leave the carnal imagination of the early Mormonism to one side. See "Plural Marriage
     and Families in Early Utah," https://www.lds.org/topics/plural-marriage-and-families
     -in-early-utah?lang=eng.

60   Ulrich, *A House Full of Females*, 85.

61   Givens, *The Viper on the Hearth*, 92.

62   On the plainspokenness of Smith's revelations, and especially on their characteristic
     running-together of divine and quotidian purpose, see again Bushman's "The 'Little,
     Narrow Prison' of Language," in *Believing History*. There Bushman notes how "Smith's
     most provocative and mysterious" revelations keep easy company with the homely (as
     when a revelation "rebukes Frederick G. Williams for letting his children get out of
     hand" or when "the Lord seems to micro-manage the everyday affairs of the Church").
     For Bushman, the effectiveness of Smith's mode lies in the way "the lives of plain people
     are caught in the same rhetorical space where God's voice speaks of coming calamities
     and the beginning of the marvelous work and a wonder" (257).

63   Quoted in Givens, *People of Paradox*, 133.

64   "Any power overwrites bodies with the fictions that its mechanisms require," is how
     Mark Jordan elegantly summarizing this central aspect of Foucault. See Jordan's *Con-
     vulsing Bodies: Religion and Resistance in Foucault* (Stanford: Stanford University Press,
     2015), 55.

65   The point I have been pursuing here is coordinate with Givens's argument, in *The Viper
     on the Hearth*, about the nature of the Mormon affront to orthodox nineteenth-century
     religiosity, and its construction as heresy. For Givens, it is that collapsing of the space
     of sacred distance, and with this "the re-presentation of sacred beginnings," that "effec-
     tively constitute the transgression of orthodoxy, at least in the increasingly secularized
     world in which Mormonism appeared and grew" (96). For me, the consequences of that
     collapse are less abstract than rigorously *material*: alive in the vision of earthly matter,
     the material world, and what the body is.

66   Brodie, *No Man Knows My History*, 294.

67   Brodie, *No Man Knows My History*, 300.

68   My sense of Smith as a theologian in love with life is heartened by, and in dialogue with,
     Samuel Morris Brown's reading of him as "roaring in the face of death," in his *In Heaven
     as It Is on Earth*, 12.

CHAPTER THREE

———————

1   Nathaniel Hawthorne, *The Blithedale Romance* (New York: Penguin, 1983), 17. Cited internally hereafter.

2   Joan Wallach Scott, "Secularism and Gender Equality," in *Religion, the Secular, and the Politics of Sexual Difference*, ed. Linell E. Cady and Tracy Fessenden (New York: Columbia University Press, 2013), 25–45, 27.

3   Linell E. Cady and Tracy Fessenden, "Gendering the Divide," in Cady and Fessenden, *Religion, the Secular, and the Politics of Sexual Difference*, 3–24, 5.

4   See Saba Mahmood, *Politics of Piety: The Islamic Revival and the Feminist Subject* (Princeton: Princeton University Press, 2005); Cady and Fessenden, *Religion, the Secular, and the Politics of Sexual Difference*; Molly McGarry, *Ghosts of Futures Past: Spiritualism and the Cultural Politics of Nineteenth-Century America* (Berkeley: University of California Press, 2008); Lila Abu-Lughod, *Do Muslim Women Need Saving?* (Cambridge: Harvard University Press, 2013); and Joan Wallach Scott, *Sex and Secularism* (Princeton: Princeton University Press, 2018).

5   Nancy Bentley, "Marriage as Treason: Polygamy, Nation, and the Novel," in *The Futures of American Studies*, ed. Donald E. Pease and Robyn Wiegman (Durham: Duke University Press, 2002), 341–70, 350.

6   Quoted in Laurel Thatcher Ulrich, *A House Full of Females: Plural Marriage and Women's Rights in Early Mormonism, 1835–1870* (New York: Knopf, 2017), 156. Cited internally hereafter.

7   One way we do *not* best keep on guard against those secularizing impulses, I think, is by scaling the activities of early Mormon women according to the presence, absence, or mitigation of what is called "agency." I follow Saba Mahmood in regarding the Westernized metrics of "agency" as often more obscuring than clarifying, especially in relation to the forms of power claimed by women at one or several removes from secular imaginaries of authority. So while I am heartened by work like Catherine A. Brekus's "Mormon Women and the Problem of Historical Agency," and Susanna Morrill's "Mormon Women's Agency and the Changing Conceptions of the Mother in Heaven," I offer here a consequentially different conceptual vocabulary, one that works to keep in focus forms of power that do not default to secular rubrics. See Mahmood, *Politics of Piety*; Brekus, "Mormon Women and the Problem of Historical Agency," *Journal of Mormon History* 37, no. 2 (2011): 59–87; Morrill, "Mormon Women's Agency and the Changing Conceptions of the Mother in Heaven," in *Women and Mormonism: Historical and Contemporary Perspectives*, ed. Kate Holbrook and Matthew Bowman (Salt Lake City: University of Utah Press, 2016), 121–35. A strong parsing of the problems of agency-talk in the context of nonsecular imaginaries appears in Aimee Evans Hickman's "Narrating Agency," in Holbrook and Bowman, *Women and Mormonism*, 301–11.

8   I am fortified in this work by a long and vibrant tradition of feminist scholarship on Mormonism. Exemplary texts for me, in addition to the works already cited, include the essays gathered in *Women and Authority: Re-emerging Mormon Feminism*, ed. Maxine Hanks (Salt Lake City: Signature Books, 1992), Jill Mulvay Derr, Janath Russell

Cannon, and Maureen Ursenbach Beecher, *Women of Covenant: The Story of Relief Society* (Salt Lake City: Deseret Book Company, 1992), and Martha Sonntag Bradley and Mary Brown Firmage Woodward's *4 Zinas: A Story of Mothers and Daughters on the Mormon Frontier* (Salt Lake City: Signature Books, 2000), as well as two fine historiographic collections featuring work from the archive of feminist inquiry: *Mormon Feminism: Essential Writings*, ed. Joanna Brooks, Rachel Hunt Steenblik, and Hannah Wheelwright (New York: Oxford University Press, 2016), and Holbrook and Bowman, *Women and Mormonism*.

9   Quoted in Bradley and Woodward, *4 Zinas*, 158. Cited internally hereafter as *4 Zinas*.

10 Peter Coviello, *Tomorrow's Parties: Sex and the Untimely in Nineteenth-Century America* (New York: New York University Press, 2013), 126. The work of D. Michael Quinn would be especially important here, most particularly his *Same-Sex Dynamics among Nineteenth-Century Americans: A Mormon Example* (Urbana: University of Illinois Press, 1996). See also the strong work gathered in Maxine Hanks's collection *Women and Authority: Re-emerging Mormon Feminism*.

11 See especially Smith's remarks in "Observations Respecting the Priesthood," in *EJS*, 160–64. On women and priesthood, see Smith's remarks to the Female Relief Society; see also Kathleen Flake, "The Emotional and Priestly Logic of Plural Marriage," *Arrington Annual Lecture*, paper 15 (Logan: Utah State University Press, 2009). On wives married to several men—Zina Diantha Huntington Jacobs Smith Young would be the exemplary figure here—see Todd Compton, *In Sacred Loneliness: The Plural Wives of Joseph Smith* (Salt Lake City: Signature Books, 1997); Richard S. Van Wagoner, *Mormon Polygamy: A History* (Salt Lake City: Signature Books, 1989); Bradley and Woodward, *4 Zinas*; and Kathryn M. Daynes, *More Wives Than One: Transformation of the Mormon Marriage System, 1840–1910* (Urbana: University of Illinois Press, 2001).

12 See also "Revelation, 12 July 1843 [D&C 132]," Joseph Smith Papers, http://www .josephsmithpapers.org/paper-summary/revelation-12-july-1843-dc-132/1.

13 On these emergences, see Mary Ryan's *Cradle of the Middle Class: The Family in Oneida County, New York, 1790–1865* (New York: Cambridge University Press, 1981).

14 Fanny Stenhouse, *Exposé of Polygamy: A Lady's Life among the Mormons*, ed. Linda Wilcox DeSimone (Logan: Utah State University Press, 2008), 122.

15 On divorce in Mormon polygamy, see also Kathryn M. Daynes, *More Wives Than One: Transformation of the Mormon Marriage System, 1840–1910* (Urbana: University of Illinois Press, 2001), 141–59.

16 As Ulrich writes, "In Masonic iconography, a key represented *the ability to keep a secret*" (*A House Full of Females*, 60, emphasis added).

17 "Nauvoo Relief Society Minute Book," p. 88, Joseph Smith Papers, http://www.joseph smithpapers.org/paper-summary/nauvoo-relief-society-minute-book/85. Further materials around the Relief Society Minute Book can be found among the documents collected at *The First Fifty Years of Relief Society*, a resource that has been indispensable to me in my work here. See https://www.churchhistorianspress.org/the-first-fifty -years-of-relief-society?lang=eng.

18 "Nauvoo Relief Society Minute Book," p. 4, http://www.josephsmithpapers.org/paper -summary/nauvoo-relief-society-minute-book/4.

19 The scandal concerned Bennett's public accusation that Smith had proposed polyga-
    mous marriage to Sarah Pratt, Orson's wife. Pratt, unwilling to disregard his wife even
    in the name of believing the prophet, was excommunicated with his brother in August
    of 1842, though he was later reinstated. On this affair see Van Wagoner, *Mormon Polyg-
    amy*, 29–40.

20 "Nauvoo Relief Society Minute Book," pp. 80, 79, http://www.josephsmithpapers.org
    /paper-summary/nauvoo-relief-society-minute-book/77.

21 "Nauvoo Relief Society Minute Book," p. 22, http://www.josephsmithpapers.org/paper
    -summary/nauvoo-relief-society-minute-book/19.

22 See also "Nauvoo Relief Society Minute Book," p. 36, http://www.josephsmithpapers
    .org/paper-summary/nauvoo-relief-society-minute-book/33.

23 Richard Lyman Bushman, *Joseph Smith: Rough Stone Rolling* (New York: Knopf, 2005),
    447.

24 On this development, see especially Ulrich, *A House Full of Females*, 123.

25 Van Wagoner, *Mormon Polygamy*, 44. I refer to her as Zina Diantha following the
    precedent set by Bradley and Woodward in their indispensable volume *4 Zinas*. I am
    informed here as well by Derr, Cannon, and Beecher, *Women of Covenant*, especially
    127–50; Ulrich, *A House Full of Females*; Van Wagoner, *Mormon Polygamy*; Daynes,
    More Wives Than One; and perhaps most of all by Marilyn Higbee, "'A Weary Traveler':
    The 1848–50 Diary of Zina D. H. Young," *Journal of Mormon History* 19, no. 2 (Fall
    1993): 86–125.

26 Daynes, *More Wives Than One*, 10.

27 Few would dispute that plural marriage, as it was invented as a social practice in Nau-
    voo, came under the sway of a more deliberate structuring, or even that this more rigor-
    ous systematization tracks with the centralization of priesthood authority that followed
    Smith's death. But Zina Diantha's story shows us, too, how that centralization worked
    also as a special kind of patriarchalization: a more and more complete rendering of
    the celestial sphere, too, as subject to the strict hierarchies of gender. For meticulous
    work that means to bring into focus precisely the undersystematized conceptions of
    authority circulating in early Mormonism, with "liturgical" and "ecclesiastical" and
    "priesthood" authorities running unevenly together in the terrain of what the author
    calls "cosmological priesthood," see Jonathan A. Stapely, "Women and Authority," in
    Holbrook and Bowman, *Women and Mormonism*, 101–17, 103–4. For an account that
    maps a similar confinement of women's authority but dates it differently—figuring
    nineteenth-century Mormonism as featuring a "more egalitarian gender status" that,
    however, "became bogged down in the twentieth century, subordinated to a continua-
    tion of the previous century's dominant 'cult of domesticity'"—see Gary Shepherd and
    Gordon Shepherd, *Binding Earth and Heaven: Patriarchal Blessings in the Prophetic
    Development of Early Mormonism* (University Park: Pennsylvania State University
    Press, 2012), 104. Shepherd and Shepherd argue that "the religious status and organi-
    zational roles of LDS women were relatively progressive for their time and place," at
    least "compared to many other nineteenth-century Christian women" (104). Though
    in some measures surely true, such a claim nevertheless invisibilizes the great chasm

between the forms of authority early Mormon women had reason to imagine *might* be directly accessible to them and the roles (locked, typically, within steeply hierarchized distributions of gendered power) they were given.

28 Van Wagoner, *Mormon Polygamy*, 44.

29 These words are Zina Diantha's recollection, from 1894. Quoted in Bradley and Woodward, *4 Zinas*, 113.

30 Richard Bushman, "Joseph Smith as Translator," in Bushman, *Believing History: Latter-day Saint Essays*, ed. Reid L. Neilson and Jed Woodworth (New York: Columbia University Press, 2004), 233–47.

31 This is the first line, from 3 November 1848, in her diaries for 1848–50. They are reproduced in Higbee, "'A Weary Traveler,'" 91–125. Cited internally as "Diary."

32 John G. Turner, *Brigham Young: Pioneer Prophet* (Cambridge: Belknap Press of Harvard University Press, 2012), 215. Turner continues, "Kahpeputz, or Sally as Clara called her, quickly became acquainted with Young's extended family," though as Turner points out she "did not live as Young's other children," subject as she was to different treatment (215–16). She would go on to marry a chief Native ally of the Mormons, Ute leader Kanosh. On the context of the Native slave trade and the Mormon role there, see also Jared Farmer's *On Zion's Mount: Mormons, Indians, and the American Landscape* (Cambridge: Harvard University Press, 2008), 54–104, and Ned Blackhawk, *Violence over the Land: Indians and Empires in the Early American West* (Cambridge: Harvard University Press, 2006), especially 226–66. For more on Sally Kahpeputz's life within Mormonism, and her role inside Young's shifting allegiances with Native figures like Kanosh and Wakara, see Max Perry Mueller, *Race and the Making of the Mormon People* (Chapel Hill: University of North Carolina Press, 2017), especially 197–211.

33 Bushman, "Joseph Smith as Translator," 239, 240.

34 See especially Amy Hollywood, *Sensible Ecstasy: Mysticism, Sexual Difference, and the Demands of History* (Chicago: University of Chicago Press, 2001), as well as the work collected in Hollywood's *Acute Melancholia and Other Essays: Mysticism, History, and the Study of Religion* (New York: Columbia University Press, 2016).

35 On Henry's fate, see also Ulrich, *A House Full of Females*, 285–86; Van Wagoner, *Mormon Polygamy*, 44–46; Turner, *Brigham Young*, 154–55.

36 Henry's final extant letter to Zina Diantha, from 1852, was to find him less sanguine and generous than wounded, Job-like, and sorrowing, baffled by a heartbreak that would not release him. "I think of you often very often Zina," he wrote, in what was essentially a long exhalation of grief, "when I sleep the sleep of death then I will not for get you and my little lambs I love my Children. O Zina will I ever get you again answer the question please If you are at Liberty to answer the question write me soon as you get this my troubles her ar great greatere than I can bar." Shortly after this, Brigham Young forbade Zina Diantha any further correspondence with Henry. On this episode, and on the multiple and sometimes conflicting family recollections that comprise much of its archive, see Bradley and Woodward, *4 Zinas*, 197–202, 198.

37 Quoted in *4 Zinas*, 132. Young's vision of divorce in the name of access to a man with higher priesthood authority complicates, though it does not overturn, readings of the

church's policy on divorce as especially beneficial to women. For such readings see especially Daynes, *More Wives Than One*, 141–70; and Ulrich, *A House Full of Females*, 279–83.

38 For more on the Quorum of the Anointed, in its several early permutations, see D. Michael Quinn, "Latter-day Saints Prayer Circles," *BYU Studies* 19 (Fall 1978): 84–96.

39 Turner, *Brigham Young*, 159, including the quotation from Woodruff's journal.

40 From a document reproduced in the web archive *The First Fifty Years of Relief Society*, https://www.churchhistorianspress.org/the-first-fifty-years-of-relief-society/part-1 /1-13. The website reproduces passages from Brigham Young, Discourse, 9 March 1845; taken from the Record of Seventies, Book B, 1844–1848, pp. 77–78. The original of that document is here: https://content.ldschurch.org/bc/content/PDF/1-13-Brigham -Young-Discourses-Mar-9-1845-CHL-CR-3-51.pdf.

41 These passages reproduce Brigham Young, Discourse, 9 March 1845; from the Nauvoo High Priests Quorum Record, 1841–1845. That document is reproduced here: https:// dcms.lds.org/delivery/DeliveryManagerServlet?dps_pid=IE6158773&page=96.

42 Quoted in Turner, *Brigham Young*, 158, 159.

43 Turner, *Brigham Young*, 113.

44 Turner, *Brigham Young*, 3. See also the precursor biography to Turner's, Leonard J. Arrington's *Brigham Young: American Moses* (New York: Knopf, 1985).

45 Quoted in Turner, *Brigham Young*, 158.

46 See also Jill Mulvay Derr and Carol Cornwall Madsen, "Preserving the Record and Memory of the Female Relief Society of Nauvoo, 1841–92," *Journal of Mormon History* 35 (Summer 2009): 88–117.

47 Turner, *Brigham Young*, 237.

48 Ulrich, *A House Full of Females*, 212.

49 Richards is writing to her husband in August of 1846; quoted in Ulrich, *A House Full of Females*, 156.

50 Bentley, "Marriage as Treason," 350.

51 See Cady and Fessenden, *Religion, the Secular, and the Politics of Sexual Difference*; McGarry, *Ghosts of Futures Past*; Mahmood, *Politics of Piety* and *Religious Difference in a Secular Age: A Minority Report* (Princeton: Princeton University Press, 2015); Tracy Fessenden, *Culture and Redemption: Religion, the Secular, and American Literature* (Princeton: Princeton University Press, 2006); and Scott, *Sex and Secularism*.

52 Quoted in Turner, *Brigham Young*, 363.

53 On Indian Relief Societies and Mormon colonization, see Ulrich, *A House Full of Females*, 297–305; and Turner, *Brigham Young*, 207–18. On the ecology of early Mormon colonial relations to indigenous people, see Farmer, *On Zion's Mount*, especially 54–104; on biophilanthropy, see Kyla Schuller, *The Biopolitics of Feeling: Race, Sex, and Science in the Nineteenth Century* (Durham: Duke University Press, 2017), 134–70.

54 Turner, *Brigham Young*, 128–30.

55 Orson Pratt, "Celestial Marriage—an Excerpt," in *The Essential Orson Pratt* (Salt Lake City: Signature Books, 1991), 275.

56 James E. Talmage, *The Essential James E. Talmage*, 128–32, 128; originally in *Young Woman's Journal* 25 (October 1914): 600–604, 600.

57 See, for instance, Martha Pierce, "Personal Discourse on God the Mother," in Hanks, *Women and Authority*, 247–56, as well as the wide-ranging observations collected, in the same volume, in "Emerging Discourse on the Divine Feminine" (257–96). See also Edward Jones III, "The Mystical Body of God the Mother," *Sunstone Magazine*, 11 February 2014, https://www.sunstonemagazine.com/the-mystical-body-of-god -the-mother/; as well as Margaret Toscano, "Heavenly Mother: Silences, Disturbances, and Consolations," *Sunstone Magazine*, 3 April 2012, https://www.sunstonemagazine .com/heavenly-motherhood-silences-distrubances-and-consolations/. My own sense is that Heavenly Mother discourse, though valuable inasmuch as it counteracts the marginlessness of the identification between authority and masculinity, does very little to unwrite the confining of femininity, and especially feminine divinity, to the sphere of reproductivity.

58 To be clear: the matter is not that Zina Diantha suddenly has the notion of submission *pressed upon her*, and is therefore expelled from some more properly, robustly "feminist" position. It is rather that within Mormonism she had found the possibility of a noncontradiction between certain kinds of female duty and submission *and a female power unto godliness*. That possibility, I have been arguing, is what Young works so effectively to foreclose. Here and throughout the chapter I have before me the analytic example of Mahmood's anthropology, her refusal of "resistance" and nonsubmissiveness as the sine qua non of feminist subjectivity, and her admonition that "the desire for freedom and liberation is a historically situated desire whose motivational force cannot be assumed a priori, but needs to be reconsidered in light of other desires, aspirations, and capacities that inhere in a culturally and historically located subject." See her "Feminist Theory, Embodiment, and the Docile Agent: Some Reflections on the Egyptian Islamic Revival," *Cultural Anthropology* 16, no. 2 (2002): 223.

59 Quoted in Turner, *Brigham Young*, 108.

60 Quoted in Terryl Givens, *People of Paradox*, 133.

61 See Jan Shipps, *Mormonism: The Story of a New Religious Tradition* (Urbana: University of Illinois Press, 1985), 77. Shipps's pathbreaking work is rooted in the conviction that "recognition of a fundamental theological tension within Mormonism" allows us a fuller understanding of its "radical character," without which, as she writes, "Mormonism can all too readily be misunderstood as little more than an elaborate idiosyncratic strain of the nineteenth-century search for a primitive Christianity" (77, 68). Precisely this protean doubleness of early Mormon theology is at the heart of the work I have attempted here. For an interesting updating of Shipps's propositions, see J. Spencer Fluhman's account of Mormonism's vibrantly vexed relation to nineteenth-century Protestantism, which for him put illuminating pressure on the definitions of American "Christianness" itself. Fluhman, *"A Peculiar People": Anti-Mormonism and the Making of Religion in Nineteenth-Century America* (Chapel Hill: University of North Carolina Press, 2012).

62 On these points see, again, Flake, "The Emotional and Priestly Logic of Plural Marriage." See also, in Hanks, *Women and Authority*; Linda P. Wilcox, "The Mormon Concept of a Mother in Heaven," 3–21, 3; as well as Margaret Merrill Toscano, "Put On Your Strength O Daughters of Zion: Claiming Priesthood and Knowing the Mother,"

411–37. See also Martha Sonntag Bradley, *Pedestals and Podiums: Utah Women, Religious Authority, and Equal Rights* (Salt Lake City: Signature Books, 2005).

63 Bentley's work is, here again, exemplary; see her "Marriage as Treason."

CHAPTER FOUR

————————

1 An especially rich account of the origin-stories surrounding the Book of Mormon, its necromancy and its entanglement with Smith's own youthful history of chicanery, appears in Richard Lyman Bushman's *Joseph Smith: Rough Stone Rolling* (New York: Knopf, 2005)—though for my purposes the fact that the plates are retrieved from the very earth of North America, the soil of the stolen and misnamed "New World," is crucial for what I will call Mormonism's efforts toward the indigenization of Christianity.

2 Paul C. Gutjahr provides a strong taxonomy of approaches to the Book of Mormon in his excellent study *The "Book of Mormon": A Biography* (Princeton: Princeton University Press, 2012). He identifies three major "schools" of response: the "supernaturalist or revelatory school," the "plagiarist school," and the "naturalist school" (45). Part of my claim here is that secular premises, premises about the hard and legible distinctions between the fictive and the real, the "enchantedly" magic and the disenchantedly rational, fuel the status-disputes around the Book of Mormon.

3 Jared Hickman, "*The Book of Mormon* as Amerindian Apocalypse," *American Literature* 86, no. 3 (September 2014): 434.

4 Alfreda Eva Bell, ed., *Boadicea: The Mormon Wife; Life-Scenes in Utah* (Baltimore, Philadelphia, New York, and Buffalo: Arthur R. Orton, 1855), 81, emphasis added.

5 "The Mormons," *Putnam's Monthly* 5, no. 27 (March 1855): 225–36, 234.

6 Jack London, *The Star Rover* (New York: Macmillan, 1963), 131. This passage is important to the readings of many excellent scholars of race and Mormonism. See especially Nancy Bentley, "Marriage as Treason: Polygamy, Nation, and the Novel," in *The Futures of American Studies*, ed. Donald E. Pease and Robyn Wiegman (Durham: Duke University Press, 2002), 341–70; Matthew Rebhorn, *Pioneer Performances: Staging the Frontier* (New York: Oxford University Press, 2012); and W. Paul Reeve, *Religion of a Different Color: Race and the Mormon Struggle for Whiteness* (New York: Oxford University Press, 2015).

7 See Hickman, "*The Book of Mormon* as Amerindian Apocalypse"; Bentley, "Marriage as Treason"; Reeve, *Religion of a Different Color*; and J. Spencer Fluhman, "*A Peculiar People": Anti-Mormonism and the Making of Religion in Nineteenth-Century America* (Chapel Hill: University of North Carolina Press, 2012).

8 Quoted in John G. Turner, *Brigham Young: Pioneer Prophet* (Cambridge: Belknap Press of Harvard University Press, 2012), 197. It is Hickman's point throughout his pathbreaking essay that the Book of Mormon was legible in the register of anti-imperial critique not only to early Mormons but to a great range of indigenous and/or nonwhite figures. His essay accordingly takes up both the "affirmations of Amerindian cultural and spiritual identity" that one might mine from the Book of Mormon, and its affordances for a

wealth of nonwhite theologies keyed to anti-imperial liberation (see especially 435–36). My interest here lies less in the liberationist possibilities of the Book of Mormon than in the collision of scriptural anti-imperial critique, on the one hand, and on the other the multifaceted colonizing practices of Mormons in the latter half of the nineteenth century.

9   Resources for thinking about race, modernity, and the regime of the secular are plentiful. Some of the works that have been most galvanizing to me include José Casanova, *Public Religions in the Modern World* (Chicago: University of Chicago Press, 1994); Talal Asad, *Formations of the Secular: Christianity, Islam, Modernity* (Stanford: Stanford University Press, 2003); Gil Anidjar, "Secularism," *Critical Inquiry* 33, no. 1 (2006): 52–77; J. Kameron Carter, *Race: A Theological Account* (New York: Oxford University Press, 2008); Saba Mahmood, *Politics of Piety: The Islamic Revival and the Feminist Subject* (Princeton: Princeton University Press, 2011); and Vincent Lloyd, ed., *Race and Political Theology* (Stanford: Stanford University Press, 2012).

10 Joseph Smith, *The Book of Mormon: Another Testament of Jesus Christ* (Salt Lake City: Church of Jesus Christ of Latter-day Saints, 1981), 66. Cited internally hereafter, by chapter, book, and verse.

11 Max Perry Mueller, *Race and the Making of the Mormon People* (Chapel Hill: University of North Carolina Press, 2017), 17, 52. Mueller's claim is that this version of the redeemability of the Lamanites—this "proto-postmodern view of race as a historical construct" (12)—makes for a "restorative racial universalism" (17) that "proved too ambitious to be tolerated in antebellum America" (20). In the next chapter I will engage more directly with Mueller's work, which I think is especially strong on the affordances of Mormon theology for a variety of *specific* Native and nonwhite believers. The idea, however, that there is a kind of redemptive radicality to thinking of race as extrabiological and therefore mutable, subject to alteration via redemption, seems to me tremendously misapprehending; what it misapprehends, in the first instance, is the familiar genocidal logic of universalizing colonial redemption. Whatever the possibilities for anti-imperial critique that lie within the Book of Mormon—and my claim here is that they are many, and immensely forceful, and underread—do not emerge in the promise that redeemed Lamanites might themselves become white and delightsome. For a revisiting of this nexus of problems, as they played out in the twentieth century, see Matthew Garrett's *Making Lamanites: Mormons, Native Americans, and the Indian Student Placement Program, 1947–2000* (Salt Lake City: University of Utah Press, 2016). Here, for instance, is a the voice of a Native graduate of the ISSP, "a graduate student and . . . Southwest Indian missionary," speaking as against "would-be traditionalists" who in 1969 had been protesting at BYU: an Indian, John Rainer remarked, "is a mistaken identity which some individual students are trying to shackle the other students with on this campus by making them learn these old dances, learn these old traditions, which are not the true identity of the Lamanite" (186–87).

12 The reading I offer here of race and narrative form in the Book of Mormon has been enabled by the work of many generations of careful textual critics. Of particular importance to me have been Terryl L. Givens, *By the Hand of Mormon: The American Scripture That Launched a New World Religion* (New York: Oxford University Press,

2002); Grant Hardy, *Understanding the Book of Mormon: A Reader's Guide* (Oxford: Oxford University Press, 2010); Elizabeth Fenton, "Open Canons: Sacred History and American History in *The Book of Mormon*," *J19: The Journal of Nineteenth-Century Americanists* 1, no. 2 (2013): 339–61; and, most crucially, Hickman, "*The Book of Mormon* as Amerindian Apocalypse."

13 Hardy, *Understanding the Book of Mormon*, 15, 13.

14 Hardy, *Understanding the Book of Mormon*, 54–55.

15 Hickman, "*The Book of Mormon* as Amerindian Apocalypse," 447; Avi Steinberg, *The Lost Book of Mormon: A Journey through the Mythic Lands of Nephi, Zarahemla, and Kansas City, Missouri* (New York: Doubleday, 2014), 9.

16 Hardy astutely describes Zeniff's comments at this moment in Mosiah as "nothing less than an explanation of the war—*from the Lamanites' perspective*" (*Understanding the Book of Mormon*, 129).

17 Hardy, *Understanding the Book of Mormon*, 130; Hickman, "*The Book of Mormon* as Amerindian Apocalypse," 450–55.

18 Hickman, "*The Book of Mormon* as Amerindian Apocalypse," 441.

19 Hickman, "*The Book of Mormon* as Amerindian Apocalypse," 448. Mueller, too—following Hickman—writes of the Nephites' "ethnocentrism, perhaps even racial antipathy." In his rendering, this is what causes them to "reject the message of salvation that will come through belief in Christ," where that "message" signifies in the register of a deracialized universalist future; I am less persuaded by the redemptive possibilities of racial (which is really *deracinating*) universalism than I am eager to attend to the Nephites' damnation, the linking of their fall and destruction *to* the racism that they cannot avow or narrate, but that their *text* manages to stage. Mueller, *Race and the Making of the Mormon People*, 51.

20 As Hickman puts it, there is one voice "the Nephite narrative does *not*, at least not willingly, include—the prophetic voice of the Lamanite" ("*The Book of Mormon* as Amerindian Apocalypse," 452).

21 Herman Melville, *Moby-Dick; or, The Whale* (New York: Penguin, 1992), 193.

22 Gutjahr, *The "Book of Mormon": A Biography*, 66.

23 Jan Shipps, *Mormonism: The Story of a New Religious Tradition* (Urbana: University of Illinois Press, 1985), 77.

24 Gutjahr, *The "Book of Mormon": A Biography*, 29, 32. With respect to the initial printing, Gutjahr goes on, "Grandin needed to think long and hard before becoming the publisher of a text many would consider an upstart rival to, and thus critique of, the book American Christians held most dear" (29).

25 Frederick Douglass, *The Narrative of the Life of Frederick Douglass, an American Slave*, ed. Houston Baker Jr. (New York: Penguin, 1982); Harriet Jacobs, *Incidents in the Life of a Slave Girl, Written by Herself*, ed. Jean Fagan Yellin (Cambridge: Harvard University Press, 1987), 52.

26 Frederick Douglass, "Oration Delivered in Corinthian Hall, Rochester, July 5th, 1852" (Rochester: Lee, Mann & Co., 1852), 28, 29.

27 Henry Highland Garnet, "Address to the Slaves of the United States," in *Walker's Appeal, with a Brief Sketch of His Life* . . . (New York: J. H. Tobitt, 1848), 91. See also *Pamphlets*

of Protest: An Anthology of Early African-American Protest Literature, 1790–1860, ed. Richard Newman, Patrick Rael, and Philip Lapsansky (New York: Routledge, 2001), 160–64, 161.

28 See Eddie S. Glaude Jr., *Exodus! Religion, Race, and Nation in Early Nineteenth-Century Black America* (Chicago: University of Chicago Press, 2000), especially 155–59. Hickman's account of both Garnet and Glaude's response appears in Jared Hickman's *Black Prometheus: Race and Radicalism in the Age of Atlantic Slavery* (New York: Oxford University Press, 2017), 356–63. Both Glaude's and Hickman's formulations follow in important ways from Albert J. Raboteau, *Slave Religion: The "Invisible Institution" in the Antebellum South* (1978; New York: Oxford University Press, 2004).

29 Few are persuaded, at this stage, by the earlier accounts of the tale as, in essence, a sympathetic portrait of American innocence confronting the demonic treacheries of genuine Evil—where "Evil" is identified with Babo's mercilessness and deception and not, say, the enslavement that necessitates both. Some canonical counterreadings would be found in Jean Fagan Yellin, "Black Masks: Melville's 'Benito Cereno,'" *American Quarterly* 22 (Fall 1970): 678–89; Carolyn Karcher, *Shadow over the Promised Land: Slavery, Race, and Violence in Melville's America* (Baton Rouge: Louisiana State University Press, 1980), 127–59; Michael Rogin, *Subversive Genealogy: The Politics and Art of Herman Melville* (New York: Knopf, 1983), 208–20; Robert S. Levine, *Conspiracy and Romance: Studies in Brockden Brown, Cooper, Hawthorne, and Melville* (Cambridge: Cambridge University Press, 1989), 199–210; Eric Sundquist, *To Wake the Nations: Race in the Making of American Literature* (Cambridge: Harvard University Press, 1993), 136–64; H. Bruce Franklin, "Slavery and Empire: Melville's 'Benito Cereno,'" in *Melville's Evermoving Dawn: Centennial Essays*, ed. John Bryant and Robert Milder (Kent: Kent State University Press, 1997), 147–61; and Geoffrey Sanborn, *The Sign of the Cannibal: Melville and the Making of a Postcolonial Reader* (Durham: Duke University Press, 1998).

30 Herman Melville, *"Billy Budd," "Bartleby," and Other Stories* (New York: Penguin, 2016), 55, 90. Cited internally hereafter. Passages from my introduction to that edition were adapted from the argument offered here.

31 Eve Kosofsky Sedgwick, in a telling passage about a different Melville text, observes that "the inexplicit compact by which novel-readers voluntarily plunge into worlds that strip them, however temporarily, of the painfully acquired cognitive maps of their ordinary lives . . . on condition of an invisibility that promises cognitive exemption and eventual privilege, creates, especially at the beginning of books, a space of high anxiety and dependence. In this space a reader's identification with modes of categorization ascribed to her by a narrator may be almost vindictively eager." Melville exploits precisely these dependencies and precisely these affects in "Benito Cereno"—terror, exemption, assurance, induced credulity—in ways tuned explicitly to the problems of a racialized theodicy, and *its* manifold problems of omniscience. My reading in this respect means to speak across to the reading Hickman offers in *Black Prometheus*, of "*Benito Cereno*'s discrediting of the omniscient narrative voice and, by implication, the Euro-Christian/God as imbecilically racist" (348), with Sedgwick's insight as a kind of narratological pivot. See Sedgwick, *Epistemology of the Closet* (Berkeley: University of California Press, 1990), 197.

32 This is the argument of my own essay "The American in Charity: 'Benito Cereno' and Gothic Anti-Sentimentality," *Studies in American Fiction* 30, no. 2 (2002): 155–80, 166.

33 Karcher, *Shadow over the Promised Land*, 131; Hickman, *Black Prometheus*, 318.

34 William R. Jones, *Is God a White Racist? A Preamble to Black Theology* (Boston: Beacon Press, 1998), ix; Hickman, *Black Prometheus*, 134–35. This is secularism as "the fulfillment of a Euro-Christian eschatological fantasy of becoming-god vis-à-vis non-Euro-Christians others" (145–46). Hickman's acute sense of the mixed and racially overcharged meanings of human divinization and the humanization of gods in a planetary space suddenly fragilized by the contact of 1492—*immanentized*, to use Hickman's idiom—stands behind much of my work in these chapters. My interest differs from Hickman's chiefly in that I hope to track the "eschatological fantasy" that is secularism not solely as it divides the world into a zero-sum Manichean cosmic race war but as it *materializes* itself, as it lives through bodies marked not only racially but as gendered, as sexed. Secularism, for me as for Hickman, is an eschatological fantasy propagated by the imperial victors of 1492, what I will call here the racialized theodicy of a liberalism on its way to becoming hegemonic; but it *lives* in the nineteenth century, I hope to show, as a biopolitics. I am especially fortified here by Sylvia Wynter's work on what she calls "nonhomogeneity" in the order of life, and its ontologized metastasization *as* race, in "1492: A New World View," in *Race, Discourse, and the Origin of the Americas*, ed. Vera Lawrence Hyatt and Rex Nettleford (Washington, DC: Smithsonian Institute Scholarly Press, 1995), 5–57.

35 Hickman, *Black Prometheus*, 54.

36 Hickman, *Black Prometheus*, 53–54.

37 Jared Farmer, *On Zion's Mount: Mormons, Indians, and the American Landscape* (Cambridge: Harvard University Press, 2008), 59.

38 Turner, *Brigham Young*, 153. On the Mormons at Winter Quarters, see also Richard E. Bennett, *Mormons at the Missouri, 1846–1852: "And Should We Die . . ."* (Norman: University of Oklahoma Press, 1987).

39 Quoted in Turner, *Brigham Young*, 120.

40 Quoted in Turner, *Brigham Young*, 120, emphasis added.

41 Bennett, *Mormons at the Missouri*, 92.

42 Farmer, *On Zion's Mount*, 57, emphasis added.

43 Farmer, *On Zion's Mount*, 92. For something of a prehistory of "Lamanism," see also Samuel Morris Brown's account of early Mormon "Indianism." "Mormon Indianism," he accurately remarks, "led to conflict with white neighbors, particularly their apocalyptic emphasis on Indian restoration." Brown, *In Heaven as It Is on Earth: Joseph Smith and the Early Mormon Conquest of Death* (New York: Oxford University Press, 2012), 109.

44 Farmer, *On Zion's Mount*, 92–93.

45 Parley P. Pratt, *Mormonism Unveiled: Zion's Watchman Unmasked, and its Editor, Mr. L. R. Sunderland, Exposed* (Painesville, OH, 1838), 12. For more on the force of these eschatological disidentifications with the American state, from which they understood themselves to be in flight, see especially David L. Bigler and Will Bagley's *The Mormon Rebellion: America's First Civil War, 1857–1858* (Norman: University of Oklahoma Press,

2011), as well as Bigler's slightly less polemical *Forgotten Kingdom: The Mormon Theocracy in the American West, 1847–1896* (Logan: Utah State University Press, 1998). Both accounts are anchored in a reading of early Mormonism's forceful and (in their views) too easily sidestepped *anti*-Americanism—though they are anchored, too, in a strikingly undercritical sense of the general beneficence of "republican systems of rule," at least as they are set in contrast to those more "theocratic" in nature (Bigler and Bagley, *The Mormon Rebellion*, 17). See also, on early Mormon eschatology, Grant Underwood, *The Millenarian World of Early Mormonism* (Urbana: University of Illinois Press, 1999).

46 Woodruff's speech, quoted in Farmer, *On Zion's Mount*, 94, was printed in the Mormon *Journal of Discourses* in 1856. "Woodruff castigates the Saints," Farmer observes, "for treating the Indians the way the Gentiles had treated the Mormons" (93–94).

47 Quoted in Farmer, *On Zion's Mount*, 102.

48 Quoted in Farmer, *On Zion's Mount*, 134.

49 *Encyclopedia of Latter-day Saint History*, ed. Arnold K. Garr, Donald Q. Cannon, and Richard O. Cowan (Salt Lake City: Deseret Book Company, 2000), 600–601. As Bigler summarizes the "Walker War" of 1853–54, which was in essence a fight over territorial power and the ability to set the terms of commerce and exchange there, especially of Native slaves: "The conflict was less a war in the customary sense than a series of atrocities by both sides, ambushes and mutilations by one and out right executions, sometimes billed as 'skirmishes,' by the other" (*Forgotten Kingdom*, 74).

50 Ned Blackhawk's work on "allegiance" would be especially pertinent here—see Blackhawk, *Violence over the Land: Indians and Empires in the Early American West* (Cambridge: Harvard University Press, 2006). For more recent approaches to "conversion" (of which we will see a good deal more in chapter 5), see Tisa Wenger, *We Have a Religion: The 1920s Pueblo Indian Dance Controversy and American Religious Freedom* (Chapel Hill: University of North Carolina Press, 2009) and Vera B. Palmer, "The Devil in the Details: Controverting an American Indian Conversion Narrative," in *Theorizing Native Studies*, ed. Audra Simpson and Andrea Smith (Durham: Duke University Press, 2014), 266–96.

51 Blackhawk, *Violence over the Land*, 230, 241, 238. My sense of the intertribal geopolitics of the region, and of the Mormons' unstable place there, is deeply informed by Blackhawk's work, especially 226–66.

52 Kyla Schuller, *The Biopolitics of Feeling: Race, Sex, and Science in the Nineteenth Century* (Durham: Duke University Press, 2018), 161–66.

53 Apologizing accounts of the settler practices of Mormonism are many, and are keyed typically to the forms of liberal consensus of their moment. The Mormons appear in these as heroic colonizers (this is especially vivid in early accounts of Mormonism such as John Gunnison's, as we shall see) but then, later, as a wounded people who, in their relation with Native peoples, appear to great advantage when contrasted with federal authorities. (Here some of the salient details are adoptions, Native conversions, and the scripturally mandated regard for Lamanites—which are especially prominent in accounts like those of Turner, in *Brigham Young*; of Reeve, in *Religion of a Different Color*; and, somewhat more critically, of Mueller, in *Race and the Making of the Mormon People*.) Historians of the West who tend to side against the Mormons, such as Bagley

and Bigler, find themselves in a complexly uncomfortable position: that of chastising the early Mormons in the name of a democratic ethos they traduce, while also having to recognize that the Mormons, in their relations to Natives in the West, were unnervingly *like* the Americans, whose secular republican virtue does not, in such scenes of colonial terror and expropriation, show to great advantage. One strong counternarrative to these accounts, keyed especially closely to the environmental aspects of Mormon settlement, appears in Farmer's excellent *On Zion's Mount*; another, in Blackhawk's *Violence over the Land*.

54 Quoted in Reeve, *Religion of a Different Color*, 91–92. For more on Hurt, see also Bigler, *Forgotten Kingdom*, especially 87–102.

55 Reeve, *Religion of a Different Color*, 90.

56 On Young's meetings with representatives of the Shoshone and Southern Paiute, see Reeve, especially 95–97. On the shifting and crossed allegiances between Mormons and Native peoples, as routed through the Saints' hunger for self-rule, see Bigler and Bagley, *The Mormon Rebellion*, 31–73, as well as Bigler, *Forgotten Kingdom*, 63–85, 121–58.

57 On the pornography of antipolygamy novels, and the racial dynamics that animate them, see again Bentley's exceptional essay "Marriage as Treason: Polygamy, Nation, and the Novel."

58 Reeve, *Religion of a Different Color*, 55.

59 Turner, *Brigham Young*, 229. Or again, in a way that makes such racial contextualism plain: "Given the racial context of the mid-nineteenth-century United States and the attitudes of other Mormon leaders, it makes little sense to lay the entire blame for the church's discriminatory policies as the feet of Brigham Young" (229).

60 Reeve, *Religion of a Different Color*, 16, 6, 9.

61 Tavia Nyong'o, *The Amalgamation Waltz: Race, Performance, and the Ruses of Memory* (Minneapolis: University of Minnesota Press, 2009), 83; Schuller, *The Biopolitics of Feeling*, 11.

62 Quoted in Turner, *Brigham Young*, 120, emphasis added.

63 Bigler and Bagley, *The Mormon Rebellion*, 73.

64 Lewis Henry Morgan, *Ancient Society* (1877; Tucson: University of Arizona Press, 1985), 505. For especially perceptive readings of Morgan's indigenization of spirituality, see Mark Rifkin's *When Did Indians Become Straight? Kinship, the History of Sexuality, and Native Sovereignty* (New York: Oxford University Press, 2011), 143–47; and John Lardas Modern, *Secularism in Antebellum America* (Chicago: University of Chicago Press, 2011), 183–238.

65 See especially Daniel Heath Justice, Mark Rifkin, and Bethany Schneider, "Introduction," *GLQ: A Journal of Lesbian and Gay Studies* 16, nos. 1–2 (2010): 5–39, 17, and Deborah A. Miranda, "Extermination of the *Joyas*: Gendercide in Spanish California," *GLQ* 16, nos. 1–2 (2010): 253–84, as well as Rifkin's indispensable *When Did Indians Become Straight?* See also Scott Lauria Morgensen's *Spaces between Us: Queer Settler Colonialism and Indigenous Decolonization* (Minneapolis: University of Minnesota Press, 2011), as well as his "The Biopolitics of Settler Colonialism: Right Here, Right Now," *Settler Colonial Studies* 1, no. 1 (2011): 52–76, and J. Kehaulani Kauanui, *Hawai-*

ian Blood: Colonialism and the Politics of Sovereignty and Indigeneity (Durham: Duke University Press, 2008). A strong and internationally comparativist approach to these questions appears in T. J. Tallie, "Queering Natal: Settler Logics and the Disruptive Challenge of Zulu Polygamy," *GLQ* 19, no. 2 (2013): 167–89. We will return in the next chapter to the settler-colonial fusing of a demand for erotico-familial normalcy in Native peoples—for, in short, private-property-holding monogamy—with a specific rebuke of Native *religion*, as seen especially clearly in the 1883 statement on the rules governing the "Court of Indian Offenses," which helped prepare the way for the Dawes Allotment Act of 1887.

66 We need think here only of the violent suppression of the Ghost Dance at the end of the century, which, as Louis S. Warren argues throughout *God's Red Son: The Ghost Dance Religion and the Making of Modern America* (New York: Basic Books, 2017), was at its core an attack on *Native religion*, newly formulated and reenvisioned in response to the changing historical pressures of American colonization.

67 London, *The Star Rover*, 131.

68 For more on faltering Mormon claims for sovereignty, see Brent M. Rogers, *Unpopular Sovereignty: Mormons and the Federal Management of Early Utah Territory* (Lincoln: University of Nebraska Press, 2017).

69 Quoted in Richard S. Van Wagoner, *Mormon Polygamy: A History* (Salt Lake City: Signature Books, 1989), 135.

70 Talal Asad is commanding on this point, observing that "religion" only *counts* as having gone "public," and in this way as having violated the necessary democratic codes of privatization, when it is organized around principles that do not cohere in and with hegemonic liberal sociality. So a variety of Protestantisms can be supersaturated with explicitly political aim and intent while remaining dutifully "secular"; whereas any effort of a rival structure of belief to find traction for itself *as against* its secular erasure can only emerge, in such terms, as a listing toward "theocracy." See Asad, *Formations of the Secular*, especially 181–94. Bigler and Bagley, who apprehend in the Mormons a frightening "theocratic" refusal of the benevolent principles of republican governance, offer perhaps the most vivid version of these secular mechanics, in *The Mormon Rebellion*.

71 Hickman, "*The Book of Mormon* as Amerindian Apocalypse," 434.

72 This is an especially prominent feature in John W. Gunnison's important *The Mormons, or, Latter-Day Saints, in the Valley of the Great Salt Lake* (Philadelphia: Lippincott, Grambo & Co., 1852).

CHAPTER FIVE

1 On the "Mormon War" of 1838, see William G. Hartley, "Missouri's 1838 Extermination Order and the Mormons' Forced Removal to Illinois," *Mormon Historical Studies* 2, no. 1 (Spring 2001): 5–27, as well as the essays collected in *The Missouri Mormon Experience*, ed. Thomas M. Spencer (Columbia: University of Missouri Press, 2010).

2   Quoted in Thomas M. Spencer, "'Was This Really Missouri Civilization?' The Haun's Mill Massacre in Missouri and Mormon History," in Spencer, *The Missouri Mormon Experience*, 100–118, 106.

3   W. Paul Reeve, *Religion of a Different Color: Race and the Mormon Struggle for Whiteness* (New York: Oxford University Press, 2015), 54. Reeve recounts "the most infamous and perhaps well-known use" of the phrase "*nits make lice*," which was attributed to Colonel John M. Chivington, who "led a cavalry charge into a village of Arapaho and Cheyenne Indians, killing nearly 140 of them," including numerous children. Chivington's soldiers, Reeve writes, "were reportedly spurred on by his command, 'kill and scalp all, big and little; nits make lice'" (54).

4   Quoted in Reeve, *Religion of a Different Color*, 72.

5   On the Utah War, see especially David L Bigler and Will Bagley's *The Mormon Rebellion: America's First Civil War, 1857–1858* (Norman: University of Oklahoma Press, 2011), as well as Bigler's *Forgotten Kingdom: The Mormon Theocracy in the American West, 1847–1896* (Logan: Utah State University Press, 1998), which contains a detailed account of the massacre (159–80). The canonical text on Mountain Meadows is Juanita Brooks's *The Mountain Meadows Massacre* (1950; Norman: University of Oklahoma Press, 1991). A more recent volume, *Massacre at Mountain Meadows*, by Ronald W. Walker, Richard E. Turley, and Glen M. Leonard, provides an account marginally more exonerating in respect to Brigham Young (New York: Oxford University Press, 2011). John G. Turner, in *Brigham Young: Pioneer Prophet* (Cambridge: Belknap Press of Harvard University Press, 2012), is judicious on both matters; see especially 265–300.

6   Turner, *Brigham Young*, 283, 274.

7   Michel Foucault, *"Society Must Be Defended": Lectures at the Collège de France, 1975–1976*, trans. David Macey, ed. Mauro Bertani and Alessandro Fontana (New York: Picador, 2003), 51.

8   I am heartened in this turn by Elizabeth Freeman's work on the way sects like the Mormons "threatened to replace parental and marital bonds with affinities between same-sex peers and undermine the patriarchal family and church as means of social control." See Freeman, *The Wedding Complex: Forms of Belonging in Modern American Culture* (Durham: Duke University Press, 2002), 127.

9   Reeve, *Religion of a Different Color*, 166.

10 Quoted in Richard S. Van Wagoner, *Mormon Polygamy: A History* (Salt Lake City: Signature Books, 1989), 129.

11 Such a disposition is especially prominent in those accounts that look to push back against maligning dismissals of the Saints on the grounds of their zealotry, their orthodoxy, their illiberality, chiefly by presenting them as *already liberal*, as early practitioners of a devotion already in line with the dictates of liberalism—in line with what I have been calling *religion by the lights of secularism*—and covetous of their "religious liberty." Bushman's *Joseph Smith: Rough Stone Rolling*, Reeve's *Religion of a Different Color*, Turner's *Brigham Young*, and Ulrich's *A House Full of Females* are only four of the very most accomplished recent works in this liberalizing tradition.

12 Jan Shipps, *Mormonism: The Story of a New Religious Tradition* (Urbana: University of Illinois Press, 1985), 77. Cited internally hereafter.

13 Quoted in Leonard J. Arrington, *Brigham Young: American Moses* (Urbana: University of Illinois Press, 1986), 233–34 (quoted also in Turner, *Brigham Young*, 244).

14 Turner, *Brigham Young*, 245.

15 Turner, *Brigham Young*, 245. For a fuller explanation of these circumstances, see also Turner's "Unpopular Sovereignty: Brigham Young and the U.S. Government, 1847–1877," in *Mormonism and American Politics*, ed. Randall Balmer and Jana Riess (New York: Columbia University Press, 2015), 14–31. Bigler and Bagley's *The Mormon Rebellion* offers perhaps the most full-throated account of the Mormons as seditious rebels, more or less spoiling for a war that would pit against one another "theocratic and republican systems of rule" (17). Looking at the longish road to the Utah War, as it was fomented in the 1850s, they remark on "the growing body of evidence from the six years prior to the nation's first civil war *in support* of President Buchanan's decision to confront a defiant theocracy" (42, emphasis added).

16 J. Spencer Fluhman, *"A Peculiar People": Anti-Mormonism and the Making of Religion in Nineteenth-Century America* (Chapel Hill: University of North Carolina Press, 2012).

17 John C. Bennett, *The History of the Saints; or, An Exposé of Joe Smith and Mormonism* (Boston: Leland and Whiting, 1842), 218. Cited internally hereafter.

18 Bennett writes that in 1839 "their leaders had formed, and were preparing to execute, a daring and colossal scheme of rebellion and usurpation throughout the North-Western states of the Union" (5).

19 "The Mormons," *Putnam's Monthly* 5, no. 27 (March 1855): 225–36, 234.

20 Fanny Stenhouse, *Exposé of Polygamy: A Lady's Life among the Mormons*, ed. Linda Wilcox DeSimone (Logan: Utah State University Press, 2008), 85.

21 "The Mormons, strong already in their number and their zeal, are increasing like the rolling snowball, and will eventually fall with the force of an avalanche upon the fair fabric of our institutions, unless the people, roused to resist their villainy, quit the forum for the field, and, meeting the Mormons with their own arms, crush the reptile before it has grown powerful enough to sting them to the death." Bennett, *History of the Saints*, 307.

22 As in Jacob 2:24 of the Book of Mormon, which reads: "Behold, David and Solomon truly had many wives and concubines, which thing was abominable before me, saith the Lord."

23 Laurel Thatcher Ulrich, *A House Full of Females: Plural Marriage and Women's Rights in Early Mormonism, 1835–1870* (New York: Knopf, 2017), 240.

24 Orson Pratt, "Polygamy," 24 July 1859, *Journal of Discourses* 6:349–64, 360, http://jod .mrm.org/6/349. See also *The Essential Orson Pratt* (Salt Lake City: Signature Books, 1991), 256–82.

25 Udney Hay Jacob, *The Peace Maker* (Nauvoo: J. Smith, 1842), 5, 6.

26 From a document reproduced in the web archive *The First Fifty Years of Relief Society*, https://www.churchhistorianspress.org/the-first-fifty-years-of-relief-society/part-1 /1-13. The website reproduces passages from Brigham Young, Discourse, 9 March 1845; the original of the document, from the High Priests Quorum record, can be found here: https://dcms.lds.org/delivery/DeliveryManagerServlet?dps_pid=IE6158773& page=96.

27 Alfreda Eva Bell, ed., *Boadicea: The Mormon Wife; Life-Scenes in Utah* (Baltimore,
    Philadelphia, New York, and Buffalo: Arthur R. Orton, 1855). In their 2016 annotated
    edition of the text, editors Michael Austin and Ardis E. Parshall observe that "the per-
    son listed as the editor, 'Alfreda Eva Bell,' is also a part of the fiction," going on to note
    that, given that "no person of this name can be found in any of the records of the day,"
    we do well to consider this personage "the fictional editor of a fictional narrative cre-
    ated by an author who is claiming (with little probability) to be simply reporting the
    truth." They argue that the "most likely candidate" for authorship of *Boadicea* is Arthur
    R. Orton, a prolific pamphleteer of the time. (The text, they note, was "printed on cheap
    newsprint with no cover, with the final page advertising another tawdry 'true' story";
    in this, *Boadicea* "was more like an illustrated pamphlet than a novel.") See Austin and
    Parshall, "A Critical Introduction," in *Boadicea: The Mormon Wife; Life-Scenes in Utah*,
    ed. and annotated Michael Austin and Ardis E. Parshall (Salt Lake City: Greg Kofford
    Books, 2016), xi–xii, xii, xi.
28 Bell, *Boadicea*, 81.
29 Joan Wallach Scott, *Sex and Secularism* (Princeton: Princeton University Press, 2018),
    102.
30 From a discourse of Young's on 12 March 1848, quoted in Turner, *Brigham Young*, 158.
31 Quoted in Bigler, *Forgotten Kingdom*, 164.
32 Tisa Wenger, *We Have a Religion: The 1920s Pueblo Indian Dance Controversy and
    American Religious Freedom* (Chapel Hill: University of North Carolina Press, 2009),
    35. Wenger traces out the competing investments in such evolutionary mappings of
    Native peoples by rival sets of missionaries, working variously "to assimilate the Indians
    into mainstream American life" and, by extension, progressive Christian modernity. As
    Frederick E. Hoxie summarizes the social evolutionary theory of late-century America,
    exemplified by Morgan as well as "reformers" like Alice Fletcher, all of whom would
    prove greatly influential as Grant's explicitly Christianizing "Peace Policy" gave way
    to the visions of Henry Dawes: "'Civilization' was sure to sweep across the West, and
    those who understood its impact had an obligation to minister to its victims. Fletcher
    argued that Native Americans should embrace individual landownership, literary, and
    exclusive monogamy." See Hoxie's *A Final Promise: The Campaign to Assimilate the
    Indians, 1880–1920* (Lincoln: University of Nebraska Press, 1984), 28. See also Lewis
    Henry Morgan, *Ancient Society* (1877; Tucson: University of Arizona Press, 1985). For
    an exquisite account of the racializations of nonmonogamy—keyed to the problems
    of mobility and labor in the late-nineteenth-century West—see Nayan Shah's *Stranger
    Intimacy: Contesting Race, Sexuality, and the Law in the North American West* (Berke-
    ley: University of California Press, 2011). My sense of racialization as a *repertoire* of
    responses to shifting forms of sociality, themselves emerging around transforming
    demands for labor, is deeply indebted to Shah's work, especially 153–88.
33 Among those crucial differences: the Mormons were shielded from dispossessions
    keyed to their *laziness*, which in the rhetoric of Indian affairs was the designation for
    Native resistance to the dictates of private property. Though the Mormons were indeed
    communitarian, and though that committed economic communitarianism disquieted
    some merchants and lawmakers in the later nineteenth century, few were ready to

racialize the Mormons on the grounds of their insufficient industriousness, or their faltering commitment to capitalism. On the "spread of a communitarian gospel," see Bigler, *Forgotten Kingdom*, 259–79, 260.

34 Daniel Heath Justice, Mark Rifkin, and Bethany Schneider, "Introduction," *GLQ: A Journal of Lesbian and Gay Studies* 16, nos. 1–2 (2010): 5–39, 17. This passage is taken from Schneider's portion of the introductory essay. Rifkin turns this point especially directly in *When Did Indians Become Straight? Kinship, the History of Sexuality, and Native Sovereignty* (Oxford: Oxford University Press, 2011), 153: "One of the chief mechanisms [of dispossession] was the institutional erasure of native forms of kinship and the collective geographies established and maintained through these webs of attachment/obligation. Not only were allotments parceled out to each 'head of family,' thereby soldering occupancy to a particular vision of what constitutes a family unit, but the act mandated that the 'law of descent and partition in force in the State or Territory where such lands are situated shall apply thereto,' creating a barrier to native efforts to merge land claims through extended chains of familial belonging or to maintain ties of tribal identification through the transfer of land along alternate lines of descent / affiliation." On possession, dispossession, and white sovereignty—inflected by a strong engagement with Foucault's biopolitics—see also Aileen Moreton-Robinson, *The White Possessive: Property, Power, and Indigenous Sovereignty* (Minneapolis: University of Minnesota Press, 2015), especially 125–35. On the larger problematics of dispossession on the terrain of Marxist conceptions of primitive accumulation, see Glen Sean Coulthard, *Red Skin, White Masks: Rejecting the Colonial Politics of Recognition* (Minneapolis: University of Minnesota Press, 2014).

35 Deborah A. Miranda, "Extermination of the *Joyas*: Gendercide in Spanish California," *GLQ: A Journal of Lesbian and Gay Studies* 16, nos. 1–2 (2010): 253–84; Kyla Schuller, *The Biopolitics of Feeling: Race, Sex, and Science in the Nineteenth Century* (Durham: Duke University Press, 2018), 134–70. In relation to the conditions Mirada describes as gendercide, see as well as Rifkin's *When Did Indians Become Straight?*; Scott Lauria Morgensen's *Spaces between Us: Queer Settler Colonialism and Indigenous Decolonization* (Minneapolis: University of Minnesota Press, 2011); and J. Kehaulani Kauanui's *Hawaiian Blood: Colonialism and the Politics of Sovereignty and Indigeneity* (Durham: Duke University Press, 2008). See also the work collected in *Gender and Sexuality in Indigenous North America, 1400–1850*, ed. Sandra Slater and Fay A. Yarbrough (Charleston: University of South Carolina Press, 2011).

36 On the "gentle genocide" of the Peace Policy, which shifted the management of Indian affairs to a range of Christian missionizing organizations—and "effectively placed Indian reservations under Church control"—see Robert H. Keller Jr., *American Protestantism and United States Indian Policy, 1869–82* (Lincoln: University of Nebraska Press, 1983), 1–2, 159. That work forms an important backdrop for Wenger, *We Have a Religion*.

37 "Developed by colonial anthropology and other life sciences, race demarcated the accumulated physical effect of a group's relative achievement of the seven cultural traits defined as defined as determinant of civilization: sexual differentiation, monogamous marriage, Christian faith, arts and literacy, domestic architecture, capitalist accumula-

tion, and democratic government" (*The Biopolitics of Feeling*, 12). Schuller is summarizing here the works of E. B. Tylor and, especially, Lewis Henry Morgan. For more on sexual differentiation as racial attainment, see 101–33. See also Scott Lauria Morgensen's "The Biopolitics of Settler Colonialism: Right Here, Right Now," *Settler Colonial Studies* 1, no. 1 (2011): 52–76.

38 "Code of Indian Offenses," Department of the Interior, Office of Indian Affairs, https:// en.wikisource.org/wiki/Code_of_Indian_Offenses. The text would note by way of preface both the prevalence of polygamy and the saving power of a propertied and male head of house: "The value of property as an agent of civilization ought not to be overlooked. When an Indian acquires property, with a disposition to retain the same, free from tribal or individual interference, he has made a step forward in the road to civilization. One great obstacle to the acquirement of property by the Indian is the very general custom of destroying or distributing his property on the death of a member of his family. . . . I am informed by reliable authority that frequently the head of a family, finding himself thus stripped of his property, becomes discouraged, and makes no further attempt to become a property owner."

39 Peter Coviello, *Tomorrow's Parties: Sex and the Untimely in Nineteenth-Century America* (New York: New York University Press, 2013), 127.

40 Orson Pratt, "Celestial Marriage—an Excerpt," in *The Essential Orson Pratt*, 275.

41 John Cradlebaugh, *Utah and the Mormons* (Washington: L. Towers & Co., 1863), 4.

42 Reeve, *Religion of a Different Color*, 165.

43 Again, the finest anatomization I know of these crossed dynamics in anti-Mormon sentimentalism appears in Nancy Bentley's "Marriage as Treason: Polygamy, Nation, and the Novel," in *The Futures of American Studies*, ed. Donald E. Pease and Robyn Wiegman (Durham: Duke University Press, 2002), 341–70.

44 For a full text of Young's sermon "An Act in Relation to Service," see http://www.utlm .org/onlineresources/sermons_talks_interviews/brigham1852feb5_priesthoodand blacks.htm. (This text is drawn from the archives of the LDS Church Historical Department—in "Brigham Young Addresses, Ms d 1234, Box 48, folder 3, dated Feb. 5, 1852.") See also the transcription in *The Mormon Church and Blacks: A Documentary History*, ed. Matthew L. Harris and Newell G. Bringhurst (Urbana: University of Illinois Press, 2015), 37–40, 37. I have learned a great deal from Harris and Bringhurst's tracking of Young's evolving positions on blackness, as I have from Bringhurst's historiographic essay "The 'Missouri Thesis' Revisited: Early Mormonism, Slavery, and the Status of Black People," in *Black and Mormon*, ed. Newell G. Bringhurst and Darron T. Smith (Urbana: University of Illinois Press, 2004), 13–33. Full accounts of the proceedings, with corresponding quotations, appear as well in Turner, *Brigham Young*, 218–29; and Reeve, *Religion of a Different Color*, 152–61. For further commentary on the act, see also Max Perry Mueller, *Race and the Making of the Mormon People* (Chapel Hill: University of North Carolina Press, 2017), 189–93.

45 Brigham Young, "Intelligence, Etc.," 9 October 1859, *Journal of Discourses* 7:282–91, 290, http://jod.mrm.org/7/282.

46 "An Act in Relation to Service," http://www.utlm.org/onlineresources/sermons_talks _interviews/brigham1852feb5_priesthoodandblacks.htm.

47 Here is the full quote, from Wilford Woodruff's account of Young's address on 4 February 1852: "Some may think I don't know as much as they do, but I know that I know more than they do! The Lord will watch us all the time. The Devil would like to rule part of the time, but I am determined he shall not rule us at all, and Negros shall not rule us." See *The Teachings of President Brigham Young*, vol. 3, *1852–1854*, ed. Fred C. Collier (Salt Lake City: Collier's Publishing, 1987), 49, 30–50. See also Turner, *Brigham Young*, 226.

48 Turner, *Brigham Young*, 297.

49 Quoted in Turner, *Brigham Young*, 362.

50 This contest is detailed in Turner, *Brigham Young*, 327–29, 328, as well as in Bigler, *Forgotten Kingdom*, 213–17. Bigler writes of reports that Young had called him a "black-hearted abolitionist," adding for good measure, "If he attempts to interfere with my affairs, woe! woe! unto him" (215).

51 It is worth noting that these grammars of Mormon self-defense come to be repeated, in an uncanny way, by those scholarly accounts that take anti-Mormonism to be rooted in what is, finally, a specious misrecognition, an intolerance of religion dressing itself up in the more violent language of racial and sexual disapprobation: less a telling reminder of *what race is*, of its constitution in and through the biopoliticized mechanics of secular distinction, than an instance of "religious discrimination cloaked in racial garb," as Reeve concisely puts it. Reeve's account, in *Religion of a Different Color*, of the persecutors of early Mormons as, in their racializations, "intent upon seeing a difference where none existed," is exemplary here (9, 10).

52 Gunnison's death took place in the midst of a fraught jockeying for position among Native nations, and as part of the ongoing hostilities between the Mormons and the Ute chief Wakara, known as the "Walker War." The Mormons were suspected of aiding the Pahvants, in the hope of discouraging emigration. For an account of these conflicts with Wakara, and especially of the place of the death of Gunnison, see Bigler, *Forgotten Kingdom*, 73–85.

53 John W. Gunnison, *The Mormons, or, Latter-Day Saints, in the Valley of the Great Salt Lake* (Philadelphia: Lippincott, Grambo & Co., 1852), 156, 136.

54 Turner, *Brigham Young*, 3.

55 See Scott, *Sex and Secularism*, 96. See also Carole Pateman, *The Sexual Contract* (Stanford: Stanford University Press, 1988).

56 Stenhouse, *Exposé of Polygamy*, 106.

57 Preface to Frederick Douglass, *The Narrative of the Life of Frederick Douglass, an American Slave*, ed. Houston Baker Jr. (New York: Penguin, 1982), 34.

58 See, paradigmatically, Albert J. Raboteau, *Slave Religion: The "Invisible Institution" in the Antebellum South* (1978; New York: Oxford University Press, 2004). See also sharp updatings in Sylvester A. Johnson, *African American Religions, 1500–2000* (Cambridge: Cambridge University Press, 2015), 128–45; and, in a different key, Vincent W. Lloyd, *Religion of the Field Negro: On Black Secularism and Black Theology* (New York: Fordham University Press, 2017). On Stowe's fear not for the soul of the slave but for her own complicit white salvation, see James Baldwin's "Everybody's Protest Novel," in Baldwin, *Notes of a Native Son* (Boston: Beacon Press, 1955), 13–23.

59 See especially Givens's *The Viper on the Hearth: Mormons, Myths, and the Construc-tion of Heresy* (New York: Oxford University Press, 1997). Excellent work on apostasy appears, too, in *Standing Apart: Mormon Historical Consciousness and the Concept of Apostasy*, ed. Miranda Wilcox and John D. Young (New York: Oxford University Press, 2014). I am especially informed by Matthew Bowman's "James Talmage, B. H. Roberts, and Confessional History in a Secular Age," in *Standing Apart*, 77–92.

60 Jan Shipps's work is perhaps the most conceptually rich in its address to this critical ter-rain. It is preceded by the important work of scholars like Hugh Nibley (in books such as *"Lehi in the Desert" and "The World of the Jaredites"* [Salt Lake City: Deseret Book Company, 1952] and *Since Cumorah: The Book of Mormon in the Modern World* [Salt Lake City: Deseret Book Company, 1967]) and worked out, in more and less esoteric versions, by scholars like John L. Brooke (in *The Refiner's Fire: The Making of Mormon Cosmology, 1644–1844* [Cambridge: Cambridge University Press, 1994]), as well as in the works we have seen by Paul Gutjahr, J. Spencer Fluhman, and Terryl L. Givens.

61 I follow here especially closely upon the work of John Lardas Modern, and his explora-tions of "the discursive alignment of Protestant subcultures" and its contribution to what he calls "the power of a nonspecific Protestantism" (*Secularism in Antebellum America* [Chicago: University of Chicago Press, 2011], 32). In his skeptical responsive-ness to Mark A. Noll's *America's God: From Jonathan Edwards to Abraham Lincoln* (New York: Oxford University Press, 2002) and his estimation of the "evangelical syn-thesis," I take Modern to be following here in the vein of Tracy Fessenden's *Culture and Redemption: Religion, the Secular, and American Literature* (Princeton: Princeton University Press, 2007).

62 Jared Hickman, *Black Prometheus: Race and Radicalism in the Age of Atlantic Slav-ery* (New York: Oxford University Press, 2017), 39, 37, 134. He is in conversation with Enrique Dussel, *The Invention of the Americas: Eclipse of "the Other" and the Myth of Modernity*, trans. Michael D. Barber (New York: Continuum, 1995); Édouard Glissant, especially the works in *Caribbean Discourse: Selected Essays* (Charlottesville: University Press of Virginia, 1999); Walter D. Mignolo, *Local Histories/Global Designs: Colonial-ity, Subaltern Knowledges, and Border Thinking* (Princeton: Princeton University Press, 2000); and—to my mind most saliently by far—Sylvia Wynter, "1492: A New World View," in *Race, Discourse, and the Origin of the Americas*, ed. Vera Lawrence Hyatt and Rex Nettleford (Washington, DC: Smithsonian Institute Scholarly Press, 1995), 5–57. See also Alexander G. Weheliye's reading of Wynter in *Habeas Viscus: Racializing Assemblages, Biopolitics, and Black Feminist Theories of the Human* (Durham: Duke University Press, 2014), 24–29.

63 Wynter, "1492," 41.

64 Van Wagoner, *Mormon Polygamy*, 131.

65 Quoted in Van Wagoner, *Mormon Polygamy*, 128–29. For more on the political circum-stances surrounding the emergence of the Manifesto, in the context of what he describes as the "Americanization of the Kingdom," see also Bigler, *Forgotten Kingdom*, 341–62.

66 Quoted in Van Wagoner, *Mormon Polygamy*, 135.

67 See Rifkin, *When Did Indians Become Straight?*, 99–142.

68 Daniel Heath Justice, Mark Rifkin, and Bethany Schneider, "Introduction," *GLQ: A Journal of Lesbian and Gay Studies* 16, nos. 1–2 (2010): 5–39, 17.

69 See Lora Romero, *Home Fronts: Domesticity and Its Critics in the Antebellum United States* (Durham: Duke University Press, 1997), especially her chapter on James Fenimore Cooper, "Vanishing Americans," 35–51.

70 See Justice, Rifkin, and Schneider, "Introduction," 20, emphasis added.

71 Louis S. Warren, *God's Red Son: The Ghost Dance Religion and the Making of Modern America* (New York: Basic Books, 2017), 55. Warren's book telegraphs the point that the United States government set out to *suppress a religion* when it sent the army among the Western Sioux. And his work makes clear as well the national perception of Mormon entanglement with the Ghost Dances: "Taken aback by the joyful reception of the Ghost Dance among Mormons living near Nevada, and recalling that Mormons had conspired with Indians to attack other white settlers in the Mountain Meadows Massacre of 1857, some influential voices speculated that the Mormon church had created the Ghost Dance as part of a large conspiracy." Hence, General Miles's pronouncement about Mormon plotting (55, and see also 96–100).

72 DeWitt Talmage, *A Sermon on "Mormonism"* (Milnsbridge: J. S. Illingworth, 1880), 8–9, 9–10.

73 On the proximity of Ghost Dance protests and the extirpation of Mormon polygamy, see Bigler, *Forgotten Kingdom*, 341–62. Like Bigler—though more in the key of theology than of political history—Max Perry Mueller notes the crossings between "Book of Mormon theologies of Lamanite people building" and Ghost Dances (*Race and the Making of the Mormon People*, 178). I take Louis S. Warren's careful and nondismissive skepticism, in relation to hasty and somewhat simplified claims of "influence," to be instructive; see *God's Red Son*, especially 96–100.

74 Listed on the LDS webpage as incorporated into Doctrine and Covenants, and entitled "Official Declaration 1," the text of Woodruff's 1890 Manifesto can be found at https://www.lds.org/scriptures/dc-testament/od/1.

75 Woodruff quoted in Matthias F. Cowley, *Wilford Woodruff* (Salt Lake City: G. Q. Cannon and Sons, 1909), 571.

76 Kathleen Flake, *The Politics of American Religious Identity: The Seating of Senator Reed Smoot, Mormon Apostle* (Chapel Hill: University of North Carolina Press, 2004).

77 Jared Hickman, "*The Book of Mormon* as Amerindian Apocalypse," *American Literature* 86, no. 3 (September 2014): 434.

78 Quoted in Van Wagoner, *Mormon Polygamy*, 143. See also Davis Bitton, *George Q. Cannon: A Biography* (Salt Lake City: Deseret Book Company, 1999), 270–334. There Cannon is quoted as saying, also in 1885, that if the Saints "were to repudiate this principle, our Church would cease to be the Church of God, and the ligaments that now bind it together would be severed" (275).

79 Quoted in Van Wagoner, *Mormon Polygamy*, 146.

80 Givens, *The Viper on the Hearth*, 82. For one strain of Mormon historiography, this sacrality is linked to an unexpurgated origin in what gets called, in various iterations, *magic*. Brooke's *The Refiner's Fire* would be crucial here, as well as D. Michael Quinn's

Early Mormonism and the Magic World View (Salt Lake City: Signature Books, 1987), though I am wary of the secular mechanics that would pronounce some internal and apprehensible division between practices that get conceptualized as "religion" and those that appear as "magic." See also, for the placement of Mormonism within a larger metaphysical tradition, Catherine L. Albanese, *A Republic of Mind and Spirit: A Cultural History of American Metaphysical Religion* (New Haven: Yale University Press, 2007), 136–50.

81 Disputes over certain of then-President John Taylor's statements about the doctrine of plural marriage would help foment the post-Manifesto fundamentalist turn. See Van Wagoner, *Mormon Polygamy*, 153–63.

82 The canonical account of nation-time appears in Benedict Anderson, *Imagined Communities: Reflections on the Origin and Spread of Nationalism* (New York: Verso, 1991). It finds vigorous updating in Lauren Berlant and Elizabeth Freeman, "Queer Nationality," *boundary 2* 19, no. 1 (1992): 149–80; and Wai Chee Dimock, *Through Other Continents: American Literature across Deep Time* (Princeton: Princeton University Press, 2006).

83 Fluhman, *"A Peculiar People,"* 13–14; Harold Bloom, *The American Religion: The Emergence of the Post-Christian Nation* (New York: Simon and Schuster, 1992). Bushman, despite what I have marked as his exemplary commitment to a liberal rendering of early Mormonism, nevertheless resists the collapsing of that liberalism into "Americanism" full-stop. See his useful speculations in "A Joseph Smith for the Twenty-First Century," in Bushman, *Believing History: Latter-day Saint Essays*, ed. Reid L. Neilson and Jed Woodworth (New York: Columbia University Press, 2004), 262–78.

CHAPTER SIX

1 "The Family: A Proclamation to the World," First Presidency and Council of the Twelve Apostles of the Church of Jesus Christ of Latter-day Saints, presented by President Gordon B. Hinkley, 23 September 1995, https://www.lds.org/topics/family-proclamation?lang=eng&old=true.

2 Elder Dallin H. Oakes, "The Plan and the Proclamation," https://www.lds.org/general-conference/2017/10/the-plan-and-the-proclamation?lang=eng.

3 On Charles Taylor's deference to an occluded metaphysics of choice, see John Lardas Modern, "The Sun Shone Fiercely through the Window at Starbucks," *The Immanent Frame*, 9 September 2010 https://tif.ssrc.org/2010/09/09/through-the-window-at-starbucks-i/. As Modern writes, "For at the end of the day, Taylor's story of the nova effect of choice vis-à-vis the concept of religion is premised upon a self that has the potential to fulfill such promises and fuel such harmonic processes in and through its inherent sovereignty and its capacity for immediate access to itself and the world around."

4 Ben Williams, "Utah's Always Had Queer Marriage," *Q Salt Lake Magazine*, 24 January 2014, https://qsaltlake.com/news/2014/01/24/utahs-always-queer-marriage/. I am fortified here, again, by Taylor G. Petrey's work in "Toward a Post-Heterosexual Mormon Theology," *Dialogue: A Journal of Mormon Thought* 44, no. 4 (2011): 106–41, in which

he explores "how Mormons might imagine different kind of sealing relationships other than heterosexual marriage" (107).

5 Elder M. Russell Ballard, "The Trek Continues!" https://www.lds.org/general-conference /2017/10/the-trek-continues?lang=eng.

6 Elder Quentin L. Cook, "The Eternal Everyday," https://www.lds.org/general-conference /2017/10/the-eternal-everyday?lang=eng. Elder Cook proclaimed, "Anyone who claims superiority under the Father's plan because of characteristics like race, sex, nationality, language, or economic circumstances is morally wrong and does not understand the Lord's true purpose for all of our Father's children."

7 Molly McGarry, *Ghosts of Futures Past: Spiritualism and the Cultural Politics of Nineteenth-Century America* (Berkeley: University of California Press, 2008). McGarry cautions us to be on our guard against the misapprehensions that nest within neat secularization stories, observing that "histories of secularism structurally underwrite histories of sexuality *and function to elucidate some forms of sexual subjectivity while occluding others*" (155, emphasis added).

8 Peter Coviello, *Tomorrow's Parties: Sex and the Untimely in Nineteenth-Century America* (New York: New York University Press, 2013), 104–28.

9 I am riffing freely here on Lauren Berlant's work, in both *Cruel Optimism* (Durham: Duke University Press, 2011) and its precursor, *The Female Complaint: The Unfinished Business of Sentimentality in American Culture* (Durham: Duke University Press, 2008). My subtitle is a small homage to Berlant's peerless work on sentimentality as (among other things) a *genre* that stages the simultaneous promises and sharp curtailments of liberalism in the racial state.

10 Jasbir Puar, *Terrorist Assemblages: Homonationalism in Queer Times* (Durham: Duke University Press, 2007), 4. See also Lisa Duggan, "The New Homonormativity: The Sexual Politics of Neoliberalism," in *Materializing Democracy: Toward a Revitalized Cultural Politics*, ed. Russ Castronovo and Dana D. Nelson (Durham: Duke University Press, 2002), 175–94.

11 An early genealogy of the queer turn toward normalcy, and a lastingly powerful rebuke to its politics, appears in Michael Warner's *The Trouble with Normal* (Cambridge: Harvard University Press, 1999).

12 On the Mormon moment, see as one exemplary text Walter Kirn, "The Mormon Moment." *Newsweek*, 5 June 2011, http://www.newsweek.com/mormon-moment-67951. This passage of heightened attention was taken to crystallize a push toward a number of liberalizing moves in the church; retrenchment—complete with excommunication for feminist Mormon women such as Kate Kelly, and the insistences on sexual normativity we have already seen—marked, for many, the end of such a moment. See, for instance, Cadence Woodland's op-ed, "The End of the 'Mormon Moment,'" *New York Times*, 14 July 2014. Woodland wrote succinctly: "This crackdown marks the end of the 'Mormon Moment'—not just the frenzy of interest that rose (and largely faded) with Mitt Romney's campaigns for the presidency, but a distinct period of dialogue around and within the Mormon community." See also, on "the Mormon ecumenical moment," Stephen H. Webb, *Mormon Christianity: What Other Christians Can Learn from the Latter-day Saints* (New York: Oxford University Press, 2013).

13 The text of Proposition 8 is available online at the California attorney general's website: http://www.ag.ca.gov/cms_pdfs/initiatives/i737_07-0068_Initiative.pdf.

14 Jesse McKinley and Kirk Johnson, "Mormons Tipped Scale in Ban on Gay Marriage," *New York Times*, 14 November 2008.

15 Jennifer Dobner, "New Mormon Policy Makes Apostates of Married Same-Sex Couples, Bars Children from Rites," *Salt Lake Tribune*, 6 November 2015, http://archive.sltrib .com/article.php?id=3144035&itype=CMSID.

16 James E. Talmage, *The Essential James E. Talmage*, ed. James Harris (Salt Lake City: Signature Books, 1997), 128–32.

17 For more on Socarides—author of such memorable texts as *Homosexuality: A Freedom Too Far*—see Simon LeVay, *Queer Science: The Use and Abuse of Research into Homosexuality* (Cambridge: MIT Press, 1996). For a fortifying rebuke to psychologized "treatment" of queer kids, see Eve Kosofsky Sedgwick's "How to Bring Your Kids Up Gay," in Sedgwick, *Tendencies* (Durham: Duke University Press, 1993), 154–64.

18 Jason Park, *Helping LDS Men Resolve Their Homosexual Problems: A Guide for Families, Friends, and Church Leaders* (Salt Lake City: Century Publishing, 1997), 34, 157–58.

19 Transcription of the speech available as "Elder Bruce C. Hafen Speaks on Same-Sex Attraction," at *Newsroom*, the official LDS organ, http://www.mormonnewsroom.org /article/elder-bruce-c-hafen-speaks-on-same-sex-attraction.

20 Modern renderings of the Book of Mormon have revised the passage, so that it reads "a *pure* and a delightsome people." See https://www.lds.org/scriptures/bofm/2-ne /30.6?lang=eng.

21 Max Perry Mueller, *Race and the Making of the Mormon People* (Chapel Hill: University of North Carolina Press, 2017), 159. The Mormon regard for the Indians as Lamanites ready to be metamorphosed into God's agents in the new dispensation appears in a range of histories of the Saints in the West, but Mueller's takes on most directly the language of redemptive metamorphosis proper to the early Mormon racial imaginary. See especially Jared Farmer, *On Zion's Mount: Mormons, Indians, and the American Landscape* (Cambridge: Harvard University Press, 2008). For a similarly ambivalent account of the transformative fantasies of early Mormonism as they carried over into the twentieth century, and especially into the Indian Student Placement Program, see Matthew Garrett, *Making Lamanites: Mormons, Native Americans, and the Indian Student Placement Program, 1947–2000* (Salt Lake City: University of Utah Press, 2016).

22 Mueller, *Race*, 164.

23 Mueller, *Race*, 17, 161, 27, 165.

24 Regarding "secular redemptive politics," Asad underscores the "readiness to cause pain to those who are to be saved by being humanized." This, for Asad, is "the violence of universalizing reason itself." Or again: "The anguish of subjects compelled under threat of punishment to abandon traditional practices," Asad writes, in terms that bear directly upon the case of Native peoples in the Americas, "could not therefore play a decisive part in the discourse of colonial reformers." For "in the process of learning to be 'fully human' only some kinds of suffering were seen as an affront to humanity, and their elimination sought. This was distinguished from suffering that was *necessary* to the process of realizing one's humanity." See Talal Asad, *Formations of the Secular:*

Christianity, Islam, Modernity (Stanford: Stanford University Press, 2003), 61–62, 59, 110–11. On the expressed wish of nineteenth-century missionaries to transform Native peoples into "white Christians," see Robert H. Keller Jr., *American Protestantism and United States Indian Policy, 1869–82* (Lincoln: University of Nebraska Press, 1983).

25 "Elder Bruce C. Hafen Speaks," http://www.mormonnewsroom.org/article/elder-bruce -c-hafen-speaks-on-same-sex-attraction.

26 On that decline see Garrett, *Making Lamanites*, 204–34.

27 Michel Foucault, *The Birth of Biopolitics: Lectures at the Collège de France, 1978–1979*, trans. Graham Burchell, ed. Michel Senellart (New York: Picador, 2004), 3, emphasis added.

28 Puar, *Terrorist Assemblages*, 29.

29 Asad, *Formations of the Secular*, 61. For more on this figure, and on this rendering of homophobia in the work of Puar, Joseph Massad, and others, see Coviello, "The Wild Not Less Than the Good: Thoreau, Sex, Biopower," *GLQ: A Journal of Lesbian and Gay Studies* 23, no. 4 (Fall 2017): 509–32, especially 521–22.

30 Puar, *Terrorist Assemblages*, 31.

31 Puar, *Terrorist Assemblages*, 1–36, 25.

32 Rey Chow, *The Protestant Ethnic and the Spirit of Capitalism* (New York: Columbia University Press, 2003), 3. See Puar, *Terrorist Assemblages*, 24–25.

33 On debility and capacity, see Puar's work in "The Cost of Getting Better: Suicide, Sensation, Switchpoints," *GLQ: A Journal of Lesbian and Gay Studies* 18, no. 1 (2012): 149–58, and in *The Right to Maim: Debility, Capacity, Disability* (Durham: Duke University Press, 2017). This latter work asks us to consider Palestine not as a scene of exceptionality but, to the contrary, as something of an experimental theater for new millennial biopolitics, in which multiple modes of extraction from a racialized surplus population are *tried out*, tested for their viability across several registers of functionality. Given the conditions of secular stagnation that prevail in global capitalism, and its concomitant production of huger and huger swaths of the earth as unassimilable surplus, precisely this extractive biopolitical economy—the leveraging not only of making live and letting die but of maiming, fracturing life, partializing it—seems a template for the future of liberal power. On surplus population and its racialization, see especially Ruth Wilson Gilmore, *Golden Gulag: Prisons, Surplus, Crisis, and Opposition in Globalizing California* (Berkeley: University of California Press, 2007); for more on the management of racialized surplus under conditions of secular stagnation, and scenes of revolt, see Joshua Clover, *Riot. Strike. Riot: The New Era of Uprisings* (New York: Verso, 2016).

34 See Dana Luciano, *Arranging Grief: Sacred Time and the Body in Nineteenth-Century America* (New York: New York University Press, 2007); Kyla Wazana Tompkins, *Racial Indigestion: Eating Bodies in the 19th Century* (New York: New York University Press, 2012); and Kyla Schuller, *The Biopolitics of Feeling: Race, Sex, and Science in the Nineteenth Century* (Durham: Duke University Press, 2017).

35 DeWitt Talmage, *A Sermon on "Mormonism"* (Milnsbridge: J. S. Illingworth, 1880), 8–9; Boggs quoted in William G. Hartley, "Missouri's 1838 Extermination Order and the Mormons' Forced Removal to Illinois," *Mormon Historical Studies* 2, no. 1 (Spring 2001): 5–27; "The Mormons," *Putnam's Monthly* 5, no. 27 (March 1855): 225–36, 234.

36 Orson Pratt, "Celestial Marriage—an Excerpt," in *The Essential Orson Pratt* (Salt Lake City: Signature Books, 1991), 275.

37 Michel Foucault, *"Society Must Be Defended": Lectures at the Collège de France, 1975–1976*, trans. David Macey, ed. Mauro Bertani and Alessandro Fontana (New York: Picador, 2003), 61, emphasis added. Cited internally hereafter.

38 On Foucault and empire, see Ann Laura Stoler's pioneering *Race and the Education of Desire: Foucault's History of Sexuality and the Colonial Order of Things* (Durham: Duke University Press, 1995). In differing inflections, Foucault's genealogical project shapes Dipesh Chakrabarty's *Provincializing Europe: Postcolonial Thought and Historical Difference* (Princeton: Princeton University Press, 2007), as well as the works of Puar and Chow we have already seen. On what he calls "the nuclear situation," see Foucault's *History of Sexuality*, vol. 1, *An Introduction*, trans. Robert Hurley (New York: Vintage, 1978). On imperial neglect, see Christopher Taylor, *Empire of Neglect: The West Indies in the Wake of British Liberalism* (Durham: Duke University Press, 2018).

39 Jared Hickman, *"The Book of Mormon* as Amerindian Apocalypse," *American Literature* 86, no. 3 (September 2014): 434.

40 Biopolitical society's "only problem is this: it is threatened by a certain number of heterogeneous elements which are not essential to it, which do not divide the social, or the living body of society, into two parts, and which are in a sense accidental" (Foucault, *Society*, 80–81). In the rhyme between Foucault's sense of the murderous racialization of "heterogeneous elements" and Sylvia Wynter's argument about colonial racialization and "heterogeneity" in life, we find a measure of the strong mutuality of biopolitical and anticolonial and antiracist critique, as well as of the (still-suppressed) status of theorists like Foucault and Wynter as *peers*, differently situated theorists of race, power, and life. See here especially the work gathered in *Sylvia Wynter: On Being Human as Praxis*, ed. Katherine McKittrick (Durham: Duke University Press, 2014).

41 See again Coviello and Hickman, "Introduction: After the Postsecular," *American Literature* 86, no. 4 (December 2014): 645–54, especially for the account of Tracy Fessenden's bracing reading of contemporary work in the "religion and literature tradition." See Fessenden's "The Problem of the Postsecular," *American Literary History* 26, no. 1 (2014): 154–67.

42 That Foucault himself was keenly interested in producing some critical escape velocity in respect to secularism's propensities for capture has been suggested to me perhaps most forcefully by Behrooz Ghamari-Tabrizi's great work in *Foucault in Iran: Islamic Revolution after the Enlightenment*, which takes up Foucault's interest in revolutionary Islamic foment as a potentially countersecularizing mode of "political spirituality" (Minneapolis: University of Minnesota Press, 2016), 117.

43 Saba Mahmood, *Religious Difference in a Secular Age: A Minority Report* (Princeton: Princeton University Press, 2015), 114. Mahmood is examining the isomorphic interiorization of *both* religion and sexuality under conditions of secular liberalism, and of the turning of them both into the master keys with which we are granted access to what she calls elsewhere "a valorized interiority." See Mahmood, "Sexuality and Secularism," in *Religion, the Secular, and the Politics of Sexual Difference*, ed. Linell E. Cady and Tracy Fessenden (New York: Columbia University Press, 2013), 47–58, 50. Pertinent here,

too, would be the work of Ann Pellegrini and Janet Jakobsen, in *Love the Sin: Sexual Regulation and the Limits of Religious Tolerance* (New York: New York University Press, 2003), and Joan Wallach Scott's *Sex and Secularism* (Princeton: Princeton University Press, 2018).

44 I'm indebted here to a long tradition of scholarship thinking black religiosity in relation to the shifting norms of a de facto white Christianity. See Albert J. Raboteau, *Slave Religion: The "Invisible Institution" in the Antebellum South* (1978; New York: Oxford University Press, 2004); Eddie S. Glaude Jr., *Exodus! Religion, Race, and Nation in Early Nineteenth-Century Black America* (Chicago: University of Chicago Press, 2000); J. Kameron Carter, *Race: A Theological Account* (New York: Oxford University Press, 2008); *Race and Political Theology*, ed. Vincent Lloyd (Stanford: Stanford University Press, 2012); Judith Casselberry, *The Labor of Faith: Gender and Power in Black Apostolic Pentecostalism* (Durham: Duke University Press, 2017); and Vincent W. Lloyd, *Religion of the Field Negro: On Black Secularism and Black Theology* (New York: Fordham University Press, 2017).

45 I am thinking here with Hortense Spillers's investigation of the Obama legacy in "Destiny's Child: Obama and Election '08," *boundary 2* 39, no. 2 (2012): 3–32. See also Kathryn Lofton, on evangelicalism and the rise of Trump, in "Understanding Is Dangerous," published online in *The Point* in 2016, https://thepointmag.com/2016/politics/understanding-is-dangerous.

46 Joseph A. Massad's furious critique of what he calls the "Gay International," on the ground of its implantation and reproduction of an explicitly Westernized "gayness" in and through the bodies of working-class Arab men who have sex with other men, offered in the name of rescuing them from illiberal despotisms, is partial, contentious, and still absolutely trenchant and necessary. See Massad, *Desiring Arabs* (Chicago: University of Chicago Press, 2007), especially 160–90.

47 A very fine accounting of Mormonism as a kind of externalization of this-worldly glory, and of Smith as a man in this way "roaring in the face of death," see Samuel Morris Brown, *In Heaven as It Is on Earth: Joseph Smith and the Early Mormon Conquest of Death* (New York: Oxford University Press, 2012), 12.

48 The utopian horizon has not closed. See, most hearteningly, José Esteban Muñoz, *Cruising Utopia: The Then and There of Queer Futurity* (New York: New York University Press, 2009).

INDEX

settler-colonialism (*cont.*)
ism, 162, 176; and secularism, 43–44; state
policy, 41–42, 187. *See also* "Code of Indian
Offenses"
sexuality: and carnal life of the spirit, 235–36;
Foucault on, 6, 31, 39–40, 42, 76–77, 217,
235; and secularism, 39–40, 42, 236, 287n7
Shah, Nayan, *Stranger Intimacy*, 280n32
Shipps, Jan: *Mormonism*, 18–19, 84, 176,
259n22; and postpolygamy transformation
of Mormon history to scriptural, 208; on
theological dividedness of early Mormonism, 129, 147–48, 196, 206–7, 269n613
slavery: and racialized theodicy, 148–55; and
white deification, 196–98
Smith, Emma, 114; dispute of church's claim
to Smith's estate, 117; and Female Relief
Society, 97; relation to polygamy, 78–79, 81
Smith, Hyrum, 248n19
Smith, Joseph: 1842 address to Female Relief
Society, 99–102, 108, 238; assassination
of, 1, 15, 54, 106, 172, 248n19; carnality as
vehicle for joyousness, 75, 76; charges of
licentiousness brought against, 57–58,
69–70, 77–78; difficulties of dealing with
ambition of various Elders, 101; and difficulty of Mormons to believe and receive
concepts of polygamy and exaltation, 20,
80, 86, 210; and direct revelation, 59–60;
and earthly pleasures, 86–88, 108; exhor-
tation to "make yourselves Gods," 8, 57, 67,
83, 200; fractures with other members of
inner Mormon circle, 69; and friendship,
76; and gendered counterpossibilities,
99–102, 116, 118, 120, 121, 238; on his history, 53, 79, 83; hyperidentification with
"ancient saints," 62, 71, 207; King Follett
Discourse, 57, 66, 69, 85, 246n8, 258n8; letter to Nancy Rigdon, 75, 80, 88; marriages
to Fanny Alger, Lucinda Pendleton, and
Emma Smith, 257n3; marriage to Louisa
Beaman, 51–52, 69; mixing of quotidian
detail and divine revelation, 14, 61, 84–85,
259n16, 263n59; on nature of priesthood authority, 99–100, 109; on need for

secrecy of plural marriages, 81; pairing
of polygamy with godliness, 57–59; "The
Principle and Doctrine of Having Many
Wives and Concubines," 78–79, 197–98;
prophecies of fate of American nation,
158, 159; and redemption, 63–64, 67, 80,
85, 226; rejection of three-person God,
58–59; and sexualized scandal of 1842,
98; shame and misgiving in practice of
polygamy, 80–81; "The Vision," 262n48;
writings to Whitney family, 80–81. *See
also* exaltation to divinity; Mormonism,
early theology; polygamy; polygamy
revelation of 1843
Smith, Sardius, 171
Smith, William, 117
Smoot, Reed, seating of in senate, 204
Snow, Eliza, 3, 92, 98, 99, 101, 114, 118
Socarides, Charles, 221
Sowiette, father of Utes, 160–61
Spillers, Hortense, 23, 44; "All the Things You
Could Be by Now if Sigmund Freud's Wife
Was Your Mother," 45; "Destiny's Child,"
291n45
Spivak, Gayatri, 34
Stansbury Expedition, 193–94
Stanton, Elizabeth Cady, 121, 123
Stein, Jordan, 26
Steinberg, Avi, 144
Stenhouse, Fanny: *Exposé of Polygamy*, 196–97;
Tell It All, 18, 95, 179, 182
Steptoe, Edward, 176–77
Stowe, Harriet Beecher, *Uncle Tom's Cabin*, 18,
95, 197, 283n58
Sunstone magazine, 247n18

Talmage, DeWitt, 229
Talmage, James E., "The Eternity of Sex," 125,
198, 203, 221
Taylor, Charles, 6; and "the nova effect," 26,
250n8, 286n3; *A Secular Age*, 25–27, 43, 44,
250n13, 250nn7–8; *Sources of the Self*, 25
Taylor, John, 82, 200, 201, 205, 216, 286n81
Teller, Henry M., 186
Tompkins, Kyla Wazana, 228

Young, Brigham: "An Act in Relation to Service," 189–90, 282n44, 283n47; and alienation from American nation, 166, 176–77;
alternating violence toward and paternalistic treatment of Native Americans, 165;
on bodily pleasures, 86; denunciation of
Female Relief Society, 115–17, 119, 181–82;
and divorce, 267n37; extralegal treaties
with Omahas and Otoes, 1, 157, 172; family
compound, 113; "Indian Relief Societies,"
124; on influence of women, 118, 183;
initial reaction to concept of plural marriage, 82; marriage to Louisa Beaman, 52;
misogyny, 115–19, 181–83; and Mormon
westward migration, 16; prophesy of
downfall of American government, 139,
156–58, 174; and reinstitution of Female
Relief Society, 124; rejection of revelations by women, 120; revision of Smith's
remarks to Female Relief Society, 118–19;
sermon on tenth anniversary of Smith's
death, 128; on slavery and racial hierarchy,
189–92, 206, 229, 282n44, 283n47, 283n50;
specification of hierarchized gendered
order of Mormon life, 115–16, 128–29, 183,
187, 269n58; systemization of plural patri-

archal marriage and authority of men,
112–13, 115–19, 128, 187, 191, 266n27
Young, Clara, 107
Young, Mary Ann, 114
Young, Zina Diantha Huntington Jacobs
Smith, 3, 92, 93; account of early days in
Brigham Young's compound, 112–14, 205,
238, 266n27, 269n58; baptism of parents
into Mormonism, 105; biography of,
102–10; estrangement from Henry Jacobs,
106, 110–12, 267n36; identification with
prophetic power, 102; interpretation and
speaking in tongues, 105–8; interweaving
of daily and divine, 108; journey west to
Great Salt Lake, 106–7; married to Henry
Jacobs "for time," March 1841, 102, 104;
proselytizing, 107; receipt of endowment
and admission to Holy Order, 111–12;
recreation of Smith's prophetic power
and authority, 107–10; resealed to Joseph
Smith, 2 February 1846, 102; "sealed for
time" to Brigham Young, 2 February 1846,
102, 106, 110; "sealed" to Joseph Smith for
eternity, 27 October 1841, 102, 103, 104–5;
self-reconstitution into central figure in
female support network, 119–20

Lightning Source UK Ltd.
Milton Keynes UK
UKHW020716011119
352682UK00002B/5/P